TOWARD THE

Toward the
Poems of Mallarmé

Expanded Edition

By Robert Greer Cohn

UNIVERSITY OF CALIFORNIA PRESS
Berkeley, Los Angeles, London

University of California Press
Berkeley and Los Angeles, California

University of California Press, Ltd.
London, England

ISBN 0-520-03846-0
Library of Congress Catalog Card Number 65-25352

Printed in the United States of America

1 2 3 4 5 6 7 8 9

To Susan, my mother

PREFACE

❖⚜❖⚜❖⚜❖⚜❖

   This study examines almost all of the more demanding *Poésies* (poems in verse) of Stéphane Mallarmé. The sequence is Mallarmé's, except for the *Faune* which I feel serves as a good introduction, and the especially difficult *Prose* which has been put last. Otherwise I can find no significant reason for changing the poet's order. He himself obviously had an eye to gradually inducing us into complexities roughly following his own natural growth, that is, chronologically. I try to take advantage of this for the reader. But practically everything comments on everything in Mallarmé's highly unified poetic universe, and ideally he should be read in this spirit.

   The translations are merely literal guides to the French, following it slavishly, line by line and, as far as possible, word by word, with some intercalated clarifications (in square brackets).

   Although the juxtaposition of the French and English texts (plus the intercalations) often distorts the shape of the poems, this arrangement seemed most helpful to the interpretive purpose; the reader should be able to consult the unblemished texts in any of the various editions.

   All page references without symbol are to the standard Pléiade edition of 1945. Other abbreviations are:

   C: *L'Oeuvre de Mallarmé: Un Coup de Dés;* Cohn
   N: *Les Noces d'Hérodiade,* edited by Davies
   LL: *Les Lettres;* special numbers (9, 10, 11) on Mallarmé
   MI: *Mallarmé plus intime,* edited by Mondor
   ML: *Mallarmé lycéen,* edited by Mondor
   EL: *Eugène Lefébure,* Mondor
   Corr.: *Correspondance de Mallarmé,* edited by Henri Mondor and
                                                 Jean-Pierre Richard
   Biog.: *Vie de Mallarmé;* Mondor
   Propos: *Propos sur la poésie,* edited by Mondor
   f.: the *feuillet* of the text of *Tombeau d'Anatole*
   W: *The Writer's Way in France;* Cohn
   Page (capitalized): the double page of *Un Coup de Dés*
   Italics in quotations are, unless otherwise specified, our own.

   This volume is a companion to the *Oeuvre de Mallarmé: Un Coup de Dés.* As I explain in the *Introduction,* the subject of that book connects in many ways with the subject of this, and the cross-references are correspondingly numerous; they are guidelines toward a more complete view.

Appendixes A, B, and C are extracts from *L'Oeuvre de Mallarmé* which are especially useful to our interpretations of the *Poésies*.

After many years of indebtedness, it is a particular pleasure to be able to express here my gratitude to a distinguished and warmly admired colleague and brother in arms, Judd Hubert, for his continuing encouragement, advice, and support.

I am also indebted to Valentina Adams for various assistance with the manuscript, and to Mary Hurt for typing it.

R. G. C.

POSTSCRIPT FOR THE EXPANDED EDITION

Asterisks in the margins indicate added material, listed according to page and line in an appended section entitled "Revisions." These include fresh insights, some important discoveries by others, and a few emendations. Other corrections have been made in the text proper.

An Epilogue, "Mallarmé's Poetic Vision," traces the main way that leads from these *Poésies* to the Great Work.

Finally, there are commentaries on four additional poems: *Apparition, Brise Marine, Petit air II*, and *Remémoration d'Amis belges*. .

More appreciation is due: to George Mulford, for some acute criticism; to my wife, Valentina Cohn; to *Yale French Studies* and *Romantic Review* for permission to use material first printed in their pages.

CONTENTS

Introduction 1

1. *L'Après-midi d'un faune* 13

2. *Salut*, sonnet 33

3. *Le Pitre châtié* 37

4. *Sonnet* ("Sur les bois oubliés") 43

5. *Don du Poème* 47

6. *Hérodiade*

    Introduction 52

    I. *Ouverture ancienne d'Hérodiade* 56
    II. *Scène* (La Nourrice—Hérodiade) 67
    III. *Cantique de Saint Jean* 81

7. *Sainte* 91

8. *Toast Funèbre*, à Théophile Gautier 96

9. *Éventail* de Madame Mallarmé 111

10. *Autre Éventail*, de Mademoiselle Mallarmé 113

11. *Petit Air, I* ("Quelconque une solitude") 117

12. *Quand l'ombre menaça de la fatale loi* 120

13. *Le vierge, le vivace et le bel aujourd'hui* 124

14. *Victorieusement fui le suicide beau* 133

15. *Ses purs ongles très haut dédiant leur onyx* 138

16. *La chevelure vol d'une flamme* 147

17. *Le Tombeau d'Edgar Poe* 153

18. *Le Tombeau de Charles Baudelaire* 158

19. *Tombeau* (de Verlaine) 170

20. *Hommage* (à Richard Wagner) 177

21. *Hommage* (à Puvis de Chavannes) 186

22. *Toute l'âme résumée* 189

23. *Au seul souci de voyager* 192

24. Triptyque:
    I. *Tout orgueil fume-t-il du soir* 197
    II. *Surgi de la croupe et du bond* 201
    III. *Une dentelle s'abolit* 206

25. *Quelle soie aux baumes de temps* 218

26. *M'introduire dans ton histoire* 223

27. *A la nue accablante tu* 229

28. *Mes bouquins refermés* 237

29. *Prose* (pour des Esseintes) 240

    Appendixes:
    A. A Translated Extract from *L'Oeuvre de Mallarmé* . 261
    B. A Translated Extract from *L'Oeuvre de Mallarmé* . 263
    C. A Letter Table 265

NEW TEXT 281

1. More Poems

    I. *Apparition* 283
    II *Brise marine* 288
    III *Petit air II* 292
    IV. *Remémoration d'Amis Belges* 294

2. Epilogue: Mallarmé's Poetic Vision 299

3. Revisions 312

    Bibliography 323

INTRODUCTION

Mallarmé's poems are the culmination of a long evolution of French lyricism which began in the Middle Ages, took notable shape in the sixteenth century and, after gathering subtle resources of articulation in the classic period, leaped into Romanticism and its finer heir, Symbolism. Elusive as the development obviously is, nonetheless, if we take a panoramic perspective, certain main lines of direction become relatively clear. As we proceed over the years into the thick of the nineteenth century, there is a discernible movement downward toward the instinctual realm, the emotional roots, immediate childlike sensuality, the simplicity of nature; all this in one direction and simultaneously, in the other, toward complexity, a special imaginative form of intellect and a corresponding delicacy or refinement of language.

The familiar formula of "increasing individualism" which historians apply to Romanticism, is closely bound up with this phenomenon of up-and-down dialectical growth on a vertical psychic plane: the "ivory tower" (and "ivory well") of subjective, self-involved feeling or consciousness. Inevitably, given the radically opposite urges, between the mind and body of the isolated lyric poet, there is often a dramatic, or even agonizing, tension (which is somewhat characteristic of civilized men generally). The faculty of the Imagination then takes on increasing importance, in a sort of synthesizing mid-region of the human spirit, as a mode of reconciliation or integration. A corollary horizontal tension between the artist and society occurs, so to speak, at right angles to the primary one, and the poet's classic impulses move, in another kind of reconciliation, along this axis, from the concentration of pure poetry through a more realistic verse, toward rhetoric and, eventually, to rhymed prose. There is a constant fluctuation between these two spiritual dimensions: even in the most art-for-art's-sake Symbolists a line replete with rich, crystallized imagery (proceeding from the warring depths and heights) will be occasionally followed by a relatively rhetorical or calmly discursive line, classic in tone. But, on the whole, in the nineteenth century, the seminal development from Lamartine through Hugo and Baudelaire to the Symbolists (with major stimulus from coeval English and German writers and the American, Poe) is pre-

1

dominantly an intensification of romanticism, with classicism in a supporting role.

With Mallarmé, the romantic intensity reaches its all-time apogee as expressed, for example, in the unprecedented vibrancy of his images. And the moments of release, like a lightning flash between intolerably opposed poles of being, are correspondingly joyous: "Glory of the long desire." A representative poem in this respect is *Hérodiade,* where, clearly, the central figure is a sublime, unyielding, starry-eyed virgin, hard and cold as ice. Yet (as Mauron insists), the poem is one of the most "submarine" in the French language, with its obsessive infantile milk imagery, the summer leaves under the frozen pond, the fountain in the mirror, the trembling prospect of disrobing, the persistent suggestions of imminent thaw. The moral struggle results in some memorable instances of those organic crystallizations which are the basic substance of poetry (arising, as we said, in that resolving mid-region, the imagination):

> Ô miroir!
> Eau froide par l'ennui dans ton cadre gelée
> Que de fois et pendant des heures, désolée
> Des songes et cherchant mes souvenirs qui sont
> Comme des feuilles sous ta glace au trou profond,
> Je m'apparus en toi comme une ombre lointaine,
> Mais, horreur! des soirs, dans ta sévère fontaine,
> J'ai de mon rêve épars connu la nudité!

The agon of the lofty and sensual attractions of this art is epitomized in the final word *nudité.* Is it, as in *Igitur,* the nakedness of her soul she sees in this familiar moment of self-confrontation? Or is it the *blancheur animale* (*Faune*) of her body that she glimpses in the dusky narcissistic mirror? Ambiguously, poetically, it is both: like her cousin the faun, with his goat's legs and demigod's torso, torn between wildly permissive urges and a complex, inhibitive mind, she is caught in the above-below dilemma of romanticism. With this excruciating word, *nudité,* the whole exciting passage reaches a climax, and the taut vibrancy of the image-series—the frustrating yet inviting mirror, the suspended leaves, the hovering between present and past, between motion and rest —melts into gratifying esthetic release.

As we read on in Mallarmé, the single image, or image-cluster (as in the just-quoted verse) ultimately joins with other images, in a vast network, to form the total scope of the poet's vision. Mallarmé is squarely in the mystic—the romantic-ideational—tradition which goes back to Plato and which includes prominently his immediate spiritual forebears, Lamartine, Hugo, Nerval, Poe, and Baudelaire. He shares their belief in universal analogy, in the ultimate harmony or connectivity of all reality. The things of this world can rise—like his famous flower —by "magic" artistic alchemy or distillation, to membership in a paradisiacal order, akin to Plato's realm of pure essences but closer to the one revealed by Proust's "privileged moments" or Joyce's "epiphanies"; and, true to the paradoxical principle of advanced lyricism, the objects plunge earthward toward a natural simplicity, take on a full Keatsian weight, become more vividly concrete and present, even as they aspire upward to the shores of light: "the Word remains . . . more massively bound to nature" (522). The patent persistence of the idealist in Mallarmé, or the "algebraist" Valéry saw, should never cause us to scant the solid being who wrote a friend: "To be really man or nature when thinking, one must think with all one's body." Even the haunting *azur* of the early poems, which is consistently interpreted as an ideal absolute, can flow into supreme sensuality as the lost-paradisiacal mother's milk:

> Et la bouche, fiévreuse et d'azur bleu vorace,
> Telle, jeune, elle alla respirer son trésor,
> Une peau virginale et de jadis! . . .
> (*Les Fenêtres*)

In this sense, contrary to the critics, the *azur* persists throughout the later Mallarmé as well, through *Hérodiade; Don du poème; Le vierge, le vivace* . . . and *Mes bouquins* . . . , right up to the *Coup de Dés*. It is unthinkable for Mallarmé to have abandoned a symbol whose roots descended so deeply into his infantile psyche; rather, it kept growing, with the other symbols, in subtle ramifications toward the full rounded foliage of the universal "tree."

To meet these ambitious requirements, in addition to the more usual exigencies of verse, Mallarmé had to be extremely patient and meticulous in choosing his words (which helps account for the scantiness of his production); only so many of them possess the polyvalent virtualities, the all-around availability requisite to joining in the *Jeu suprême*. Like an over-eager huntsman, the greedy grasp of the will could only frighten the delicate prey, get in the way; the best chance of success in the game was to gently stalk and lie in wait, "céder l'initiative aux mots." As distinguished, for example, from the hard-and-fast sculptural language of the Parnassians, pinned down to immovable objects, his words and the images they delineate (symbols) reach out in all directions (including the mentioned high-low) toward other words and images of the "net," in a constellar pattern, resembling the web at the center of which he saw himself installed as a "sacred Spider." His words are richly connotative, fluid, ambiguous, suggestive; they saturate the air with overtones which emerge when they marry the overtones of other terms.

* All of his favorite symbols, flower, window, feather, siren, bird, star, hair, and so on, are at a crossroads of cognate polarities—up-down, static-kinetic, light-dark, male-female, cold-hot—that emanate from a parent pair, Being and Nothingness, as we have detailed at length in our *L'Oeuvre de Mallarmé.* This imperialistic esthetic clearly implies, not a vagueness, as is sometimes thought, but a greater precision which, inevitably, offers initial resistance, and hence involves a prolonged process —"deviner peu à peu"—of understanding or participation on the part of the reader. The initial moment of mystery makes for a delightful sense of infinite possibilities, a sort of swimming in the lucidity (or the white page) surrounding each artistocratically chosen word. But this "feeling" phase is eventually followed by a form of artistic apprehension closer to the word "knowing." So that if we say that Mallarmé is a musical poet—implying, primarily, the expression of delicate harmonies as well as the more usual melodiousness of verse—we must add that his is a highly articulated, or intellectual, *verbal* music, a point Mallarmé was at some pains to make critically (particularly in his essay on Wagner).

These salient and better-known qualities of Mallarmé are complemented, as we said earlier, by certain classic tendencies, apparent enough for Claudel to dub him "the crown of the French classic tradition." He generally uses a quite standard vocabulary — however selective — and established verse forms, and refers to things everybody knows. Together with flashes of inspiration he believes in and practices self-critical, patient craftsmanship. He is eager to communicate with the many, eventually, on his own élite terms, and even to transform his society by "purifying the dialect of the tribe" as well as by expanding its total vision or myth. Occasionally he is rather rhetorical, in a refined way, as in *Toast funèbre.* He was, for a poet, a surprisingly decorous citizen and a good family man. In this broad direction, we may put the gentle and kindly, if not always appreciated, English teacher; the charming, though impecunious, Parisian host of the *mardis,* friend to many a minor (as well as major) painter, musician, and versifier; the editor of a fashion magazine, and author of the love poems to Méry and the amiable *vers de circonstance;* and, finally, the warm master of Valvins, with his donkey cart and his little sailboat.

The psychic tension we discussed earlier, which is primordially be-
* tween mind and body, extends, particularly in mature artists of the rare Symbolist type, to the relation between the two personae, classic and romantic. Hence the "glory of the long desire" is all the sweeter in Mallarmé for his being so hesitant, so conscious and careful, so "classic" in his métier. The third version of *L'Après-midi d'un faune* is more grati-

fying than the first. Or, as a clearer example, if we compare almost any poem of Hugo (excepting a few like *Booz endormi*) with almost any by his "cher poète impressioniste," we find that, contrary to a common notion, in the former the emotional impact of the imagery tends to be canceled, rather than furthered, by the shapes and sounds of the words. Let us pursue these comparisons briefly to get some further historical bearings on our poet.

From Baudelaire to Mallarmé the gains are not as apparent as in the foregoing example, but they are, nonetheless, there, not only in the weightier individual poems like *L'Après-midi d'un faune* or *Toast funèbre* or *Hérodiade* but, more, in the conception and partial execution of an overall *Oeuvre* (which his poems helped prepare). Conversely, the architecture of the *Fleurs du mal* is arbitrary and unimportant; Baudelaire shifted poems around in a way that precludes any precision of total scheme and, at most, there is a loose anecdotal or fairly obvious thread binding the various parts. Altogether Baudelaire is a more easy-going figure, often even casual—he knocked off many poems on set themes to fill gaps in his collection—though unquestionably a very great one.

Baudelaire is usually a realistic poet, implying a warm middle style that is closer to prose; Mallarmé is more often a "pure" or a poetic one, implying a more taut style, greater distillation and radiancy. The reader who prefers novels, or theater, to poetry finds Baudelaire naturally more congenial; those who put poetry above the other genres are apt to find it more difficult to choose between the two.

Mallarmé's miraculous younger contemporary, Rimbaud, is a considerably less-developed poet, in the sense of steady craftsmanship and conscious control. This seems likely enough, given the brevity and the precociousness of his career. Rimbaud opens up areas of childhood and immediate experience of nature and dream or hallucination that are entirely original; there has never been anything quite like him. Mallarmé, nonetheless, shares a good deal of the fresh ingenuousness of Rimbaud's vision, as can be seen from the early poem *Le Sonneur*:

> Cependant que la cloche éveille sa voix claire
> À l'air pur et limpide et profond du matin
> Et passe sur l'enfant qui jette pour lui plaire
> Un angelus parmi la lavande et le thym, . . .

This kind of transparency pervades Mallarmé's later writing as well, though less exclusively. *Le Sonneur* indicates he could have trodden further along the earthy Rimbaldian path and also raises the distinct possibility that Rimbaud took an important cue here (it appeared in the

Parnasse contemporain of 1866, which he is known to have read atten-
tively; he "pastiched" Mallarmé's *Les Fleurs* from the same group).
Le Sonneur, incidentally, illustrates Mallarmé's remarkable hidden resources of vitality: he had an extraordinary capacity for deep inner
change, metamorphosis, and could assume manner after manner,
whether derivatively (the Baudelaire or Banville vein) or unprece-
dentedly. Almost every poem in the *Poésies* represents a start in a radically new direction. This is particularly noticeable in the earlier poems,
as the later ones are increasingly a part of the developed Mallarméan
idiom, the verbal net being woven to include all reality in the one
Grand' Oeuvre.

A few words on Valéry will round out this summary review. Valéry
often, and fervently, stated his immense debt to Mallarmé, in remarks
like: "I don't know what I would have become if he hadn't existed."
Moreover, one need merely line up his own favorite verse (the section
beginning with "Ô douceur de survivre à la force du jour") from *Fragments d'un Narcisse,* with a comparable passage from the *Faune* (for
example: "Ainsi quand des raisins j'ai sucé la clarté," or "Tu sais ma
passion que pourpre et déjà mûre" and the few lines that follow), to
see that Mallarmé is the original and concentrated phenomenon, Valéry
the extremely talented disciple. Valéry does, at times, extend sensibility to new areas, certain timbres and luminosities all his own or fil-
tered from other sources. His verse, particularly in *La Jeune Parque,*
or the numerous didactic passages of the *Cimetière marin,* often tends
toward a Racinian (occasionally Villonesque) discursive horizontality or
bel canto melodiousness and is generally therefore less "crystallized," in
the sense we defined previously, less purely poetic than Mallarmé's,
more classic and sometimes even monotonously so. This is, of course,
an entirely relative matter, and there is no questioning Valéry's pre-
ëminence in the twentieth century. All the more reason why we ought to
take him seriously when he tells us that Mallarmé is "the most perfect"
poet who ever held a pen.

I began putting together a study of Mallarmé's *Poésies* in 1948.
Before the study got very far on paper I became absorbed in the *Coup
de Dés.* This was newer and more challenging territory and it occupied
me for the next few years. The amassed notes on the *Poésies* served this
project as the *Coup de Dés* synthesizes, to a considerable extent,
Mallarmé's lifetime poetic efforts. But, of course, everything did not
get into the synthesis, and in any case the earlier poems were very interesting works of art in their own right, and deserved independent
comment despite Mallarmé's modest insistence that they were mere
exercises.

Meanwhile others have been publishing their own interpretations in numerous books and articles, to be crammed onto an already full shelf on the subject. Occasionally, using the new material that has come to light, they have duplicated my own dormant discoveries. Still, I will surprise no one if I announce that there is a great deal remaining to be turned up and appreciated in these poems. And no one will surprise me by the news that, having read my book, the reader discovers some harmonies and possible meanings I missed.

I should like to make plain, nonetheless, that I do not believe there are various possible interpretations of Mallarmé: this is a view held by individuals who do not, I am convinced, care much about Mallarmé or probably even art (though they may very well care about equally important values), and when Valéry claimed the contrary (Preface to *Charmes*), I can only assume he was in an unusually insouciant and desultory mood. There is only *one* meaning to a Mallarmé poem, or any other authentic poem. True, the meaning may be exceedingly complex, polyvalent, ambiguous (in the well-known Empsonian sense); it may be constructed in places like music, with overtones achieved through a sort of verbal equivalent to chords; moreover, the poet himself is not always fully aware of his meaning, at the conscious level. All this makes for added problems of interpretation, but it does not alter the basic condition of *integrity,* or authenticity, or inner harmony. Of course, even the most eager critic may not *find* the complete meaning at the first or even the tenth reading. Still, as we know in our depths that there is only one best way of expressing a given idea (we may try a dozen drafts before approaching it), just so, although it cannot be dogmatically stated that a given interpretation for each poem is the ultimate, nevertheless, assuming the postulate of integrity, one is naturally inclined to keep on trying when others have abandoned the chase. Is this not, after all, what is meant by "faith"?

My aim is to be as simple, and readable, as is possible under the circumstances.

That Mallarmé is a difficult writer everyone agrees. Above all, however, he is an exquisite poet. The problem then is, first, always to evoke the single total impact of intellectually refined beauty (with, ultimately, the simultaneity or unity of effect achieved by, say, the impressionist painters he knew and appreciated), which impact depends largely on certain key effects clustered in a central constellation of interrelated word-images. The commentator must try, therefore, to indicate this dominant shape of delight in each poem; or, since he, like his subject, necessarily, *faute de mieux,* proceeds in the linear pattern of words, he must show the "main way" of meaning or art through each poem.

Secondly, without overloading his pages, the "guide" will attempt to point out some secondary threads of meaning which link the primary ones radiating from the center of the "web" (where Mallarmé saw himself installed as the "sacred Spider"). Third, since not a few passages are still obscure, despite the many attempts to dispel that obscurity, the critic must elucidate these, bringing in some proof, primarily by quoting from other poems or prose writings.

When to all this are added various other considerations of *explication de texte,* such as comments on felicities of expression or attitude, rhyme-schemes, rhythms, revelation of sources, snatches of general literary history, or biography, the going can get heavy for the reader. What to do? One partial solution is to ruthlessly reduce the scholarly apparatus. For example, we must resist the temptation to bring in excessive amounts of substantiating material from Mallarmé, or from others. The heavy guns of exegesis should be reserved for the truly resistant passages. Any extra material of this sort, which is of secondary interest, will go into notes at the end of each chapter.

Generally, our ambition here is to concentrate on the poetry as such. Biographical or literary-historical material is kept down to the bare minimum, not because we do not believe in it—we do, and often rely on it—but this can be found *in extenso* in worthy studies by Mondor, Wais, Michaud. On the other hand, we hope to have brought new insights to not a few of these *Poésies,* however often they have been gone over before.

I am indebted to many previous commentators and exegetes; whenever I am conscious of a direct borrowing, I mention the name. I have found, on the whole, Thibaudet and Mauron to be the most gifted of the earlier critics on the subject. Reservations about both of them were expressed in our *L'Oeuvre de Mallarmé: Un Coup de Dés,* and those reservations extend to their work on the *Poésies.* Thibaudet, immensely talented, was handicapped by the then unavailability of much important material. A graver deficiency was his excessive eagerness to *deal* with Mallarmé, labeling him as an "idealist" and the like. Mauron's attempt to psychoanalyze Mallarmé is worthwhile as a loose study of some emotional roots of his art, though, in truth, the superbly aware Mallarmé had gone farther into this subterranean domain and himself provides all the main clues. For example, why speak of *revealing* a dead-sister complex in a man who himself said in his correspondence that he was haunted by his sister and his mother and that his future work would be a sacrificial offering to them, and who often spoke consciously in his critical writings of the major obsessions of the *id*? The obviously mature approach is to work *with* Mallarmé in this respect.

More recently numerous others have added considerably to our knowledge of Mallarmé: Madame Noulet has made solid contributions, Mondor has brought much new material to light, Wais has not a few perceptive pages, as do Chisholm, Gengoux, Davies, Michaud, Fowlie; it all helps immensely. In sum, there is no monopolizing our poet.

The monumental work of Jean-Pierre Richard, *L'Univers imaginaire de Mallarmé,* deserves special mention. It appeared when my manuscript was receiving its final touches. On the whole, despite numerous reservations, it is gratifying to see the emergence of a scholar who is willing to approach Mallarmé with the minuteness and patience he deserves. Although he often fails to draw the full or adequate conclusions, particularly in regard to the *Coup de Dés,* at almost every point he confirms my remarks on that *Poème*—though in a roundabout and often inadvertent way—as well as on these *Poésies.* How the new material that he discusses and his parallel views bear on the *Coup de Dés* we hope to show in a future little book.

Richard's volume is remarkable, but chiefly, as we have come to expect of him, as a study of the man (a sort of inner biography) or, rather, of the "everypoet" in Mallarmé. This is scientific and general *pre*-criticism, or aesthetics, rather than criticism and does not rise to the full specificity of the individual works. How often an image pinned down by a dozen quotations will change under the impact of neighboring images in a given poem! But, while much space is allotted to juvenilia or repetitious documentation, the poems themselves receive a few lines (or, at most, a couple of pages) each. Richard chooses to ignore, for practical purposes, Mallarmé's biggest single effort at a poetic work, the *Coup de Dés.* In this way, *he,* Richard—as he candidly admits to be his aim—becomes the owner of the ambitious syntactical or "totalizing" vision which is properly Mallarmé's. God protect us from our friends!

But, within his limits, on his chosen terrain, Richard is impressive and an almost flawless scholar. He provides an excellent checklist of themes and images, a few new insights which I have acknowledged, and an up-to-date bibliography with only a few noteworthy omissions.

To his friend, Verlaine, Mallarmé (in what is now known as the *Autobiographie*) wrote the following concerning his *Poésies:*

> . . . l'époque . . . est trop en désuétude et en effervescence préparatoire pour qu'il y ait autre chose à faire qu'à travailler avec mystère en vue de plus tard ou de jamais et de temps en temps à envoyer aux vivants sa carte de visite, stances ou sonnet . . . (664)

Well, like all mortals, Mallarmé was inconsistent. He obviously cared about his *Poésies* rather more than the above "carte de visite" or, as he termed them elsewhere, "études en vue de mieux, comme on essaie les becs de sa plume" (76), would indicate. No doubt, like all geniuses he occasionally sighed to be simpler, to resemble more ordinary men, even to achieve a sort of popular success—or why else would he have tried to write a stage version of the *Faune* for the *Comédie Française* or, later, have the poem reviewed by a well-placed friend of a friend? He undoubtedly derived considerable pride from these poems which were read and appreciated by many, even in his lifetime. He worked and reworked them and occasionally published them in more than one place. In a letter to Gosse he spoke of them as "des points de repère très exacts de mon esprit," meaning that although they were not actually the final thing, they were pretty good indicators of what that crowning work would be like. He particularly cared about the *Faune* which he mentions apart in the *Bibliographie* (77); and indeed, it may well be, as the young Valéry enthused, the most accomplished poem in the French language. Another long poem, *Prose (pour des Esseintes)* is clearly ambitious too, a kind of interim report on the poet's dream of a *Grand 'Oeuvre;* it crams in many of the framentary artistic crystallizations that arose in him through the years of waiting and working toward the major effort. *Toast funèbre* is comparably weighty, and it is the favorite of some fine readers; it is in a fairly official or rhetorical vein yet bears many of the unmistakable marks of this highly particular poet. And, of course, *Hérodiade*—the whole *Mystère,* or dramatic poem —is a lifetime project second only to the *Livre. Hérodiade* stands, so to speak, halfway between his total vision and the more ordinary verse (for instance, his love poems to Méry). It was still very much on his mind just before he died.

The more elusive later poems, since roughly the *Igitur* crisis (1866-1869), all reflect, as in some sense everything he wrote does, his central vision—even when he denies it, as in the case of *Ses purs ongles.* Sometimes these *cartes de visite* are fantastically rich in poetic substance, as if, despite their occasional nature, he had tried to do his best anyway, to dazzle the reader and derive heightened glory from the apparent casualness. Some seem overstuffed, like the *Tombeau de Charles Baudelaire*—though here the subject perhaps called for this jammed late-nineteenth-century quality—but, when we are up to him, even these denser and more challenging sonnets can come alive in a rare way. Mallarmé was certainly ambitious and some will say pretentious — that key mid-twentieth-century word by which we console each other for our mediocrity—but fortunately he had the resources to back his ambitions, which is to say that he was a hard-headed and even shrewd realist as well as (or fused with) a dreamer, and knew there was no substitute for the achieved poetic result, line by line, word by word, (and even letter by letter, space by space). To understate the matter in our American way, we may say in sum that he almost never short-changed. Moved by a deep sense of debt—to his beloved dead, to the spiritual fathers, to life—with pride and humility, he very often gave us in these *Poésies* something like his all.

1. L'APRÈS-MIDI D'UN FAUNE

◇⟡◇⟡◇⟡◇⟡◇

The young Valéry called this dramatic monologue the best poem in French literature, and it may well be the king of the anthologies. Mallarmé tended to set it apart from his other *Poésies;* perhaps only *Hérodiade* could rival it in his own mind (aside, of course, from the vastly more ambitious *Coup de Dés*).[1] It is certainly very French, alexandrines in the lineage of La Fontaine (*Adonis*) and Racine (*Phèdre*), classically clear, or as clear as great poetry can or ought to be; after all, even reading Racine takes effort. Yet look what richness late romanticism (Symbolism's substance) has brought to the French tradition! One of the best guides to the mood of the poem is Debussy's *Prelude* which, as is well known, was inspired by it and was admired in turn by the inspirer. The introduction via Debussy can be helpful mainly because the more obvious, physically-gripping qualities of such music[2] offset the sad mistake of approaching Mallarmé as if he were coldly intellectual, an "algebraist" of literature, and so forth. He is indeed (to invoke a still-useful cliché) as precise as the mathematician in his own, literary fashion. But the thing about poetry is that it manages to fuse such analytic exactness or minuteness with warmth, or love, or passion at every step, all the way. The critic and the reader owe it to the masterpieces to approach them with the best of *both* these resources— intellect and feeling—they can muster, and preferably in a mood approaching those rare moments when all our faculties seem as one, as branches of a single tree of Being, with the sap rising full.[3]

There exist three major versions of the *Faune,* which were written over a period of ten years. It first appeared in 1876. We take note of some important variants, but for the complete texts and detailed comparisons, I refer the reader to Mondor's *Histoire d'un faune.* *

The title owes something to a new appreciation of subtle *états d'âme* beginning, say, with Watteau, "le peintre des fêtes d'après-midi dans les parcs" (Baudelaire, "Théophile Gautier"). *

Le Faune	The Faun
Ces nymphes, je les veux perpétuer.	These nymphs, I want to perpetuate.

The opening line has the joint possibilities of procreation and creation; to perpetuate in the flesh or in the spirit. Together they con-

13

14 L'APRÈS-MIDI D'UN FAUNE

stitute an image of the play between nature and its mirrored aspect in art; they depict the process of the distillation of reality. The faun—like the poet in Eliot's conception, "both more primitive and more civilized" —is very sensual and yet very hesitant or unsure; in other words, he represents or reflects the complex, intellectually-refined, voluptuous psyche of his author. *Perpétuer,* in sum, is of the essence of art. We may think of the *Metamorphoses* of Ovid, whose central myths—so fertile in the Western tradition—tell us how the sensitive being, fleeing from some forbidden or frighteningly direct form of love, is converted into something permanent, within which is hidden, like the nymph in the willow trunk, the suffering, thwarted, but consenting human soul. The specific Ovidian myth here invoked is the story of Syrinx, who runs away from Pan, and is at last turned into a reed among reeds which, plucked, become the instrument of music. Laforgue, remembering his Mallarmé in a *Moralité légendaire* about this classic woodland pair, summed up the underlying theme as "l'art c'est le désir perpétué."

The primitive aspect, the innocent candor of the faun—half-beast, half-deity, like Hugo's satyr, whose transparent aim is to obliviously treat himself to the ravishing of nature's Queen—is expressed by the direct "je les veux."[4]

As we said, *perpétuer* (with its petulant, swelling *p*'s) is, like so much in this poem, of initially uncertain meaning (Mallarmé's richer words are rather like musical chords, many-leveled and harmonious): bring them back in the flesh, prolong them in his memory, perpetuate them in art, perpetuate them in offspring.

Si clair,   So clear,
Leur incarnat léger, qu'il voltige dans   Their light incarnadine, that it lilts in
   l'air   the air
Assoupi de sommeils touffus.   Drowsy with tufted slumbers.

The broken line adds space, purity, airiness; it also puts some more variety, movement, vitality into the alexandrine, as do the different type sizes; thus new dimensions of art are introduced, usually for meaningful reasons. The jump here is in the spirit of the *voltige,* of the vaulting arabesque of flute melody, as Debussy caught it. It sets off the first petulant statement from the blob of watery color of *si clair.* The artfulness, the musicality of the intent is underlined by the fact that *Si* (one of Mallarmé's favorite words; C, p. 305) is one of the tone symbols of solfeggio (cf. *qui cherche le la,* below).

Mallarmé uses the same combination of words, *si* and *clair,* partly because of their bright sounds, for a similar effect in *Sur les bois oubliés:* "Âme, au si clair foyer tremblante."

Altogether the opening lines are in a Renoir-like atmosphere of

lightness—rosy flesh, light, air—and heavy darkness—the woods' tufted
slumbers at drowsy noon (including the slumber of nymphs). Mallarmé
wrote Debussy in reference to the *Prelude:* "Vraiment vous m'avez
dépassé en lumière et nostalgie." The lilting, soaring, bubbly, flute melo-   *
dy in the upper reaches—the *lumière*—contrasts with the deep-throated,
moaning, amorous cellos — the *nostalgie* — throughout the orchestral
transcription. Similar tonal contrasts are found in typical Renoir: lyric
freshness and swirling washes of voluptuousness. In the poem the effect
is achieved by contrasts of imagery: *Si clair / Leur incarnat léger qu'il
voltige dans l'air* is contrasted with *Assoupi de sommeils touffus.*
Further, the bright sounds of the acute *é* and *er* of *léger* (and the *i* of
voltige) or the transparent *ar* cluster (*air-clair-incarnat*) are pitted
against the darkest non-nasal vowel in the language, the *ou* in *assoupi*
and *touffus.*[5]

Aimai-je un rêve?   Did I love a dream?

The doubt is in the question, and the dream-mood of *rêve* permeates
the poem.

Mon doute, amas de nuit ancienne, s'achève	My doubt, accumulation of old night, ends
En maint rameau subtil, qui, demeuré les vrais	In many a subtle bough, which, [having] remained the true
Bois mêmes, prouve hélas! que bien seul je m'offrais	Woods themselves proves, alas, that all I offered myself
Pour triomphe la faute idéale de roses.	For triumph was the ideal fault [sin] of roses.

In his study of the poem, Chisholm comments: "The heaviness of sleep
(*amas de nuit ancienne*) has left the faun uncertain. But his uncer-
tainty seems to be dispelled (*mon doute s'achève*) as he grows more
lucid and alert." This is fine but scarcely sufficient. An earlier version
of the poem, *Improvisation d'un Faune,* had:

> Mon doute, loin ici de finir, se prolonge
> En de mornes rameaux; qui, demeurés ces vrais
> Massifs noirs . . .

In other words, made possible by the ambiguity of the final choice
s'achève, we may become aware of a counterpointed theme of familiar
Mallarméan metaphysics: Old Night pushes fingers of negation, like the
ink strokes of the tree etching that is created herewith, into awareness
as doubt or analytic consciousness which tells the faun he must have
been dreaming: "Un doute . . . la goutte d'encre apparentée à la nuit
sublime" (481).[6] The effect is startling because there is a jump from one
category of apprehension, the analytic faculty—"maint rameau subtil"

—to another, the direct sensing of nature—"les vrais bois"—an effect
very like the one Marianne Moore gets with her "imaginary garden with
live toads" or Rimbaud's "j'ai vu quelquefois ce que les hommes ont
cru voir" (*Le Bateau Ivre*), which is pretty much what Mallarmé was
saying in *Prose*:

> Oui, dans une île que l'air charge
> De vue et non de visions

The most direct meaning is that the reality of the woods—as opposed to the nonexistent nymphs (represented perhaps only by roses
which he mistook for them)—proves his "fault" (love-act) was only an
"ideal" or unreal one, with a sort of "spectre of a rose," as in Gautier's
*   familiar poem.

"Rose" is always feminine for Mallarmé (in *Hérodiade,* in the
poems to Méry, and so forth), as it had been for Guillaume de Lorris,
Ronsard, and many another poet. The association "Roses . . . nids" (in
Ce que disaient les trois cigognes) indicates an intimate reason for this
ancient symbolism. Note the *o*.

Triomphe: implies an experience of floral beauty which we find in
other Mallarmé poems—still, this was obviously not quite *it*.

The orchestration of sounds is almost consistently remarkable in the
Faune. The dark *ou* of *doute* reinforces the blackness specifically stated
in *amas de nuit ancienne*. The delicate acute *u* and *i* of *subtil* add to the
subtlety as does the faint diphthong of *maint* which is a vibrant word
(unity in multiplicity) appropriate to the unsure mood. The rounded *b*
and *o* of *bois* are possibly reminders that these are suavely-rounded
French woods, though ostensibly Sicilian. The *p* and *o* of *pour* and
triomphe (and of the *o* of *roses*) are a favorite Mallarmé effect, for
swelling Eros, as in "L'or de la trompette d'Été," "Grandissait trop
pour nos raisons," "le trop grand glaïeul." (*Prose*); and, as in "Dame
sans trop d'ardeur à la fois enflammant / La rose . . ." (*Sonnet*).

Réfléchissons . . .   Let us reflect . . .

> ou si les femmes dont tu gloses   or what if the women you expound
> **Figurent** un souhait de tes sens fabu- Represent a wish of your fabulous
> leux!   senses!

The meaning of the *ou si* is somewhat obscure; we might read: "Let
us reflect . . . or [the problem is] whether the women you are puzzling
about are a mere wish-dream of your fabulous senses." (Acoustically,
the *ou si* is one of those steep contrasts that afford sudden artistic jolts,
like the *si plonge* of *Petit Air, I* or Debussy's plunging harp glissando, in
his *Prelude,* instantaneously fusing the upper and lower.)

fabuleux: is both "wonderful" and "the faun is a creature of fable."

femmes dont tu gloses: the meaning can also be secondarily "women you gossip (unkindly) about" or "complain of"; because of the *gl, gloses* has some of the feeling of the similar outburst in *Gloire du long désir (Prose):* "G . . . une aspiration simple . . . le désir, comme satisfait par *l* exprime avec la dite liquide . . . joie, lumière, etc." (938): compare *blancs sanglots glissants* (in *Apparition*).

Faune, l'illusion s'échappe des yeux bleus
Et froids, comme une source en pleurs, de la plus chaste:

Faun, the illusion escapes from the blue
And cold eyes, like a tear-welling spring, of the chaster [nymph]:

It is not clear whether the "illusion" that "escapes from the blue eyes" of the chaster nymph is enhanced or dissipated—and so much the better poetically. Mauron plumps for the heightening, Chisholm the lessening, why not either, in the faun's oscillating mind? Considering that Mallarmé is indeed, as Chisholm avers, trying to "take back his own" from music in this piece, such a fluttering, tentative query, perhaps in an unsteady key or mode, or through the unresolved chords of "deceptive cadence," is of the essence of good music (Brahms, Debussy), and poetry can afford some of it.

The ambiguous meaning is then that the illusion is dissipated by the clear reminiscence of the blue-eyed nymph; that the illusion *was* an illusion, emerging from a dubious blue-eyed nymph who could be also a mere "spring in tears"; Syrinx, incidentally, was a fountain-nymph.

Note the brightness or lucidity of *i* and *u* in *illusion. Source en pleurs* is a fine effect of brimming-over of water; as if from the tense container of *u* (cf. *urne*) which is a receptacle in shape but a concentration in sound, a release of expression seems to well up and spill over in the liquid *r* which, graphically, is a sort of brimming or spilling-over in both words.

Mais, l'autre, tout soupirs, dis-tu qu'elle contraste
Comme brise du jour chaude dans ta toison?

But, the other [nymph], all sighs, do you say she contrasts
Like a hot breeze of the [hot] day in your fleece?

Continuing the hypothesis for the previous lines, that is, "if the cold nymph existed, perhaps, merely as spring water, then shall we say that the warm one existed perhaps only as a summer breeze in my fleece?" The faun is *very* unsure. (Note the dark *ou*'s in *tout soupirs* for the brunette.)

On the whole the unsureness itself is the theme. In the first version of the poem these lines read: "L'illusion, Sylvain, appelle les yeux bleus / Et verts, comme les fleurs des eaux, de la plus chaste," and the main effect is the impressionistic painting of a luminous inner landscape in which the longed-for woman's transparent spring-watery eyes are seen, the very color of artistic, illusory—dreamed-of—airily transcendent desire. Illusion is naturally associated with the naive nymph, the limpidity of her blue eyes, the ingenuousness of her soul: "bleus . . . couleur d'illusion, du temps et de l'azur" (859).

Que non! par l'immobile et lasse pâmoison	But no! through the motionless and weary fainting [heat effect]
Suffoquant de chaleurs le matin frais s'il lutte,	Suffocating with heat the fresh morning, if it struggles [up with a breath of air],
Ne murmure point d'eau que ne verse ma flûte	Murmurs no [sound of] water but that which my flute pours
Au bosquet arrosé d'accords; et le seul vent	Into the grove sprinkled with chords; and the only wind
Hors des deux tuyaux prompt à s'ex-haler avant	[Coming] Out of the two pipes prompt to exhale itself before
Qu'il disperse le son dans une pluie aride,	It disperses the sound in an arid rain,
C'est, à l'horizon pas remué d'une ride,	Is, on the horizon unstirred by so much as a wrinkle,
Le visible et serein souffle artificiel	The visible and serene artificial breath
De l'inspiration, qui regagne le ciel.	Of inspiration, which regains heaven.

Meaning that there was not even any water except the "liquid" sounds formed by my flute, nor any breath of wind except that exhaled from the instrument (*souffle artificiel de l'inspiration*); hence there was nothing at all but my dream; or since there was no water nor breeze, perhaps there were real nymphs.

The faun is still not at all certain . . .

The modulations between nature, or reality, and art (with an intermediate phase of fiction or dream), are very knowing here, with fluid transpositions between sound and sight. In *bosquets arrosés d'accords,* for example, there is imagined a "visible" sprinkle of notes (like the visible wrinkle of wind below). The art theme, of inspiration returning, like the smoke of a burnt offering, to its mother-source is parallel to the image in *Toast funèbre:* the sunlight reflected in the window of Gautier's tomb seems to be the light of his genius returning in death to its sun-source. (Cf. *Le Cantique de Saint Jean:* "au même / Principe qui m'élut / Penche un salut".)

Note the defeated flatness of the *a* in *lasse* and *pâmoison;* the delicate diphthong of *frais* and the breezy *f* as in *souffle;* we may remember Hugo's "Un frais parfum sortait des touffes d'asphodèles / Les souffles de la nuit flottaient sur Galgala" (Plato, in his *Cratylus,* commented on the same windy effect of the Greek *f*). Then there is the more traditional onomatopoeia of *murmuré*: soft summery *m*'s, flute-like *u*'s, liquid *r*'s. The verse has a transparency in the *ver* (*verre,* cf. *hiver lucide* in *Renouveau*) that is furthered in the prominent *ar* group: *pluie aride-arti-ficielle-inspiration* (with a corollary effect in *serein*); compare the transparent grape skin later, with its seven *ar* effects.

aride: since it is not true rain (Fowlie).

matin frais s'il lutte: the struggle of morning freshness against the heat.

Ô bords siciliens d'un calme marécage	O Sicilian banks of a calm marsh
Qu'à l'envi de soleils ma vanité saccage,	That my vanity plunders like the [recurrent] suns,
Tacite sous les fleurs d'étincelles, CONTEZ	Tacit [the marsh], under the flowers of sparks, TELL

(The Sicilian setting is a vestige of Theocritus, the ancient practitioner par excellence of pastoral poetry such as this.)

Meaning: that the faun seeks explanation from the site—O tacit banks of the marsh that my vanity (overweening desire, or desire for truth) like the burning sun, plunders (seeking the facts, or the reeds, or the nymphs) TELL (what happened). The italics indicate a change to the more fragile mood of a memory.

Note the flat *a*'s of *calme marécage;* the impressionistic imagery of "flowers of sparks" evokes the play of a dazzling light at high noon.

"*Que je coupais ici les creux roseaux domptés*	*That I was cutting here the hollow reeds tamed*
"*Par le talent; quand, sur l'or glauque de lointaines*	*By talent; when, on the glaucous gold of distant*
"*Verdures dédiant leur vigne à des fontaines,*	*Greeneries dedicating [clinging] their vine to wellsprings,*
"*Ondoie une blancheur animale au repos:*	*Undulates an animal whiteness in repose:*
"*Et qu'au prélude lent où naissent les pipeaux*	*And [Tell] that at the slow prelude with which the pipes are born [start up]*
"*Ce vol de cygnes, non! de naïades se sauve*	*The flight of swans, no! of naïads flees*
"*Ou plonge . . ."*	*Or plunges . . ."*

The reeds "tamed by talent" refer to the old Pan-Syrinx myth: taming nature into art, or the faun's ingenious appropriation of the reeds.

dédiant: implies the finger-like clutch of the vines (etymology: *digitus,* cf. *Ses purs ongles*).

blancheur animale: (with its mat effect of the two *a*'s) is an aston-
ishing expanse of sensual whiteness in the woods. The confusion of
swans and naked maidens, with the corollary confusion of purity and
voluptuousness, recalls the early poem *Loeda:* "Sous son aile il
dépose / La nymphe frémissante: ils ne forment qu'un corps" (ML).
Note the combined effect of *naissent* and *naïades,* evoking a tone of
milky whiteness (mother's milk linked to the birth theme: see Appendix
A) in the nymph or swan flanks.

ou plonge originally read *y plonge*: the *ou* adds a downward dark
tone, a rounded *o*, a pendulous *u,* to the sense of *plonge* with its
caressing *g;* compare *Quelconque une solitude:* "Mais langoureusement
longe / Comme de blanc *linge* ôté / . . . si *plonge.*"

Inerte, tout brûle dans l'heure fauve	Inert, all burns in the tawny hour
Sans marquer par quel art ensemble détala	Without showing by what art [ruse] together ran off [the nymphs]
Trop d'hymen souhaité de qui cherche le *la*:	Too much hymen [with the nymphs] desired by [me] the one who seeks the *la*:
Alors m'éveillerai-je à la ferveur première,	Then I'll awaken to the first fervor,
Droit et seul, sous un flot antique de lumière,	Straight and alone, under an ancient flood of light,
Lys! et l'un de vous tous pour l'ingénuité.	Lily! [or lilies] and one of you all [lilies] in point of candor.

This tuning up refers to both the musician and the seeker after a
simpler harmony of the flesh. *Trop d'hymen* is the hyperbolic desire for
two (or many) nymphs, with a suggestion that it is the excessiveness
of his (typically creative) desire that makes him lose the reality. The
"Alors m'éveillerai . . ." refers to his acute erotic tension within which
he remains pure and intact (though unintentionally) and his whole
person stands up rigid with desire. The phallic overtones have been
noted by Huysmans (in *À Rebours*) and, though denied by some, are
clearly a Mallarméan side effect. The corresponding passage of the first
version of the *Monologue* has "je suis donc la proie / De mon désir
torride, et si trouble qu'il croit / Aux ivresses de la sève? Serais-je pur?"
The lily metaphor, white and tall (emphasized by the vertical exclamation mark) is used elsewhere by Mallarmé (*Toast funèbre*) contrasted
to the eternally-feminine rose that is here associated with the nymphs.

"L'un de vous tous pour l'ingénuité" means "I am one of the lilies
in white candor, purity"; (the version called *Improvisation* had "Lilies;
and amid you all, beautiful with candor").

Note the rendering of transparently empty (of nymphs) summer air in the line: *Sans marquer par quel art ensemble détala,* with its three *ar* effects.

   trop: is swelling and hyperbolic, as in the *trop grand glaïeul* of *Prose,* or the *trop* expressing the hubris of the *prince amer de l'écueil* of the *Coup de Dés; m'éveillerai-je* is bright and rising. *Droit* has overtones of *roi, roide,* and *froid. Lys* is based on the acute *i* sound, reinforced by the narrowness of the word and the exclamation mark. The *vous tous* has the more subdued tone (*ou*) of a background crowd (of lilies) contrasted to the bright *lys!* and *ingénuité;* the plural, as always in Mallarmé (e.g., "l'absente de *tous bouquets*"—note also the two *ou*'s), helps render this "background" quality; see under *s* in Appendix C.

Autre que ce doux rien par leur lèvre ébruité,	Other than the sweet nothing [the kiss] rumored by their lips,
Le baiser, qui tout bas des perfides assure,	The kiss, which quietly assures of the perfidious ones,
Mon sein, vierge de preuve, atteste une morsure	My breast, virgin of proof, attests a bite,
Mystérieuse, due à quelque auguste dent;	Mysterious, due to some august tooth;

   doux rien: is the mere possibility of a remembered or dreamed-of nymph's kiss; the *morsure mystérieuse* is possibly a memento of the nymphs but primarily refers to the faun's failure, something like his original guilt ("remorse" stems from "re-morse," "again-bite," as in the Old English phrase "agenbite of inwit," or the prick of conscience: "remords . . . la dent [du] crime," *Angoisse*); compare the "frayeur secrète de la chair," below (primarily the nymph's but also hinted to be the faun's) and the *vagues trépas,* later, which made him loosen his arms and lose the nymphs; in this sense the *auguste dent* is of a deity, the "biter" of his conscience. Note the hard *t*'s of *atteste, auguste,* and *dent,* and *d*'s of *du* and *dent* for the bite; the *ou* and *a* of *tout bas.*

Mais, bast! arcane tel élut pour confident	But, enough! such a mystery chose for confident
Le jonc vaste et jumeau dont sous l'azur on joue:	The vast and twin reed on which one plays under the azure:
Qui, détournant à soi le trouble de la joue,	Which, turning to itself [the reed-flute] the trouble of the cheek,
Rêve, dans un solo long, que nous amusions	Dreams, in a long solo, that we were beguiling
La beauté d'alentour par des confusions	The surrounding beauty [of nature] by false [fictitious] confusions
Fausses entre elle-même et notre chant crédule;	Between itself [the beauty] and our credulous song;
Et de faire aussi haut que l'amour se module	And [dreams] to make, as high as love modulates,

Évanouir du songe ordinaire de dos	Vanish [distill] from the ordinary dream of a back
Ou de flanc pur suivis avec mes regards clos,	Or a pure flank followed by my closed looks,
Une sonore, vaine et monotone ligne.	[Distill] A sonorous, vain and monotonous line.

The mystery of guilt troubles him, and he diverts his trouble from his cheek into the flute, converting nature—or the real naked body (*ordinaire*)—by a distillation, into melody, or (through synesthesia) arabesquing lines in the air. The imagery is magnificently archetypal or phenomenological: the depth of Mallarmé's vision—universal analogy —allows him to play, or modulate, between categories of being with masterly inclusiveness and control. He beguiles the beauty of the surroundings [nature] by "des confusions / Fausses entre elle-même [beauty of nature] et notre chant crédule," that is, he amuses nature with its distillation in his art (fiction: *confusions fausses*), and he modulates, or plays, back and forth between the two realms; in *Prose* he similarly compares nature's beauty to that of his feminine companion.

The series of *o*'s in *solo long* and *sonore, vaine et monotone ligne* are the "bubbles" of his flute notes, visible sound.[7] *trouble* is also pleasantly burbly; "gonfler sa flûte indécise / Du trouble" (111).

crédule: implies that an original naïve belief in the power of art to magically influence nature is leading to a disenchantment *(vaine)*.

regards clos: inner vision, dreams, but also a suggestion of the artistic half-look.

Note the series of *j*'s in *jonc . . . jumeaux . . . joue;* a form of *i,* it also has a jabbing or thrust quality, suited to the reed or flute. The twisting soaring rise of *évanouir* (*ou* to *i*)—duplicated in a memorable moment of Debussy's score—is like the *ou-i* rising wind effect Mallarmé described to George Moore (C, p. 96); or *épanouir* with its corollary effect, the convoluted spiralling-up of bloom.

Tâche donc, instrument des fuites, ô maligne	Try then, instrument of flights, O wicked
Syrinx, de refleurir aux lacs où tu m'attends!	Syrinx, to reflower [as reeds again] at the lakes where you await me!

In a fitful gesture, the faun flings aside the flute of which he is now tired, and tells it to become a reed again; the *tu m'attends* refers to the reeds which wait to be plucked by him: "[moi, un homme] qui coupe, en imagination, une flûte, où nouer sa joie" (405).

instrument des fuites: is ambiguous—the original flight of the mythical Syrinx; the flight of the faun's nymphs; the flight of this fantasy in melody (which he now sees as an escape from more direct approaches to love).

The *u*'s and *i*'s of *instrument* and particularly of *fuites* (close to *flûte* or our English "fweet") are very effective. Note also the *f* for the wind instrument, as in "enfle sa flûte" (112).

Moi, de ma rumeur fier, je vais parler longtemps	I, proud of my rumor [sounds I made], am going to speak at length
Des déesses; et par d'idolâtres peintures,	Of [these?] goddesses; and by idolatrous portrayals,
A leur ombre enlever encore des ceintures:	Lift still more girdles from their shadow.

He is going to talk, and analyze, to solve his problems; or paint the nymphs verbally back into reality. The *ombre* is multiple—the mystery, the shady woods into which they disappear; their sleep; their "shade" (spectres); their sex (cf. the *ombre* at the end of the poem; this cluster is treated at length in Appendix B). The *ceintures* are like the veils (morning mist) Rimbaud removes successively from the goddess of dawn in *Aube;* or Salomé's; they remind us also of Venus's girdle in classic myth. Venus, of course, is *the* queen, *the* nymph (like Rimbaud's maternal goddess of dawn, cf. *Les Déserts de l'Amour*) whom the faun will try to seduce in his fantasy (like Hugo's Satyr), and this overweening desire, with more than a hint of the Oedipal, turns into guilt in all three poets: Mallarmé's *blasphème* meets with its *sûr châtiment.*

Ainsi, quand des raisins j'ai sucé la clarté,	Thus, when I have sucked from grapes the brightness,
Pour bannir un regret par ma feinte écarté,	To banish a regret [which is] by my ruse put aside,
Rieur, j'élève au ciel d'été la grappe vide	Laughing, I raise to the summer sky the empty cluster
Et, soufflant dans ses peaux lumineuses, avide	And, blowing in its luminous skins, avid
D'ivresse, jusqu'au soir je regarde au travers.	For drunkenness till evening I look through them.

In place of the nymphs, the faun has the infantile pleasure of staring through the empty grapes. The image is powerful: it is the mystery of the Source:[8]

> Je fuis et je m'accroche à toutes les croisées
> D'où l'on tourne l'épaule à la vie, et, béni,
> Dans leur verre, lavé d'éternelles rosées,
> Que dore le matin chaste de l'Infini
>
> Je me mire et me vois ange! . . .
>
> (*Les Fenêtres*)

This mystery is the fountainhead of the light that streamed through the stained-glass windows in the church at Combray and the various other "magic casements" of poetry. All of us can recall celebrating this rite as children, gazing entranced through slivers of ice, fragments of colored bottle glass or (for me preferably orange) lollipops.

pour bannir un regret par ma feinte écarté: is the childish pathetic prolonging of disappearing delight (making up for the loss of the consumed or, in this case, the nymphs); "banish a regret" by a ruse (*par ma feinte*) which sets the regret aside (*écarté*).

The transparent tone is set by the direct meanings of pure look in *regarde* and *travers,* by the openness of *ciel* and *grappe vide,* the luminosity of *u* and *i* in *lumineuses,* by the *ar*'s in *raisin, clarté, par, écarté, grappe, regarde, travers;* also by the glass-overtone (*verre*) in *travers,* the brightness of *u* and *é* in *sucer,* the *i*'s of *avide d'ivresse* (the *r,* which is part of the *ar*-effect, renders a fluid tenderness, as in Verlaine's most typical poems).

Ô nymphes, regonflons des SOUVE-NIRS divers.	O nymphs, let us reinflate some diverse MEMORIES.

A subtle modulation from the grapeskins to the reinflated balloons or bubbles of memory occurs here. *SOUVENIRS* is capitalized as a sort of motif and title of the following section (cf. the capitalized words of *Un Coup de Dés*); a certain simple variety or vitality is also obtained by the device.

The *o*'s of *regonflons* are effective.

"Mon oeil, trouant les joncs, dardait chaque encolure	"My eye, piercing the reeds, darted at each immortal
"Immortelle, qui noie en l'onde sa brûlure	Neck, which drowns in the water its burning
"Avec un cri de rage au ciel de la forêt;	With [on my part] a cry of rage to the forest roof [or sky];
"Et le splendide bain de cheveux disparaît	And the splendid bath of hair disappears
"Dans les clartés et les frissons, ô pierreries!	In the brightnesses and the shivers, o jewels!"

Again, delicate dream-like italics indicate a remembered episode (as in the art section of *Un Coup de Dés,* Pages 6 to 9). The flashing dazzling effect of light-jeweled water and drowning hair is partly obtained by the many bright vowels: *brûlure, cri, splendide, clarté, frissons, pierreries* (cf. Valéry's: *maint diamant d'imperceptible écume*); the *ss* of *frisson,* as in the *tressaille,* later, is a graphic shivering effect (often used by Verlaine, Baudelaire, Mallarmé).

"J'accours; quand, à mes pieds, s'en- | "I run up; when, [whereupon] at my
trejoignent (meurtries | feet, are clasped (bruised
"De la langueur goûtée à ce mal | From the languor tasted of this [pain
d'être deux) | or] evil of being two)
"Des dormeuses parmi leurs seuls | [Two] Sleeping women amid their
bras hasardeux; | mere [they are naked] random
 | arms;"

mal d'être deux: implies the frustrated conjunction. They are not a true amorous couple but merely juxtaposed. There is a further allusion to a more general separation between any two realities short of total union in pure love, not present in this life. The duality of the nymphs —like the two girls in Rousseau's famous "Idylle des Cerises"—is of the essence of the faun's hesitation; Hamlet's "sicklied o'er with the pale cast of thought." Thus in Mallarmé's essay on Hamlet: "Ce promeneur d'un labyrinthe de troubles et de griefs en prolonge les circuits avec le suspens d'un acte inachevé" (300). Rousseau's "poison that spoiled my desires" has an equivalent in the faun's *frayeurs secrètes de la chair.* The faun is, like both his predecessors, a son of late civilization, a *homo duplex* torn between extreme opposites: half beast, half deity, virile yet passive, both voluptuous and impotent, in the image of his creator. Mallarmé's duality, as expressed by two female types— blond and brunette—was similarly evoked in an early prose poem discovered by Eileen Souffrin.[9]

In the more general sense, the *mal d'être deux* is the principle of negation that separates, as in "nous ne serons jamais une seule momie" (*Tristesse d'Été*). It is present in the *Mon crime c'est d'avoir divisé la touffe,* below. Mallarmé saw this principle everywhere. It is reminiscent of the Biblical serpent of the Fall, a sort of black line separating man from the All, the "vieux mal de vivre" (*Tombeau d'Anatole,* f. 168), the "omniprésente Ligne" of *La Musique et Les Lettres,* associated with the sullying mark the artist is forced to make on the pure white sheet and representing his limited and clumsily intervening human will (linear), contrasted with the purity of the infinite—"virginité [the page] . . . elle-même s'est comme divisée en ses fragments de candeur, l'un et l'autre, preuves nuptiales de l'idée" (387). In other words, the violation of purity is linked with the feminine principle of duality, or the negative role of masculine intervention, or of the male "serpent" of will, or phallus.

seuls bras: implies the nakedness.

hasardeux: implies "casually this and that way" and perhaps also the vulnerability, the scant protection.

"Je les ravis, sans les désenlacer, et
vole
"À ce massif, haï par l'ombrage
frivole,
"De roses tarissant tout parfum au
soleil,
"Où notre ébat au jour consumé soit
pareil."

"I ravish them [snatch them up]
without disentangling them, and
flee
To this clump, hated by the frivolous shadow,
Of roses yielding up all perfume to
the sun, where may our
[Amorous] Sporting be like the
consumed day."

haï: is the blackness of shadow contrasted with the bright sun; a similar use of *haï* occurs in *Hérodiade: le ciel sinistre ait les regards haïs de Vénus* (the star or goddess).

frivole: has the airiness felt amidst the impressionistic leaves. The idea of love as consuming, as flowers yielding up their perfume, is parallel to the emptying of the grape (or "comme le fruit se fond en jouissance," Valéry): "may our amorous disport be consumed in the day" or in the sun, the source of love and the consuming destroyer of it. as in the ambivalent myth of Apollo.

Je t'adore, courroux des vierges, ô
délice
Farouche du sacré fardeau nu qui se
glisse
Pour fuir ma lèvre en feu buvant,
comme un éclair
Tressaille! la frayeur secrète de la
chair:
Des pieds de l'inhumaine au coeur de
la timide

Que délaisse à la fois une innocence,
humide
De larmes folles ou de moins tristes
vapeurs.

I adore you, wrath of virgins, O
ferocious delight
Of the sacred naked burden which
slides
To flee my lip on fire drinking in, as
a lightning thrust
Quivers! the secret terror of the flesh:
From the feet of the inhuman [cold,
nymph] to the heart of the timid
one
Who is abandoned at once by an [her]
innocence, humid
With mad tears or less sad vapors.

The complex character—voluptuous but troubled—of the faun is evidenced by the sadism: "I adore you, wrath of virgins"; the tug of opposites creates the baroque shiver, a lightning flash, but a trembling one: *tressaille!* (the flash of the *éclair,* is reinforced by the exclamation mark; the shiver of the *tressaille* by its *ss*). The *frayeur* is primarily the nymph's, but also the faun's.

délaisse is double: her innocence emanates; it also departs.

moins tristes vapeurs: are no doubt erotic fluids.

"Mon crime, c'est d'avoir, gai de
vaincre ces peurs

"My crime, is to have, gay at van-
quishing these treacherous fears,

"Traîtresses, divisé la touffe échevelée	*Divided the dishevelled tuft*
"De baisers que les dieux gardaient si bien mêlée:	*Of kisses that the gods kept so well mingled:"*

crime: the meaning is complex, referring first to the separation of the two kissable nymphs, joined in innocent slumber; then to the *violation* implied—here the symbolism of *touffe* is obvious if we compare the act of the paperknife, destroying a "virginity" in "solennités toute intimes, l'une: de placer le couteau d'ivoire dans l'ombre que font deux pages jointes d'un volume" (718), "un sacrifice dont saigna la tranche rouge des anciens tomes; l'introduction d'une arme, ou coupe-papier, pour établir la prise de possession" (381). We recall also the just-cited "virginité . . . elle-même s'est divisée." This whole theme is treated at length in Appendix B.

"Car, à peine j'allais cacher un rire ardent	*"For hardly was I about to hide an ardent laugh*
"Sous les replis heureux d'une seule (gardant	*Under the happy folds of one (keeping*
"Par un doigt simple, afin que sa candeur de plume	*By a simple finger, so her featherlike candor*
"Se teignît à l'émoi de sa soeur qui s'allume,	*Might be colored by the emotion of her sister which is beginning to catch fire,*
"La petite, naïve et ne rougissant pas:)	*The little one, naive and not blushing):*
"Que de mes bras, défaits par de vagues trépas,	*When from my arms, undone by vague deaths,*
"Cette proie, à jamais ingrate se délivre	*This prey forever ungrateful frees itself*
"Sans pitié du sanglot dont j'étais encore ivre."	*Without pity for the sob with which I still was drunk."*

rire: is an oral-erotic outburst, typical of the poet, whether warmly personal as in *M'introduire: rire très haut sa victoire,* or metaphysical and impersonal, as in the *Coup de Dés: rire . . . que si c'était le nombre, ce serait le hasard.* It also subtly stands here for more obvious erotic acts as it does in *M'introduire* or in another sonnet addressed to Méry: "Cette frigidité se fond / En du rire de fleurir ivre" (59).

doigt simple: is marvellously concrete: a sort of provisional hold on the potential sexual partner, a delicate promise of more—this combination of refinement and greed jars and amuses—by something neither altogether physical nor mental, but midway (as in the half-euphuistic expression "to give someone's hand in marriage"); Mallarmé often uses hand or feather (occasionally heel) to express this artistically sublimated (yet still sensual) gesture or impulse.

candeur de plume: the naive nymph, virginally white, reminds us of Mallarmé's earliest visions of sensually-intense innocence (C, p. 139). The feather, an ideal expression of this ambiguity, develops into one of his major symbols.

trépas: a typical male contretemps, provisional impotence.

Tant pis! vers le bonheur d'autres m'entraîneront	So much the worse! towards happiness others will pull me along
Par leur tresse nouée aux cornes de mon front:	By their tresses knotted to the horns of my forehead:

There is something very warmly, even maturely, human in this attitude of Mallarmé: life goes on (contrast, for example, the defeat at the close of the *Bateau Ivre*). The image of the tresses entwined in the faun's horns is good-humored and prettily pleasant, as well as erotic. The hair is the ideal emanation of the woman's sensuality (as in *Pelléas et Mélisande*), as the horn is the sublimated (upper) male symbol (W, p. 252); their union is gratifying. All this provides an excellent transition to the physical warmth exuded in the next episode.

"Tresses" is always a good word for hair (the sinuous *ss*), compare Baudelaire's *fortes tresses, soyez la houle* (*La Chevelure*).

Tu sais, ma passion, que, pourpre et déjà mûre,	You know, my passion, that, purple and already ripe,
Chaque grenade éclate et d'abeilles murmure;	Each pomegranate bursts and murmurs with bees;
Et notre sang, épris de qui le va saisir,	And our blood, smitten with whoever will take it,
Coule pour tout l'essaim éternel du désir.	Flows for all the eternal swarm of desire.

The "tone poem" modulates into a heavier, swelling-to-bursting passionate key, reminding us of Keats's *Ode to a Nightingale*.

The "swarm"—like a murmurous summer hum of bees—is a perfect evocation of the mood when all the honeyed cells of one's being are joined in the single desire: "l'essaim de . . . joies" (Villiers, *Isis*, Crès, p. 231). The bursting pomegranate is an obvious image applied elsewhere by Mallarmé to a woman's lips (*Hérodiade*); here the faun himself becomes the fruit being consumed, crushed into flowing juice by whoever will seize it—"comme le fruit se fond en jouissance"—in the maturing sun.[10]

Note the swelling *p*'s of *passion* and *pourpre;* they play a comparable role in *comme mourir pourpre la roue,* the climax of the erotic sonnet addressed to Méry Laurent, *M'introduire,* and in *Prose: Triomphalement ne sais-tu / Te lever . . . Grandissait trop pour nos raisons . . . le trop grand glaïeul.*

À l'heure où ce bois d'or et de cendres se teinte
Une fête s'exalte en la feuillée éteinte:

At the hour when this wood with gold and ashes is tinted
A festival is excited in the extinguished foliage:

The festival is: the fantasy he offers himself as substitute gratification, the dream of possessing Venus (see below)—this love-light flares up as the leaves darken; and the festival of sundown, Mallarmé's favorite spectacle. The effect of light being gradually extinguished in the leaves is wonderfully caught; the fresh cool-of-the-evening paling light sifts through the growing shadows of the leaves, like dying firelight through ashes; the faint diphthongs of *teinte* and *éteinte* render the subtle mood (as in Lamartine's *Isolement*: "Son éloigné qu'affaiblit la distance / À l'oreille incertaine apporté par le vent,"); or the dying strains in the contrapuntal closing pages of Debussy's score. Mallarmé had "taken back our own" from music, and now poetry could teach music a thing or two: as Dukas surmised, Debussy learned previously-unheard timbres from the text: vibratos, hums, shakes, tinklings. The *cendres* lead to the image of Etna:

Etna! c'est parmi toi visité de Vénus
Sur ta lave posant ses talons ingénus,

Quand tonne un somme triste ou s'épuise la flamme.

Etna! It is amid you visited by Venus
On your lava placing her candid heels,

When a sad slumber thunders or the flame exhausts itself.

The bursting-pomegranate image has been blown up to a thunderous volcano. The *somme triste* is a sort of reminiscence of the *frayeurs de la chair;* the imminent release is not without guilt, as it comes from the dark region of the hidden underground soul from which animal passion leaps to expression, as the faun succumbs to summer heat. Sexuality is often thought of by Mallarmé as sad, a premature loss of strength or of beauty, as in "la sottise . . . pressée de dégorger son éclair . . . la prostitution" (322); also in *Angoisse* and in *Tristesse d'été*. But the sadness here more likely has to do with the pathos of his solitary satisfaction.

Etna: Sicily, and hence Etna, is invoked because of Theocritus; also there was a legend that Venus ascended Etna, where her spouse, Vulcan, forged. Compare Nerval's *Myrthô:*

Je sais pourquoi, là-bas, le volcan s'est ouvert . . .
C'est qu'hier tu l'avais touché d'un pied agile,
Et de cendres soudain l'horizon s'est couvert.

The delicate symbolism of the heel resembles that of the earlier-mentioned finger.

Note the *v*'s of *visité-Vénus-lave;* see Appendix C.

Je tiens la reine!   I hold the queen!

"I hold the queen!" is a fantasy of triumph the faun belatedly, desperately, and with pathetic braggadocio, offers his frustrated desires. This is very reminiscent of Hugo's *Satyre* and Rimbaud's *Aube* or *Les Déserts de l'amour* (the Rimbaud pieces were unknown to Mallarmé at the time).

Venus is the queen, the queen of nature, a goddess. The remoteness of the deified woman who springs from forbidden incest is threatened in this fantasy. Compare Delmore Schwartz: "I [took] Venus on a cloud" (*Shenandoah: a Verse Play*).

Ô sûr châtiment . . .   O sure punishment [to come] . . .

His extreme hubris, even in the mere imagination, meets with its only possible reward, extreme guilt. Note the graphic fall (as in the *Coup de Dés: aile* . . . [then a drop] *retombeé*).

Non, mais l'âme	No, but the soul
De paroles vacante et ce corps alourdi	Empty of words and this weighted body
Tard succombent au fier silence de midi:	Succumb late to the proud silence of noon:
Sans plus il faut dormir en l'oubli du blasphème,	Without any more ado we must sleep in forgetfulness of the blasphemy,
Sur le sable altéré gisant et comme j'aime	Lying in the thirsty sand and as I love
Ouvrir ma bouche à l'astre efficace des vins!	To open my mouth to the wine-making star [the sun]!
Couple, adieu: je vais voir l'ombre que tu devins.	Couple, adieu; I'll see the shadow you became.

The afternoon has worn on to its close: the *tard* refers to the lateness of the day; the faun has gradually succumbed to the heat that reached its peak during the "proud silence" of the summer woods at noon. The cycle of desire and light, which began in morning freshness, is almost over.

He seeks to forget his guilt—*blasphème*—in sleep. Yet his thirst remains: lying in the hot ("thirsty") sand he keeps his mouth open towards the declining sun, source of the wine of life: "l'art c'est le désir perpétué" (Laforgue): "Le Vin, fils sacré du Soleil" (Baudelaire, *Le Vin du Chiffonnier*).

Note the lassitude of the *a*'s in *âme, parole, vacante;* the heaviness of *our* in *alourdi,* as in "la *lour*deur triste de l'*ours*" (276).

ombre: is like its earlier evocation, multiple: sleep, and the sleep of the nymphs; the dark woods into which the nymphs disappeared with its shadow further deepening toward night; the mystery of their disappearance and of love and guilt generally; the black shadow of their feminine secrets.

Note the dark nasal of *ombre.*

devins: has a hint of *divin (couple).*

NOTES

1 Mallarmé called the *Faune* his summer poem, *Hérodiade* his winter poem, but this should not be overemphasized; each is both a summer and a winter poem, though the emphasis differs.

2 Because of the varied type-size and other "musical" effects, some have invoked the influence of Wagner; but that influence came only later, and we must not forget Hugo's *Djinns,* Gautier's *Symphonie en Blanc Majeur,* quite successful attempts to "take back from music our own," before Mallarmé's. Moreover the "music of verse" is a quite different affair from music (aside from certain relatively superficial effects), as Suzanne Bernard properly insists in her *Mallarmé et la musique,* and T. S. Eliot before her, in a well-known article on the subject, "The Music of Verse." Or, in our own terms, "The musician ... may invent other challenges or resistances, but none so meaningful as the forging of art from rational communication, keeping as reward for the additional effort much of the original ideational substance" (W, p. 42). Mallarmé is closer to Debussy than to Wagner; Debussy enjoys and exploits the sensual quality of music to the full, yet with the (French) refinement of control that comes from intellect. Nor is this just a matter of "form"; the sparkling intellect speaks to us in a subtle way from the music; the whole range of us (as in Brahms) is involved, even though not with the usual intellectually-communicative means, that is, we sense that a simple man would not hear the full range of this art as an intellectual (who appreciates music) does.

3 If an individual does not care to commit his best resources in this way, he can always read something else, lesser poetry, or prose, and save himself for other causes with entire justification. The only wrong thing would be to pretend that one is *reading* Mallarmé or comparable poets with less than the mentioned rich commitment.

4 This reminds us of the boyish boast "je courus ... j'ai vu" of Rimbaud's *Bateau Ivre.*

5 Cf. *Les Mots anglais:* "*I,* éclaircissement ... *Iou,* assombrissement" (983). For a more complete discussion see Appendix C. Our appreciation of letter-values in Mallarmé is explained and documented (largely from *Les Mots Anglais*) in our *Oeuvre de Mallarmé;* see also, in reference to other poets, my article "The ABC's of Poetry" in *Comparative Literature,* No. 2, 1962.

6 Which does not contradict Chisholm so much as increase our admiration for the old magician, Mallarmé. One must insist here that this is not just an arid game—though the exegete, forced to delve into proofs, may seem to be playing one—for a sensitive reader undoubtedly intuits these concurrent and fluidly interwoven themes just as he does in music, though he might be hard put to demonstrate them.

7 Jacques Rivière spoke of the *Faune* as being all, or mere, bubbles, which is nonsense, nonsense that did not even convince him; he has seldom spoken so poorly and

arbitrarily and with such obviously bad conscience, as the very unclearness of his remarks indicates.

8 "When Perceval stares tranced at the sight of blood on snow, or when Mallarmé's *Faune* gazes raptly at the translucent grape, they are delighting in the reduction of life to its essences and so celebrating-by-profaning the one mystery of spirit and matter become presence: love, light, into life . . ." (W, p. 78). "The crushing act of love, the shedding of blood, extracting essences: 'comme le fruit se fond en jouissance' (Valéry), 'breaking the grape's joy' (Dylan Thomas), are related cele- brations of the mystery" (W, p. 78).

9 In *French Studies*, January, 1950. The two women symbolize opposite poles of northern and southern types (as in Gide, Mann, etc.); there have been many equivalents in art: Keats's *Endymion*, Boucher's painting *Faun and Nymphs*, Rousseau's "Idylle des Cerises," Banville's *Diane au bois*.

10 Aubanel's collection of Provençal poems, *The Half-Opened Pomegranate*, may have been an influence here.

2. SALUT

Mallarmé was asked, in 1893, to offer a toast at a gathering of young writers. The result was this "sonnet de circonstance," a miniature crystalline marvel, which Mallarmé placed at the head of his collection as a sort of introduction.

His poem first alludes modestly to itself as a nothing; and then from this nothing—this microcosmic cup, like the "wooden O" of *Henry V*—distills a fleeting magic image of an oceanscape, the site for the lonely voyage of the creator, which is the central motif. From the champagne-sea foam there arise flashes of nude sirens—symbols of the airy yet sensual art which the poet favored and of its sophisticated and ingenuous *femme fatale* allure of perfection. Next, Mallarmé depicts himself as the old master "taking a back seat" as the young become the *avant fastueux,* or the dazzling *avant-garde*. Playfully, he holds his cup aloft, without fearing the "rocking of the boat," his drunkenness which is his glory in the moving paternal moment, or the intoxication of the wine he brandishes. The boat is life, or the vocation, summed up in the familiar figure of the lonely captain, Man (including men's representative, the Poet). At the end, he offers his rising young companions a highly condensed version of his perfectionistic and heroic artistic credo. The title *Salut* means "greeting," "toast," or (true to its etymology) "health to you." It further implies "this is the artist's salvation." Hence "ce salut: solitude, récif, étoile."

*

Rien, cette écume, vierge vers	Nothing, this foam, virgin verse
À ne désigner que la coupe;	To designate naught but the cup;
Telle loin se noie une troupe	Thus far-off drowns a troop
De sirènes mainte à l'envers.	Of sirens many upside down.

Rien: from Latin *rem* (obj. of *res*), "thing," the word vibrates between two meanings here as it almost always does for Mallarmé: a nothing-something, a sacrificially pure beauty—"un rien, fait de songes intacts" (286); "un rien d'aigre et d'ingénu" (382); "le Rien qui est la vérité" (C, p. 375). Nonetheless we feel that modesty prevails here; Mallarmé is apologizing for the slightness of the offering compared to the lifelong Dream he had not yet offered to the public and, particularly, to his youthful admirers.

écume: "l'écume qui n'est rien" (594), the champagne foam is also the "froth," the inconsequential—and bright, light, airy—patter of this occasional verse. This is a favorite word of Mallarmé: "Si peu d'écume sur un golfe / C'est cela ce rire" (113). Frothy laughter leads to (or from) champagne—"on s'attend même au champagne / Si d'autre rire ne coulait" (181). Some mythologists believe that seafoam, seen from a distance (hence *loin*) was the origin of sirens. Mallarmé has likely profited from this notion. For the wider resonance of *écume*, see Appendix A, and C, p. 274 under *u*.

vierge vers: "Quel génie pour être un poète . . . la vie, *vierge* en sa synthèse et illuminant tout" (Propos, p. 164). *Vierge,* implying an innocent, unspoiled perfection, is a favorite word of Mallarmé. There is an obvious weaving between *vierge* and *vers;* something of the vivacious sparkling of champagne is achieved in the *v*'s, as in "Le vierge, le vivace et le bel aujourd'hui" (C, p. 312).

à ne désigner que la coupe: literally, all his verse does is designate the toast, the synecdochic "cup"; we may recall the *coupe* in which a similar (but more serious) emptiness prevailed, the vessel of his funeral toast to Gautier, wherein, instead of frolicking sirens, there shone a suffering "golden monster," a *Chimère.*

A secondary sense is that the foam, that heady nothingness, "designates," by bubbling around, the rim (like Keats's "beady bubbles winking at the brim") of the cup.

A distant possible echo is the "pause," *coupe,* of official verse.

Telle loin: Mallarmé obviously enjoyed the harmony of *tele* (Greek: "far") with the *loin;* compare, in the *Tombeau d'Edgar Poe,* "Telle . . . enfin . . . éternité" or "Telle, jeune . . . jadis" (*Les Fenêtres*).

noie: the subtle element *oie,* "goose," goes with the nude whiteness of the sirens like that *blancheur animale* of the swan-nymphs in the *Faune,* or the "noyé . . . flanc enfant d'une sirène" of *A la nue;* "ondoie . . . blanc . . . soie au soleil blondoie" (23).

troupe: the slight overtone *croupe* is brought out by the neighboring *mainte à l'envers.*

sirènes: as super- and infrahuman creatures (like the demigod faun, with his goat's legs), they typify art; a fantastically rich word or image, a favorite of Mallarmé's era (Heine, Gautier, Debussy, Régnier, Redon); noteworthy are sinuous *s,* the *rène-reine* echo; see our complete discussion in *L'Oeuvre de Mallarmé* (C, pp. 324-327), also *A la nue,* under *sirène.*

mainte à l'envers: a playful and painterly touch with some serious suggestion of the eternal down-movement following the waves of reality, as in the image of the "drowning" siren of *A la nue,* or the one on Page 8 of the *Coup de Dés.* Compare "de loin [on] croit voir . . . une culbute" (Les *Néréides,* Gautier).

Nous naviguons, ô mes divers	We navigate, O my diverse
Amis, moi déjà sur la poupe	Friends, I already on the stern
Vous l'avant fastueux qui coupe	You the festive prow that cuts
Le flot de foudres et d'hivers;	The wave of lightnings and winters;

This old man-young man, wide-narrow (feminine-masculine) opposition is prominent in the *Coup de Dés;* for example, the *Maître* versus his son, the *ombre puérile* (C. pp. 193-194): "Vieillard presque ou adolescent ... la saute ... d'une époque à la suivante, comme marche le temps" (406). The essays "Confrontation" and "Conflit" explore the relation historically.

fastueux: an allusion to the festive occasion, as well as the art of his youthful friends. Is there a hint of "showy"?

poupe: dark *ou* for the stern versus cutting *v* for the prow (*vous, l'avant*).

foudres: the lightning that both emerges from and strikes proud eminences is described on Page 7 of the *Coup de Dés,* in a similarly marine and stormy setting, in association with the lonely poet, *prince amer de l'écueil* [cf. *récif* below] ... *s'en coiffe* [d'une haute vision]: *plume / en foudre* (C, p. 286).

hivers: the season of stormy voyaging; there is an overtone of snowy ocean foam and perhaps of old age (C, pp. 186-187).

Une ivresse belle m'engage	A beautiful drunkenness incites me
Sans craindre même son tangage	Without fearing even its rocking
De porter debout ce salut	To carry erect this greeting [or toast, or health]
Solitude, récif, étoile	Solitude, reef, star
À n'importe ce qui valut	To whatever was worth [the effort of]
Le blanc souci de notre toile.	The white care of our [sail-] cloth.

ivresse: the drunkenness is his sense of glory in his poetic vocation, that he would share with these spiritual sons: "un cloître, mental, aux arceaux d'âge en âge, qu'illumine l'instant fugitif d'élus ... avec ceux [the young], déjà, le futur" (406).

belle: the reversing of the usual order adds a (drunken) freshness to the word.

tangage: his intoxication. Also the rocking of the boat on the "sea of life," which is seldom calm and is increasingly unsure as he nears the final shoals of death. But Mallarmé is courageous: *sans craindre.*

ce salut: Au seul souci is likewise "ce salut," a calling to the young.

solitude, récif, étoile: these three points—the fearful reef of risk, below; the alluring distant star of aspiration toward perfection, above; the solitary man of art, between—trace his vertical (subtly heroic, comic-tragic) stance.[1] The *salut* offered to Gautier was similarly devoid of sentimentality. Compare "La voile / Que sillonnait l'éclair, et qu'à l'écueil / Poussait le vent" (ML, pp. 173-174).

n'importe: the insouciant air is rather like that of "Au seul souci de voyager," the adventurous spirit of Mallarmé, who had no sentimental hopes and who expected nothing or anything; compare the *n'importe / où vaine* referring to the drowning Master (Man), on Page 4 of the *Coup de Dés* (C, p. 189) or, referring to the death of his beloved Villiers: "*n'importe*, tout cela n'est pas, les maux, puisque subis et que seul maintenant ignore, qui mourut, *n'importe*" (502).

blanc souci: the ambivalence of serious art, recalling the *hilarité et horreur* of the creator, on Page 6 of the *Coup de Dés;* the stark contrast of darkness and brightness—shadow in the billowing sail—is like that of the *blanche agonie* of the swan in "Le vierge, le vivace et le bel aujourd'hui."

toile: cloth, of sail with an associated idea of artistic "canvas" or white paper and, further, the white tablecloth of the banquet. Mallarmé has elsewhere played between these: "la page blanche de la voile" (Biog., p. 796). Part of the reason is that vellum (*vélin* occurs in various fragments of *Hérodiade,* etc.,) is made of cloth and echoes *vela,* the Latin source of *voile.*

The development from sail-cloth to table-cloth (of the banquet here; compare the same double image in *Le Livre,* p. 80) and to related imagery was foreshadowed by Gautier:

> Cette étoupe qu'on file et qui, tissée en toile,
> Donne une aile au vaisseau dans le port engourdi,
> À l'orgie une nappe, à la pudeur un voile,
> Linceul, revêtira mon cadavre verdi!
>
> (*Stances*)

The veil-shroud aspect, which will be developed in *Ouverture ancienne, Tombeau* (de Verlaine) and, particularly, *Un Coup de Dés* (C, pp. 219-229), is at most a minor overtone in *Salut.*

NOTE

[1] Mais celui qui regarde, intrépide et tranquille
Les hommes et les flots, à qui la mer stérile
Toujours offre un écueil,
Il s'y dresse en silence et lutte solitaire.
Toute voile pour lui n'est au fond qu'un suaire,
Tout esquif qu'un cercueil.

(Villiers, *À mon ami*)

Hugo is another important predecessor of this manner, in *Matelots, Matelots, Oceano Nox,* and in many another poem. Earlier there are Lamartine and a long tradition.

3. LE PITRE CHÂTIÉ

Le Pitre châtié goes back to 1864; it was not published, however, until 1887, much rewritten. A first version, which we include in the notes, helps to clarify it.[1] Despite the syntactical difficulties and the density of the idiom, the poem crystallizes some of Mallarmé's most compelling imagery. Eventually it captivates.

A clown (representing, in a self-deprecatory way, the artist) has abandoned his Muse in favor of a real woman and plunged into the lakes, her eyes. He feels refreshed when the trumpery clown paint is washed off him in the metaphorical water, which experience is a sort of baptism in love (-death)—a rebirth. Alas, he discovers that the dirty paint was essential to his art, was even "all of (my) genius."[2] This is partly a confession of provisional personal failure to win through to the highest realms, but mainly it is an exaggeration of the truism that pure intentions are not enough, that art requires perspiration (as well as inspiration), compromise, technique, showmanship. The central theme is simply the need to stay "down here" in order to create (as in *Les Fenêtres,* or "Le vierge, le vivace et le bel aujourd'hui"), the need to remain a mere performer, a "clown." An idea that is disappointing in terms of Mallarmé's wildest ambitions, but which speaks for his wisdom.

In "Mimique" Mallarmé tells us that true art depends on a balance between various positions: "entre le désir et l'accomplissement [etc.] ... Tel opère le Mime, dont le jeu se borne à une allusion perpétuelle sans briser la glace" (310). The violent escape to any extreme, for example, to an active life (as in excessive realism, or in journalism) upsets this balance of art, brings down this high-wire act; *Les Fenêtres* warns us again that if we break through the window of the absolute we risk falling throughout eternity, as happened notably to one named Lucifer, with his excessive pretentions, or hubris. In the sonnet the sexual act carries with it this corollary of escape into a metaphysical absolute, a quasi-religious leap to purity. The artist, of course, is occasionally tempted to try anyway, fortunately for human fate.

The attempt was undertaken by that other eager early figure, the faun, who came into being about the same time as the first version of the *Pitre.* The faun, we remember, tried to make love to Venus, which was pretentiousness with a vengeance, leading to a *sûr châtiment*. In a fragment of the *Après-midi d'un faune* (part of a section to be entitled "Réveil du faune", when the whole was conceived as a "poème scénique"), published in *Empreintes*,[3] we come upon the baptismal motif in terms so close to those of *Le Pitre châtié* that we might call this the true first version of it:

> Je veux, dans la clarté transparente, innover
> Une âme de cristal pur que jette la flûte
> Et je fuis immortel, vainqueur en cette lutte,
> Les femmes qui pour charme ont aussi de beaux pleurs.
> N'est-ce pas moi qui veux, seul, sans que les douleurs
> Me forcent, Idéal limpide?
>   À la piscine,
> Des sources, à l'horreur lustrale qui fascine
> L'azur, je vais déjà tremper l'être furtif
> Qui de leur glace va renaître, primitif!

Here the love motif is separated from the rebirth, though it hovers in the background as a possible way.

Here, now, is the definitive sonnet:

Yeux, lacs avec ma simple ivresse de renaître	Eyes, lakes with my simple fervor to be reborn
Autre que l'histrion qui du geste évoquais	Other than the [poor] actor who with his gesture evoked
Comme plume la suie ignoble des quinquets,	For feather the ignoble soot of Argand lamps
J'ai troué dans le mur de toile une fenêtre.	I have pushed through the wall of cloth [tent] a window.

Yeux, lacs: by simple juxtaposition (apposition) Mallarmé achieves a clean syntax, avoiding cluttering connectives such as "like." This is good symbolism. The sign and the designatum interpenetrate fluidly, weave together; eyes have naturally much in common with water[4] and, further, with the window onto the infinite suggested in *fenêtre* (cf. *Les Fenêtres*). We may feel that eyes and lakes are two links (or meshes) in one universal chain (or net) of Being. The *lacs* is connected further with the *glacier* below (which contains it; compare these two words in "Le vierge, le vivace et le bel aujourd'hui"). It also bears the direct overtone of its other dictionary meaning: "trap."

Baudelaire had, as often, preceded Mallarmé here: "tes yeux verts, / Lacs où mon âme tremble et se voit à l'envers" (*Le Poison*).

renaître: in *Les Fenêtres* there is:

>   ... je meurs, et j'aime
> —Que la vitre soit l'art, soit la mysticité—
> À renaître ...

The aim of every original artist, of every growing spirit, is to be reborn: Gide's palingenesis, Malraux's metamorphoses. The highest aim is obviously not attained, but growth occurs precisely through the effort: one may at least "shuffle off another skin," as Goethe said, and "faire peau neuve." The baptismal-death motif is prominent in the *Cantique de Saint Jean:* "Selon un baptême / Penche un salut" (the cut-off head bows).

l'histrion: This idea goes back to Poe's statement, in *The Poetic Principle,* about the humble tricks-of-the-trade every poet occasionally needs: "les plumes de coq, et tout le maquillage de *l'histrion littéraire*" (Baudelaire's translation). The artist-clown association owes something to Baudelaire's *Vieux Saltimbanque* (echoed again in Mallarmé's prose poem *Réminiscence*) as well as Banville's *Tremplin.* Incidentally, at the stage of his career when Mallarmé began the poem, he was particularly discouraged, in spells, as his letters show. In a letter to Cazalis (1862), he refers to himself as a "ridicule Hamlet," in another as a "cadavre."

du geste évoquais: the verb ending is in the first person in accord with the subject of the whole sentence, *Je* (fourth line). The syntax is "who [myself] evoked." The probable meaning of the whole is that the actor who, with his ham-acting gestures, evoked [produced the effect of] a mock-hero, whose plume of glory [e.g., Hamlet's feather, see below] was only the plume of sooty smoke rising from the Argand lamps used as stage lights in a cheap traveling show.

plume: it reminds us of the "plumes de coq" of the Poe article we alluded to but, more importantly, also of Hamlet who wore a *toque* with a feather waving in it, according to a Banville poem and a Manet portrait, with both of which Mallarmé was very familiar (he quotes the former in his "Hamlet" and owned the portrait). Hence the *mauvais Hamlet* below. In the *Coup de Dés,* the plume on the Hamlet figure is prominent (C, p. 250). Here the soot image implies that the feather is dark; the Banville poem had the lines:

> Le vent fait voler ta plume noire
> Et te caresse, Hamlet, ô jeune Hamlet

le mur de toile: part of the cheap sideshow atmosphere, a backdrop, probably one wall of a tent, compare "trouer . . . ainsi qu'une vaporeuse toile" (crude realities spoiling art, in reference to a poor performance of *Hamlet;* 301).

fenêtre: the same motif of escape to an absolute is the core of *Les Fenêtres:*

Est-il moyen . . .
D'enfoncer le cristal . . .
Et de m'enfuir, avec mes deux ailes sans plume
—Au risque de tomber pendant l'éternité?

We recall also the "briser la glace" of "Mimique," previously cited, and the unbroken *glace* of "Le vierge, le vivace et le bel aujourd'hui" to which we may add Hérodiade's ice-block of impenetrable mirror (the opposite of Alice in Wonderland's).

De ma jambe et des bras limpide nageur traître,	With my leg and my arms limpid traitorous swimmer,
À bonds multipliés, reniant le mauvais	In multiple bounds, denying the bad
Hamlet! c'est comme si dans l'onde j'innovais	Hamlet! it's as if in the wave I innovated [created]
Mille sépulcres pour y vierge disparaître.	Countless tombs in which to disappear [a] virgin.

The swim-love association is archetypal: "Amants, il [le guignon] . . . vous plonge en une mare / Et laisse un bloc boueux du blanc couple nageur" (*Le Guignon*); "ta chevelure est une rivière tiède . . . Où noyer sans frissons l'âme qui nous obsède" (*Tristesse d'été*); "comme un bon nageur qui se pâme dans l'onde / Tu sillonnes gaîment l'immensité profonde / Avec une indicible et mâle volupté" (Baudelaire, *Élévation*). Baudelaire's image combines the love and the mysticism, as in the sonnet. This "swimming in the Source" idea occurs at the end of the *Tombeau* (*de Verlaine*) and was the core of the *Faun* fragment.

le mauvais Hamlet: Hamlet was his central figure of spiritual heroism, associated with Poe, Villiers, and others; here he is the symbol of the poet with large aspirations who is impotent to realize his dreams. The *mauvais* implies that he lacks, in defeat, the tragic nobility of Hamlet. Perhaps the English echo "ham-Hamlet" stayed in his ears. In a letter to Cazalis, of 1862, he refers to himself as a "ridicule Hamlet"; compare "cette ombre d'Hamlet imitant sa posture . . . cet histrion" (Baudelaire, *La Béatrice*).

The flight, accordingly, is a desperate effort to master fate by a violent risk, a psychic suicide, losing all with the tacit hope of a miraculous total gain, or at least the attainment of dignity.

innovais: "Je veux, dans la clarté transparente, innover / Une âme de cristal pur" (*Réveil du faune*). He kept the word, for a slightly different use, in the sonnet, perhaps because of the incisive *v* (again in *vierge disparaître*).

sépulcres: the love-death or baptismal theme—each hollow made in the "water" by his "swimming" stroke is a sort of minuscule tomb-womb: "Toi [la femme] qui sur le néant en sais plus que les morts" *(Angoisse);* Villiers had also used this image in "Le vent creuse un tombeau dans les sillons amers" *(Exil).*

vierge: emphasizes the feeling of sexual union and the paradoxical innocence it brings and, visually, the swimmer's white *nudité.* The *v,* together with the *y,* creates an effect of plunge.[5]

Hilare or de cymbale à des poings irrité,	Hilarious cymbal-gold irritated by fists,
Tout à coup le soleil frappe la nudité	Suddenly the sun slaps the nudity
Qui pure s'exhala de ma fraîcheur de nacre,	Which, pure, exhaled itself from my nacreous freshness,
Rance nuit de la peau quand sur moi vous passiez,	Rancid night of the skin [sex-experience or the dirty paint] when you passed over [off] me,
Ne sachant pas, ingrat! que c'était tout mon sacre,	[Me] Not knowing, ingrate! that it was all my sacred rite [genius],
Ce fard noyé dans l'eau perfide des glaciers.	This paint drowned in the perfidious water of glaciers [ice-cold].

Hilare or de cymbale: The sun-cymbal association is part of an important cluster (C, p. 119); here we will cite only the "C'est [le soleil] le premier coup de cymbale de l'automne."[6] Note the *o* of *or* for the sun-disk; in the various Saint John fragments there are allusions to the sun as a golden plate and to other roundnesses: "l'éblouissant / Nimbe là-bas très glorieux arrondissant" (N, pp. 55-56).

irrité: the jarring, vibrant quality of cymbal-clash is well conveyed by this word; the three bright vowels shed light.

Rance nuit de la peau quand sur moi vous passiez: the love-act seen in retrospect is soured: "[le guignon] vous plonge en une mare / Et laisse un bloc boueux du blanc couple nageur" (*Le Guignon*). The night of the skin is also ambiguously the paint (*fard*) which darkens it; compare "un fétide torrent de fard mêlé de vin" (14). This three-line phrase, "When the rancid night of the skin passed over [or off] me who didn't know, etc.," is all dependent on the main verb "slaps."

sacre: the first version read "tout le génie" (see note 2); the religious term indicates the depth of Mallarmé's concern for authenticity in art: "La poésie, sacre" (372), *dernier point qui sacre,* the "dot on the i," so to speak, of a work, of cosmic or personal creation (*Coup de Dés,* Page 11).

glaciers: the absolute purity is expressed likewise as *glaciers* in the *Cantique de Saint Jean:* "pur . . . ô glaciers!"; or "glaciers vierges" (Biog., p. 91). The word echoes the *lac* of the first line (as in "Le vierge, le vivace") and contains a note of hard, steely coldness in the element *acier* (rhymed with *glacier* in *Ouverture ancienne*).

NOTES

[1] Pour ses yeux,—pour nager dans ces lacs, dont les quais
Sont plantés de beaux cils qu'un matin bleu pénètre,
J'ai, Muse,—moi, ton, pitre,—enjambé la fenêtre
Et fui notre baraque où fument tes quinquets.

Et d'herbes enivré, j'ai plongé comme un traître
Dans ces lacs défendus, et, quand tu m'appelais,
Baigné mes membres nus dans l'onde aux blancs galets,
Oubliant mon habit de pitre au tronc d'un hêtre.

Le soleil du matin séchait mon corps nouveau
Et je sentais fraîchir loin de la tyrannie
La neige des glaciers dans ma chair assainie,

Ne sachant, pas, hélas! quand s'en allait sur l'eau
Le suif de mes cheveux et le fard de ma peau,
Muse, que cette crasse était tout le génie!

[2] The first version, "tout le génie," registered the main sense, the disenchanted half-truth about art being showmanship; Lefébure, Mallarmé's friend, objected to this. He therefore chose something more ambiguous which allowed for two possibilities: "tout mon sacre" could mean the general truth about art being showmanship or, secondly, that that is all the art *he* had (1415).

[3] *Empreintes*, no. 5, pp. 12-13.

[4] In Hérédia's sonnet, *Antoine et Cléopâtre*, the famous line "Ses yeux òu fuyaient des galères" vibrates in symbolist fashion between the liquid eyes and the sea (in her fatal eyes Anthony read the future naval disaster of Actium).

[5] The Y-shape of his diving siren in the *Coup de Dés* (Page 8) is analogous; cf. "y plonge" in an early version of the *Faune*.

[6] Valéry reported this remark by Mallarmé (Biog., p. 796).

4. SONNET ("Sur les Bois Oubliés")

There is relatively little to say explicatively about this posthumously published poem; it is, nonetheless, remarkable. Mallarmé wrote it for an unidentified friend, in 1877,[1] to commemorate the latter's deceased wife. She speaks—hence the quotation marks—and says, in essence, to her husband who is kept apart from her, held "captive" by the "sill," of the house door (and possibly the tomb), on this winter's day, that he should not grieve because there are no flowers on her grave. She remarks (second quatrain) that he is staying up at midnight, sitting in an armchair, in the hope of catching a glimpse of her in the fireplace, which would then be illuminated by a "supreme firebrand" of vision or stirred-up memory. She admonishes that whoever wants to be Visited (by a dead loved one) must not put too many—tangible—flowers on the tombstone that "my finger lifts with the apathy of a defunctive strength." This is a moving image of the woman's effort to return to life to console her husband. Finally (last tercet), she adds that as a "Soul trembling (in eagerness, or as an insubstantial flame-like shadowy spectre) to come to rest in the so-bright fireplace"—to satisfy his desire to see her amid the flames—"all that I need do to live again is borrow from your lips the breath of my name murmured through an evening."

SONNET

(*Pour votre chère morte, son ami*)

2 novembre 1877

(*For your beloved deceased lady, her friend*)

2 November 1877

—"Sur les bois oubliés quand passe l'hiver sombre
Tu te plains, ô captif solitaire du seuil,
Que ce sépulcre à deux qui fera notre orgueil

Hélas! du manque seul des lourds bouquets s'encombre.

Sans écouter Minuit qui jeta son vain nombre,

"When the somber winter passes over the forgotten woods
You complain, O solitary captive of the threshold,
That this tomb for two which will be our pride [when we are joined there]

Alas! is laden with but the absence of heavy bouquets.

Without heeding midnight which casts its vain number,

43

Une veille t'exalte à ne pas fermer l'oeil
Avant que dans les bras de l'ancien fauteuil
Le suprême tison n'ait éclairé mon Ombre.

Qui veut souvent avoir la Visite ne doit
Par trop de fleurs charger la pierre que mon doigt
Soulève avec l'ennui d'une force défunte.

Âme au si clair foyer tremblante de m'asseoir,
Pour revivre il suffit qu'à tes lèvres j'emprunte
Le souffle de mon nom murmuré tout un soir."

A vigil incites you to not close your eyes
Before [with you sitting] in the arms of the old armchair
The supreme firebrand has lit up my shadow.

Whoever wishes to have the Visit [of the dead] often must not
With too many flowers burden the stone that my finger
Lifts with the apathy of a defunctive strength.

Soul trembling to rest in the so bright fireplace,
To revive it suffices for me to borrow from your lips
The breath of my name murmured through an evening."

In tone and setting the poem is close to Poe's *Raven,* which was being translated by Mallarmé about this time. There is the midnight Visit to a mourning husband—sitting in his armchair before the fireplace in a bleak season—though here the message is optimistic and it is the woman herself who speaks. The setting is found elsewhere in Mallarmé: for example, in *Igitur* and in *Tout orgueil,* though not as frequently as Claudel claims in his unduly-praised article, *La Catastrophe d'Igitur.* Davies has rightly observed that Mallarmé is a poet of the outdoors as much as the indoors, of day as well as, or more than, night.

A comment on Poe by Mallarmé reads: "elle (a lady friend of the young Poe) mourut . . . La pensée de la morte solitaire remplit son coeur d'un chagrin profond et incommunicable. Quand les nuits étaient lugubres et froides . . ." (232). But if we speak of a Poe-like mood in the sonnet, we must also observe the infinitely finer texture of Mallarmé.

Another echo is of Baudelaire's "Servante au grand coeur": on a winter night, lying snugly in his warm bed, he thinks, with uneasy conscience, of his old servant Marietta who is buried in a cold, cold grave, near other skeletons:

> Sans qu'amis ni famille
> Remplacent les lambeaux qui pendent à leur grille
> Lorsque la bûche siffle et chante, si le soir,
> Calme, dans le fauteuil je la voyais s'asseoir,
> . . . .
> Grave, et venant du fond de son lit éternel

Mallarmé copied this poem into a private anthology (Cellier, p. 36).

In one of his earliest pieces, *Ce que disaient les trois cigognes,* Mallarmé evoked this mood and added the image of the powerless finger: "je plains les pauvres morts qui, cousus dans leur linceul pâle, sans le pouvoir soulever du doigt, sentent par les fentes de la bière suinter régulièrement les gouttes lentes et mystérieuses de la neige fondue" (MI, p. 32).

bois oubliés: forgotten, unvisited by humans in winter. A fine effect of a rounded (though stripped) tree-bush is in the *o*'s and *b*'s; the dark *ou* complements the somber nasal of *sombre;* the flat *a* of *passe* is corollary; there is a dull moaning sound in *ain* of *plains.*

Chassé has pointed out an etymological overtone in *oublier* of "livid," the wintry discoloration.

Seuil: sill of the house door and threshold of the tomb; the latter usage is duplicated in "seuil éternel" (523).

manque seul de lourds bouquets: one of Mallarmé's well-known pure-presence-as-absence effects, as in "L'absente de tous bouquets" (857) "anciens fruits ... [leur] docte manque" (*Mes bouquins refermés*).[2] The *ou* of *lourds* and *bouquets* underscores the rounded heavy impression.

The notion that flowers would add to the burden of her task emphasizes the "weakness" of dead fingers and also the antimateriality of her message. This one-sided idealism, of course, is not Mallarmé's full doctrine.

minuit: there is the same effect of a clock casting forth empty numbers as in *Igitur*: "minuit [jeta] ... sa vacante sonorité" (435); *minuit* is inevitably bright by its sound, see our comment on *Ses purs ongles.*

veille: compare "la veillée amère" of *Surgi de la croupe,* in which a supreme flash of beauty—"une rose dans les ténèbres"—is likewise awaited.

suprême: the wave-movement of a flare-up is delicately suggested by the circumflex, as in "écume ... suprême" (337) or on Page 5 of the *Coup de Dés.*

Ombre: in the *Tombeau de Charles Baudelaire,* there is a similar cluster of ideas about this word: the returning spectre as a flame-shadow with the word *asseoir* (*rasseoir*) used in a similar way, with a dramatic leap from the immaterial to the concrete. Its sound is dark (nasal), contrasting vividly with the bright sounds of *éclairé.*

trop: the heavy effect is supported by the swelling *op* as in the *trop grands glaïeuls* of *Prose; trop* is in a "flower"-cluster, *tropical-trope-héliotrope* (C, pp. 267-268).

doigt: the single finger is a fine gesture of the quiet inner self, as in *Sainte;* it is more *penetrating* than the hand.

si clair: the *i* sharpens the brightness; the *s* suggests twisting flame and perhaps, through its sound, the hissing log; *clair* features the *ar*-effect which we have discussed in the chapter on the *Faune.*

souffle: f is the breezy or windy letter for Mallarmé, as it was for Plato.

mon nom: "Un nom sur un cercueil òu je ne puis pleurer / Un nom! qu'effaceront le temps et le lierre! / Un nom . . . Et tout est dit. Oh! non, doit-on donc l'oublier? / Qui sut se faire aimer ne meurt pas tout entier" (8). Also: "[enfant] qu'un mot de nous peut réveiller" (*Prière d'une mère*). Mallarmé's early griefs (here for a girl-friend) are in the lineage of the sonnet, though not as simply or directly as Mauron, Wais, or Cellier claim.

The discretion, tact, refinement called for in the final tercet are of the essence of Mallarmé.

NOTES

1 Cellier thinks that the man is the husband of Ettie Yapp. She had been the fiancée of Cazalis, and there are indications of unusual sympathy, even *amitié amoureuse,* between her and Mallarmé.

2 Cellier's (and Adam's) idea that the *manque* refers to the lover's absence from the grave is obviously incorrect; he would hardly be on top of the tomb (or "encumber" it); nor would the woman refer to the flowers again, unless she were consoling him for their absence.

The date of the poem is noteworthy: November 2 is All Souls' Day.

5. DON DU POÈME

Though published later, in 1883, it is clearly established that this poem was written at the time of—it is a comment on the birth pains of —*Hérodiade,* that is to say, around 1865. It was originally entitled *Le Jour,* referring to the theme of daybreak. The "gift" in the definitive title is of that dramatic poem to Mallarmé's public, so far consisting of just his wife, with the usual apologies on the part of Mallarmé for its not being what he had ideally hoped for.

Je t'apporte l'enfant d'une nuit d'Idumée!	I bring you the child of a night of Idumea!

This is a night on which he worked, apparently fruitlessly, on his poem: "[mon travail] acharné sur *Hérodiade,* ma lampe le sait!" (Corr., p. 207). Hérodiade is a princess of Edomite (Idumean) ancestry, as some have suggested; the word is used also because it is attractive and has three bright sounds (there are some more in *nuit*) to go with the idea of inspiration under bright, yet soft (the *m* of *Idumée* and *lampe*), lamp-light. Vigny in his *Chant de Suzanne au Bain* seems to have used it for similar, factually tenuous and poetically effective, reasons:

> Les fuseaux ont tissé la toile d'Idumée;
> Le passant dans la nuit voit sa lampe allumée.

Mallarmé undoubtedly knew this, for a version of *Ouverture ancienne* (N, p. 144) had "la tapisserie iduméenne."

Noire, à l'aile saignante et pâle, déplumée,	Black, with pale bleeding wing, unplumed,
Par le verre brûlé d'aromates et d'or,	Through the glass burned with aromatics and gold,
Par les carreaux glacés, hélas! mornes encor	Through the icy panes alas! still dreary,
L'aurore se jeta sur la lampe angélique	The dawn threw itself on the angelic lamp,
Palmes! . . .	Palmes! . . .

The dawn rays (recalling slightly Homer's "rosy-fingered") are, as in *Ouverture ancienne* (*aurore au vain plumage noir*), associated with wings, reaching through the window mingled still with streaks of black

night and cold morning air; the morning sun—like the poor poem—
is an unfledged ("unplumed") bird, fallen prematurely from its nest,
with bleeding (its red rays), pale wing.[1] Note that in *Igitur* the visita-
tion of a haunting thought at night is associated with a bird, like Poe's
raven. Mallarmé used the term "unplumed wing" for immature art, on
at least one other occasion: "mes deux ailes sans plume" *(Les Fenêtres)*.

"Glass burnt with aromatics and gold" is probably the oil-filled
glass of the glowing lamp, but mingled artfully with the sunrays shining
through the window *(carreaux)*, and there is a perfume, an incense
in the air as if emanating from his dreamed of oriental princess with her
hair "de l'or, à jamais vierge des aromates" (unsmelled perfumes are
sweeter); compare "la lampe, qui verse le calme doré de l'huile" (736).
The radiant and clear-lined (like spokes with intervening cold dark)
dawn's wings are suggestive of the fingers radiating from the palm
(paume) of a hand and, more aptly, the spray of branches of a palm tree
(recalling the oriental setting of this poem); the dawn rays fling themselves onto the lamp rays. And since *palme* has all the letters of *lampe,*
the union of natural and artificial light is consummated in the words
with masterly effect.[2] Nature (natural light) has overwhelmed human
creation (interior light: lamp). The poet's yearning for the instinctive
—a violent reaction to his stubborn artificing—will now modulate to
a thirst for the natural origin of life: paradisiacal milk, musical intimate
woman, the milky *azur*. A similar movement is the central theme of
Las de l'amer repos.

In *palme* there is also a hint of glory[3] (the dawn's if not the poet's);
compare "les saintes ont des palmes" (264); a palm-wing loose linkage is found in *Le Démon de l'Analogie:* "des palmes jaunes et les ailes
enfouies en l'ombre, d'oiseaux anciens" (273); the words *plume* and
palme are obviously close poetically because of their shape both as objects and as words, hence in *Le Démon,* "plume ou rameau" (273) and
"aile . . . palme . . . doigt" (272). The *déplumé* has an overtone not
only of dawn's dreary aspect but the "un-penned" poet, impotence
(see note 1).

lampe angélique: light as an angel is traditional; compare Rimbaud's
Mémoire where *mille anges* are the sun's rays (W, pp. 321-324).

The *or* tonality is particularly important here, in *aromates, or,
mornes, encor, aurore*—the gold of the light of day, of the lamp, of the
dreamed-of Hérodiade's tresses.

. . . et quand elle a montré cette relique	. . . and when it [the solitude] showed this relic [the poor poem]
À ce père essayant un sourire ennemi,	To this father [Mallarmé] trying a hostile smile,

	[The way fathers often do at their newly-born misshapen heirs]
La solitude bleue et stérile a frémi.	The blue and sterile solitude shivered.

The last line is a transparent evocation of matutinal air, both lovely and cold, hence the vibrant poetic *frémi*. The blue sky *(azur)* always has this doubleness with Mallarmé—its purity allures and mocks him. And though there is an added nuance of morning chill, still it is a fetching line despite the sterility (it shivers delightfully, thrills). The purity of the air (unsullied solitude) is in strong contrast with the all-too-human "abortion." A clear implication is that pure nature shivers in horror at the poet's weak imitation of Creation.

The theme of male birth, or parthenogenesis (Saurat), occurs later in the *Tombeau d'Anatole* (f. 40).

There is a scintillating cold precision in the *i, u, é, i, é, i.*

Ô la berceuse, avec ta fille et l'innocence	O cradling-woman [his sleeping wife] with your baby daughter and the innocence
De vos pieds froids, accueille une horrible naissance	Of your cold feet, receive a horrible birth [his poem]
Et ta voix rappelant viole et clavecin,	And [you with] your voice recalling viola and harpsichord,
Avec le doigt fané presseras-tu le sein	With your faded finger will you press the breast
Par qui coule en blancheur sibylline la femme	Through which flows in sybilline whiteness the woman
Pour les lèvres que l'air du vierge azur affame?	For the lips [of the poor-bird-poem] that the air of the virgin azure famishes?

The azure instilled the hunger of aspiration in his baby "bird" with its feeble wings (like the exiled impotent swan of the sonnet or of *Ouverture ancienne,* Hérodiade herself). Having failed as an artistic creator, Mallarmé turns to the natural creator, his wife, and asks her to feed his poem, with some pathetic irony. But these literal meanings are underpinned by more complex associations: the real and poetic hunger here is for the supremely sensuous Infinite which may arise in the unsatisfied flesh or perhaps after too long a struggle in the upper realms of artificing, particularly in shivery morning, as in Baudelaire's ostensibly fatigued but still subtly desirous:

> . . . l'âme, sous le poids du corps revêche et lourd,
> Imite les combats de la lampe et du jour.
> L'air est plein du frisson des choses qui s'enfuient,
> Et l'homme est las d'écrire et la femme d'aimer
> (*Crépuscule du matin*)

or

> Quand chez les débauchés l'aube blanche et vermeille
> Entre en société de l'Idéal rongeur,
> Par l'opération d'un mystère vengeur
> Dans la brute assoupie un ange se réveille.
>
> *(L'Aube spirituelle)*

This most intimate thirst is for the original paradisiacal milk:

> Si tu me vois les yeux perdus au paradis,
> C'est quand je me souviens de ton lait bu jadis.
>
> *(Hérodiade)*

Therefore it evokes the equally intimate, and more usually acceptable, beauty of music, which he associates in turn with the intimacy of the voice—what is more penetrating?—of a woman, his wife, who is at one with nature, innocent, asleep. Hunger and woman are one for the poet: *femme-affame,* and the wife-mother expands into something as eternal and ambiguous as the azure. The "virgin azure" is pure like her, and in one sense, by its ideality, brings the need for a violent reversal toward the flesh, yet it subtly flows with its own milkiness, as in *Les Fenêtres:*

> Et la bouche, fiévreuse et d'azur bleu vorace,
> Telle, jeune, elle alla respirer son trésor,
> Une peau virginale et de jadis! encrasse
> D'un long baiser amer les tièdes carreaux d'or.

In *Une dentelle* this same birth-window—bellied, fertile (*naître-fenêtre*)—music (bellied instrument)-milk-paradise cluster is paramount. In fact, we are here in, or near, the central network (or constellation) of Mallarmé's poetic universe, first identified by Mauron. It is close in mood to Coleridge's richest poem, *Kubla Khan,* where the "damsel with a dulcimer" is linked to the "milk of paradise."

In *Don du poème* the music and woman are joined not only in her voice and milk but in the word *berceuse,* "singer of lullabies." The *viole* is another link, being a bellied instrument (with a sensual overtone of *viol*) like the *mandore* of *Une dentelle.*

A milk-dawn association is found in *Les Dieux antiques:* "l'Aurore qui est nourrice du soleil" (1272).

The "cold feet" add a touch of innocence and purity and solicitous tenderness on the part of Mallarmé—and a bit of guilt for fleeing the natural by staying up and working cerebrally, with a greed for private glory. Compare "je vous baise, ô pieds froids de ma mère endormie" (Hugo, *Contemplations;* Cellier).

fané: part of his guilt, the "faded" hands of the housewife he is exploiting.[4] Compare the "mains sans paresse" of Madame Mallarmé in *Éventail*.

Note the three *i* sounds of *sybilline:* the white bright fierce jet of milk; compare "blanchit l'étoile sybilline" (258), "sanglots sybillins" (*Hommage à Richard Wagner*) which adds the sobbingly sensual quality of exultation as in "blancs sanglots glissant" (*Apparition*) or "tu fis la blancheur sanglotante des lys" (*Les Fleurs*). The *g* has much to do with this effect (see Appendix C). The best example of the whiteness of the *i* is, of course, the "sonnet in *i*," "Le vierge, le vivace et le bel aujourd' hui."

NOTES

[1] Compare Baudelaire's "enfant des noirs minuits" (*Sed non satiata*), which may have mildly influenced the baby-bird and baby-dawn and dawn-bird associations. The bird as traditional phallic symbol is only a minor undertone here and elsewhere in Mallarmé. We have noted it in connection with various passages of the *Coup de Dés* (e.g., C, p. 251) and explored it, but only as one link in a vast net of poetic Being.

The wing as symbol for psychic aspiration and defeat (hence closely linked with the rise and fall of light, or the inclination of light rays), runs throughout Mallarmé. It is a key image, on Page 3, of the *Coup de Dés*, further linked with the movement of waves. A possible source is "Psyché . . . laissait s'abattre ses plumes jusqu'à ce que ses ailes traînassent en la poussière" (tr. of Poe, 197). Actually, the symbol is as ancient as myth and literature. It reaches particular prominence in the Renaissance and in the Romantic era.

[2] "lampe . . . calme" (736) and "lampe . . . palmes" (*Don du poème*) are two links in a cluster; the circle is completed in Valéry's *Palme* with its repeated echo "palme . . . calme". All these words depend heavily on the flat, calm *a* for their poetic effect; see Appendix C and our article "The ABC's of Poetry" in *Comparative Literature*, no. 2 (1962).

[3] "Pourquoi, Stéphane, lui disions-nous un jour, avez-vous mis 'Palme' au bas de cette page?—Pour évoquer l'idée de *gloire*, répondait-il" (H. Roujon,—*La Galerie des bustes*, p. 21).

[4] "Je crois lui [à Marie] voler un temps qui lui appartient" (Biog., p. 71).

6. HÉRODIADE

❖❖❖❖❖❖❖❖❖❖

INTRODUCTION

Hérodiade (the *Scène*) was begun in 1864, in Mallarmé's twenty-second year, about the same time as the *Après-midi d'un faune* and not long before the famous metaphysical crisis. In other words, it represents the Mallarmé of late adolescence (generally prolonged in poets), beginning to hit his full stride of artistic manhood, shaking off the Baudelaire and Parnassian influences, finding his own voice, gingerly approaching a dazzling total vision that will grace and, for a while, throw him. Accordingly, *Hérodiade* duplicates many of the images, and the underlying artistic "ideas," found in the *Faune,* in the slightly later *Igitur,* in many of the *Poésies,* and even in *Un Coup de Dés. Hérodiade,* the whole *Mystère* (dramatic poem with spoken parts), indeed came close to being the capital work itself, so deeply were its themes rooted in Mallarmé's psyche. It might be identified as *the* main branch off the trunk which leads, from the 1866-1869 vision (most fully represented at that time by *Igitur*), to the *Coup de Dés,* a branch that reaches parallel to the trunk right up to the poet's final years, at which time he continued his work on *Hérodiade* where he had left off a few decades before.[1]

"*Hérodiade* où je m'étais mis tout entier sans le savoir," he then said. The central figure is, accordingly, a sort of sister to his other "masks" of the poet:[2] Igitur, the Faun, Hamlet, Poe, Villiers.[3] She haunts him as a creature of sheer beauty, a dream of perfect poetry. The concomitant of this beauty is cold cruelty and its price, suffering. Hérodiade appears to be largely ambivalent in one direction of the spirit, and somewhat androgynous in another. She is delight and pain, she is woman and something of man. But this spiritually-virile—sharp, lucid, aspiring, saintly, even godlike—aspect will emerge more fully in the figure of Saint John, projected, as it were, from the central figure of *Hérodiade* by "decomposition."[4]

Hérodiade is disturbingly complex: she is a child, "reine enfant"— yet one who is hovering on the edge of womanhood; feminine—yet a descendent of warriors with something of their metallic hardness; cold as "icicles"—yet she "burns"; narcissistic, yet "dying" to give herself.

In sum, she is human—and yet more than (and less than) human, as we have learned (from Eliot and others) to expect of art. As a figure of the poetic imagination, she emerges from a creative dream-zone in which words and sensations are strangely mixed: "la plus belle page de mon oeuvre sera celle qui ne contiendra que ce nom divin *Hérodiade.* Le peu d'inspiration que j'ai eu, je le dois à ce nom, et je crois que si mon *héroïne* s'était appelée Salomé, j'eusse inventé ce mot sombre, et *rouge* comme une *grenade* ouverte, *Hérodiade.* Du reste, je tiens à en faire un être purement rêvé et absolument indépendant de l'Histoire." (EL, p. 341).

Red is the color of life-blood and passion, fierce dark passion in this case; and the poetic effect depends largely on the clustered elements of *Hérodiade-héros* (or *héroïne* in the letter above)[5]-*Eros-rose* as in "des héros et des roses" (520) or

> . . . pareille à la chair de la femme, la *rose*
> Cruelle, *Hérodiade,* en fleur du jardin clair,
> Celle qu'un *sang* farouche et radieux arrose!
> (*Les Fleurs*)

The *héros-Eros* association can be traced back to Plato's *Cratylus,* which claims they are etymologically connected (it is primarily no doubt a matter for Mallarmé of rhyme-echo, a primitive and advanced form of knowledge). The *Eros-rose* association goes with the imagery of love and blood-suffused cheeks.

Why the *grenade* of the correspondence? Well, it rhymes with the word Hérodiade; it is the ripe, and dark red, fruit of bursting passion in a woman's parted lips ("ma bouche de grenade"; MI, p. 30) or as in the *Faune:*

> Tu sais, ma passion, que pourpre et déjà mûre,
> Chaque grenade éclate et d'abeilles murmure;
> Et notre sang, épris de qui le va saisir,
> Coule pour tout l'essaim éternel du désir.

(Note the *sang* of the *Faune,* recalling that of *Les Fleurs:* "Hérodiade . . . / celle qu'un sang farouche," etc.) A source of the blood-red feeling hovering about *grenade* is undoubtedly the echo *grenat* (garnet). *Grenades* is used once in a revealing way in the *Ouverture ancienne:* "ses promenades . . . quand le soir méchant a coupé les grenades" with a variant *"entr'ouvre* les grenades" (N, p. 150). Underneath all this related imagery is the secret connection between sexual consummation and blood-sacrifice (W, p. 78). The "ferocious" desire of Hérodiade, the blood in her rosy cheeks and lips, will lead to the decapitation of the Male,[6] as well as her own "sang déshonorant" (N, p. 206).   *

Another important effect—of crystal purity, sparkling hardness—
is the *diade* (hard *d*'s, bright *i*) with its overtones of *diamant* or
diadème, hence "Hérodiade au clair regard de diamant" (*Scène*) and
the final jewel-image of the *Scène,* or

> Pierres où mes yeux comme de purs bijoux
> Empruntent leur clarté mélodieuse.

In the just-quoted letter to Lefébure, Mallarmé adds "Je n'invoque
même pas tous les tableaux des élèves du Vinci et de tous les Florentins
qui ont eu cette maîtresse et l'ont appelée comme moi." This is a mild
attempt to justify the name historically, but it is obvious from his preceding statements about "une créature purement rêvée," that all he retained from the Bible story was a composite figure of a cruel woman,
Hérodiade (the mother who asked her daughter Salomé to dance for
Saint John's head), coalesced with her daughter Salomé, plus the saint.
Mallarmé's Hérodiade, then, is a virgin girl who secretly yearns for
a strange union with Saint John, involving his decapitation.[7]

The first part of the *Mystère,* often referred to as the *Ouverture
ancienne,* was begun early by Mallarmé and was later much reworked,
but it remained unfinished at the time of his death. Mallarmé was
clearly not satisfied with the piece and thought of abandoning it for
other possible openings. Nevertheless, the fragment is often intrinsic-
ally rewarding and is particularly rich in suggestions of future de-
velopments.

The whole of the *Ouverture ancienne* is one long soliloquy by
Hérodiade's nurse. The nurse, as in *Phèdre,* represents (again, by a sort
of projection of Hérodiade) the voice of woman and the flesh, the
Ewig-Weibliche in the mature state, the "flesh that always says yes"
(Joyce)—the milk-giver or nourisher (there is a curious sub-theme involving the present sterility of her breast). In a late fragment she
represents to Hérodiade the future woman she will not become, "vain
fantôme de moi-même celle que je ne serai pas" (N, p. 98). She is in
touch with the dark and instinctive roots of Being. And so she utters
her incantation, trying to appease her concern about a crisis and ritually
ease a passage from virginity to womanhood: will Hérodiade successfully emerge from her solitary chrysalis into a mature sexual being?
She, Hérodiade, seems slated for a special destiny, perhaps doom. After
all, she is not an ordinary young woman. She is the creation of a poet,
representing his *anima,* or an aspect of the poet himself, both less and
more than ordinary women. She will not have any ordinary lover, but
Saint John, the pure Godlike spirit whose transfixing Look could alone
(and, according to certain fragments, did) possess her. To which her

dangerously feminine response is decapitation.[8]

In other words, to the male-female (*animus-anima*) polarity of Hérodiade and Saint John, we must add the youth-age polarity of Hérodiade and her nurse.[9] On the whole, *Hérodiade* reflects the drama of Mallarmé's own complex evolution toward maturity. Throughout, Hérodiade hovers between male and female—the princess with flowing hair and robe versus the "inviolate reptile," the cruel lion-taming Diana —and between a youthfully egocentric inward vision (vertical, extreme) and the opposite impulse of the self toward the Other. The solitary, narcissistic maiden can also be the one who awaits the man with warm imaginings despite her "horror," who at the end admits she has been lying through the "naked flower of my lips" and inwardly observes her cold jewels begin to "separate" and break up in thaw.[10]

The poem, of course, is even more involved than that. It is all alive with as much vibrancy between various states as is the *Après-midi d'un faune.* Amidst the taut tensions of the manifold drama, as evidenced through Manichean imagery like *toi qui brûles de chasteté,* there are interspersed gentler moments—wafts of perfume, ashen light through foliage, touches of summer softness—for a crisis mood cannot well be kept constant through such long stretches of poetry. On the whole, though, it is notably intense, blowing very hot and cold.

Along with the icy diffidence, then, we find the typical Mallarméan image of melting jewels: *clarté mélodieuse;* her hair is "gold . . . with a cold sterility of metal," but it is a running "torrent" (in the same way as the frozen mirror can melt into a gushing "fountain"). She is as afraid to grow and flow as Hamlet, in Mallarmé's essay, is to "become" (instead of be, or not to be), and clings to her youthful hardness, at least on the surface, as adolescents often do—but the nurse knows better. Eventually the girl bursts out with a deeply narcissistic form of pure Flow: the image of milk drunk at the nurse's breast. She invokes the idea of her unveiling before the warm summer sky (though she refuses it, the effect is there and all the more powerful for her refusal) and when she says "Je déteste moi le bel azur," we think she detests or protests too much. And there is sensuality enough in:

> . . . aroma of ferocious delight
> The white shiver of my nudity would come out of the petals of my dress

The image of the weeping melting wax is primarily hers; the "naked flower of my lips" is surreptitiously inviting. After first breaking down and admitting to herself "you lie," the final image is of total yielding, eruption of a whole childhood's long-buried instincts:

the supreme bruised sobs
Of a childhood feeling amidst its reveries
At last separate its cold jewels.

It is very like the *Gloire du long désir* of *Prose,* or "l'enfant près de finir jette un éblouissement" (406).

Underneath *Hérodiade,* in sum, is the dream of a prolonged childhood: a fiercer struggle than most, a tenser drama leading to a more explosive resolution and a richer result, the maturity of the artist or his work's ripeness.

Rémy de Gourmont called the *Scène* "le poème le plus pur, le plus transparent, de la langue française"; if he was wrong, it is only a matter of nuance.

The mood of the *Cantique de Saint Jean* is quite different. It is fiercely univalent, fanatically pure, though a certain pathos may be read into it.[11]

(In the text of the *Ouverture* which we present here, the reader may note several discrepancies from the Pléiade edition; in all these cases, the Davies edition (N) is clearly more reliable.)

I. Ouverture Ancienne d'Hérodiade

La Nourrice
(Incantation)

Abolie, et son aile affreuse dans les larmes

Abolished [the dawn: i.e., defeated —threatening disaster broods over the whole scene], and its frightful wing [steeped] in the tears

Du bassin, aboli, qui mire les alarmes,

Of the fountain-basin, abolished [the basin shares in the air of general defeat] that mirrors the alarms,

Des ors nus fustigeant l'espace cramoisi,

Of the bare gold [of sunrise] whipping the crimson space,

Une Aurore a, plumage héraldique, choisi

A Dawn has—heraldic plumage— chosen

Notre tour cinéraire et sacrificatrice,

Our tomb-like [cinerary] and sacrificial tower,

Lourde tombe qu'a fuie un bel oiseau, caprice

Heavy tomb which a beautiful bird has fled [one of the images of Hérodiade who has deserted her room and, in a mysterious crisis, walks the palace gardens], solitary

Solitaire d'aurore au vain plumage noir . . .	Caprice of dawn with vain black plumage . . . [the act of fleeing was a sudden capricious deed in the dawn; the bird image of Hérodiade merges with the wing image of the dawn rays, still mingled with night, hence "black"]

Don du Poème uses the same image for sun rays at dawn: "Noire, à l'aile sanglante et pâle, déplumée, / . . . L'aurore se jeta sur la lampe angélique."

This is a dubious dawn still streaked with night-blackness, in a dying season, *l'automne éteignant en elle [l'eau] son brandon.* Clearly, it is the defeated rays that reach down into the basin (and not clouds, contrary to Davies), as in *Soupir:* "Octobre . . . aux grands bassins . . . laisse, sur l'eau morte . . . Se traîner le soleil jaune d'un long rayon."

The wing image is usually an aspiration—kinetic, soaring—in Mallarmé, but it can be an aspiration that failed; both aspects are found on Page 3 of the *Coup de Dés.* Both aspects are also present here: the "heraldic plumage" of a dawn's rays move upward as well as down into the basin and through the window. The escutcheon-like feathery spray of rays—as on the Austrian crest—are elsewhere described as "heraldic," in "coucher héraldique du soleil" (482).

plume(s): is a haunting word for Mallarmé. It is found often in his writings from the earliest (angel wings in *L'ange gardien*) through *Réminiscence* and especially *Le Démon de l'Analogie* (feathers in a shop window) and *Igitur* (the mysterious visitant bird); *plume* is prominent in his jottings for *Igitur,* as published by Bonniot.[12] It is a key word of the *Coup de Dés* (Page 7).

Aboli: one of his favorite terms, implying a tragically noble defeat, as in Nerval's famous line "Le prince d'Aquitaine à la tour abolie"; compare *Ses purs ongles:* "aboli bibelot d'inanité sonore" and *Une dentelle s'abolit,* which opens on a similar note of dubious daybreak; also the *Coup de Dés: N'ABOLIRA.*

Note the round effect of *b* in *bassin, abolie . . . aboli* as in Keats's "Beady bubbles winking at the brim"; the *bol* in *aboli* echoes *bassin.*

The downcast wing may remind us of Poe's *Ulalume:* "laissant s'abattre ses plumes jusqu'à ce que ses ailes traînassent en la poussière" (tr., 197); or Baudelaire's *Albatros:* "piteusement leurs grandes ailes . . . traînaient."

*

Ah! des pays déchus et tristes le manoir!	O! this mansion of sad dejected country!
Pas de clapotement! L'eau morne se résigne,	No slapping of water! The dreary water resigns itself,

| Que ne visite plus la plume ni le cygne | [The water] No longer visited by feather [of birds] or by the |
| Inoubliable: | Unforgettable swan: |

Note the *plus-plume* echo, prominent in the notes or jottings published by Bonniot together with *Igitur*. The theme of deserted, listless water will be treated later. The *b*'s of *inoubliable* go very well with the swan image. The mansion recalls the *Fall of the House of Usher*, a Mallarmé favorite, echoed in the *Coup de Dés*, Page 8.

l'eau reflète l'abandon	the water reflects the abandonment [dying dejection]
De l'automne éteignant en elle son brandon:	Of the autumn extinguishing its fire-brand in it: [i.e., the last ray of dying light of the year]
Du cygne quand parmi le pâle mausolée	[And reflects the dejection] Of the swan when amidst the pale mausoleum
Ou la plume plongea la tête, désolée	Or [which is] its feathers the swan-head buried itself, desolated
Par le diamant pur de quelque étoile, mais	By the pure diamond of some star, but
Antérieure, qui ne scintilla jamais.	Past, and which never scintillated.

This desperate image of a dead star which *could* have shone is the "issu stellaire . . . EXISTÂT-IL / autrement qu'hallucination éparse d'agonie" of Page 9 of the *Coup de Dés;* it is the tragic beauty of the swan song[13] that runs throughout *Hérodiade*.

There is a swan and naked girl association which haunts the lower recesses of his memory with a troubling mixture of purity (perhaps that of his dead innocent sister) and sensuality, as in the early poem *Loeda:*

Loeda voit à son front scintiller une étoile!
"Qui donc es-tu? qui donc? cygne au baiser de miel?"
Dit-elle en palpitant. "Ton amant!—"Oh! dévoile
Ton nom, coeur enivrant!"—"Loeda, le roi du ciel!"

Jupiter! . . . à ce nom, mollement son sein rose
Plein d'amour se noya dans le sein ondoyant
Du cygne au col neigeux qui sur son coeur riant
Cueille d'ardents baisers. Sous son aile il dépose

La nymphe frémissante: ils ne forment qu'un corps.
Loeda se renversa, la paupière mi-close,
Les lèvres s'entrouvrant . . . sourit dans cette pose . . .
—Et la nuit tomba noire et voila leurs transports.
(*Loeda,* in *Mallarmé lycéen*)

Although the swan is primarily associated with the princess

Hérodiade in the *Ouverture*—her naked image in the mirror (*Scène*) is subtly foreshadowed by the water-reflected image here—from the *Loeda* excerpt we may see that the swan is an unusually complex, and ambiguous, motif. Is it too much to say that the adolescent Mallarmé (of *Loeda*) himself aspired to be that swan, a God-Beast? Then, years later (*Hérodiade*, etc.), like the magnificent exiled creature depicted in "Le vierge, le vivace," he, no doubt, dreamed of such lost voluptuous innocence involving the forbidden glimpse of a naked girl. This would be primarily a memory of his sister (a secret then buried from the young poet: *la nuit tomba noire*). But it could be something even subtler. In other words, the naked phantom in a mirror (duplicated in the nixie of *Ses purs ongles*, the dreamed-of woman in *Frisson d'hiver*) is not only feminine. It is the forbidden "nakedness" of himself, as in *Igitur*, the narcissistic image of his orphaned childhood, or of his lamented future ghost (with a physical, erotic undertone).[14] This drama of self-love involves the doubleness of *animus* and *anima*. The creature in the mirror, like the swan itself, is somewhat androgynous. All this will be summed up in the ambiguous *sirène* on Page 8 of the *Coup de Dés* (C, pp. 320-336). Mauron has preceded us into these subterranean realms, but only partially and certainly less fully then did Mallarmé himself. What Mallarmé makes of all this is something far more conscious, artistically-willed and structured than Mauron cares to believe.

Crime! bûcher! aurore ancienne! supplice!	Crime! Funeral pyre! Ancient dawn! Torture!
Pourpre d'un ciel! Étang de la pourpre complice!	Purple of a sky! [or roof] Pond accomplice of [reflecting] the purple!
Et sur les incarnats, grand ouvert, ce vitrail.	And on these rose tints, wide open, this stained-glass window.

The scene is set outdoors and, as in a cinematic pan-in, we enter, through the frame of the window, Hérodiade's abandoned room. There may be, as Mme. Ayda says, the suggestion of a transition from the water surface, with a stained-glass effect in its reflection of the colorful evening sky.

The dawn of the fateful approaching crisis is dramatic, "old"—heavy with past and mystery—like the death-of-a-hero myths described by Mallarmé in *Les Dieux antiques*. It is paralleled in:

> Victorieusement fui le suicide beau [crime-suicide]
> Tison de gloire [bûcher], sang par écume, or, tempête . . .

The excited baroque dramatic agonized giddy creamy bloody piercing experience of love-death up there is the same in both.

La chambre singulière en un cadre, attirail	The strange room in a frame [the window through which we look], [with its] trimmings

De siècle belliqueux, orfèvrerie éteinte,	Of a warlike century, [its] tarnished gold,
A le neigeux jadis pour ancienne teinte,	Has as its ancient color the snowy yesteryear [i.e., pale faded effect of tapestries, metals, etc.],
Et sa tapisserie, au lustre nacré, plis	And its tapestry, with pearly luster, useless folds
Inutiles avec les yeux ensevelis	With the buried [in the folds] eyes
De sibylles offrant leur ongle vieil aux Mages.	Of sybils offering their old fingernails to the Magi [some vaguely familiar—Biblical?—motif of hieratic female figures with uplifted hands moving toward some master].

Mallarmé often uses synecdoche: for example, the fingernail for finger (or hand), because it is delicate, discreet, subtly penetrating, as in *Ses purs ongles*. The uplifted nail image is found again at the end of the poem, and a similar one in *Sainte* (the finger held up against the plumage).

plis inutiles: mainly because the room is abandoned by the heroine, but also to create a general atmosphere of dejection or fatality; for Mallarmé, a twisted line is often a sign of futility, or man's useless squirm in agony at his fate, the *torsion* of the siren in the *Coup de Dés* or of the *chimère* in *La Musique et les Lettres* (648).

Une d'elles, avec un passé de ramages	One of them [sybils, one embroidered on the Nurse's dress], with embroideries of flowery vines
Sur ma robe blanchie en l'ivoire fermé	On my dress bleached in the closed ivory [an old dress, long kept in a chest]
Au ciel d'oiseaux parmi l'argent noir parsemé,	[And] With a bird-filled sky scattered amid the black silver [old embroidery]
Semble, de vols partis costumée et fantôme,	Seems, garbed in risen bird flights and phantom [adj.],
Un arôme qui porte, ô roses! un arôme,	Like an aroma which carries, O roses! an aroma,
Loin du lit vide qu'un cierge soufflé cachait,	Far from the empty bed that a blown-out candle hid [stood in front of? did not light?],
Un arôme d'os froids rôdant sur le sachet,	An aroma of cold bones [the nurse's strange old, cold odor] prowling on the sachet [a sachet enclosed in the ivory chest smells like roses, like the roses in a vase in the room],

Une touffe de fleurs parjures à la lune,	A bunch of flowers unfaithful to the moon [the bunch has its flower heads turned away from the disappearing moon],
(À la cire expirée encor s'effeuille l'une,)	(By the extinguished candle one of them [the flowers] is shedding its petals)[15]
De qui le long regret et les tiges de qui	Whose [the flowers] long regret [i.e., they fade and wilt] and stalks
Trempent en un seul verre à l'éclat alangui . . .	Steep in a single glass with a languishing gleam . . .
Une Aurore traînait ses ailes dans les larmes!	A Dawn dragged its wings in the tears! [of the fountain-basin, parallel to the water in the flower glass].

A variant jotting for this passage read "[the nurse disappears] s'en fut / non par une fente des tapisseries / mais évanouie en sa trame usée / dans un effroi de—licorne / de fleur ramagée" (N, p. 128); compare "les murs, plutôt de quelque épaisseur isolées les tentures, vieillies en la raréfaction locale; pour que leurs hôtes déteints avant d'y devenir les trous . . . balbutiassent ou radotassent, seuls, la phrase de leur destin . . . fantômes" (329-330). In short, the feeling is of lovely old tapestry from which ghost-like human figures seem to emerge—or into which they disappear again—in an air of fine symbolist mystery. The sibyls are vague prophetesses of the fateful crisis.

But why this lyric outburst specifically in reference to the nurse's dress?[16] It probably indicates some familiar nostalgia of the poet for the smell of female clothing, together with the fascination of death in the sterile habit of a "wintry nurse" (Scène). His mother had died when he was very young, and he obviously got great satisfaction from dressing women in his imagination, as has been observed in the pages of La Dernière Mode (we are reminded of Baudelaire's remarks on the poet-as-child, raised amidst feminine finery, perfumes, furs).

The dangerously deep nostalgia for an infantile paradise (paradis . . . ton lait bu jadis; Scène) is clearly entangled with death.

Further fragments (N, pp. 198, etc.) indicate that it is indeed the nurse's dress: for example, Hérodiade has just dismissed the nurse, at the end of the Scène, in the following fragment:

> mes froides pierreries
> À tout et même à toi [the nurse] n'ai-je pas dit adieu
> Que restes-tu

followed by a cluster of possible choices:

> [où as-tu] glissé au doux sachet

d'os légers et de cendres
quoi tu n'es pas évanouie en la tapisserie?

The strange smell of the nurse's dress—"sweet sachet of light bones and
ashes"—is confirmed here; compare "son [the nurse's] sachet de vieille
faille / rôde" (N, p. 196). "Sachet exhalé sur qui rôde le nom" [de
Saint Jean] (N, p. 197)—this last association hints that the death of
Saint John is also implied in the os froids.

Yet though it is certainly the nurse, an ambiguity persists. After all,
the nurse is a sort of projection of Hérodiade herself, her maturity; the
fantôme of the Ouverture ancienne is echoed in a fragment that makes
precisely this point: "vain fantôme de moi-même celle que je ne serai
pas" (N, p. 98). The following reference to his dead sister, Maria, "ce
pauvre jeune fantôme, qui fut treize ans ma soeur" may make us medi-
tate, in passing, that she too, like Hérodiade, had no future and is, perhaps, vaguely remembered here, along with the dead mother (nurse)
and the poet's own childhood. The main persona here is the poet's own
soul, anxious about its fate: can it emerge into real life (or a sublimated
equivalent of it, the successful poetic reality)? Or will it remain a
phantom "half sick of shadows" like Tennyson's Lady of Shalott, held
by the mirror in a death-like narcissistic limbo?

The element ro is repeated many times in these lines: "robe . . .
ivoire . . . arôme . . . porte . . . ô roses . . . arôme . . . arôme . . . os froids
rôdant" and sounds one of the main tones of the whole poem, as the ro
(and the letters of roide) of Hérodiade; the cluster is ro-or (often repeated and often connected with Hérodiade's hair) and further, roi-
froide-roide-ivoire, compare "roide de froid" (941). The last-mentioned
elements of stiffness and coldness, the hard virile aspect of the virgin,
passes somewhat into the wintry nurse, and is connected with the sound
and imagery of ivory (stiff cold bones); hence the ivoire and "os froids
* rôdant sur le sachet." This links with the later image of the shroud and
of the warrior-father. The "sachet" and the "rose" involved in the
aroma are the other side of the cluster, the soft warm flowing delight,
depending on the liquid harmonious r and or (the wintry nurse's milk
* flows, or did once, as Hérodiade's golden hair may flow).

Ombre magicienne aux symboliques charmes!	Magic shadow with symbolic charms! [haunting thought: the mystery of Hérodiade]
Une voix, du passé longue évocation,	A voice, long [also: from far away] evocation of the past,
Est-ce la mienne prête à l'incanta-tion?	Is it mine ready to break into incan-tation?

The nurse is about to be seized with the mystic vision. The poet's own processes are obviously recounted here (recalling the tear-secretion in Valéry's *La Jeune Parque*). A variant (N, p. 147), intercalating *mandore* after *la mienne,* links the original "voice" with the music-milk-birth-feminine voice theme we discuss under *Don du poème* (cf. also *Une dentelle*).

Encore dans les plis jaunes de la pensée	Still in the yellow folds of thought [merely stagnant and potential, the vision]
Traînant, antique, ainsi qu'une toile encensée	Dragging, old, like a perfumed cloth [woven texture: the network of thought]
Sur un confus amas d'ostensoirs refroidis,	Over a confused mass of cold monstrances, [the vision is like the cold unused items of a rite, now to be revived]
Par les trous anciens et par les plis roidis	Through the old holes and the stiffened folds [again the stiff "fabric" of thought with its spaces]
Percés selon le rythme et les dentelles pures	Pierced just like the rhythm and the pure lacework
Du suaire laissant par ses belles guipures	Of the shroud letting through its beautiful stitches
Désespéré monter le vieil éclat voilé	The old veiled dazzle desperately mount
S'élève: (ô quel lointain en ces appels célé)!	Rises: (oh, what a distance is hidden in those calls!)
[Le vieil éclat voilé . . .]	[The old veiled dazzle . . .]

The fabric of thought covering the cold vision—now about to rise and glow—is compared to a shroud which lets through some gleam of the buried life. Mallarmé refers to a stagnant state of mind as "pensée jaune" in a letter (Corr., p. 93; Richard): "cuivre jaune" evokes decadence in *Plainte d'automne;* in *Soupir,* the dying sunlight is "jaune."

This hovering on a threshold is very typical of Mallarmé. In the *Sonnet, Pour votre chère morte,* it is between life and death (as in various tales of Poe); in *Le nénuphar blanc,* and numerous other texts, it is between presence and absence.

Le vieil éclat voilé du vermeil insolite,	The old veiled dazzle of the strange gilt,
De la voix languissant, [sic], nulle, sans acolyte,	Of the languishing voice, empty, without acolyte [the poor nurse, like the poet, is alone in this "heretical" attempt to resuscitate Truth]
Jettera-t-il son or par dernières splendeurs,	Will it cast its gold in last splendors [an apocalypse],

Elle, encore, l'antienne aux versets demandeurs,
À l'heure d'agonie et de luttes funèbres!

[Will] It [rise] still, the hymn with pleading verses,
In the hour of agony and deathly struggles!

The peak of inspiration, struggling to rise, has been reached; now the fall. (The idea of an apocalypse, of himself as a "last" poet, is quite common in Mallarmé and in the artists closest to him).

Et, force du silence et des noires ténèbres
Tout rentre également en l'ancien passé,
Fatidique, vaincu, monotone, lassé,
Comme l'eau des bassins anciens se résigne.

And, through silence and the black shadows
All alike goes back into the ancient past,
Fatal, vanquished, monotonous, tired,
As the water of ancient basins grows resigned.

The rise and fall (resignation) is like the parabolically curving neck of the swan who will figure prominently in the imagery here.

The wave motion or rhythm of reality is here expressed by water as in the *Coup de Dés:* "rien n'aura eu lieu que le lieu / inférieur clapotis quelconque / comme pour disperser l'acte vide." A blast of golden light is also a major theme in Mallarmé: "illuminait telle divination longtemps voilée, lucide tout-à-coup" (395); "l'or de la trompette d'Été" (*Prose*) "tout-à-coup l'éruptif multiple sursautement de la clarté, comme les proches irradiations d'un lever de jour" (648); the most important example is Page 1 of the *Coup de Dés* (C, pp. 119-121), where the theme of defeated aspiration is pursued on Page 3 and throughout the Poem.

In the next section, the *Elle* which begins it is the voice (cf. the *elle* six lines back) announcing the vision of Truth or Poetry and also the *She* who represents it for the nurse (and for Mallarmé): Hérodiade herself, the swan-like solitary princess.

Elle a chanté, parfois incohérente, signe

She [and/or the voice] has sung, at times incoherent, [a] sign [which is]

Lamentable!

Lamentable! [The distraught princess's swan-song presages something awful—a crisis, the death-marriage with decapitated Saint John]

le lit aux pages de vélin,
Tel, inutile et si claustral, n'est pas le lin!

the bed with vellum pages,
Such, useless and so claustral, is not linen! [the nurse is worried because Hérodiade walks out at night; her bed remains empty, and unwrinkled, unused; it is like blank paper: virgin, sterile]

Qui des rêves par plis n'a plus le cher grimoire,

Which [linen] no longer has the dear writing of dreams in its folds, [the rumpling—"writing" on the sheets —of a tossing, dreaming woman would be promise of life]

Ni le dais sépulcral à la déserte moire,
Le parfum des cheveux endormis. L'avait-il?

Nor has the sepulchral dais with the abandoned watered silk,
The perfume of sleeping hair. Did it have it? [was Hérodiade at all in her bed?]

The linen-vellum-text-*grimoire* cluster is part of an intricate network which is discussed at length in the chapter on *Une dentelle s'abolit.*

Froide enfant, de garder en son plaisir subtil
Au matin grelottant de fleurs, ses promenades,
Et quand le soir méchant a coupé les grenades!

Cold girl-child, to keep [up] as her subtle pleasure
In the morning shivering with flowers, her walks,
And [also to walk] when the wicked evening has cut the pomegranates! [when evening spills red on the skies]

Le croissant, oui le seul est au cadran de fer
De l'horloge, pour poids suspendant Lucifer,
Toujours blesse, toujours une nouvelle heurée,
Par la clepsydre à la goutte obscure pleurée,
Que, délaissée, elle erre, et sur son ombre pas
Un ange accompagnant son indicible pas!
Il ne sait pas cela le roi qui salarie

Depuis longtemps la gorge ancienne et tarie.
Son père ne sait pas cela, ni le glacier

The crescent moon, yes the only one is on the iron dial [dark night]
Of the [sky] clock, with Lucifer [morning star] as a weight,
Always wounds [strikes a new hour], [and] always another hour-full
[Is] Wept by the water-clock with a dark drop,
[And still] Abandoned, she wanders, and over her shadow no
Angel [is] accompanying her inexpressible step!
He does not know this, the king who has hired

For years the ancient and dried breast [the nurse].
Her father does not know this, nor [does] the fierce glacier

Farouche reflétant de ses armes l'acier,
Quand sur un tas gisant de cadavres sans coffre
Odorant de résine, énigmatique, il offre
Ses trompettes d'argent obscur aux vieux sapins!
Riviendra-t-il un jour des pays cisalpins!

Reflecting the steel of his arms,
When over a heap of corpses
Without resinous caskets, enigmatic he offers up [the sound of]
His trumpets of dim silver to the old firs!
Will he come back one day from the cisalpine lands!

Assez tôt? car tout est présage et mauvais rève!

Soon enough? For all [here] is omen and bad dream!

The Pléiade edition has "est tarie" but Davies (N) offers a better reading, "et tarie." The weeping water-clock—lamenting time's passing —is repeated in "souvent une heure, prompte et que sanglotait la clepsydre" (613). The *croissant oui le seul* means that it is not only a replica but the real moon, which itself is crossing the sky, "moving like the luminous hand of a clock across the grim dark face of night (*au cadran de fer*). And now the counterweight of that nocturnal clock is becoming visible, in the form of the morning star, Lucifer" (Chisholm). Compare: "le cadran des étoiles" (197); "Cadran lunaire" (215).

*   *Grenade:* compare "ce mot sombre, et rouge comme une *grenade* ouverte, *Hérodiade*" (EL, p. 341).

À l'ongle qui parmi le vitrage s'élève

Upon the fingernail which amid the stained-glass window is raised

Selon le souvenir des trompettes, le vieux

According to the memory of the trumpets, [the image of the raised finger recalls by analogy the image of the raised trumpet] the old

Ciel brûle, et change un doigt en un cierge envieux.

Sky burns, and changes a finger into an envious candle, [the glare of sunrise makes an imitative—"envious"—glow on the finger in the stained-glass window]

Et bientôt sa rougeur de triste crépuscule
Pénétrera du corps la cire qui recule!

And soon its redness of sad dusk
Will penetrate the wax of the shrinking candle's body! [bring total destruction]

This candle is echoed by the one that brings the *Scène* to a close.[17] It is the theme of consuming love. To the virgin adolescent, the thought of adulthood, the death of childhood, can be a cause for tears; something precious is passing away. The awareness of the infinite claims of the body can bring a sense of horror—the plunge into the menacing waters of reality—of diminishing spirit, of disaster; this is the tone of this section of the poem.

De crépuscule, non, mais de rouge lever,

Of dusk, no, but of red dawn, [in this strange apocalyptic setting, dawn and dusk seem confused]

Lever du jour dernier qui vient tout achever,
Si triste se débat, que l'on ne sait plus l'heure

Dawn of the last day which comes to end all,
So sadly it struggles [the "redness" of the next line], that one no longer knows the hour

La rougeur de ce temps prophétique qui pleure	The redness of this prophetic time that weeps
Sur l'enfant, exilée en son coeur précieux	Over the girl-child, exiled in her precious heart
Comme un cygne cachant en sa plume ses yeux,	Like a swan hiding in its plumage its eyes,
Comme les mit le vieux cygne en sa plume, allée,	As the old swan put them [its eyes] in its plumage, like a pathway,
De la plume détresse, en l'éternelle allée	[In the] Distress of the plumage, in the eternal departure
De ses espoirs, pour voir les diamants élus	Of its hopes, to see the elite diamonds
D'une étoile, mourante, et qui ne brille plus!	Of a dying star, and which no longer shines!

This, aside from the strange usage of the word *allée* (pathway in the feathers?) is quite clear: the unsure setting of an apocalyptic crisis during which the swan-princess, Hérodiade, turns on herself in hopeless solitude, despairing of life itself—and then from this despair diamond-stars shine forth, her beauty; "Loeda voit à son front / scintiller une étoile" *(Loeda, ML)*. The nurse is fearful that she will never grow into a Queen.[18] The evocation of an unsure hour is found elsewhere in the fragment "vespérale ou matinale—on ne saura (N, p. 139)." Its *rougeur* is part of the consummation theme; compare the opening lines.

II. SCÈNE

La Nourrice—Hérodiade

N.

Tu vis! ou vois-je ici l'ombre d'une princesse?	You are alive! [after braving the lions] Or do I see here the shade of a princess?
A mes lèvres tes doigts et leurs bagues et cesse	To my lips your fingers and their rings and cease
De marcher dans un âge ignoré . . .	Walking in an unknown age [the mysterious legendary past of the *anciens rois,* the lions she visits in the dungeon] . . .

H.

Reculez.	Stand back [even the nurse should not touch her].
Le blond torrent de mes cheveux immaculés	The blond torrent of my immaculate hair
Quand il baigne mon corps solitaire le glace	When it bathes my solitary body freezes it
D'horreur, et mes cheveux que la lumière enlace	With horror [even the touch of her hair alarms the virgin], and my hair enlaced with light
Sont immortels. O femme, un baiser me tûrait	Is immortal. O woman, a kiss would kill me
Si la beauté n'était la mort ...	If beauty were not death ...

The tension of the virgin seeking her own intimate essence, yet quivering on the threshold of maturity, gives off a vibrant radiancy of beauty-horror;[19] almost everything is in terms of extreme opposites: her golden hair is a "flowing torrent" yet it is coldly immaculate, freezes with remoteness and inviolability; compare the later lines, "je veux / Vivre parmi l'effroi que me font mes cheveux" (ambivalent—beauty-gold and horror-cold).

cheveux . . . immortels: her hair is metallic, gold, hard as her youth (and hair *is* generally enduring); the element *or* has much to do with the choice of words; it is prominent in the poem, particularly in the passages having to do with her locks.

Un baiser me tûrait: so the virgin thinks, and often approximately so expresses herself—"j'ai horreur de ça"—in real life; this points to the deep ambiguity of authentic Eros in a limit-situation, its entanglement with death.

Si la beauté n'était la mort: we speak of a "stunning" beauty, "dressed to kill," a "crush," a "lady-killer," and Cupid comes armed with arrows. Hérodiade, a narcissistic girl par excellence, obviously, according to her words, slays herself by her own sight—but she is really surrounding herself with violent beauty for our sakes.

Par quel attrait	Led by what attraction
Menée et quel matin oublié des prophètes	And [do I know] what morning forgotten by prophets
Verse, sur les lointains mourants, ses tristes fêtes,	Pours, on the dying distances, its sad festivals,
Le sais-je? tu m'as vue, ô nourrice d'hiver,	Do I know [any of this—what impelled me, what day it is]? you have seen me, O wintry nurse
Sous la lourde prison de pierres et de fer	[Enter] Under the heavy prison of stones and iron

Où de mes vieux lions traînent les siècles fauves	Where the tawny centuries [an age-old tradition] of my old lions drag
Entrer, et je marchais, fatale, les mains sauves,	Enter. And I walked, fatal, untouched,
Dans le parfum désert de ces anciens rois:	In the deserted perfume of those former kings [the lions]:
Mais encore as-tu vu quels furent mes effrois?	But did you see how frightened I was?

The "morning forgotten by prophets" is an evocation of the fateful dawn of the *Ouverture,* the crisis of the emergence into life (or poetic fulfillment) which she dreads and desires (will she have the strength to "make it"?). And *oublié des prophètes* implies the original, back-to-the-source nature of the naked experience, predating even the Bible (recall the *sans acolyte* of the *Ouverture*). Further, there is the suggestion of a pure, free morning untouched by prophetic castigation (perhaps a foreshadowing of Saint John, and a setting of a Biblical tone). The "sad festivals" of a twilight is like that of the *Après-midi d'un faune:* "ashes and gold . . . festival in the extinguished foliage"; and the "dying distances" is another touch of this mysterious half-light and shade (compare Debussy's *Fêtes* with the first frail spray of horns, in the unsure distance).

nourrice d'hiver: her cold old age, perhaps her costume, certainly her (former) white milk, specifically referred to later, are part of the "winter."

Siècles: are the lions *that* old? Reference is made here rather to the stone enclosure and setting and the tradition of the lions; the "Judah is . . . an old lion" of the Book of Genesis—and their dignified old bearing and their color; tawniness, of the lions and the prison stones, evokes age as in "toute la vétusté presque couleur encens / . . . , je sens / Que se dévêt . . . la pierre veuve" *(Remémoration).* Mauron speaks of an atmosphere of fallen temporal power or grandeur (linking the *fauve* lions with the *fauve agonie* of the leaves in *Soupir,* which is less convincing).

Je m'arrête rêvant aux exils, et j'effeuille	I stop, dreaming of exiles [the adolescent princess is naturally idealistic], and I strip
Comme près d'un bassin dont le jet d'eau m'accueille,	As if near a basin whose fountain welcomes me,
Les pâles lys qui sont en moi, tandis qu'épris	The pale lilies which are in me [an actual flower; her pure thoughts—she likes to drop petals in water, dreamily], while smitten
De suivre du regard les languides débris	Through following with their glance the languid debris [of lily-petals]

Descendre, à travers ma rêverie, en silence,	Falling, through my revery, silently
Les lions, de ma robe écartent l'indolence	The lions push aside the indolence [slack] of my dress
Et regardent mes pieds qui calmeraient la mer.	And watch my feet which would calm the sea.

The "feet which would calm the sea" is a Bible-legendary image, as in "tes pieds qui calmeraient la mer" (15); compare also Rimbaud's "sans songer que les pieds lumineux des Maries / Pussent forcer le mufle aux Océans poussifs" (*Bateau Ivre*). The virgin's traditional power to tame the unicorn is vaguely remembered in this encounter with the lions.

There is a possible allusion to disrobing in the lily petals but it makes for difficulties (see notes 16 and 17).

Calme, toi, les frissons de ta sénile chair,	Calm the shivers of your senile flesh,
Viens et ma chevelure imitant les manières	Come and [since]my hair [is] imitating the too ferocious appearance
Trop farouches qui font votre peur des crinières,	Which causes you to fear manes,
Aide-moi, puisqu'ainsi tu n'oses plus me voir,	Help me, since you no longer dare to look at me that way [unkempt],
A me peigner nonchalamment dans un miroir	To comb myself nonchalantly in a mirror.

The princess before her mirror is a familiar narcissistic image. Note the slow caressing effect of *nonchalamment* (with its soft *ch*); *chevelure* has a similar quality; note the shiver of *ss* in *frisson;* the *f* of *farouche* and *font* offer a mane effect akin to the one of curving feather we describe in our Letter Table. (This English teacher almost seems to have been aware of the effect on us of *manière,* compare *morne* below).

N.

Sinon la myrrhe gaie en ses bouteilles closes,	If not the gay myrrh in its closed bottles,
De l'essence ravie aux vieillesses de roses,	[Then the dark effect] Of the essence stolen from old roses,
Voulez-vous, mon enfant, essayer la vertu	Will you, my child, try the dark
Funèbre?	Effect?

Mallarmé (as in *Frisson d'Hiver, Symphonie Littéraire*) occasionally speaks of the "grace of faded things," having perhaps learned from Baudelaire this charming decadence, vaguely Byzantine in mood.[20] But rather than of "decadence" (that much-abused term) it is better to speak of the enhanced depth that time brings to antique objects—the serious coloration of the partial death involved in aging.

H.

Laisse là ces parfums! ne sais-tu
Que je les hais, nourrice, et veux-tu
que je sente
Leur ivresse noyer ma tête languissante?
Je veux que mes cheveux qui ne sont
pas des fleurs
A répandre l'oubli des humaines
douleurs,
Mais de l'or, à jamais vierge des aromates,
Dans leurs éclairs cruels et dans leurs
pâleurs mates,
Observent la froideur stérile du
métal,
Vous ayant reflétés, joyaux du mur
natal,
Armes, vases depuis ma solitaire enfance.

Leave the perfumes! Don't you know
I hate them, nurse, do you wish me
to feel
Their drunkenness drown my lan-
guishing head?
I want my locks which are not
flowers
[Meant] To spread oblivion of hu-
man pain
But gold, forever pure of scent,

In their cruel lightning and their mat
[dull] paleness,
[I want my hair] To observe the cold
sterility of metal,
Having reflected you, adornments of
my native walls,
Weapons, vases since my solitary
childhood.

As we observed earlier, she protests too much and we should not
take her too literally; beneath her outer coldness she is clearly trembling
with sensuality, about to erupt, and herself admits, just before the end,
that she has been lying with her lovely lips.

Note the (metallic) flat *a*'s of *pâleur, mat, métal, natal, armes, vases;*
the wavy *ss* of *ivresse* and *languissante;* the bright acute *é* and *u* and *i* of
éclairs cruels, stérile; the *v* of *veux* and *cheveux* is a very feminine
effect, pouting—reflecting the overall feminine effect of the letter.

She is the scion of a warlike race, and some of this quality passes
into her hair, as in various fragments (N, pp. 157, 158, 161) and
Victorieusement fui.

N.

Pardon! l'âge effaçait, reine, votre
défense
De mon esprit pâli comme un vieux
livre ou noir . . .

Pardon! Age was erasing, queen, your
interdiction
From my mind which has become
pale as an old book, or black . . .

Either the print is faded or the page is grimy—in either case the
book of her memory is unreadable . . .

The mind as text has been discussed under *Ouverture ancienne.*

H.

Assez! Tiens devant moi ce miroir,
                    O miroir!

Enough! Hold this mirror up to me,
                    O mirror!

Eau froide par l'ennui dans ton cadre gelée	Cold water frozen by ennui in your frame,
Que de fois et pendant des heures, désolée	How many times and for hours, distressed
Des songes et cherchant mes souvenirs qui sont	By dreams and seeking my memories which are
Comme des feuilles sous ta glace au trou profond,	Like leaves under your ice with its deep hole,
Je m'apparus en toi comme une ombre lointaine,	I appeared in you like a distant shadow,
Mais, horreur! des soirs, dans ta sévère fontaine,	But horror! evenings, in your severe fountain,
J'ai de mon rêve épars connu la nudité!	I have recognized the nakedness of my scattered dream!
Nourrice, suis-je belle?	Nurse, am I beautiful?

The narcissistic girl, seeking the secret of her being, has looked in the mirror (as we all have done): "j'étais obligée pour ne pas douter de moi de m'asseoir en face de cette glace"; "se cherchant dans la glace devenue ennui [note *ennui* above] et se voyant vague et près de disparaître" (439-440); "je t'avoue du reste . . . que j'ai encore besoin . . . de me regarder dans cette glace pour penser, et que si elle n'était pas devant la table où je t'écris cette lettre, je redeviendrais le Néant." (*Propos*, p. 78). The imagery of the correspondence just quoted (dated May, 1867), of *Igitur*, written about that time, and of *Hérodiade*, all concords notably here, showing once again how close this princess is to his central Hamlet-figure, who is himself.

The mirror has the depth of ourselves. The sustained tension of its frustrating impenetrable surface—a hard *fact*—versus its infinite distance of mirrored perspective (light and shadow)—an utterly inviting, yielding *appearance* (as in *Alice in Wonderland*)—breeds a huge vertigo of sensation, as we know. The *ennui* is the long waiting and repeated frustration—as in *Igitur*—before the barred threshold of flight; all the past dreams crystallize into a frozen block of delightful impotence, the *glacier* of "Le vierge, le vivace," or the *cristal* of *Les Fenêtres*.

The cold hardness of the *glace* (both "mirror" and "ice") is like Hérodiade's virginity (which glass symbolizes in Hebrew ritual), unyielding as the "inviolate reptile" she will soon see herself to be; but it may refreshingly flow and even gush, as a fountain.[21]

Note the effect of Ô in *Ô miroir!* (We think of Mallarmé's clearly round *glace de Venise* in *Frisson d'Hiver*, "profonde comme une froide fontaine"; or Baudelaire's "miroirs profonds," *Invitation au Voyage*.)

A fine effect of dainty halftone is in the diphthong of *fontaine* and *lointaine;* an even subtler effect is the overtone *tain* in both, reflecting the substance with which the mirrors are coated.

The naked girl is sublimated—a ghost *(ombre)*, yet, as with all adolescent ghosts, there is a violent sensuality underneath . . .[22] "ta glace de Venise . . . plus d'une femme a baigné dans cette eau le péché de sa beauté; et peut-être verrais-je un fantôme nu si je regardais long-temps" (271). Compare the *nixe* of *Ses purs ongles.*

Nakedness is purity, whiteness and, like these qualities, it connotes fierce opposites: if white is the color of sterility it also is pregnancy, containing all the colors, like Hegel's pure Nothing which is potentially All. Bareness is the condition of both death and love. The color white can be, as Melville knew, most redolent of evil.

The "scattered dream" is the familiar spectral (ectoplasmic) effect of particles of dusk and light when one looks into a mirror in the gloaming. Compare *Igitur:* "le frémissement amorti, dans de l'oubli, comme une chevelure languissante, autour du visage éclairé de mystère, aux yeux nuls pareils au miroir de l'hôte, dénué de toute signification que de présence" (436); "le péché de voir le *Rêve* dans sa *nudité* idéale" (Corr. p. 270). The long waiting of adolescence, with its sense of un-reality, approaches a crisis point, a fear of total disappearance. But Hérodiade is not quite ready to yield to life.

N.

Un astre, en vérité	A star, in truth
Mais cette tresse tombe . . .	But this tress falls [the nurse starts to replace the fallen tress—horror!] . . .

H.

Arrête dans ton crime	Restrain yourself in your crime
Qui refroidit mon sang vers sa source, et réprime	Which chills my blood back to its source, and repress
Ce geste, impiété fameuse: ah! contemoi	This gesture, a notorious profanation: ah! tell me
Quel sûr démon te jette en le sinistre émoi,	What sure demon throws you into the sinister emotion,
Ce baiser, ces parfums offerts et, le dirai-je?	That kiss, those proffered perfumes and, shall I say it?
Ô mon coeur, cette main encore sacrilège,	O my heart, that hand further sacrilegious,
Car tu voulais, je crois, me toucher, sont un jour	For you wanted, I believe, to touch me [all these things make or] are a day
Qui ne finira pas sans malheur sur la tour . . .	Which will not finish without misfortune on the tower [her room is in a tower, we learned in *Ouverture ancienne*] . . .
Ô jour qu'Hérodiade avec effroi regarde!	O day that Hérodiade regards with fright!

There is no doubt some tradition for the idea of a sacrilege involved in the gesture of touching locks; hair has long been an object of superstition; we all remember the example of Samson. It is prominent in the child's earliest experience of the mother. In any case, a woman's hair is a leading expression, a sort of gesture, of her intimacy (we may think of the *accroche-coeur*), especially for Mallarmé, witness all the sonnets to Méry and various other ladies.

N.

Temps bizarre, en effet, de quoi le ciel vous garde!	Queer times, indeed, from which heaven protect you!
Vous errez, ombre seule et nouvelle fureur,	You wander, solitary shadow and new furor [a fresh agitation],
Et regardant en vous précoce avec terreur:	Looking into yourself precociously with terror:
Mais toujours adorable autant qu'une immortelle,	But always adorable as an immortal,
Ô mon enfant, et belle affreusement et telle	O my child, and terribly beautiful and such
Que . . .	That . . .

Note the *or* effects and the baroque contrasts of terror and beauty. In *belle affreusement* we have luxurious prolongation as in *belle indolemment* of *Les Fleurs*.

H.

Mais n'allais-tu pas me toucher?	But were you not going to touch me?

N.

. . . J'aimerais	I'd like
Être à qui le destin réserve vos secrets.	To be the one to whom destiny reserves your secrets [your confidante—compare Phèdre's Oenone].

H.

Oh! tais-toi!	Oh! Be silent!

N.

Viendra-t-il parfois?	Will he come at times?

H.

Étoiles pures,	Pure stars,
N'entendez pas!	Do not listen! [Hérodiade herself would be a pure star, "froide d'oubli et de désuétude" (*Coup de Dés*)—compare "le froid scintillement de ta pâle clarté" later in the *Scène*]

N.

Comment, sinon parmi d'obscures Épouvantes, songer plus implacable encor Et comme suppliant le dieu que le trésor De votre grâce attend! et pour qui, dévorée	How, if not among obscure Fears, dream [as being] still more implacable [than you, or the stars] And like a suppliant the god whom the treasure Of your grace awaits [what kind of godlike man must he be to win you, and how begging]! and for whom [do you, who are] devoured
D'angoisses, gardez-vous la splendeur ignorée Et le mystère vain de votre être?	With anguish, keep the unknown splendor And the vain mystery of your being?

H.

Pour moi.   For me.

N.

Triste fleur qui croît seule et n'a pas d'autre émoi Que son ombre dans l'eau vue avec atonie.	Sad flower that grows alone and has no other feeling But its shadow seen in the water tone- lessly [another version of the nar- cissus theme, but with a sad narcis- sism—the nurse is, of course, biased].

H.

Va, garde ta pitié comme ton ironie.	Go, save your pity as well as your irony.

N.

Toutefois expliquez: oh! non, naïve enfant, Décroîtra, quelque jour, ce dédain triomphant . . .	Still, explain: Oh no, naive child [you were wrong], Some day, this triumphant disdain will fall . . .

H.

Mais qui me toucherait, des lions respectée? Du reste, je ne veux rien d'humain et, sculptée, Si tu me vois les yeux perdus au paradis, C'est quand je me souviens de ton lait bu jadis.	But who would touch me, me re- spected by the lions? Besides I want nothing human, and, sculptured, If you see me with my eyes lost in paradise, It's when I remember your milk drunk of yore [momentarily, a vaguely Parnassian (sculptured, impassive) Hérodiade—yet this stone melts into milk].

N.

Victime lamentable à son destin offerte!	Lamentable victim offered to its fate!

H.

Oui, c'est pour moi, pour moi, que je fleuris, déserte!	Yes it is for me, for me I bloom, alone!
Vous le savez, jardins d'améthyste, enfouis	You know this, amethyst gardens, hidden
Sans fin dans de savants abîmes éblouis,	Without end in knowing dazzling abysses [the subconscious],
Ors ignorés, gardant votre antique lumière	Unknown golds, keeping your ancient light
Sous le sombre sommeil d'une terre première,	Under the sombre sleep of a primeval earth [all this is her buried dazzling love, soon to erupt],
Vous, pierres où mes yeux comme de purs bijoux	You, [precious] stones from which my eyes like pure jewels
Empruntent leur clarté mélodieuse, et vous	Borrow their melodious brightness, and you
Métaux qui donnez à ma jeune chevelure	Metals which give to my young hair
Une splendeur fatale et sa massive allure!	A fatal splendor and its massive allure!

Note that the brightness, though hard, diamantine, is potentially (and somewhat already) flowing, therefore *mélodieuse;* compare "ouïr dans sa chair pleurer le diamant" (*Sonnet: Dame sans trop d'ardeur*) which is very like the weeping or melting that the diamonds of Hérodiade will more specifically do at the end of the poem.

The "obscures / Épouvantes" are a foreboding of St. John and the love-death theme associated with his decapitation.

The *r* is a liquid element already present in *clarté;* compare "Hérodiade au clair regard de diamant" later, and "Hérodiade en fleur du jardin clair" (in *Les Fleurs);* note the *a*'s, for matness, massiveness; the bright *i, é, u,* for the jewels.

Quant à toi, femme née en des siècles malins	As for you, woman born in wicked times
Pour la méchanceté des antres sibyllins,	For the meanness of sybilline caves,
Qui parles d'un mortel! selon qui, des calices	[You] Who speak of a mortal! [a mere man as my lover] according to whom, from the petals
De mes robes, arôme aux farouches délices,	Of my dresses, aroma with ferocious delights,
Sortirait le frisson blanc de ma nudité,	Would come the white shiver of my nudity

Prophétise que si le tiède azur d'été,	Prophesy [this is a command] that if
Vers lui nativement la femme se dévoile,	the warm summer azure —Toward it woman natively [spontaneously] unveils—
Me voit dans ma pudeur grelottante d'étoile,	Sees me in my shivering star's modesty
Je meurs!	I die!

"Wicked times / For the meanness of sybilline caves" is mainly just an insult—"you are wicked"—but with a hint of the nurse's ancient mystic chthonian role as nourisher, deeply rooted in sensual being: "le sein / Par qui coule en blancheur sybilline la femme" (*Don du Poème*).

The male-sun association is traditional and frequent in Mallarmé, particularly in *Les Dieux antiques,* where the sun-god is seen as the archetype of all mythical heroes. Moreover, the sun traditionally fecundates, being the eternal "male" element of nature, according to countless myths of various cultures; literary embodiments would include Lucretius' *De Rerum Natura,* Shakespeare's *Hamlet,* Rimbaud's *Soleil et chair.*

The haunting, and eventually piercing, aspect of the absolute is in the *azur* which in *L'Azur* punches holes through the barrier (*plafond*) erected by the fog or the poet's fancy: "Il . . . traverse / Ta native agonie ainsi qu'un glaive sûr." It is like the divine sword which stabbed St. Paul on the road to Damascus, or in Rimbaud's *Bannières de mai* ("Si un rayon me blesse je succomberai sur la mousse").

The calyx-robe association is found in other poems; for example, in *Sonnet: Dame sans trop d'ardeur,* as well as in *Ouverture ancienne.*

Note the series of feminine (virginal) *v*'s in *vers, nativement, dévoile, voit,* and (in the next lines) *vierge, veux, vivre, cheveux, inviolé,* very much associated with the image of the "white shiver of my nudity." The root of *nativement—naître,* "to be born"—adds a primitively intimate feeling of naked *bas-ventre,* the place of birth; the association of "native" and "nakedness" is found in *native nue (Quelle soie).*

The grave accent on *tiède* adds to the feeling of languourous tepidness as in *rivière tiède* of *Tristesse d'Été;* the *ou(r)* of *farouche* is darkly sensual, as in *amour-mourir-pourpre-lourd.*

J'aime l'horreur d'être vierge et je veux	I love the horror of being virgin and I wish
Vivre parmi l'effroi que me font mes cheveux	To live amid the fright that my hair gives me
Pour, le soir, retirée en ma couche, reptile	So as to, in the evening, retired to my couch, a snake
Inviolé sentir en la chair inutile	Inviolate, feel in my useless flesh

Le froid scintillement de ta pâle clarté	The cold scintillation of your pale clarity
Toi qui te meurs, toi qui brûles de chasteté,	You who die unto yourself, you who burn with chastity,
Nuit blanche de glaçons et de neige cruelle!	White night of icicles and cruel snow!

Again the deep tension: between fire and ice (as in Rimbaud's *Matinée d'Ivresse*) and, more subtly, between the cold-horror and the gold-beauty in *effroi* (overtones *froid, roi, or*). But this tension is about to be released, and a hint of the warm flow to come is already present, as we have indicated previously.

The snake is often a phallic symbol, though its undulations are feminine; here it is too cold and isolated (*inviolé*) not to emphasize the virile quality of this *virgo intacta*. She may remind us of Nerval's Mélusine, fairy-become-snake in *El desdichado,* or Coleridge's *Cristabel,* which similarly features the familiar dream-reversal of beauty into horror, warm to cold, woman to man. Baudelaire knew this troubling image: "la taille fringante / Ainsi qu'un reptile irrité" (*Une martyre*);
* another version of it occurs in *Le serpent qui danse.*

There are many bright *i*'s, *u*'s, and *é*'s to go with this frosty passage.

Et ta soeur solitaire, ô ma soeur éternelle,	And your solitary sister, O my eternal sister [moon: Diana],
Mon rêve montera vers toi: telle déjà	My dream will mount toward you: such already [alone like you]
Rare limpidité d'un coeur qui le songea,	—Rare limpidity [lucidity] of a heart that dreamed it [this idea]—
Je me crois seule en ma monotone patrie	I believe myself alone in my monotonous native land
Et tout, autour de moi, vit dans l'idolâtrie	And all about me lives in idolatry
D'un miroir qui reflète en son calme dormant	Of a mirror that reflects in its sleeping calm
Hérodiade au clair regard de diamant . . .	Hérodiade with the lucid stare of a diamond . . .
Ô charme dernier, oui! je le sens, je suis seule.	O final charm, yes! I feel it, I am alone.

"Sister" could be a solitary star but it is more likely the moon, Diana, the chaste huntress, an eternally feminine orb. The moon as a sort of paler companion of the sun has long, in the egocentric mind of man, been a symbol for womankind. Here the cold virginal Diana image of the moon is undoubtedly associated with its solitude lost in the night wastes.

The monotonous "native land" is Idumea; "idolatry" is a possible reference to pagan heresies in that dissident land; primarily the sense is that the royal narcissistic girl sees her mirror-image as the supreme creature of the region, whom all idolize, adore.

The *diade-diamant* echo is prominent here (with hard *d*'s and *t*'s), as is the *ar*-cluster: *clair, regard, charme;* compare *Les Fleurs:* "éclair, chair, Hérodiade, jardin clair, farouche, radieux, arrose."

N.

Madame, allez-vous donc mourir?   My lady, are you then going to die?

H.

Non, pauvre aïeule,	No, poor old woman,
Sois calme et, t'éloignant, pardonne à ce coeur dur,	Be calm and, while going away, pardon this hard heart,
Mais avant, si tu veux, clos les volets, l'azur	But first, if you please, close the blinds, the seraphic azure
Séraphique sourit dans les vitres profondes,	Smiles in the deep panes,
Et je déteste, moi, le bel azur!	And I, I hate the beautiful azure!
Des ondes	**Waves**
Se bercent et, là-bas, sais-tu pas un pays	Are tossing [in the sea—nearby?] and, yonder [beyond the sea] do you not know a land
Où le sinistre ciel ait les regards haïs	Where the sinister sky has [gets] the hated looks
De Vénus qui, le soir, brûle dans le feuillage:	Of Venus [bright star, angry at the darkness] who, in the evening, burns in the leaves.
J'y partirais.	I'd go there [if it was so].

N.

Hérodiade still wants to be alone (she thinks, or claims), and guards herself against the male fecundity of the sun. Guy Michaud has seen a connection here with Mallarmé's fear of the alluring azure which mocked his weakness with its purity *(L'Azur)*. This leads in turn to the Look of Saint John.

vitres profondes: are *eidetic* in quality, reach towards one, according to an optical law that makes bright objects seem nearer, or even dart into the eye (they may seem to belly out as in *Une dentelle*); they may also have the depth of the mirror, as partial reflectors (as in *Les Fenêtres:* "je me mire"); and the depth is prolonged by their opening —driven by the compression of the frame—in a plunging perspective to the outdoors.

The land (her desire is like Mignon's *Connais-tu le pays?* except that she thinks she wants the opposite of a summer sky) might be Sicily, as in *L'Après-midi d'un faune.* There, too, the sky was darkened by volcanic ash and Mount Etna was traditionally visited by Venus (her spouse, Vulcan, forged there, it is said); but Venus is here primarily the evening star: "étoile . . . Vénus" (270); "deux suaves, scintillantes Vénus" (208); "Vénus brille à travers les branches ténébreuses" (Villiers, *Hymne à Vénus*). *Haïs* means that the Goddess of Love is frustrated in this barren setting and, secondly, that the dark sky is violently *against* the bright star, as in this effect of the *Faune:* "ce massif, haï par l'ombrage frivole . . . / au soleil."

Allume encore, enfantillage	Yet [one more service] light, childish
Dis-tu, ces flambeaux où la cire au feu léger	[Though] You say [it is], those candles where the wax with light fire
Pleure parmi l'or vain quelque pleur étranger	Weeps amid the vain gold some alien tear
Et . . .	And . . .

N.

Maintenant?	Now?

H.

Adieu.	Goodbye.
Vous mentez, ô fleur nue	You lie, O naked flower
De mes lèvres!	Of my lips!
J'attends une chose inconnue	I await an unknown thing
Ou peut-être, ignorant le mystère et vos cris,	Or perhaps, unaware of the mystery and your cries [spontaneously, in spite of her not knowing why and of her cries of protest],
Jetez-vous les sanglots suprêmes et meurtris	You [lips] are flinging out the supreme bruised sobs
D'une enfance sentant parmi les rêveries	Of a childhood feeling amidst the [its] reveries
Se séparer enfin ses froides pierreries.	At last its cold jewels [thaw and] separate.

As Mauron early noted, the melting candle weeping an "alien" tear may be a symbol (though not crudely so) of the strange male; it can also, better, be a symbol of the melting Hérodiade herself—the "vain gold" is her own virginal (vain, sterile) sheen.

Note the fine effect of the liquid *r* in *pleure,* spilling over, as if from the cuplike candletop, from the *u,* welling up like the *source en pleurs* of the *Faune;* compare *ouïr dans sa chair pleurer le diamant (Dame, sans trop d'ardeur).*

The "you lie" breaks down the whole pose of self-sufficiency not only now, but referring back, by definition, to all its previous manifestations in the poem, that is to say, "you *have been* lying all along, for you are waiting for Something, or Somebody." Is the "unknown thing" a new transcendent realm of poetry and truth (Michaud, Davies), or the coming of the lover? Why not both? This is a poem and can (or better, should) suspend such opposites, vibrantly. Mallarmé himself, for a long while, was clearly unsure of the meaning. The exegetes try too hard to pin down a univalent meaning, which is particularly futile with symbolism. What Mallarmé clearly sought in all his poetry was *"l'ambiguïté* de quelques figures belles" (647). Most of the key images of this poem are double (like the pure yet sensual *nudité),* and it is fitting that the poem end on an unresolved "chord," especially since it was *à suivre.*

On whatever level, the whole last image is indisputably of thaw and of the warm light that is about to break forth, in love, from this apparently cold precious stone. It is all very much like the *roue* of *M'introduire dans ton histoire* (chariot wheel, Saint Catherine's wheel, fireworks, peacock tail, hair, sunburst, explosion of erotic joy), a circular cluster, or constellation, of frigid jewels thawing; "comme mourir pourpre la roue," compare "éclata en pierreries d'une couronne" (531). The jewels are by definition originally buried dazzlement dug up, as in *Au seul souci:* "un inutile gisement / Nuit, désespoir et pierrerie" (stars in the night, delight to be dug from obscurity by the poet), or the "trésor enfoui" ("Offices"), the unknown poet's work; "Maint joyau dort enseveli / Dans les ténèbres et l'oubli" (Baudelaire, *Le Guignon).*

III. CANTIQUE DE SAINT JEAN

The hymn is sung by the Saint. It tells us of his decapitation. Whether it is sung before (in anticipation), during, or after (by his spectre) is not quite clear. Mallarmé seems to have envisaged various positions in the verse-drama for the piece.

Hérodiade is a virginal woman; Saint Jean is the noblest of men. During their gory confrontation, he is a mere head with a piercing gaze (as in Gustave Moreau's painting); she is a complete feminine creature, with a magnificent body (she dances, in one fragment). This relatively secondary outer drama is complemented by an inner meaning. As we said earlier, the Saint represents, like Igitur (Hamlet, Poe, Villiers), the pure male ideal: knife-sharp virility of intellect (the *idée)* or spirit (*esprit* is both in French and is closer to Mallarmé's meaning); he is something near to Divinity — a pure transfixing Look by which Hérodiade desires to be transfixed, judged, and *possessed* and which she at the same time, fears. Her infinitely womanly role is to be possessed and to destroy her possessor.[23] Mallarmé has said in a letter to Villiers that the subject of his work was Beauty and "the apparent object is only a pretext for going towards Her [Beauty]" (N, p. 16). In these terms, the marriage of Hérodiade and Saint Jean is that of his *animus*—transcendent male genius—and his *anima*—his passively "feminine," or more warmly human, sense of beauty (Davies). Mallarmé has described a similar union in "Vénus . . . subira la chaîne de Vulcan, ouvrier latent des chefs-d'oeuvre, que la femme ou beauté humaine, les synthétisant, récompense par son choix" (334).

Le Soleil que sa halte	The Sun which its halt
Surnaturelle exalte	Supernatural[ly] exalts
Aussitôt redescend	Immediately redescends
Incandescent	Incandescent

This is the supreme, total (at the moment of death or sacrifice) *éclair* of the Saint, or the poet-genius who imagines him, during which time stops, as in Proust's so-called privileged moments. The "supernatural halt" seems to echo the Book of Joshua of the Old Testament wherein God stopped the sun.[24] As the variant, "L'astre bas que prolonge / Mal un pompeux mensonge" (N, p. 184) clearly indicates, the halt occurs at the horizon as in "le soleil repose avant de s'évanouir" (270), Mallarmé's favorite spectacle of sunset.

It is evident that the supreme flash of genius is the main *raison d'être* of Saint John. Various fragments refer to it, for example, "le glaive vain a aidé à l'éclair—fulguration" (N, p. 129). Another association is between the sun disk and the golden plate on which the head will be carried according to various fragments in the *Noces* (N, pp. 170, 174); compare the sun as cymbal in *Le Pitre Châtié*.[25]

Je sens comme aux vertèbres	I feel as if in my vertebrae
S'éployer des ténèbres	Dark shadows spread out [like wings]
Toutes dans un frisson	All in a shiver
À l'unisson	In unison.

The moment of decapitation releases, soaring like a dark bird's wings (*ployer* has this wing connotation), spreading out from his vital center in a radiant shock, the dawn of Death; all these subordinate shadows raying out are finally brought together in a vast black shadow of agony, into one "unison." Moreover, the joy of the first strophe and the blackness of the second are joined together, finally reconciled peacefully, we sense, in this *unisson* as in the following passage from "Catholicisme": "maintes vibrations de certitude et ténèbres jointes en un méditatif unisson" (390). A union of opposites occurs in a further sense, in the *Cantique;* the (relatively vertical) opposition of head and body is overcome, "les anciens désaccords avec le corps." Compare "Quand l'ombre menaça de la fatale loi [death: the fatal law of all life] / Tel vieux rêve, désir et mal de mes vertèbres." In *Quand l'ombre,* Death's wings are fought actively—life goes on—by the flights of Eros, faith: the old dream "afflicted at perishing . . . bent its indubitable [undying faith] wing in me."[26] Though Saint John perishes with his flash of total vision, clearly there is a paradox here too: life goes on as poetry. This is the miraculous reversal Mallarmé sought by the psychic suicide described in *Igitur* and in various of his other texts. Like Hegel, Schopenhauer, Nietzsche, he believed that the submerging of the individual will into cosmic consciousness was the only way to create in the deepest sense, to rival the original Creation (he, no more than any other poet, could never be sure it is possible to do so, but this was the flame of glory he never ceased to approach, like Goethe's drunken moth). This idea of a reunion with nature, expressed in a somewhat less radical form but illustrating well the use of the word *unisson,* is found in a letter to Lefébure: "je crois que pour être bien l'homme, la nature en pensant, il faut penser de tout son corps, ce qui donne une pensée pleine et à *l'unisson"* (EL, p. 353).

The shivers in *ss* of *frisson, unisson* are graphic.

Et ma tête surgie	And my head [which has] surged up
Solitaire vigie	[Like] A solitary lookout
Dans les vols triomphaux	In [from] the triumphant flights
De cette faux	Of that scythe

At decapitation, the head flies up separated from the rest like a lookout on a mast: "solitary lookout"; compare the variant "proud lookout" (N, p. 180). A secondary possibility: *vigie* can mean "buoy," which would merely emphasize the feeling of an isolated being, surging up from the ocean-mass.

The sentence is completed in the next strophe: "my head . . . as a clean break, cuts off the old discords with the body"; that is to say, being free of the body, the saintly head (spirit) is rid of the old ascetic tension. The same moment is referred to in a fragment: "Tout ambiguïté . . . fuie" (1448).

The scythe is the weapon of execution, the traditional emblem of death, the Grim Reaper. There is a negative overtone of "betrayal" in   * the word *faux;* compare *"Triomphaux* . . . faux [scythe] . . . faux [false]" (76); the implication is of a lie-of-life (*Lebenslüge;* Mallarmé's "Glorieux Mensonge") as in "pompeux mensonge" of the variant of strophe number 1 (N, p. 184); this is reinforced by the feeling of "something stolen" in the word *vols,* as in "les visites d'Hélios aux hauteurs du ciel. Le vol du nectar et de l'ambroisie répond au vol du feu par Prométhée" (1225); "à l'archange noir tu comptes un grand vol!" (9).

Comme rupture franche	[My head] As a clean break
Plutôt refoule ou tranche	Rather suppresses [forgets] or cuts off
Les anciens désaccords	The old discords
Avec le corps	With the body

A variation for line number 1 read "In a clean separation" (N, p. 181).

plutôt: as Richard suggests, is probably used with the meaning "suppresses or cuts the discords with the *body,*" rather than, "flying up physically to pure space." The transcendence occurs on earth.

Qu'elle de jeûnes ivre	[Rather] Than it drunk with fasting
S'opiniâtre à suivre	Stubbornly follow
En quelque bond hagard	In some haggard bound
Son pur regard	Its pure look

Qu'elle: goes with the *plutôt;* a *ne* is implied, as in the variant "Qu'elle ne pourra suivre" (N, p. 181).

There are two further possible translations, according to two syntactic possibilities, undoubtedly both intended:

A.	B. (probably better)
[The body] Which it [the saint's head] drunk with fasting	Let it [my head] drunk with fasting
Stubbornly follows [to the ground]	Stubbornly follow [from below]
In some haggard thud and rebound	In some haggard [little] bound
[With] Its pure look [being "up there where the eternal cold does not endure your surpassing it, O glaciers all"]	Its pure look [which flies up high]

In all these versions, the cut-off head, haggard from its ordeal, hits the ground and humbly bounces ("some haggard little bound"), held to the earth, but the radiant glance follows the flight of the spirit up to the eternal cold purity above (second to last strophe).

That the physical head stays down with the humility of *Penche un salut,* and does not—contrary to Mauron and others—fly up to the glaciers, is borne out by variants (N, p. 182).

Elle de jeûnes ivre
Lourde ou de jeûnes ivre   •
[too heavy to fly]

Qu'elle ne pourra suivre
[it *cannot* go up with the
        "pure look"]
Son seul regard
        pur
        abstrait

This interpretation is confirmed by "le front pétrifié [the head] . . .
n'aura suivi les bonds de l'intérieure foudre" (N, p. 77 and p. 203).

quelque: note that Mallarmé usually uses *quelque* in a humble or
pejorative sense; "abominablement quelque idole" (*Tombeau de
Charles Baudelaire*); "inférieur clapotis quelconque" (*Coup de Dés*);   *
see Appendix C under *q.*

bond: in the *Tombeau* (*de Verlaine*), *bond* is used for the mere
material and outer ramblings of the wandering poet: "le bond / Tantôt
extérieur . . . de notre vagabond."

hagard: the look of a being suffering from an extreme ordeal; compare the *hagard musicien* of *Petit air II.*

	[The head cannot follow]
Là-haut où la froidure	Up there where the cold
Éternelle n'endure	Eternal does not endure
Que vous le surpassiez	Your surpassing it
Tous ô glaciers	O any [of you] glaciers

Meaning: no glacier can be colder than that absolute up there.
Purity expressed by glacier cold is found in *Le Pitre châtié* and its variant, "la neige des glaciers dans ma chair assainie" (1414).

Mais selon un baptême	But according to [like] a baptism [which steeps us in the original source for a rebirth: Saint John was *the* baptist]
Illuminée au même	Illuminated [the head] at the same
Principe qui m'élut	Principle which elected me [the original spark of creation]
Penche un salut.	Bows a salute [mainly, the humbly fallen head].

The spirit—in a flash—returns to the source of all light, as in *Toast
funèbre:* "la gloire ardente . . . par le carreau qu'allume un soir fier d'y
descendre [compare the sundown of Saint John] / Retourne vers les
feux du pur soleil mortel"; compare "un éclat fulgurant, l'instant de la
résurrection" (615).   *
This parallels the Icarus-curve of *Un Coup de Dés* and all its micro-

cosmic phases, for example, on Page 9, the last *illuminât-il* which drops and leads back to *HASARD* and the *écumes originelles;* this in turn recalls the total rise and fall of the cosmos in Poe's *Eureka.*

NOTES

[1] Only the *Scène* had been published, in the second *Parnasse Contemporain,* in 1871; the *Ouverture ancienne* and the *Cantique* had been written but were to be reworked. The whole *Mystère* as he envisaged it before he died included a new *Ouverture,* the *Scène,* the *Cantique* and various other parts. Gardner Davies has published all of the fragments he could find, and has attempted to reconstruct the general scheme of the whole in the *Noces d'Hérodiade: Mystère* (Gallimard, 1959). The subject needs much more attention.

Note that *Les Noces d'Hérodiade: Mystère* was to be the title of the whole work.

[2] Compare: Flaubert's "Madame Bovary c'est moi," also Valéry's *Jeune Parque.* It may be that, as Freud says, all humans have bisexual tendencies, and the sensitive man and woman particularly so; in this sense, Mallarmé represents the modern writer and modern cultured man. But this can be deceptive; for the poet (and the man) is both more feminine and more virile: "the creator has, in his narrow way, something more of both modes than his counterparts; he is at once more penetrating, virile, form-creating, and more gently available and open to the world's various impressions! ... 'this effeminate and yet indomitable character, which, floating always between weakness and courage, softness and male virtue, has till the end put me in contradiction with myself' (Rousseau, *Confessions,* Book I)." (W, p. 37).

[3] Also the *stature mignonne ténébreuse debout,* his apocalyptic poet-figure in *Un Coup de Dés.*

[4] In other words, her natural mate emerges from the unknown as he does even in the most quotidian (and nonetheless miraculous) love dramas of life.

[5] "J'ai laissé *Hérodiade* pour les cruels hivers: ... je rime un intermède *héroïque,* dont le *héros* est un Faune." (Propos, p. 50).

[6] Mme. Ayda's explanation seems far-fetched: that the *grenade* symbolizes the tubercular lungs of his dead sister and his friend Harriet, whence the line *le soir méchant a coupé les grenades.* The spilling of blood implied in the whole *mystère* is rather a fecund erotic idea of love-death:—consummation (not consumption). The *soir méchant* is the fearful "cutting" aspect of the hated and desired event. Valéry, independently, used this same erotic image in *Fragments d'un Narcisse:* "la nuit ... glisse entre nous deux le fer qui coupe un fruit."

[7] Authorities have cited possible influences: Flaubert's *Salammbô,* Villiers' *Isis,* etc. The following excerpt from Banville's *Voie lactée* seems to be a source:

> Hérodiade, svelte en ses riches habits,
> Portant sur un plat d'or constellé de rubis
> La tête de Saint Jean Baptiste qui ruisselle
> Nous résume très bien l'histoire universelle ...

*   See also note 18.

[8] According to R. de Montesquiou (*Diptyque de Flandre,* p. 235), the Look of Saint John was to be the climax of the drama. It is featured in various fragments of the *Noces d'Hérodiade.*

9 "Whenever the feeling of rejection by the parents is thorough, the son will attempt to suffice unto himself; his feminine soul flowers in the sense of beauty that brings him solace, passive bliss; the male self evolves its *libido dominandi* or will, through [sublime spiritual striving and its temperate form of] his active, rational organizing capacity. The two personae often "marry" in youthfully poetic dreams; the son becomes *qua* budding artist an androgynous angel. The danger of this too-perfect aloofness becomes, in repeated crises, apparent to the old, biological, pre-oedipal being who insists on an accounting, on a coming to grips with the father and with society, a successful action, a taking of possession, in his turn. The integration of the angelic youthful creature with the stubbornly surviving being (the original organism and its late social avatar, the bourgeois) becomes the decisive task of a key crisis as the artist enters upon his mature career. Beneath this entire spiraling evolution lies our epistemological dialectic, here operating between the four poles of male, female, maturity, youth (see also Ortega, the *Dehumanization of Art*, p. 48)." (W, p. 86).

10 Actually, there are vibrancies in other (corollary) directions or "dimensions" as well: beauty-horror, warmth-coldness, softness-hardness, purity-corruption. But these are the main ones: masculine-feminine, youth-age.

11 The theme of decapitation is linked subliminally with the notion of castration (as always), that is to say, the pure wedding *(noces)* of Hérodiade and Saint John— a virgin who yields a kiss to a bodiless sacrificial head—has an undertone of complementary radical sensuality which comes out in the fragments again and again through the milk and blood imagery running throughout the whole *Mystère* (including the associated *Don du Poème*); note also the gluttonously sensual nuptial repast (N, p. 169 and 173).

He mysteriously gets her maidenhead, according to some fragments: "l'inexplicable sang déshonorant le lys / à jamais renversé de l'une ou l'autre jambe" (N, p. 206) —and she gets his head. The necessary counterpart of a bodiless head is a headless body. Any sexual act is a sort of castration (or the larger annihilation this synecdochic deed, the part for the whole, stands for—compare the familiar theme of love-death as in *Tristan et Yseult*). The prose poem *Pauvre enfant pâle* is a fantasy mainly based on this association: "et ta complainte est si haute, si haute [cf. Saint John's hyperbolic ascension] que ta tête nue qui se lève en l'air à mesure que ta voix monte, semble vouloir partir de tes petites épaules. Petit homme, qui sait si elle ne s'en ira pas un jour, quand, après avoir crié longtemps dans les villes, tu auras fait un crime." (C, p. 283).

One of the fragments of Saint Jean has the same idea of a sort of religious complaint, a hymn, rising up violently: "A quel écho, jailli, viril, dans un tonnerre... On dirait des tréfonds...Lieu du plus noir secret...Pour voile...se frange [compare the "lace" network below]...Sinistrement blanchit et s'illumine" (N, p. 192); in other words, the idea of a brilliant flash of spiritual love, coming with death (decapitation), has its sensual undertone (C, p. 138 and Appendix A). The orgasm that accompanies execution is legendary. But something subtler is here implied: the sort of universal milk, sap of life (Hindu soma), white Eros, that we discuss in Appendix A, and that nourishes the saint's pure vision: "le renouveau vient qui allaite et vivifie la chimère" (882).   *

Another fragment (1446) has the milk image as, probably, the white cloth with which the old nurse polishes the tray on which Saint John's head will be carried: it is associated with the nurse's headdress (as well as with the curtains of a bed) and with her former milk which once spurted up (the sterility of the old nurse, linked with the death theme), and also, no doubt, with other complex possibilities (C, pp. 176-178). Compare "état de rêverie envolée ... plus haut que la coiffe même. Quelque fleur conventuelle ... pensive blancheur" (in Richard, p. 222). The *Hérodiade* fragment reads in part as follows:

> Du moins ce ponctuel décor assigne-t-il
> Comme emblème sur une authentique nourrice,
> Affres que jusqu'à leur lividité hérisse
> Un révulsif ébat vieil horrifié droit
> Selon la guimpe puis la coiffe par surcroît
> L'ordinaire abandon sans produire de trace
> Hors des seins abolis vers l'infini vorace
> Sursautant à la fois en maint épars filet
> Jadis, d'un blanc [...] et maléfique lait.

Compare this image with "seins levés ... pleins d'un lait éternel, la pointe vers le ciel" (*Le Phénomène futur*). It seems likely that the *sein-saint* echo is somewhere behind all this.

Notice that in *Igitur* the white *fraise*, or lace collar, represents the separation of head and body, hence a pure flash of vision (439). Igitur is a Hamlet figure: "sur ton front pâle aussi blanc que du lait / Le vent qui fait voler ta plume noire" (quoted by Mallarmé in his essay, *Hamlet*, 299). This rhyme *Hamlet-lait* is note-worthy. Compare "le fol ... génie ... s'en délivre, dans la voltige qu'il est, seul ... sylphe suprême" (521). This "separation" is influenced by Banville's clown (*Le Tremplin*) who leaps free into the sky (cf. *Le Pitre Châtié*, as well as Page 8 of the *Coup de Dés* and C, p. 315). Richard confirms us here, with due acknowledgement (p. 227; see also Mauron).

12 It is haunting partly because of its up-and-down ambiguity (as in the dawn-plume here) which is in turn based largely on the ambivalence of the letter *u*, acute in sound but a trough in shape; hence the *u* dominates the *Démon de l'analogie* where the association of feathers and palms is prominent.

13 The same image occurs at the end of the poem: "comme un cygne cachant en sa plume ses yeux." In *Le Cygne*, Sully Prudhomme had used a similar image: "... parmi des diamants / Dort, la tête sous l'aile."

14 Qui erre autour d'un type exceptionnel ... n'est que lui, Hamlet ... Ophélie, vierge enfance objectivée du lamentable seigneur royal" (301).

15 The flower shedding its petals—a motif of feminine yielding of grace, often sung by Mallarmé (e.g. *Les Fleurs*)—may have an overtone of a memory of Hérodiade undressing in the dark. Thus in the *Scène* we find: "j'effeuille / Comme près d'un bassin dont le jet d'eau m'accueille / Les pâles lys qui sont en moi ... " This is ambiguous: real petals or clothes; again, less ambiguously: "des calices / De mes robes, arôme aux farouches délices, / Sortirait le frisson blanc de ma nudité." Compare "les pétales de corsets délacés, un effeuillement gai" (596) and "la rose ... lasse du blanc habit ... le délace" (60).

16 One might suspect that (especially given the unfinished nature of the fragment) Mallarmé was thinking of Hérodiade herself in this passage; compare "des calices / De mes robes, arôme aux farouches délices" (*Scène*); the "s'effeuille" of a few lines down would then be connected with this notion of Hérodiade's undressing as petal-stripping, "j'effeuille / comme près d'un bassin (*Scène*); the "rose-Hérodiade" (*Les Fleurs*), also in various fragments (N, pp. 158, 161, 162). There is some link also with the floral imagery, inspired no doubt by the death of Maria, in *Ce que disaient les*

trois cigognes: "une jeune fille couronnée de roses blanches et profilant sur son suaire une forme suave et aromate." (Ayda).

[17] The *cierge-vierge* association is also important here; the inviolate white taper is like a deathly pale, pure girl, as in *Plainte d'Automne*: "la blanche créature n'est plus . . . Maria a passé là avec des cierges, une dernière fois" (217); compare "cierges soufflées" [dead] in the *Scène*; the *plus-résumant-chute* group in *Plainte d'Automne* is related to the *plus-plume* cluster of the *Démon de l'Analogie*.

[18]
> Lorsque pensive, et baignant votre sein
> Du beau cristal de vos larmes roulées,
> Triste marchiez par les longues allées
> Du grand jardin de ce royal château
> Qui prend son nom de la beauté d'une eau.
> . . . .
> Où vit maint cygne habillé tout de blanc,
> Et des hauts pins, la cime de vert peinte,
> Vous contemplaient comme une chose sainte
> . . . .
> Se promener, quand l'aube retournée
> Par les jardins poussait la matinée,
> Et vers le soir, quand déjà le soleil
> A chef baissé s'en allait au sommeil.
>   (Ronsard, *Elégie à Marie Stuart*)

The images of solitary princess, swan, mingled dawn and dusk, and even the pines, have remained.

[19] The *jeune fille* in France traditionally has "horreur" of everything. Sartre's Ivich in *L'Âge de Raison* is a good literary example.

[20] This Byzantine business has been exaggerated by unfriendly critics in the case of both poets; it applies better to minor poets like Albert Samain, or to *art nouveau* generally.

[21] Bachelard (in *Le Point*, nos. 29-30) has emphasized Mallarmé's dynamic imagery; but, obviously, all his best images are both static and dynamic, like Keats's Grecian urn, or Eliot's Chinese jar, that "moves and is ever still."

[22] There is a close connection—of which specialists in occultism are well aware— between the spooky and the erotic, particularly developed by the tensions of adolescence (horror movies are mainly made for teen-agers); for example, Henry James's *Turn of the Screw* is fraught with this double mood. The sensitive youth has for so long frustrated his basic drives that he often feels disembodied, unreal, ethereal as Puck or Ariel.

[23] As Michaud and Richard observe, Hérodiade is haunted by the absolute *azur* and its pure Look which she fears, in the *Scène*, as Mallarmé himself both feared and desired to be possessed by the Infinite.

[24] Eliot seems to have remembered these lines in

> The dove descending breaks the air
> With flame of incandescent terror
>   (*Little Gidding*)

[25] In our *L'Oeuvre de Mallarmé: Un Coup de Dés*, we have shown the connection of the original *coup* (Page 1) and an initial sunburst. All the subsequent *coups* of Man, in the cosmogonic Poem, are modified attempts to duplicate the original Creation, that is, be God: *eritis sicut dii*.

It is the original Eros which takes on many forms—dazzling light, milk, and so on —throughout Mallarmé's work (see Appendix A); thus "tout à coup l'éruptif multiple sursautement de la clarté, comme les proches irradiations d'un lever de jour" (648) and "Hilare or de cymbale...Tout à coup le soleil" (*Le Pitre Châtié*); or "tout d'un coup dans les orchestres de très beaux éclats de cuivre" (868); "illuminait telle divination longtemps voilée, lucide tout à coup" (395) these "tout à coup" expressions are related to the sudden cutting (*coupe*), the decapitation that brings the dazzling vision-in-death. Thus we find variants (N, pp. 185-186) like "les noirs coups triomphaux / de cette faux" and "coups de faux." This association of *coup* is, of course, secondary.

Since almost all of Mallarmé's important poetic clusters were included in the *Coup de Dés*, we are not surprised to find further overlappings, establishing our point: Page 8 of *Un Coup de Dés* has "scintille puis ombrage...stature mignonne ténébreuse debout...le temps de...tout de suite évaporée." This is the *coup*-flash-vision of a last poet-figure (mostly Mallarmé himself), which is linked with Saint John (Igitur, Hamlet, Villiers, Poe, etc.) in many ways (C, p. 338). In *Les Noces d'Hérodiade* (N, p. 219) we find a very similar cluster: "Le temps / dans le même éclair / révolte / aussitôt qu'assouvie / tout de suite comprimée."

The idea of sunset as the ambivalent climate of genius (the radiancy and the near darkness) is constant in Mallarmé. The dying splendor of the sun is certainly envisaged here as variants indicate. For example, "L'astre bas que prolonge / Mal un pompeux mensonge" (N, p. 184); compare "quand le soleil se repose avant de s'évanouir" (*Plainte d'Automne;* Davies).

Unlike some other commentators (Mauron, Davies), we do not see the direct connection between the head, that is to say its outer form, and the sun; rather it is the burst of inner vision; the head humbly stays on the ground.

Moreover, there is no need, that I can see, to connect the supernatural halt of the sun with the Solstice of Saint John, as Mauron does. This is really too remote an echo, and has no organic connection with the Saint John figure of the poem. The variants clearly indicate that the halt was at the horizon rather than at an apogee.

26 The wing, for Mallarmé, is the fundamental kinetic expression of spirit, negative (black) or positive (white) as in ancient mystic tradition. Compare the dove of the Bible as perpetuated in Christian tradition (the Holy Ghost); Hugo's complicated bird in *Dieu;* and Mallarmé's "vieux plumage méchant enfin terrassé, Dieu" (Propos, p. 76); the bird in *Hérodiade* and *Igitur;* Poe's raven; and so forth.

7. SAINTE

◇❄◇❄◇❄◇❄◇

A still, glowing epiphany worthy of the Italian masters, this flawless miniature presents a stained-glass window portraying Saint Cecilia, the patroness of music, as a madonna-like Muse. By a quirk of primitive perspective, she appears to be playing on the ideal harp formed by an angel's wing. The more usual instrument, the viol, and an opened hymnbook, though part of the picture, seem to have been abandoned in favor of this purer expression. We are reminded of Keats' "unheard music" frozen, visually, on a Grecian urn.[1] The sonnet thus gently represents the aspiration of Mallarmé's art that occasionally seems, or somehow manages, to express the ineffable.

Sainte is structurally crystalline, limpid, and globular, as Mallarmé's best efforts always are. That is to say, the polyvalent words connect as freely with each other—through various echoes or repetitions—as the stars of a constellation through open space. This is made possible partly through the elimination of poetically inert elements. Therefore, flatly discursive language is reduced to a decent minimum. And, since verbs are generally kinetic, as opposed to the "static" (Joyce) quality of art (particularly appropriate to this Instant caught in would-be simultaneous words), there is only one main verb in the poem. Finally, since punctuation marks are practical signs, usually carrying no esthetic weight, they are almost entirely absent.

The inspiration probably came from an unidentified stained-glass window (various approximations are known). The sonnet was apparently written for an Avignon lady named Cécile (Brunet): "lire à Madame une Sainte-Cécile que je lui avais promise. C'est un petit poème mélodique et fait surtout en vue de la musique" (letter to Aubanel; 1462). As Ernst Fraenkel observes, the fact that Madame Brunet was his daughter's godmother may have some bearing on the maternal motif of the Virgin-like *Sainte*. A manuscript of 1865, no doubt the original one, bears the title "Sainte Cécile jouant sur l'aile d'un chérubin" and a subtitle "(Chanson et image anciennes)". The poem was published in 1883, with its definitive title.

A la fenêtre recélant	In the window concealing [yet half revealing]
Le santal vieux qui se dédore	The old sandalwood losing its gilt
De sa viole étincelant	On the viol sparkling
Jadis avec flûte ou mandore,	Of yore with flute or mandolin,
Est la Sainte pâle, étalant	Is the pale saint, displaying
Le livre vieux qui se déplie	The old book which unfolds
Du Magnificat ruisselant	Of the Magnificat streaming
Jadis selon vêpre et complie:	Of yore according to [with] vesper and compline:

In the first quatrain we have the image of a musical instrument, a viol, pushed, as it were, into a background by a new silent "music," hence it is "of yore"; once it was joined in concert with flute and mandolin but no longer; this idea will be completed in the tercets.

fenêtre: obviously the same as the *vitrage* (*ce vitrage*), Mme. Noulet to the contrary notwithstanding.

recélant: is a subtle word, expressing something of both hiding and partially revealing. Accordingly, we do not agree with Mme. Noulet that the instruments disappear entirely; and their image recurs ("Nier A, c'est montrer A derrière une grille," Valéry).

santal: echoes *sainte.*

vieux: echoed by the *vieux* of the second quatrain; this parallelism is various between the two quatrains (the first version also repeated *recélant;* 1463). As Richard observed, there is a pervasive faded quality in the whole scene; the glass is charmingly ancient (probably, see *pâle* below).

jadis: always bears a hint of *paradis* (*perdu*); *jadis-paradis* is an important rhyme in *Hérodiade.* The *jadis* lends an air of "ancient instrument," as well as of the past. It may be suggested that the emblematic references to a specific "past" religion, in the window, are now subsumed into an uncluttered, total, "silent," modern poetic vision. This is the theme of various essays, such as "Catholicisme," and several poems (*Toast funèbre, Ouverture ancienne*) allude to it.

The visual contrast, male-female or line-circle, of the flute and the mandolin is complemented by the musical contrast: bright acute *u* in *flûte* (and "male" *f*) versus the warm dark *an* of *mandore* (with its feminine *o*, maternal *m*): "la flûte ou la viole de chacun" (363).

pâle . . . étalant: the broad, "faded," calm, mat effect of the *â* or *a* is supplemented by the subdued timbre of the diphthong in *sainte.* This paleness goes with the Pre-Raphaelite mood as well as with the possible worn quality of the image.

Magnificat: a hymn of the Virgin, who is naturally thought of in connection with the tender maternal *Sainte;* like the instrument, the hymnbook is now in "disuse," hence the repeated *jadis.*

ruisselant: the hymn words and probably the old-style illuminated musical notation "stream" on the rippling parchment—an apt image; the *ss* contributes much of the rippling effect; the streaming is also that of the light through the window. The effect of music on paper may remind us of the *trompettes tout haut d'or pâmé sur les vélins* of the *Hommage à Wagner.*

vêpre: the *Magnificat* is sung at vespers; together with *complie* and the later *soir,* it establishes the time as evening.

Note that the one main verb *Est* has been given; in the rest of the poem we have only a subordinate clause modifying the word *vitrage,* the window, "which is brushed by a harp," and so on. This little verb, *Est,* contributes by its modest simplicity a feeling akin to that of Verlaine's "Le ciel est, par-dessus le toit . . ."

A ce vitrage d'ostensoir	On this monstrance glass [the sunlit window]
Que frôle une harpe par l'Ange	That is brushed by [i.e., discreetly shown in the background] a harp [formed] by the Angel
Formée avec son vol du soir	Formed with his evening flight [wing]
Pour la délicate phalange	For the delicate joint [tip]
Du doigt que, sans le vieux santal	Of the finger, which, without [playing on] the old sandalwood [musical instrument]
Ni le vieux livre, elle balance	Nor [running along] the old book, [the saint] balances
Sur le plumage instrumental,	On the instrumental plumage,
Musicienne du silence.	Lady-musician of silence.

vitrage d'ostensoir: the window is sunlit like a monstrance (evening glow is suggested. The *soir* below rhymes with *ostensoir,* as in Baudelaire's *Harmonie du soir*); compare the sunset-window of *Ouverture ancienne*—"A l'ongle qui parmi le vitrage s'élève . . . le vieux / Ciel brûle, et change un doigt en un cierge envieux." A similar miraculous transformation *(ostensoir)* occurs here. The *vol du soir* may imply this descent of evening light, in a minor way.

harpe: an angel is depicted in the background, no doubt hovering over the Saint's head, somewhat remote and in a half-light, (*vol du*) *soir;* his wing is placed, in primitive perspective, in such a way as to seem to be touched by the hand, that might be playing on it as if it were a harp: "des anges blancs . . . chantent leur extase en s'accompagnant de harpes imitant leurs ailes" (264).

ange: in that other epiphany, *Apparition,* his earlier cousins, the *séraphins,* were featured, reminding us of the musical angels of the Italian primitives and their nineteenth-century avatars in the English romantics and Pre-Raphaelites or in the French Parnassian poet, Banville. Mallarmé's juvenilia were steeped in this seraphic spirit.

délicate: the element *dé* reminds us of the *ongles dédiant* of *Ses purs ongles* (q.v.).

elle balance: her finger lightly touches the wing; *elle* echoes *aile,* as frequently in Mallarmé (C, p. 144); the element *ala* in *balance* and *phalange* is part of the wing effect (C, p. 140); (Richard Wilbur calls this kind of playing "incidental fun").

phalange: Mallarmé favored the finger over the hand and the discreet—and penetrating—tip over the finger, occasionally just the tiny nail as in *Ses purs ongles* and *Ouverture ancienne:* "sibylles offrant leur ongle," where there is a similar atmosphere of flights in the background. The *doigt* is like that of an annunciatory angel—"Psyché, élevant son doigt" (197)—and has a quiet overtone, *doit.*[2]

plumage instrumental: . . . *Musicienne:* the *plume-instrument-musique* (*u*) cluster is one of the central image groups for Mallarmé (he is haunted, as we said by angels with their wings and their musical instruments in his juvenile poems); the cluster is prominent in the obsessive imagery of *Le Démon de L'Analogie* and was reinforced by some of Poe's favorite imagery, in *Israfel* and the epigraph to *The Fall of the House of Usher.*[3] Part of the underlying source is the womb-shape of mandolins, or other instruments, and the similar (womb-cradle-nest) shape of the *u,* as well as the curved, sheltering wing. The maternal *m* is close by in all three words. The feminine-maternal-music association, in connection with *Don du Poème* and *Une dentelle s'abolit,* has been noted by Mauron. Accordingly, in *Musicienne du silence* we may feel a subtle tension and release of musical "milk" from a maternal *Muse* (see *u* in Appendix C). Both Poe and Mallarmé lost their mothers as infants; Mallarmé's early writings are, like Rimbaud's, obsessed with the orphan idea, for example, *L'ange gardien:* "C'est l'ange qui étend son aile protectrice sur le berceau de l'enfant . . . bon ange . . . vous remplacez une mère qu'il a peut-être perdue" (1381). The fantasy of a cosy nest-like cabin is featured in another juvenile piece, *Ce que disaient les trois cigognes.*[4]

NOTES

[1] One of T. S. Eliot's finest images, in *Ash Wednesday* (the "slotted window"), is thought to have been inspired by *Sainte* together with *Une dentelle s'abolit* ("bellied like the fig's fruit").

[2] This association is discussed in note 12 to *Prose*. To *doigt-doit* we may add *d'oie* and the *plume d'oie* which is a symbol of this upward movement of duty or transcendence in the *Coup de Dés*. The white candle (*cierge*) carried by the dead innocent (*vierge*) sister, Maria, is a close corollary image and idea in *Plainte d'automne*. The uplifted finger of the dead woman in *Sonnet* remotely echoes all this (Mauron).

[3]
> Son coeur est un luth suspendu;
> Sitôt qu'on le touche il résonne
> (De Béranger)
> In Heaven a spirit doth dwell
> "Whose heart-strings are a lute"
> (Poe, *Israfel*)

Compare: "la voix / Du luth qui pleure un ange au ciel ravi" (vers écrits sur un exemplaire des *Contemplations*, ML). I suspect the echo *luth-lutte* reinforces the feeling of tension in the *u*.

[4] Compare this from Dickens: "I crept close to my mother's side ... and once more felt her beautiful hair dropping over me—like an angel's wing as I used to think" (*David Copperfield*, chap. 8). Bachelard has treated the theme of the nest-womb-container in *Poétique de l'espace*.   *

8. TOAST FUNÈBRE

—à Théophile Gautier

This is a solemn, somewhat rhetorical, and even "official" work. The occasion called for it: the death of Gautier, much admired by Mallarmé. He wrote the poem in 1873, at the request of Catulle Mendès, for a memorial volume, *Le Tombeau de Gautier,* which appeared later that year. "Je veux chanter," he said in his answering letter to Mendès, "une des qualités glorieuses de Gautier: le don mystérieux de voir avec les yeux (ôtez mystérieux). Je chanterai le voyant, qui, placé dans ce monde, l'a regardé, ce qu'on ne fait pas." (1465).

The poem represents a middle manner, somewhere between the relative clarity of the early *poésies* and the frequently dense obscurities of the late ones. Yet, it would be fairer to say that the poem is almost entirely clear, with a few ambiguous passages that can still stand some elucidation. The conflict between the properly lyric elements, and, on the other hand, the simplistic rhetorical situation assigned to him make for a certain *malaise,* overcome, I feel, by the weight of intermittent successes in the imagery and sound.

Is the poem the high point of Mallarmé's art, as some, including Thibaudet and Peyre, seem to think? Not for this reader, at any rate. I admire it in a special way, which goes something like this: "Bravo Mallarmé, show them what you can do along more traditional lines, whenever you want to." *Toast funèbre* probably would alone have made the reputation of some lesser figure. But Mallarmé makes us demanding about himself. The *Faune* is richer, more warmly beautiful, *Hérodiade* too, despite its apparent coldness and its Parnassian lapses (not to mention the *Coup de Dés,* which is quite apart).

Ô de notre bonheur, toi, le fatal emblème!	O of our happiness, you the fatal emblem!

A note in the "Bibliographie" Mallarmé penned for his *Poésies* said: *"Toast funèbre* vient du recueil collectif le *Tombeau de Gautier,* Maître et Ombre à qui s'addresse l'Invocation."

The dead Gautier is addressed with absolutely modern (or existential) unsentimentality. He, or his tomb, is the symbol of all horrid mortality. As an exemplary, intense representative of humanity, one who was especially alive—a poet—his amputation from the world's body is particularly shocking to Mallarmé.

The letter-values (sound, shape) are generally less vivid in this poem—though certain passages are extraordinary in this respect—than is usual in Mallarmé. As we have said, it is relatively rhetorical, depending often on some simple, broad, sweeping, booming, clanging, and other such effects. Note the all-flattening impression of death in the *a*'s of *fatal,* as in *l'avare silence et la massive nuit,* below; compare *Quand l'ombre menaça de la fatale loi* (six *a*-sounds) or the key word of indifferent negation, *LE HASARD,* in the *Coup de Dés.*

emblème: overtone of *blême,* compare "squelette, ou . . . emblème quelconque de la brièveté de la vie" (Baudelaire, "Le Tir et le Cimetière"); note the dry *è.*

Salut de la démence et libation blême,	Greeting of madness and pale libation,
Ne crois pas qu'au magique espoir du corridor	Do not think that to the magic hope of the corridor
J'offre ma coupe vide où souffre un monstre d'or!	I offer my empty cup where suffers a golden monster!

Still addressing Gautier: "do not think that I offer a toast—which would be madness and a pale, weak-spirited gesture—to a sentimental hope of immortality (the childish, magic, nonsensical hope to see your ghost); no, my cup is void of all but the dazzling monstrous awareness of the Absurd, fatality."[1]

Salut and *coupe:* remind us of the little sonnet *Salut* in which Mallarmé also refers to the emptiness of his offering, as by *Rien, cette écume, vierge vers / À ne désigner que la coupe.* In both poems, the poet is being, as usual, modest about his product (particularly in relation to the huge ambitions he harbors). He is, moreover, voicing a familiar artistic despair about ever expressing anything. In this respect, the *coupe* recalls the *pur vase d'aucun breuvage* of *Surgi de la croupe* (Gengoux) or "l'amertume / En la coupe [of life]"; (ML, p. 181). It may echo faintly the "golden cup" of the famous Goethe ballad (translated by Nerval), which was referred to by Gautier in *Caerulei Oculi:* "trésor coulé / La coupe du roi de Thulé," and by Villiers in *Isis* (Crès, p. 127). But a likelier source is "Ah! brisée est la coupe d'or! l'esprit à jamais envolé!" (tr. of Poe's *Lenore;* 200). Compare "La coupe d'or ne contient que du fiel," Leconte de Lisle, *A un poète mort* (Gautier).

The *monstre d'or* has been much discussed and never accurately explained. Mallarmé coquettishly applauded when someone suggested he made out on the poet's vessel a design of Saint George and the dragon. We see it as follows:

In *La Musique et Les Lettres,* Mallarmé writes: "Quelle agonie . . . qu'agite la Chimère versant par ses blessures d'or l'évidence de tout l'être pareil" (648) and further refers to the agonized "torsion" of this dazzling monster expressing Man's fatal limitations. Perhaps a source of the image was Gautier's own *Chimère,* a poem about the poet's eternal hopeless dream: "une jeune *chimère,* aux lèvres de ma *coupe.*" The agonizing *chimère* of perfect art is found again in "le Monstre-Qui ne peut Être! Attachant au flanc la blessure d'un regard affirmatif et pur" (541). It is roughly the tragic vision of the "Glorious Lie" Mallarmé early discovered at the heart of reality;[2] and that feeling, I believe, emerges even without comment, though obscurely or intuitively, from Mallarmé's words; a general helpless suffering and beautiful honesty before the image of death, reminding us, tacitly perhaps, of Pascal's baroque-classic credo, that human life, even crushed, is bigger than that which crushes it.

There are some subtle sound values of horror-shiver in the tremolo of *offre, souffre* and *monstre;* yet there is the harmonious glow of the quite different (unaccompanied by a consonant) *r* in *d'or.* The *ê* helps *blême* to be notably pallid. The *u* in *coupe* is active, as it is in *cruche,* according to one of France's leading contemporary poets, Francis Ponge, who said, "Pas d'autre mot qui sonne comme cruche. Grâce à cet *u* qui s'ouvre en son milieu" *(Cinq Sapates).*

Ton apparition ne va pas me suffire:	Your appearance won't suffice me:
Car je t'ai mis, moi-même, en un lieu de porphyre.	For I've put you, myself, in a place of porphyry.

The poet knows there will be no material resurrection of his master. As a sort of imaginary pallbearer, he has personally seen the remains of Gautier put away for good in the tomb.

Note the empty neuter *eu* in *lieu,* all that remains, as in the *Coup de Dés,* after the departure of Man: "rien n'aura eu lieu que le lieu."

Le rite est pour les mains d'éteindre le flambeau	The ritual is for the hands to extinguish the torch
Contre le fer épais des portes du tombeau:	Against the thick iron of the portals of the tomb:

Material hands (as opposed to the spiritual voice of the poet, below) have done their work of extinguishing the torches of hope against the uncompromising doors of the tomb; an echo is that the blaze of the dead genius is quelled. Both these feelings are expressed in *Tout orgueil:* "Torche dans un branle étouffée." In *Igitur,* the snuffed candle symbolizes psychic suicide—the end of hope or belief—the acceptance of the absurd, as in *Hamlet:* "There is within the very flame of love / A kind of wick or snuff that will abate it."

Et l'on ignore mal, élu pour notre fête	And we cannot avoid the truth, [we] elected for our [poetic] feast,
Très-simple de chanter l'absence du poëte,	A very simple one of singing the absence of the poet,
Que ce beau monument l'enferme tout entier.	That this beautiful monument encloses him entire.

This reinforces the preceding lines with a particularly Mallarméan idea of singing the poet's absence. Absence, with him, is a sort of limit-situation, an asymptotic borderline of human endeavor to grasp truth, overcoming (by including) the forces of chance or death or nothingness. Hence, it is a sort of pure essence—like Hegel's "pure Negation which is the essence of Being"—of a phenomenon. The all-too-human limitations of the clumsy ordinary knowing processes are negated away, burned up in the funeral pyre of sentimental desire and hope. And this is the central theme of the poem, that the true, even divine, Gautier is not dead but absent, in this sense: "je dis:une fleur! et, hors de l'oubli où ma voix relègue aucun contour, en tant que quelque chose d'autre que les calices sus, musicalement se lève, idée même et suave, l'absente de tous bouquets." (857).

ignore mal: mal means "à tort," according to Noulet. The sense is not changed thereby.

élu: "l'élu familier, le poète" (694).

Si ce n'est que la gloire ardente du métier,	Unless the ardent glory of the [poetic] craft,
Jusqu'à l'heure commune et vile de la cendre,	Until the common and vile hour of ashes,
Par le carreau qu'allume un soir fier d'y descendre,	Through the windowpane lit by an evening proud to descend there,
Retourne vers les feux du pur soleil mortel!	Returns towards the fires of the pure mortal sun!

This much is saved from the disaster, that the light of his art returns, like a burnt offering, to the source of our light, the sun, as in the *Faune*—"le visible et serein souffle artificiel / De l'inspiration, qui regagne le ciel." At least, it will return—his "eternally" shining glory —until all goes in an apocalypse, "l'heure commune et vile de la cendre" (recalling the *Dies irae:* "on that day the world dissolves in ashes"; C, p. 356). Hence, the sun itself is "mortal," and the "pure" refers largely to the honesty of this truth. A variant read: "l'heure dernière et vile de la cendre," confirming the notion of apocalypse, as in Poe's *Eureka,* which was a major source of Mallarmé's cosmogonic thinking, most completely expressed in the *Coup de Dés* (C, p. 337); compare also the *Cantique de Saint Jean.*

un soir fier d'y descendre: nature seems to pay a tribute to its
* pagan son.

After this introductory portion of the poem, there is a visual break and a new section, which is devoted entirely to the ordinary man (or "man")—including perhaps Gautier's ordinary mortal self. This is in contrast to the whole next (third) section, which is devoted to the Poet: "Le Maître" will dramatically introduce that final major section, which is altogether in a rising key; we note the two aspects of Gautier, essential and inessential, in the "Maître et Ombre," previously cited. Compare "l'homme et le génie" (both referring to Hugo) in *Les Gossips de Mallarmé,* no 5.

Magnifique, total et solitaire, tel	Magnificent, total and solitary, such [like Gautier]
Tremble de s'exhaler le faux orgueil des hommes.	Trembles [dares not] to exhale [express itself] the false pride of men.

Ordinary men fail to be "magnificent, total, and solitary" like Gautier, the creator whose pure art has just been evoked as returning to its source. Note the singular of the adjectives versus the dispersing, weakening plural of *hommes* (as in the just-quoted "l'absente de tous bouquets"): "cet *s* du pluriel... S... est la lettre analytique; dissolvante et disséminante par excellence" (855).

Cette foule hagarde! elle annonce: Nous sommes	That haggard crowd! it announces: We are
La triste opacité de nos spectres futurs.	The sad opaqueness of our future specters.

The crowd, "haggard" from the funeral ordeal, believes in an after-life of eternal souls of which we are, alive, mere opaque versions. In sum, it adheres to the Platonic-Christian myth, which Mallarmé early rejected, as indicated in: "ma lutte avec ce vieux et méchant plumage, terrassé, heureusement, Dieu" (Propos, p. 76); "Oublions [official religion]" ("Catholicisme," 394); "une entre les Chimères" (392); "L'Angleterre ne peut, à cause de Dieu, que Bacon, son législateur, respecte, adopter la science pure" (851). Gautier was also a pagan, atheistic.

Note the flat *a*'s of *hagard,* a favorite word with Mallarmé for spiritual disorder and distress. Contrast the bright sounds of *Magnifique.* The *ou* of *foule,* and of *Nous,* is obscure.

Mais le blason des deuils épars sur de vains murs
J'ai méprisé l'horreur lucide d'une larme,

But the heraldry of mournings scattered on vain walls,
I have scorned the lucid horror of a tear,

Mallarmé, unlike the crowd, scorns false sentiment, represented by a tear, such as one of the scattered tears depicted, on the traditional funeral decor of black velvet, by the conventional silver spangles, as in "un haillon noir y pend et pour larmes d'argent / Montre le mur blafard par ses trous" (15). Yet, something of the poet's stoic lucidity is also expressed, ambiguously, by the bright pure tear (rather, in this respect, like the solitary chandelier he could alone admire at the popular theater); compare "au bord de mes yeux calmes s'amasse une larme dont les diamants primitifs n'atteignent pas la noblesse," from his essay on Gautier (262) or, from the same, "cette larme transparente comme mon rêve lucide." Note the bright sounds of *u* and *i* in *lucide;* the sharpness and the hardness *(d)* are offset by the melting *r,* and the transparent *ar,* in *larme, épars,* and *horreur.*

épars is another favorite of Mallarmé, as in "hallucination éparse d'agonie" *(Coup de Dés),* a constellation sprinkled in a very dark night, quite close to the impression here.

Quand, sourd même à mon vers sacré qui ne l'alarme,
Quelqu'un de ces passants, fier, aveugle et muet,
Hôte de son linceul vague, se transmuait
En le vierge héros de l'attente posthume.

When, deaf even to my sacred verse which alarms him not,
Some one of those passing, proud, blind and mute
Denizen of his vague shroud, was transmuted
Into the virgin hero of posthumous expectancy.

passants: one of the passers-by of life. There is a double sense: just any man—all are equal on this terrain, as in the *"Ubi sunt?"* tradition; also a man "passing away" to the beyond, either one of the weak-spirited mass of ordinary humans or the merely bodily Gautier (cf. our comment on "pour les mains," above). The imperfect tense of *se transmuait* goes with this ambiguity: the funeral ceremony *was going on* while Mallarmé stood still within himself, stoically, and the event *was repeated* in the ordinary course of human history or of Mallarmé's experience, *"whenever a man died."* In any event, the *passant* is reaching death as a newcomer, a virgin or untried adventurer into the beyond, curious about what is there, as Hamlet was. He is "deaf . . . proud, blind, and dumb" (just as the physical death of Gautier is later referred to as "not to open the sacred eyes and to be quiet," or, again, is merely "stingy silence and massive night," in the last lines of the poem). He is "deaf even to my [Mallarmé's] verse," and this emphasizes the point that we have to do here with the non-verbal or non-spiritual, that is, with bodily demise, "dust."[3] In Villiers' *Premières Poésies,* "Don Juan," we find the following:

> Dans son orgueil sacré lorsqu'un homme succombe
> Qu'importe le néant et l'oubli d'une tombe?
> . . . .
> Grave, il repose là drapé dans son suaire,
> Sourd aux cris vagues des humains.

Mallarmé often uses the word *passant* in the main sense of it here: that is, a chance passer-by, haphazard as the wind and all outdoors, as in: "Personne! ce mot n'obsède pas d'un remords le passant" (546); or, "le texte . . . résumé de toute l'âme, la communiquant au passant" (530); compare "tombeau . . . ceux du dehors, ces *promeneurs,* en bénéficient" (502). An excellent example is "Apprenons, messieurs, au *passant,* à quiconque . . . par incompétence et *vaine vision* se trompa [about Verlaine's true nature]" (510). The *quiconque,* rather like the *quelqu'un de ces passants,* affords an idea of randomness; and note the related effect of a plural for something unessential: *passants.* In the same Verlaine essay we find the parallel idea of the contrast between the merely physical being and his essential voice: "celui qui s'y [in the tomb] dissimule pour ne pas offusquer, d'une présence, sa gloire." (510).[4]

attente posthume: the unknown fate we, like Hamlet, curiously await; and the closely corollary sense of the waiting period before a Last Judgment by fate. Davies produces good evidence for the latter sense (*Les Tombeaux de Mallarmé,* p. 46). But he is wrong in seeing this as applied only to Gautier.

The main sense is attested by: "l'attente [d'une vérité ultime] . . . faim . . . dans l'humanité" (294).

Vaste gouffre apporté dans l'amas de la brume	Vast gulf added to the mass of fog
Par l'irascible vent des mots qu'il n'a pas dits,	By the irascible wind of the words he has not spoken,
Le néant à cet Homme aboli de jadis:	The Nothing to this Man abolished of yore [says]:
"Souvenirs d'horizons, qu'est-ce, ô toi, que la Terre?"	"Memory of horizons, what, o thou, is Earth?" [so it says or]
Hurle ce songe; et, voix dont la clarté s'altère,	Howls out this dream; and, voice whose clarity breaks,
L'espace a pour jouet le cri: "Je ne sais pas!"	Space gets for plaything the cry: "I don't know!"

"Vast gulf added to the mass of fog / By the irascible wind of the

words he has not spoken" means that all the unsaid, all the inarticulateness, which characterizes the ordinary citizen as compared to the
poet, now rises up to confront him in a sort of Last Judgment; the unspoken adds to—or rather digs a fresh vivid pocket in—the general fog
of meaninglessness which goes with the awful abyss of chance or death
now facing him. This ugly wind foreshadows the "solennelle agitation
par l'air de paroles," the beautiful breath of poetry, below.   *

The unsaid haunts him, judges him—this man who was already
dead in a sense, formerly ("of yore"), that is, in his lifetime because
of his inarticulateness—and howls out to him this nightmare question:
"Memories of horizons, what, O thou, is Earth?" It seems to be a revenge for the question "Rêveur, à quoi sers-tu?" (Le Poète et la foule,
Gautier). In his early poem, Pan, Mallarmé asked "Qu'est la terre . . .
Et l'homme qu'est-il donc?.," and went on to give the "vain and stupid"
religious answers offered by a believing man (noted by Austin). In
contrast to the Maître, of the next section, this typical creature has
saved nothing from these memories of his whole life's horizons, has no
"explication orphique de la Terre" (663), has nothing to say but "I
don't know." The whole of his experience added up to a horizon—an
excellent image of man's life as a quest toward an ever-receding beyond;
a sundown is surely implied, almost always associated with the total
Question for Mallarmé (as in the Coup de Dés, Page 4); and horizon
is an ideal image for a final vision of the Earth as a ball in space as we
conceive leaving it behind in death, ultimately as blankly empty as the
"Rien n'aura eu lieu que le lieu" of the Coup de Dés (Page 10). This
precise use of horizon as the site of the ordinary man's eternally un-
answered enigma is found in "Bucolique": "la nature, Idée tangible
pour intimer quelque réalité aux sens frustes . . . communiquait à ma
jeunesse une ferveur [mais savait] en défendre l'interprétation au
lecteur d'horizons" (402)[5] A probable source is: "[Racontez] Vos
souvenirs avec leurs cadres d'horizons. / Dites, qu'avez-vous vu?"
(Baudelaire, Le Voyage).

voix dont la clarté s'altère: a spooky, echo-chamber effect of a transfigured voice. This ghostly atmosphere is prolonged in the cosmic loneliness of L'espace a pour jouet le cri "je ne sais pas"; compare "le cri de
l'étendue" (371).

In Le Guignon we have a fairly close equivalent to the irascible
vent: the wind occasionally represents to Mallarmé the threatening or
meaningless outside world.[6] Thus "un noir vent . . . dans la chair des
poètes . . . creusait aussi d'irritables ornières." In a dramatic project he
related to George Moore (Avowals), the wind stood for destiny outside
the castle, as opposed to an intimate life indoors. A good illustration

of the associated images of wind-empty-pit-inarticulateness-inauthenticity of the crowd is: "là, en public, éventée par le manque du rêve qu'elle [the flame of beauty] consume" (402); compare "le gouffre de vaine faim . . . vulgaire" (298).

The basic idea of the *gouffre* and of the whole passage is found in similar terms in Mallarmé's "Villiers" lecture: "la foule, quand elle aura, en tous les sens de la fureur, exaspéré sa médiocrité, sans jamais revenir à autre chose qu'à du néant central, hurlera vers le poète, un appel" (499); perhaps it is even clearer in: "L'âme, tacite et qui ne suspend pas aux paroles de l'élu familier, le poète, est . . . vouée irremédiablement au Néant" (694). The unsaid as a concrete negative entity, "pertes," is expressed in: "Au fond du rêve, peut-être, se débat, en tant que pertes, l'imagination de gens lui refusant un essor quotidien." (Propos, p. 162).[7]

amas de la brume: the same image of fog expressing the inarticulate masses is found in "la brume et le public" (510).

Homme: Capitalized because the *Homme* is the hero of this common drama—"L'Homme . . . le Mystère" (545)—as the *Maître* is of the poetic drama; partly because it lacks bright sounds and vertical letters, the word seems apt for this usage, as in the *Coup de Dés,* Page 4.

de jadis: associated with the simple sort of man, a hardy ancestor, in the *Coup de Dés:* "jadis il empoignait la barre" (Page 4). But this ancestor was Man and hence included the poet ambiguously, as here.

Le Maître, par un oeil profond, a, sur ses pas,	The Master, through a profound eye, has, on his foosteps,
Apaisé de l'éden l'inquiète merveille	Appeased the eden's unquiet marvel
Dont le frisson final, dans sa voix seule, éveille	Whose final shiver, in his voice alone, awakens
Pour la Rose et le Lys le mystère d'un nom.	For the Rose and the Lily the mystery of a name.

There is a dramatic contrast between the final "Je ne sais pas" (and the whole tone) of the preceding section versus the triumphant entry of *Le Maître* and the rest of the section following. We may recall the "Maître et Ombre" of the "Bibliographie" already cited: the Master of the third section is contrasted with the "Ombre," the mere shade, or spectre, of the preceding section.

Mallarmé occasionally uses the word *Maître* for the artist (e.g., pp. 498, 542).[8] This part of the poem has caused relatively little difficulty to the commentators and readers. The "eden" is the garden the poet—"ce civilisé édennique" (646)—cultivates, his field of potential poetic reality, as in "le devoir idéal que nous font les jardins de cet astre," below, and "On ne peut pas se passer d'Éden," a remark he

made to René Ghil in refutation of materialism which, as he said elsewhere, "ne prête pas un sens." (Obviously, though no sectarian, the
poet must maintain some sense of mystery in order to make beauty.)   *

The poet's field—which is ultimately life itself—is "uneasy" or
"unquiet" until it is tamed by the Master. Through this formula
Mallarmé evokes the dialectic of creativity and the process of evolu-
tionary refinement, from an original crude rhythm (or polarity) of pain
and delight (as in the simple experience of physical love), to the delicate shiver-rhythm of sound waves set in motion by the poetic voice,
the *air de paroles*. This recalls the famous phrase applied to Baudelaire
by Hugo: "frisson nouveau." The whole of the *Coup de Dés* is a prolonged version of this dialectical evolution.

Poe seems to have been an influence here: "Is not every word an
impulse on the air?" *(The Power of Words)*. My discovery here was
duplicated by Cellier, who saw a further connection in "I spoke . . .
into birth [these] brilliant flowers."

The *oeil profond* refers no doubt to the visual, somewhat Parnassian,
quality of Gautier's art (he began as a painter); he was the "poet for
whom the external world exists," as Gautier liked to say of himself;
compare "le déplaisir éclaterait . . . qu'un chanteur ne sût à l'écart et au
gré de pas dans l'infinité des fleurettes, partout où sa voix recontre une
notation, cueillir" (364).

Rose: is always a feminine entity for Mallarmé, for example, in
Les Fleurs, the *Faune,* and the various poems addressed to Méry
Laurent *(Dame, sans trop d'ardeur; Rondel II);* the lily symbolizes the
male faun: "Lys! et l'un de vous tous pour l'ingénuité"; together therefore they form a couple of universal significance.[9]

Compare "La rose aime le lys" (ML, p. 142).

Est-il de ce destin rien qui demeure,
non?
Is there of this destiny nothing which
remains. No?

O vous tous, oubliez une croyance
sombre.
O all of you, forget a somber belief.

Le splendide génie éternel n'a pas
d'ombre.
Splendid eternal genius has no
shadow.

In the "O vous tous" and the "moi de votre désir soucieux," below,
there is at least a partial—heart-warming and moving—reconciliation
with the initially scorned crowd, as in Mallarmé's later work generally;
compare "la Foule (où inclus le Génie)" (383), and particularly "Confrontation," "Conflit" and the *Coup de Dés* (C, pp. 159-166).

A juvenile poem (8) expressed the same quite conventional idea
of spiritual survival on earth (an idea especially favored by poets since
the Renaissance):

Et tout est dit. Oh! non, doit-on donc l'oublier?
Qui sut se faire aimer ne meurt pas tout entier!
On laisse sa mémoire ainsi qu'aux nuits l'étoile
Laisse une blanche lueur qu'aucune ombre ne voile.

There is a certain ambiguity in the word *ombre,* however, which may refer, like the earlier *spectre,* to sentimental belief, as opposed to the stoic credo of impersonal survival through art.

Note the bright *i-é-i-é* of the genius's light versus the dark nasals of *ombre* and *sombre,* the obscure *ou* of *vous tous.*

Moi, de votre désir soucieux, je veux voir,	I, concerned about your desire, I want to see
A qui s'évanouit, hier, dans le devoir	[Survive] The one who vanished, yesterday, in the ideal
Idéal que nous font les jardins de cet astre,	Duty set for us by the gardens of this planet,
Survivre pour l'honneur du tranquille désastre	Survive in honor [memory] of the tranquil disaster
Une agitation solennelle par l'air	A solemn agitation through the air
De paroles . . .	Of words . . .

I, concerned about your desire to have *something* conquer death, want to see it this way: the one who vanished recently—from amidst the ideal duty set for us (poets) by the gardens of this planet—is survived by a solemn agitation of words through the air (or "by the air" of expressed words, the *frisson nouveau* of Gautier's voice, sound waves) which honor, or celebrate, the quiet disaster of physical death, that is, appease the horror into something human, as art generally does —for example, those early incantatory forms of it that arise from funeral ritual.

Is this a statement of ultimate optimism, offsetting the ultimate pessimism of the first section ("soleil mortel" and so on)? This is not clear, nor could it be. Certainly it is a ringing affirmation of faith in the value of art, which outlives the body—"le buste survit à la cité," Gautier's own famous little poem, *L'Art,* had declared—even if we cannot know the final destiny of man. For obviously the artistic "message" goes down to posterity, and though we know that we die, we do not know that this will ever die.

The ancient (since Aristotle) idea of art as appeasement of fear through rhythmic incantation—which, so to speak, spreads it out, homeopathically controls it—is treated with brilliant insight in "De même": "l'orgue . . . un balbutiement de ténèbres énorme, ou leur exclusion du refuge, avant de s'y déverser extasiées et pacifiées . . . causant aux hôtes une plénitude de fierté et de sécurité" (396).

devoir: recalls "Tout en moi s'exaltait de voir / La famille des iridées / Surgir à ce nouveau *devoir*" (*Prose*).

. . . pourpre ivre et grand calice clair,	. . . drunken purple and great clear calyx,
Que, pluie et diamant, le regard diaphane	That, rain and diamond, the diaphanous look
Resté là sur ces fleurs dont nulle ne se fane,	Remaining there on those flowers of which none fades,
Isole parmi l'heure et le rayon du jour!	Isolates amid the hour and the radiancy of the day!

All this is in apposition to *paroles:* it is the epiphany of perfect poetic flowers: "La voix divine . . . chaque parole retomba, en pluie de fleurs" (631). They stand out to the pure look of Gautier, as any epiphany (meaning: "apparition," cf. Mallarmé's *Apparition*) does, or really as any authentic art does, which is "bigger than life," like the *hyperbole* of *Prose* with its *trop grands glaïeuls*.[10] An implication of *pluie et diamant* is that the poet's gaze is the "rain and sunlight" of each "absente de tous bouquets." But the main effect is the combination of liquid transparency and hard brightness (kinesis and stasis) in these mysterious—androgynous, angelic—creatures, as in "pleurer le diamant" (60).

Compare this whole glowing passage to "je laisse cette larme, transparente comme mon rêve lucide," from an early essay on Gautier (262); also "une pluie éblouissante de diamants" (673); "une clairvoyance de diamant" (Lettre à Gosse); "Hérodiade au clair regard de diamant" (*Scène*).

We note the blooming hyperbolic *p*'s of *pourpre, paroles, pluie,* as in *Prose* (*hyperbole, trompettes, trop pour, trop grands glaïeuls*); the darkly or drunken amorous red-purple of *ou* (or *our*) in *pourpre* as in the bursting pomegranates of the *Faune:* "Tu sais ma passion que pourpre et déjà mûr" (note in passing the similar *p*'s) and the erotic sonnet *M'Introduire:* "comme mourir pourpre la roue." A keen, acute tone is added by the *i* of *ivre;* note the bright *u* and *i* of *pluie,* the *d* and the *i* of *diaphane* and *diamant* (cf. the two parallel effects of hard *d* and bright *i* in the just-quoted "Hérodiade au clair regard de diamant"); a circular halo effect is supported by the *o* of *isole* and *rayon.*

C'est de nos vrais bosquets déjà tout le séjour,	It [art] is the entire abode already of our true groves,
Où le poëte pur a pour geste humble et large	Where the pure poet has as his humble and broad deed
De l'interdire au rêve, ennemi de sa charge:	To ward off from it [i.e. from the haunt] [mere] dreaming, enemy of his task:

The last section is a solemn declaration of the poet's task; of death's victory over his earthly being; and of his final triumph, transfiguration into immortal glory; both—the death and the transfiguration—are symbolized by the "beautiful monument." The *rêve* is of the sentimental variety that bred the false hopes of immortality and the inarticulateness dealt with earlier in the poem. Mallarmé usually employs the word *rêve* in a positive sense—*rêverie* (as used in the Preface to the *Coup de Dés*) is closer to his meaning—but from the context there is little doubt of his usage here, as in "sortir [la Poésie] du Rêve et du hasard" (letter to Villiers, 1866; Davies). Chisholm is helpful on this point: in his *L'Art,* Gautier had counseled against vague dreaming, "Quand flotte ailleurs l'esprit" and added "Que ton rêve flottant / Se scelle / Dans le bloc résistant!"

* The last few lines are fairly rhetorical and, to me, less successful as poetry. They may remind us of Baudelaire's statement in *Le Vin et le haschisch:* "Par l'exercice assidu de la volonté et la noblesse permanente de l'intention nous avons créé à notre usage un jardin de vraie beauté."

Afin que le matin de son repos altier,
Quand la mort ancienne est comme pour Gautier
De n'ouvrir pas les yeux sacrés et de se taire,
Surgisse, de l'allée ornement tributaire,
Le sépulcre solide où gît tout ce qui nuit,
Et l'avare silence et la massive nuit.

So that the morning of its [death's] [or "his, the poet's"] high repose,
When ancient death is as for Gautier
To not open the sacred eyes and utter no words,
There should spring, as tributary ornament of the lane,
The solid sepulchre where lies all that harms,
Stingy silence and massive night.

The sense is that, the poet having performed his duty—"so that . . . there should spring" depends on the verb *interdire,* the performance of the pure deed—there will be no harm other than to the physical body, which is summed up in the *n'ouvrir pas les yeux* and the *se taire.* Then proudly, as a monument to Gautier—*containing,* in a rich dialectical or paradoxical sense, the evil—a solid tomb, a *beau monument* [qui] *l'enferme tout entier,* where lies all that can harm (corporeal "silence" and "night," in sum the vicissitudes of human dust as opposed to immortal art), may spring up. Death and beauty are eventually inextricably linked for Mallarmé as they are for the Greek playwrights, for Shakespeare, Poe, Rimbaud, Valéry, Milosz; and the dazzling tombstone is one of his key images, particularly for poetic glory. "Every poem is an epitaph" (T. S. Eliot).

The implication of the elliptic "Afin que surgisse" is thus a tacit conversion, a miraculous change from the uncompromisingly honest, stoic acceptance of bodily death to its fitting reward—like the ultimate constellation of *Un Coup de Dés* emerging from the dark night of an apocalypse—the immortal monument of glory, art.

yeux sacrés: the implication is that the sacredness of the eyes—Gautier's particular gift—survives their physical closing, as in the *Cantique de Saint Jean* and the *Tombeau d'Anatole:* "ferme ces doux yeux . . . et tu vivras" (f. 106).

tributaire: mainly creates the image of a monument beside a cemetery lane; perhaps there is a suggestion that this *outer* shape pays tribute to the ways of ordinary mortals: "tombeau . . . ceux du dehors en bénéficient" (lecture on Villiers; 502); the uncertain meaning harmonizes with the prevailing ambiguity in this whole last section. Even the last line has a vibrant effect. Its dominant tone of massive calm expresses the flat line of death, that final horizon: "la ligne finale et calme du lourd tombeau" *(Tombeau d'Anatole,* f. 132).

NOTES

[1] The *hoir* of *Tout orgueil* is probably an echo of Villiers, who wrote: " 'La Mort est un pays inconnu d'où nul pèlerin n'a pu revenir encore' s'écrie Hamlet, dans son soliloque métaphysique. Ce qui nie absolument l'*Apparition.*" (*Chez les Passants;* note the word *passants*).

[2] The *chimère* of *Igitur*, which emerges like a vestigial constellation from the black experience of nothingness, is similar: "la clarté de la chimère en laquelle a agonisé son rêve" (436), cf. the *guirlande* of *Quand l'ombre*, the *licornes* of *Ses purs ongles.* Wallace Fowlie sees an influence of the poison-cup of *Faust.*

[3] In "Bucolique" there is an image, only partly humorous, invoking the contrast between body and spirit: "Le Monsieur, plutôt commode, que certains observent la coutume d'accueillir par mon nom" versus "moi l'esprit, là-haut aux espaces miroitant." (401).

[4] The term *passant* is several times used for Saint Jean in various fragments (N, pp. 109, etc.) in the ambiguous sense of a man who happened by (and perhaps saw Hérodiade naked) and a dying man. It is used in the sense of "the dead" in *La Dernière mode* (784), capitalized.

Ronsard, to whom Mallarmé owes much more than is realized, wrote in his *Epitaphe:* "Passant, j'ai dit, suy ta fortune / Ne trouble pas mon repos, je dors." Coppée's *Le Passant*, admired by Mallarmé, has "Je suis vraiment celui qui vient on ne sait d'où / Et qui n'a pas de but, le poète, le fou, / Avide seulement d'*horizon* et d'espace, / Celui qui suit au ciel les oiseaux et qui *passe.*" This has the ambiguous vibrancy we sense in Mallarmé's use. Even closer is "le voile obscur qui te couvre, ô passant . . . Qu'ont-ils vu? qu'est-ce qu'ils font? qu'ont-ils dit, ces fils d'Eve? Rien" (Hugo, *Contemplations,* in Cellier, p. 60).

[5] The association of wind, fear, horizon, and the unreflecting crowd is found in "un *vent* ou peur de manquer à quelque chose exigeant le retour, chasse de l'*horizon* à la ville, les gens" (388).

[6] The wintry wind of *Mes bouquins* is contrasted with the warm indoors memory of a summery classic scene. But elsewhere, of course, the wind can be something highly positive, as in "Crise de vers" where it stands for the fresh cleansing breath of the new spirit, "l'enseigne un peu rouillée ... le vent l'a décrochée, d'où soufflé" (491), cf. "bouffée unique de joie" (510). Mallarmé is a poet of the outdoors as much as the indoors, *pace* Claudel, that claudicating clod of a genius.

[7] A similar notion of unsaid words, but this time the poet's, is found in "Verlaine": "la parole haute cesse, et le sanglot des vers abandonnés ne suivra jusqu'à ce lieu de discrétion [the tomb] celui qui s'y dissimule." (510).

[8] In the *Coup de Dés* he becomes rather Man, the oft-humbled Master of the world, including, as a later development, his special representative, the poet or artist. The ambiguity is hence similar in the two works.

[9] Eternal poles in many a mystic doctrine, certainly Mallarmé's "primitives foudres de la logique" (386) which we have treated at length in our *Oeuvre de Mallarmé*. The pairing is reflected in Saint Jean, the pure upright ascetic, versus Hérodiade, "la rose cruelle" (*Les Fleurs*); also more vaguely, in *Anastase* versus *Pulchérie* of *Prose*, (q.v.). Of course, good symbolism is always a delicate matter, and to prove how elusive it can be there is: "Les demoiselles Cazalis / L'autre une rose et l'une un lys" (165). We might remind those eager to throw out symbolism and its study because of such difficulties that certain qualities associated with the male are not only found in males. The whiteness of the lily, usually associated with the male, occasionally symbolizes the purity of the *dead* woman, as in "Ce que disaient les trois cigognes."

[10] Mallarmé's vision is often eidetic; when an object is loved sufficiently it comes toward us, so to speak, like the swelling stomach of the window or mandolin in *Une dentelle*, cf. Eliot's "window bellied like the fig's fruit" (*Ash Wednesday*). Such elite apprehensions we now are apt to call "epiphanies," after Joyce. They are apart, isolated; the hyperbolic "trop grands glaïeuls" are surrounded by a "lacune / Qui des jardins les sépara"; in our more discursive terms, "an Erotic glow of 'knowing' surrounds the named object, replacing (arising as joy from sorrow) the black analytic boundary which kills its connections with the rest of reality. It is a kind of halo or aura ... a pure phenomenon of knowing ... Faith (*credo ut intellegam*) yields to a superior will, through a little death of the human will and reemerges as this transfiguration, the beauty of knowing." (W, p. 427).

9. ÉVENTAIL

◈◇◈◇◈◇◈◇◈◇◈

—de Madame Mallarmé

This poem is a slight, quietly affectionate tribute to the modest, dutiful, somewhat faded and dull lady he married, investing her, as a gift, with a little poetic glamor and playful humor. It was written and published in 1891.

Avec comme pour langage	With as if for a language [the fan's rhythm seems to give off the poetic rhythm]
Rien qu'un battement aux cieux	Nothing but a [fan's] beating in the skies
Le futur vers se dégage	The future verse arises
Du logis très précieux	From the very precious dwelling [Madame Mallarmé]

The lady's fan seems to "beat out," or scan, in the air the poetry it inspires in the observing and admiring husband; the *logis* is, no doubt, her hand which is the source of the movement; the word is chosen for its domestic qualities. Thus, in the *Tombeau d'Anatole,* the mother's cradle-rocking was the source of the poet's rhythm (pp. 56-57); an exact equivalent is the "woman"-boat of the *Coup de Dés* (C, p. 154); see also the *bercement* of the *nef* in "Le Livre," pp. 17-18.

The *avec* is chosen partly for its *v,* the fan-shape, and wing-shape, as in the later words *éventail* and *vol;* compare *Le vierge, le vivace et le bel aujourd'hui.*

Aile tout bas la courrière	With wing low the courier
Cet éventail si c'est lui	This fan if it is
Le même par qui derrière	The same by which behind
Toi quelque miroir a lui	You some mirror has glistened

The fan is, as in *Autre éventail* (q.v.), a wing, the wing of a courier (bird), that is to say, seeming to have darted across the salon into the mirror behind her. The *aile-éventail* echo is important (it is featured in many of the *Vers de circonstance,* 107-110). We observe the bright effect of *si, lui, lui,* and the round *o* of *miroir,* with its liquid, soft, light-brimming *r*'s.

*

111

tout bas: implies the discretion of the fan, a model for the poet's subtle verse (compare the "Musicienne du silence," *Sainte*).

courrière: perhaps, in part, because it may convey a lady's invitation (Chassé).

miroir: an intimate part of the domestic setting, including, no doubt, the traditional symbolism of the wife's soul as a reflection of her husband's. It further suggests the ideal light which is the source of poetry, as well as of the fan's grace.

Limpide (où va redescendre	Limpid[ly] (where will settle
Pourchassée en chaque grain	Pursued in each speck
Un peu d'invisible cendre	A little invisible ash
Seule à me rendre chagrin)	Which alone bothers me)

* *limpide* refers to the mirror: "shone . . . limpid" (apposition).

The parenthesis alludes to the fact that the fan has scattered some ashes from the poet-husband's cigarette (or cigar) as in "Ce peu d'aile [éventail] assez pour proscrire / Le souci nuée ou tabac" (108); *où:* on the mirror, where the ash will settle *(redescendre)*. And Chisholm has rightly observed that there is an allusion here to the dust of years settling on the greying couple. Richard's idea that it is the fall of his inspiration is less likely. But there is undoubtedly an allusion to the

* housewife's usual activity, dusting, *sans paresse* (below).

Toujours tel il apparaisse	Such always may it [the fan] appear
Entre tes mains sans paresse.	Between your never idle hands.

10. AUTRE ÉVENTAIL

—de Mademoiselle Mallarmé

Mallarmé expresses his exquisitely subtle, playful, yet keenly tender —with a hint of veiled voluptuousness—love for his daughter Geneviève through the voice of the fan, evoking the impressionist atmosphere of a crepuscular, vaguely ornate, late nineteenth-century salon, à la Renoir, Morisot, Vuillard, Proust, and suggesting beyond it a glimpse of (civilized, French) nature surrounding the intimate interior scene. The poem appeared in 1884, the year of its composition.

[the fan speaks:]

O rêveuse, pour que je plonge	O dreamer-girl, if you'd have me plunge
Au pur délice sans chemin,	Into pure pathless delight,
Sache, par un subtil mensonge,	Manage, through a subtle lie [fiction of a fan's flying],
Garder mon aile dans ta main.	To keep my wing in your hand.

The poet-fan is requesting a "subtle" gratification: "do this thing for me (if I am to plunge—and you too—into delight): hold my "wing" captive even as you cause its (inner) flight (of ecstasy); which is, of course, a (fatherly) fiction, or *mensonge*." By implication, the girl is also stirred into happiness. In the following strophes, it is her reactions which are featured.

The *aile* springs poetically from the final letters of *éventail;* hence: "Aile [éventail] quels paradis . . . votre pur délire (107); "aile . . . cet éventail" (57) and "l'éventail . . . cette autre aile de papier" (374); a swishing caressing quality is transmitted through the sounds of *ch* (in *chemin, sache);* the *g* of *plonge, mensonge;* the *euse* of *rêveuse;* and *ice (délice);* something brilliant and acute comes through the *u, é* and *i* of *pur délice; onge* is deeply sensual, voluptuous, as in *Petit air I.*

sans chemin: "wild"; the *indirection* of the father-daughter relationship is also discreetly implied.

Une fraîcheur de crépuscule	A freshness of twilight
Te vient à chaque battement	Comes to you at each beat
Dont le coup prisonnier recule	Whose imprisoned stroke thrusts back
L'horizon délicatement.	The horizon delicately.

The tension of the held flight—"tel que n'en jaillira le vol" *(Le Nénuphar blanc)*—corresponds to the subtly amorous mood of the poet-father. Its dynamic-static *battement* is also the rhythm of his emerging verse, scanning "space," as in *Éventail* (both poems were written originally on actual fans, gifts).

There is an effect of startling enlargement in the leap from the curved "horizon" of the fan to the total horizon it shuts out, perhaps even seems to push back gently: "l'éventail . . . cache le site pour rapporter contre les lèvres une muette fleur peinte comme le mot intact et nul de la songerie par les battements approché." (374). The poem, like the fan, excludes—or rather raises esthetically—the ordinary horizon.

The airily caressing quality is prolonged through the *ch* of *fraîcheur* and *chaque;* the *z* in *horizon* is highly suggestive of fan-folds; compare: "[Éventail] Aile ancienne, donne-moi / L'*horizon* dans une bouffée" (107).

aile is associated with *éventail* not only because of the final letters but also because of the v-shape of both "wing" and "fan," which is supported poetically by the *v* in *éventail* and helps account for Mallarmé's favoring the word *vol* for "wing"; we note the various *v*'s in *vertige, voici, vol,* and so on, below, and the similar effect of imprisoned wing-beat in *Le vierge, le vivace et le bel aujourd'hui* with its exceptionally numerous *v*'s.

Vertige! voici que frissonne	Vertigo! see how shivers
L'espace comme un grand baiser	Space like a great kiss
Qui, fou de naître pour personne,	Which, mad at being born for no one,
Ne peut jaillir ni s'apaiser.	Can neither spurt up nor be calmed.

The tension turns into vertigo; the immense emotion thus evoked is hyperbolically all space as one great kiss: "je voudrais tout confondre, dans un poétique baiser" (264). The tension is expressed again as an absurd cancellation, a futility of birth or, again, a frantic indecision between springing forth and settling back, as in *Surgi de la croupe:* "agonise . . . / mais ne consent," though here the mood is happier, more lighthearted, immediately pleasurable, from the beginning (and not in some remote constellation-after-death effect as in the most serious poems).

The echo (or even, in this playful case, "pun") *naître-n'être* is the basic absurdity and tension, to be or not to be, *ab ovo,* which is prominent in *Une dentelle.*

The *ss* of *frisson* is graphically shivery; there is a fine contrast between the bright acute sounds in *jaillir* and the flat *a* and *ai* of *s'apaiser.*

An overtone of *vertige* is *vierge,* equally tense (as in *Hérodiade*).

Compare the *vertige* of the *Coup de Dés* (C, p. 312) and of Baudelaire's *Le Flacon;* see the *v* of Appendix C.

Sens-tu le paradis farouche	Do you sense the fierce paradise
Ainsi qu'un rire enseveli	Like a buried laugh
Se couler du coin de ta bouche	Flow from the corner of your mouth
Au fond de l'unanime pli!	Deep into the unanimous fold!

The "fierce paradise" maintains the keen mood, with the tension further expressed in "buried laugh"; the fan is held folded—all its folds in one, "unanimity"—with its tip at the corner of Geneviève's mouth, a typically coquettish girlish gesture. There is a tiny hint of the gallant frustration expressed through the charming rococo (somewhat present here) of *Placet futile:* "Princesse! à jalouser le destin d'une Hébé / Qui poind sur cette tasse au baiser de vos lèvres." Compare the following lines from the *Éventail* section of the *Vers de circonstance:* "Cache . . . Ton rire" (109); "Amène contre mon sourire . . ." (108); "Dissimuler votre sourire" (110).

The tension is joyously released in the laugh, at last, "flows," but with acuteness, like a *jet d'eau:* "la vérité coule de ma bouche" (631); "le sein / Par qui coule en blancheur sibylline la femme" (*Don du poème*). Again, there is a suggestion of defeat in *couler,* "to sink," as on Page 4 of the *Coup de Dés.*

The acute *i*'s of the laugh are contrasted with the source, the *bouche* (dark *ou*); the nasal *on* of *fond* is likewise deep, and the *ou* of *farouche* adds a voluptuous depth to *paradis.*

Le sceptre des rivages roses	The sceptre of pink shores
Stagnants sur les soirs d'or, ce l'est,	Stagnant on golden evenings, this it is,
Ce blanc vol fermé que tu poses	This closed white wing you place
Contre le feu d'un bracelet.	Against the fire of a bracelet.

The closed fan is like a sceptre held by a ruler (a princess) as in "Fermé [éventail] je suis le sceptre aux doigts" (110); it is held up against the background of a sunset, with rosy shores (perhaps an echo of her lips), "stagnating," a slightly Byzantine effect, decadent, coppery as in "vapeurs de pourpre . . . ruisseaux de sang . . . nuages violets couleur du soir" (1216) or Baudelaire's curdled "sang qui se fige" for sunset streaks in his *Harmonie du soir.* The *rivage,* which is apt for such cloud effects, is so used again by Mallarmé in "le rivage . . . crépuscules . . . du soir" (1248). An actual sunset is implied, no doubt glimpsed through a window in the background—we recall the *crépuscule* of the second quatrain—but also the sunset glow of a bracelet against which the girl lays her fan in a graceful languid gesture.

The implication of *sceptre* is that this privileged maiden is nature's

Princess: "Et tout, autour de moi, vit dans l'idolâtrie / D'un miroir qui reflète . . . Hérodiade" *(Scène)*.

There is a purposefully precious conceit in the rime *ce l'est* and *bracelet;* it goes well with the semi-playful, gallant, slightly rococo mood (as in *Placet futile);* compare: "lui, ce l'est" (651) and "ce l'est" (179); is there a remote echo of *céleste?*

*

11. PETIT AIR, I

A slender airy poem, written and published in 1894, this is one of Mallarmé's best; its refinement is weighted, perhaps more fully than usually, with sumptuous sensuality.

As in *Victorieusement fui* and *Quelle soie,* the poet "abdicates" from his highest dream of glory, in favor of human love. Anyway, partly on the strength of the sacrifice, which has a rare meaning in his case, he emerges with something very superior. (As for the Dream, he really was merely reserving it, for the last).

The poet is strolling by the river, at some vague unpeopled place, with his mistress. He lowers his glance from the sunset, suggesting his abandoned dream that he now sees as "vainglory." A flash of whiteness across his vision reminds him of his human love, his mistress, as, emerging from the white slip langorously or caressingly removed from her body—like the flight of a bird—she plunges into the water and exultantly splashes in naked jubilation. Simple—and quite perfect.

Quelconque une solitude	Some indifferent solitary place
Sans le cygne ni le quai	Without the swan or the quay
Mire sa désuétude	Reflects its disuse
Au regard que j'abdiquai	In the glance I removed
Ici de la gloriole	Here from the vainglory
Haute à ne la pas toucher	Too high to touch
Dont maint ciel se bariole	In which many a sky daubs itself
Avec les ors de coucher	With the golds of sunset

The indifferent solitary place has no citified swan or quay; this site being so unpeopled, his mistress can swim nude. Its disuse "reflects," is like, the neglect of his Dream which is now, perhaps wistfully, seen as "vainglory," and, in any case, is "too high to reach." This is the mood (though then he was altogether alone and not just casting a solitary look upward) of the prose poem *La Gloire,* in which the Dream, again associated with a splendid sunset, is referred to as "superhuman": "orgueils surhumains."[1]

Quelconque: compare the "inférieur clapotis quelconque" of the *Coup de Dés* (Page 10), the slapping of water, partially rendered by the *c*'s and *q*'s (Rauhut).

All the negative effects *(sans . . . ni,* etc.), together with the bright *i*'s, crisp *c*'s and *q*'s, and the spare wording, help create a dry-point, Toulouse-Lautrec-like cleanness, a sense of absence, a cleared site ready for the vivid flash of beauty. The second quatrain, by contrast, is warmer, more ornate.

sans le cygne: his ghost, however, hovers in this absence.

regard . . . abdiquai: compare "abdiquer le regard" (1566); "regard abdiqué par la conscience des autres" (489). The word *abdiquer* implies a giving up of a kingly estate à la Rudolph of Hapsburg.

gloriole: the broader, more sumptuous and facile, warmer effects of the sunset splashes are caught in the many round *o*'s and harmonious *r*'s.

Mais langoureusement longe	But langourously runs along
Comme de blanc linge ôté	Like white linen doffed
Tel fugace oiseau si plonge	Some fleeting bird if [you] plunge
Exultatrice à côté	Exulting beside [me]
Dans l'onde toi devenue	In the water you [having] become
Ta jubilation nue.	Your naked jubilation.

Note the voluptuous, juicily caressing effects of the soft *g*'s in *longe, linge, plonge* (André Spire commented on a comparable juiciness in the *g* of the word *orange*[2]) along with the many lolling, liquid *l*'s.

langoureusement: is luxuriously long, like *exultatrice.*

oiseau: ambiguously, the slip or the woman's naked body.

si is both bright and sharp *(i),* and the brevity of the word aids the effect of crispness, the cutting dive; but the *s* is sibillant, caressing, for the entry of the water.

plonge: "je veux plonger ma tête en tes cuisses nerveuses" (15); this baptismal entry of the water-womb, in which the poet sympathetically participates, is like that of *Le Pitre châtié;* the swimmer becomes *(devenue)* her original self, her "nakedness."

Exultatrice: "un grand mot incurvé qui fait jaillir des gerbes d'eau" (Thibaudet, *La Poésie de Stéphane Mallarmé,* p. 53). See *u* in the Letter Table.

jubilation nue: the *b* is rounded like the shapes of the naked woman ("sein . . . nubile," 29); the *u*'s are feminine (wave hollows also) but excitingly acute.

The overtone *jus*—splashing foam—joins with the whiteness-cluster (*écume,* etc.). See Appendix A and *u* in the Letter Table (also C, p. 367).

*

NOTES

1 Yet he added, in this more serious piece: "ne faut-il pas qu'on en constate l'authenticité?" Which he proceeded to try to do in the *Coup de Dés*.

2 In *Plaisir poétique et plaisir musculaire*. Corti.

12. QUAND L'OMBRE MENAÇA DE LA FATALE LOI

❖⸙❖⸙❖⸙❖⸙❖

A compact masterpiece of radiant darkness, *Quand l'ombre menaça* appeared for the first time in the *Poètes maudits,* Verlaine's handsome tribute to his literary soulmates; this was in 1883. The title was originally *Cette nuit.*

The poet sees the dark shadow of night with foreboding, as the menace of death; but the old dream of beauty and truth, his artist's faith, revolts and cries out its "indubitable" "Yea!" All those scattered stars, the whole cosmos, is meaningless compared to the genius—of mankind, or the poet representing it—radiating from this earth.

In a *Moralité légendaire,* which Mallarmé had read and admired, *Salomé* (it often reads like a pastiche of *Hérodiade*) Jules Laforgue had written: "Man is only an insect under the skies, but let him respect himself and he is indeed God. A spasm of the creature is worth all of nature." The older poet must have at least approved.

Quand l'ombre menaça de la fatale loi	When the shadow [of death] menaced with the [its] fatal law
Tel vieux Rêve, désir et mal de mes vertèbres,	A certain old Dream, desire and pain [or evil] of my vertebrae,
Affligé de périr sous les plafonds funèbres	[Being] Grieved at perishing under the funeral ceilings [the recurrent night sky]
Il a ployé son aile indubitable en moi.	It [the Dream] folded in distress its indubitable [faith-full] wing inside me.

The first line features six *a* sounds, underscoring the sense of the flat line of death, like the mere nothingness, the "indifféremment LE HASARD" of the *Coup de Dés;* compare "l'avare silence et la massive nuit" *(Toast funèbre);* the sombre nasals of *Quand* and *ombre* add touches of dark negation.

ombre: the depth of death is in the total night[1] and in its emissary, the poet, stirring as the *mal* in his vertebrae, recalling that "la mort triomphait dans cette voix" *(Tombeau d'Edgar Poe)* or in that of their

120

brother Villiers who, for Mallarmé, "évoqua du geste l'*Ombre* [Poe] tout silence" (531).

Rêve: the idea of an old Dream from the past, associated with the words *Tel* and *désir,* is found in "Que sommes-nous dans le passé? / Tel rêve de notre désir," from Villiers' *Axël,* quoted by Mallarmé (501).

désir et mal de mes vertèbres: we may recall the metaphysical *mal* that inhibited Mallarmé's faun; a similar expression of the ambivalent nature of man's spine-climbing drive to glory is: "primordial instinct placé au secret de nos replis (un malaise divin)" (294). It goes to the head, as we say; thus, in the *Coup de Dés,* the plume of art, about to be put on the hero's head, is characterized by *hilarité et horreur* (Page 6). In the *Cantique de Saint Jean,* with the final burst of glory in death, the prophet proclaims: "Je sens comme aux *vertèbres* / S'éployer des ténèbres" (cf. *ployer* here). Baudelaire too may be echoed here:

> J'allais mourir, C'était dans mon âme amoureuse,
> Désir mêlé d'horreur, un *mal* particulier;
> (*Le rêve d'un curieux*)

ployé son aile: the "wing" of aspiration receives a staggering blow from the outer cosmos—heurtée à quelque choc de ses rêves déçus" (N, p. 77)—and is "folded" in resignation. There is a sacrificially resplendent retreat into the innermost recesses of tragic consciousness, the *moi (solitaire ébloui).* The movement is one of self-composure: "l'art, dans ses expressions suprêmes, implique une *solitude,* conforme, par example, au mouvement . . . de rabattre un geste *ployé* . . . sur sa poitrine à soi. Toute une volonté se compose" (171). The similar defeat of a thrust of ambition by a primordial *mal* is featured on Page 3 of the *Coup de Dés:* "aile . . . retombée d'un *mal* à dresser le vol."

indubitable: there is a certain ambiguity here, a paradoxical suggestion that the defeat cannot be doubted.

Luxe, ô salle d'ébène où, pour séduire un roi	Luxury, O ebony hall [black night of stars] where, [enough] to charm a [duped] king
Se tordent dans leur mort des guir-landes célèbres,	Twist in their death [night-agony] celebrated garlands [familiar constellations],
Vous n'êtes qu'un orgueil menti par les ténèbres	You are nought but a pride denied by the shadows
Aux yeux du solitaire ébloui de sa foi.	In the eyes of the solitary one dazzled by his faith.

luxe: this is vaguely ironic; the allure is partly meretricious. The crisp geometric effect of the *x* reminds us of a similar effect, to create a similar architectural mood, in *Ses purs ongles (onyx,* etc.).

salle d'ébène: reminds us of the dark deserted salon of *Ses purs ongles.*

pour séduire un roi: primarily, a "spectacle for a king" who, it is implied, would be impressed by this falsely alluring display; Mallarmé had a dubious respect for kings, spoke of artists being the new aristocracy (see "Cour"). This line may recall "roi de ce monde ... [présentant] le front de l'enfant aux étoiles ... 'Contemplez ce qui est plus grand que vous'" (Baudelaire, "Levana," *Paradis artificiels*).

We note in passing the series of golden glows, as in *Ses purs ongles,* in the *or* of *tordent, mort, orgueil.*

tordent: In *Igitur* the gleams of furniture in the dark chamber of the spiritual crisis are like the constellations here: "[on voit] les meubles, *tordre* leurs chimères dans le vide" (440; compare the quotation under *espace* below).

mort: the feeling of agony—the night shade—of the whole meditation; there is also the hint that stars are consuming themselves: "La vie s'alimente ... d'une mort continuelle" (901), or that the cosmos is dying, whether through entropy or an apocalypse, as in the *Coup de Dés,* where the stars are an "hallucination éparse d'agonie" (Page 9), "avant de s'arrêter" (Page 11). It may be further hinted that some stars are already dead, though we see their delayed light: "les diamants élus / D'une étoile, mourante, et qui ne brille plus" *(Ouverture ancienne);* compare "Toute naissance est une destruction et toute vie d'un moment l'agonie dans laquelle on ressucite ce qu'on a perdu, pour voir" (EL, p. 352); or, again, "sourdant que nié" *(Coup de Dés,* Page 9); "Astre qui dans la nuit immense / S'éteint" (6).

menti: used as a synonym of *démenti.*

solitaire ébloui de sa foi: this is the central theme of the prose poem *La Gloire.*

Oui, je sais qu'au lointain de cette nuit, la Terre	Yes, [a cry of affirmation!] I know that far-off into the night, the Earth
Jette d'un grand éclat l'insolite mystère,	Throws the unprecedented mystery of a great burst of light,
Sous les siècles hideux qui l'obscurcissent moins.	Under the hideous centuries that obscure it [the Earth] less [since the glow].
L'espace à soi pareil qu'il s'accroisse ou se nie	Space like unto itself whether it grow or deny itself [shrink]
Roule dans cet ennui des feux vils pour témoins	Rolls in this boredom vile fires as [mere] witnesses
Que s'est d'un astre en fête allumé le génie.	That the genius of a festive planet has lit up.

Oui: echoes *ébloui.*

éclat . . . mystère: "Illuminé au même mystère qui m'élut," (variant of *Cantique de Saint Jean,* N, p. 183), the original Eros, as in "illuminé par Eros" (first version of the *Faune)* or "les astres . . . l'Amour les meut et les assemble" (303).

l'espace à soi pareil: "Quelle agonie, aussi, qu'agite la Chimère [deepest yet illusory Vision] versant par ses blessures d'or [cf. the stars here] l'évidence de tout l'être pareil" (648); "si c'était le nombre ce serait LE HASARD" *(Coup de Dés).* Mallarmé's idea of all reality as tautological—except possibly the miracle of genius, an emanation of deity which can (paradoxically) inform all reality—was influenced by Poe's *Eureka.* The *tordent dans leur mort* of the sonnet is reflected by the same passage of "La Musique et les Lettres" which we just quoted: "tout l'être pareil, nulle torsion vaincue ne fausse ni ne transgresse l'omniprésente Ligne [cf. the *guirlande* of the sonnet] espacée de tout point à tout autre pour instituer l'idée; sinon sous le visage humain, mystérieuse, en tant qu'une harmonie est pure" (648). As in the tercets of *Une dentelle,* this *guirlande-constellation-Ligne-chimère* can also be the *ligne,* or *fil de dentelle,* of writing: "Ce pli de sombre dentelle" (1565).

qu'il s'accroisse ou se nie: "commençât-il et cessât-il . . . se chiffrât-il . . . ce serait pire / non davantage / mais indifféremment LE HA-SARD" *(Coup de Dés).*

roule: "une constellation . . . roulant" *(Coup de Dés,* Page 11).

feux vils: "selon telle obliquité par telle déclivité / de feux . . . une constellation" *(Coup de Dés);* compare: "Ces *vils* fruits ne sont que *mensonge* / Pour un oeil ravi d'épier / Tout l'éclatant jardin du songe" (117). The overtone of *feu,* defunctive, is clear from Mallarmé's conscious avoidance of the pun in "feu le grand Opéra (sans jeu de mots)" (845); the *eu* is dull, flat, as in "rien n'aura eu lieu que le lieu" *(Coup de Dés,* Page 10).

astre: the same idea of the genius of our planet—*astre*—is exploited in *Toast funèbre:* "le devoir idéal que nous font les jardins de cet astre."

NOTE

[1]
Oui le penseur en vain dans ses essors funèbres
Heurte son âme d'ombre au plafond des ténèbres.
(Hugo, in Cellier, p. 60.)   *

13. LE VIERGE, LE VIVACE ET LE BEL AUJOURD'HUI

◈◈◈◈◈◈◈◈◈

There is a comparatively clear drama in this sonnet (first published in 1885)[1]: that of the exiled swan who is caught in the ice, and who desires above all to be free, free; or, at another level, the poet who is held in the dull here-on-earth but aspires to a Platonic perfection of beauty. The *"vierge* . . . aujourd'hui" is the *new* day, morning-young, with a fresh promise of innocent delight. It is one of those winter days which carry with them (like Eliot's "midwinter spring"), according to a typically poetic ambivalence, a hint of something more exquisite than what we know on earth. And so it may tear asunder our prison of mediocrity, we hope, for a wild *(ivre)* moment: "O see the pulse of summer in the ice" (Dylan Thomas).

But the "swan" has failed to follow that impulse to freedom, in the past—a total impulse which, like that of the Manicheans, or of Tristan and Iseult, would mean death in the consummation of one pure moment (either religious or artistic or even sexual)—and this failure[2] is a continuing one, the condition of the poet's vain, merely human, existence: *exil inutile.* For it is here as with the window *(glace:* glass or ice) of *Les Fenêtres* which—"que ce soit l'art ou la mysticité"—cannot be broken without violating the conditions of art or vision, or, at another level, of life itself. The clown of *Le Pitre châtié* who broke through the tent wall was deprived of his gift; the poet figure of *Les Fenêtres* knew that if he crashed through the windowpane he would fall, like Lucifer, through eternity. This Promethean gesture is the essence of hubris, of an infringement of the rules of the human *Jeu;* a heresy, at whatever level. And so the kinetic impulse to break loose is not followed: "le jeu se borne à une perpétuelle allusion sans briser la glace" (310).

The ice in which the bird is trapped is, at one level, these frozen layers of his past history, deep, crystallized dream-memories: *un cygne se souvient.* His past is, so to speak, all around him in this static, and oddly ecstatic, moment. The whole poem is a relatively still "epiphany" rather than a dynamic drama. The defeat, in the drama, is not regarded as a merely negative element but is subsumed, circularly (in a manner

of speaking) into a harmonious effect, something like a delicious midwinter shiver: the hint of spring amid cold, a mirage of light in the ice   *
(like the infinite glint in the slivers we children used to chip from the
huge blocks icemen brought some years ago). And although the words,
in a linear progression, tell a story on the basis of their ordinary meanings, they also, like the star-words of the *Coup de Dés,* radiate among
each other—in a crystal-like or constellar pattern—to create a vibrant
atmosphere well beyond that rather commonplace message. For example, the key word *hiver* is tightly interlocked with five other words   *
all of which contain the letters *i, v, e, r,* and with numerous other words
featuring the *i* sound.

The kinetic impulse that is not followed is primarily as we have
defined it, but it has a corollary aspect of flight from the ivory tower,
from creative alienation to ordinary life. Some critics (e.g. Noulet)
have seen this as the essential meaning of *la région où vivre* as opposed
to the usual one of purity, the absolute. But I see no need to take sides
here: why not both? The "swan" is precisely at a crossroads of reality
with untaken paths in various possible directions. Just so, the clown's
mistaken flight in *Le Pitre châtié* is variously a plunge into the love-death
baptism of a sexual act or is a springing into the absolute of a mystic
experience, the poet's heaven.   *

The swan is an ideal symbol or motif. It is a natural focus of much
reality: its pure whiteness, its usually earth-bound wings, the long, aspiring, yet gracefully curving "resigned" neck, with its eternal interrogation (head meditatively bowed, it seems to be peering down and
inward at its soul secrets); its remaining behind disdainfully in winter
when the other birdlings have flown; its proud isolation on the lake and
lordlike demeanor, as contrasted to the lesser ducks; the swan song it
sings before its death (actually true for some varieties); the psychic
depth of revery of the waters it floats on; the ambiguity of the "male"
neck and the nymph-like sensuality of its naked form (see Bachelard:
L'Eau et les rêves).   *

The terrible purity aimed at, the fierce tension of the creative struggle implied, is stressed by the wintry whiteness against the swan's whiteness. And yet, we, no more than the swan, would not really leave, not
while we have our pride and strength. Like Wallace Stevens standing
on the windswept hill, we, too, cry, even as the air pangs our lungs:
"This health is holy" or Rimbaud's "que salubre est le vent!." The
first line of Mallarmé's sonnet is a pure inhalation of this pathetic,
tender, but also bracing, persistent *(vivace)* and heady challenge:
          "[O] The virgin, hardy and beautiful today"   *
The diamond-like crystalline structure of this complexly interlock-

ing sonnet, and the similar aspects of the winter day it describes (crystal-ice, cold purity) are emphasized by the fourteen rimes in *i* (bright, acute) and many other *i*'s and other hard, lucid effects.

Le vierge, le vivace et le bel aujourd'-hui	[O] The virgin, hardy and beautiful today
Va-t-il nous déchirer avec un coup d'aile ivre	Will it rend for us with a drunken wing-beat
Ce lac dur oublié que hante sous le givre	This hard forgotten lake [that is] haunted under the frost
Le transparent glacier des vols qui n'ont pas fui!	By the transparent glacier of untaken flights!

The poem begins with one of those winter mornings which, after a dreary hopeless season, offer a Promise! The sun, gleaming like a poignant mirage in the cold, may thaw the ice, rip it open, releasing the soul to a drunken flight to freedom, as in *Brise marine:* "là-bas fuir! Je sens que des oiseaux sont ivres." Yet we may know in advance there will be no taking this "easy way out" (as Rimbaud said, "on ne part pas"): all the flights that were untaken in the past (the *transparent glacier* is the frozen reservoir of *vols qui n'ont pas fui*) have led to this representative one, which will not be taken—led up through autumn of this one year, but also through all the summers and autumns of all the years, to this crucial winter: "After many a summer . . . ."

The untaken flights are primarily to freedom—"Le cygne [rendu] à l'espace" (616)—or to the Ideal: "Est-il moyen / D'enfoncer le cristal . . . et de m'enfuir, avec mes deux ailes sans plume—Au risque de tomber pendant l'éternité?" (*Les Fenêtres*). Indulging the total hubris, like Lucifer's, would have led to total Fall: "Qu'un sujet si grand vostre plume n'estonne / Plus l'argument est grand, plus Cygne vous mourrez," Ronsard wrote in his *Amours* (Garnier ed., p. 271).

The flights are, secondarily, to the direct action of others' pursuits: love, career, and so forth, as in *L'Azur*. Or, to repeat, there is a corollary possibility of, so to speak, *horizontal* flight from the ivory tower, from creative remoteness, toward conventional life. Ultimately, of course, as a poet, Mallarmé favors not fleeing from his "sweet frustrations" (Richard Wilbur), the vibrantly potential: "un noble oeuf de cygne, tel que n'en jaillira le vol" (286). The swan is very like the ballet dancer with "cette espèce d'extatique impuissance à disparaître qui délicieusement attache aux planchers la danseuse" (305). This *extatique impuissance,* to be sure, is not just plain "sterility" but a very special kind—the "negative capability" of art.

In the word *vierge* a tension, running throughout Mallarmé, is felt between an erotic "ground bass" and a heavenly purity. The tension is like that of Hérodiade, the swan princess, between her virginity and her hidden passion, between her "trembling" nakedness and her "modesty"; it is the tension of the snowy whiteness itself.[3] *Vierge-neige-cierge* (white candle) are part of a major cluster which accounts for some of the uneasy emotional power of *Plainte d'automne*, as well as of *Hérodiade*. The swan is a sensuous creature as well as pure (it reminded Proust of Albertine's naked thighs). Its curves are feminine, its whiteness nude, that startling "animal whiteness" in which nymphs and swans were confused in the *Faune;* compare "Femme et cygnes ici confondus . . . le cygne, secouant sa neige, disparaît, la vierge reste" (616). In this we sense the strange undercurrents that make the swan and the woman akin, even as the swan (with its long neck) takes a male role, as in the similarly ambiguous and powerful Leda motif:

> Un col fléxible et blanc se courbe et plonge en l'onde . . .
> . . . .
> Il ploya son blanc col moelleux comme la mousse
> Autour du sein brûlant de la nymphe qui rit
> . . . Sous son aile il dépose
> La nymphe frémissante: ils ne forment qu'un corps.
> Loeda se renversa, la paupière mi-close,
> Les lèvres s'entrouvrant . . . sourit dans cette pose . . .
> —Et la nuit tomba noire et voila leurs transports.
> (*Loeda,* in *Mallarmé lycéen*)

Compare the subtle modulation between paired females and the male-female couple in the *Faune.*

The *v*'s of *vierge* and *vivace,* and of other words, are sharp, cutting, by the outer shape and sound, like saw-teeth or icicles (in this respect they go with the tearing wing-thrust). But, oddly, they also add a quality of virginal femininity by the inner shape of receptacle (see Letter Table: *v* and *w*). This is furthered subtly by the *vierge* ("virile" yet feminine) and some overtones of *vol* (*volupté, viol, viole,* etc.). The troubling and delightful ambiguity persists.

va-t-il nous déchirer: for a moment we feel that it is *we* who are being torn; later we see that the *nous* is (also) a dative of interest: "for us (myself)."

coup d'aile: the symbolism of wing-beat as impulse, sudden aspiration, is obvious and traditional since the Renaissance, and before. The Romantics (Lamartine, Keats, Shelley) added richness to the image. To give it exclusive importance in Mallarmé, as J.-P. Weber does, is to err as much as the propagators of all the other exclusive approaches. Mallarmé likes the image because he can add his own richnesses to it, as he does, for example, with the dialectic movement of opened and closed

wings, which haunts *Igitur* and is present in the two shapes of a fan
(cf. *Autre éventail*): "un équilibre momentané et double à la façon du
vol, identité de deux fragments constitutifs" (333); compare "comme
une aile . . . bifurque" (393). The simple aspiration is expressed in
"L'éternel coup d'aile" (730), "aile l'esprit" (60)," "coups d'aile de
la pensée voulant s'élever plus haut encore" (Propos, p. 49). Compare
vols, below.

lac dur oublié: the frozen reservoir of dream, of all untaken past
impulses which had been "forgotten" and are revivified on this fresh
morning. The pure narcissistic stasis of art (a delightful mirror) can
become a stagnant, frozen *ennui,* or even horror, as in *Igitur:* "la glace
. . . pris dans son froid" (441). But there is hope of a spring, a thaw.

There is a telling vibration between *lac* and *glacier;* this is the
way a poem crystallizes. *Oublié,* Chassé observed, is attached etymologically to "livid," adding a touch of wintry discoloration as in "Sur
les bois oubliés." The *c* of *lac* is hard, crisp; the *a* is the flat surface;
the *d* of *dur* is hard; its *u* bright, like the "transparency" beneath the
hoar frost. The *o* and *b* emphasize the roundness of the lake (compare
Ô *miroir* of *Hérodiade*).

hante: the untaken acts are like those of Hamlet, *"le latent seigneur
qui ne peut devenir"* (300) and "qui *hantera* les esprits" (299). See
C, pp. 218-219.

transparent: the *ar* (and reverse, *ra*), along with its clear meaning,
establishes the word amid the *ar(t)*-cluster, as in "paroles . . . clair,
pluie et diamant, le regard diaphane" *(Toast funèbre)* or "para . . .
lucide . . . jardins sépara" *(Prose).* It was similarly used for the spiritual
depths symbolized by water in the first version of the *Coup de Dés,*
Page 3 (C, p. 153), and in an early version of *Le Pitre châtié:* "la
clarté transparente . . . Des sources." Here, of course, the water is
frozen, adding the icy diamantine quality of static art, crystallization, as
in Hérodiade's "clair regard de diamant."

glacier: echoes *acier* (they rime in *Ouverture ancienne*) as well
as *lac.*

vols: the trapped nature of the flight is somewhat present in the *v*:
"dove: colombe (oiseau dont le vol plonge)" (949); "vol . . . plonge"
(51); compare the held wing of *Autre éventail* and consult C, p. 147.

fui: "Fuir! là-bas fuir! Je sens que des oiseaux sont ivres" *(Brise
marine);* the word is very bright and acute (*u* and *i*) and dynamic (*f*).
A possible meaning noted by Chisholm is that the past untaken flights
are unforgotten, not *fled* from his memory.

Un cygne d'autrefois se souvient que c'est lui	A swan of former years remembers it is he

Magnifique mais qui sans espoir se   Magnificent but who without hope
   délivre   frees himself
Pour n'avoir pas chanté la région où For not having sung the region in
   vivre   which to live
Quand du stérile hiver a resplendi   When sterile winter's ennui shone.
   l'ennui.

cygne d'autrefois gives a time dimension in depth to the drama or
Passion; it is, in a sense, the aging poet—"vivant d'autrefois" (ML, p.
190)—remembering all his life's drama, with its typically creative extremes of magnificence and failure, or the total soaring (swan-like)
aspiration which—since it would mean death—is renounced as hopeless. Yet, like the constellation of the *Coup de Dés,* this total defeat
through an absurd dilemma springs, via a meta-paradox, obliquely, into
an unhoped-for victory, the poem.

Though it is not directly suggested in the poem, we may feel that
Mallarmé is remembering his old swan theme, in *Hérodiade.* The solitary swan-princess was close to her creator and sang a desperately resigned, pure-as-stars swan song:

> Comme un cygne cachant en sa plume ses yeux en l'éternelle allée
> De ses espoirs, pour voir les diamants élus
> D'une étoile, mourante, et qui ne brille plus.
> (*Ouverture ancienne*)

A variant of these lines emphasizes the notion of *former* power:
"fuite antique [du] cygne" (N, p. 152).

Compare: "Loeda voit à son front / Scintiller une étoile!"
                                        (*Loeda,* in ML)

The ironic quality of this scintillating "sterility" vivifies even the
"ennui of sterile winter" with a splendid sheen (the overtone of *lui:*
shone; the bright *u* and *i* illuminate *ennui* as well). The *ennui*—"l'ennui
dans le métal cruel d'un miroir" (264)—is rather like that of Hérodiade's narcissistic mirror. It, too, had the dreariness of monotonous ice
(*glace:* ice, glass mirror) or of a flat, hard, impenetrable reflecting surface
—still, its exasperating sterility could gush into a "fountain" of remembered feeling (like the *miroirs profonds* of Baudelaire's *Invitation
au voyage*). This ice in one aspect is a sensual *block,* more clearly so
than the mirror, for it is a fully three-dimensional body of crystallization,
a frozen reservoir of emotion . . . which can melt:

> Ô miroir!
> Eau froide par l'ennui dans ton cadre gelée
> Que de fois et pendant des heures, désolée
> Des songes et cherchant mes souvenirs qui sont

Comme des feuilles sous ta glace au trou profond,
Je m'apparus en toi comme une ombre lointaine,
Mais, horreur! des soirs, dans ta sévère fontaine,
J'ai de mon rêve épars connu la nudité!

This "distant shadow" of the self is the unreality that the artist is often to himself (especially before a mirror in the dusk) and is also his phantom-like almost-forgotten former self (the child, the adolescent). Both ideas are implied in the "phantom" that is the swan of the sonnet.

région: is primarily, as we said, the final one of beauty that Mallarmé always sought, the artist's perfect taunting azure *(L'Azur)*, his paradise, which one could only reach, as he often suggested, through a sort of martyrdom, losing all to gain all, becoming impersonal as a God. This is not, obviously, physical death, as of the religious martyrs who rose to sainthood. But the poet in his vicarious way, by an inner or spiritual death—absolute resignation, abnegation of will, and surpassing of the ego[4]—achieves some approximation to that beatitude in the near-perfection of his poems.

région: is also, less significantly, the ordinary life to which he might flee (the swan is at a crossroads of possible flights):

Vers toi j'accours, donne, ô matière
L'oubli de l'Idéal cruel et du Péché
A ce martyr qui vient partager la litière
Où le bétail heureux des hommes est couché
(*L'Azur*)

Angoisse and *Tristesse d'été* speak of similar escapes.
The overtone of *verre* in *hiver* reflects the *glacier, lac dur.*

Tout son col secouera cette blanche agonie	All his neck will shake off that white agony
Par l'espace infligée à l'oiseau qui le nie,	By space inflicted on the bird which denies it,
Mais non l'horreur du sol où le plumage est pris.	But not [shake off] the horror of the ground in which the plumage is caught.

Literally, the swan may shake off the snow that the Mother-heaven has thrown on it, like a taunting or mocking insult, for not having dared to fly away into it. The deeper meaning is that the bird has stoically rid itself of an impossible dream of beauty, like a flight into free space, or perhaps to unreal summer skies in the south (cf. *Prose*). It could dispel an illusion but not the hard fact of being caught in the ice on northern ground:

Ce très blanc ébat au ras du sol dénie
À tout site l'honneur du paysage faux [dreamed-of summer]
(*Mes bouquins refermés*)

The "white agony," snow, or the swan's own whiteness, is an emissary of the cruelly pure Ideal which mocks the poet for having denied it, as in *L'Azur.* In that poem he summoned up a ceiling of fog to block off the view of his tormentor. Here the poet-swan suffers defenselessly—*agonie*—and can merely shake his head in refusal, "shake it off." The whiteness of the swan and of the snow coalesce here, as in another passage: "Le cygne secouant sa neige" (616). We are forcefully reminded also of Baudelaire's *Cygne,* with its *cou convulsif* stretched toward the Ideal. This stark black-and-white effect of voluptuous agony is especially fine and has been rendered by a series of Matisse pen drawings for the sonnet.[5] Note the vibrancy between *col (cou)* and *secouera.*

*

Fantôme qu'à ce lieu son pur éclat assigne,
Il s'immobilise au songe froid de mépris
Que vêt parmi l'exil inutile le Cygne.

Phantom assigned to this place by his pure brightness,
He immobilizes himself in the cold dream of scorn
Which is put on amid the useless exile by the swan.

In the first line, the image is of the creature who by his very superiority—disdainfully he stayed behind, alone, a bit like Vigny's Moses—is assigned, or held, to this location of bitter truth. He is a phantom in various senses: a white swan in a white landscape is a spectral apparition; he is a mere shadow of his summer self in this landscape. As the adult Mallarmé, he is a wisp of his former youthful self; and, as an artist, he is somewhat unreal.

assigne implies an appropriateness of juxtaposition: white swan in white landscape; his *pur éclat* makes it fitting for him to be there. More importantly, there is the sense that this is the stoically expected and accepted fate of genius, solitude and the terrible honesty that will not allow him to escape the "absurd."

In the second line, he seems to become more and more rigidly fixed in the ice; inwardly he accepts his fate as a coldly proud isolated artist.

*

The "useless exile" is his artistic remoteness or alienation: "useless" primarily because the highest ideal is not reached: Mallarmé continuously lamented the "mediocrity" of his offered production (with terms like "exercises," "divagations," etc.) as opposed to his dreamed-of one. But another important sense is that true art—as in the doctrine of Gautier—is useless, impersonal, like the constellation *froide d'oubli et de désuétude* on the final page of the *Coup de Dés.*

lieu: a neutral word, largely because of that pallid *eu;* hence Mallarmé uses it for deserted space, as in the empty universe, of Page 10 of the *Coup de Dés:* "rien n'aura eu lieu que le lieu."

immobilise: the *o* aids the static effect; the *b* is delicately suggestive of the swan.

vêt: note that the swan is the subject, hence there is a nuance of "willed exile" or "accepted fate," *amor fati.* The circumflex is vaguely suggestive of fallen aspiration.

Cygne: the possibility of an overtone of *signe* has been suggested (the rhyme with *signe* occurs in *Ouverture ancienne*): the swan is a symbol. This, however, adds little or nothing poetically;[6] more likely is the minor vibration of the constellation *Cygne,* noted by Lawler and Champigny.

NOTES

[1] First published in the *Revue indépendante;* later, without variation, in the *Poésies* (1887). Almost everyone has written a swan poem; we naturally think first of Baudelaire's *Albatros* and, even more, *Le Cygne;* Mallarmé's sonnet undoubtedly owes something to the latter. Mondor also mentions Gautier's:

> Un cygne s'est pris en nageant
> Dans le bassin des Tuileries.
>
> (1480)

To which Cellier adds a passage from *Mlle de Maupin*: "pèlerin ... qui ... se réveillerait en hiver les jambes prises et emboîtées dans la glace." In *Magnitudo parvi,* Hugo associates the swan with snow and death (Cellier).

[2] An archetype of all our human compromises, going back perhaps to the defeat of the little boy in the family situation, but actually beyond that to a basic mystery. Still, the Oedipal idea is highly suggestive: the flight has overtones of violation of the total Mother as in the *Faune* (cf. the Hebrew marriage ritual in which glass is broken, symbolizing accession to adulthood.)

[3] White is the color of purity; but Melville, in *Moby Dick,* says it is also the color of evil, more, even, than black.

[4] This idea is common to various mystic religions or philosophies, often Oriental. Schopenhauer took it from Indian religion (Maya, Nirvana). Zen Buddhism has recently been the source for Western writers (Salinger, Kerouac).

[5] Compare the "terrible speed" of the "rapids" in the windblown white laundry in Wilbur's *Things of this World.*

[6] "Les cygnes comprennent les signes" (Hugo, *Les Misérables*). The occasionally suggested "par mille exils" adds even less.

14. VICTORIEUSEMENT FUI LE SUICIDE BEAU

◇❊◇❊◇❊◇❊◇

This celebrated love sonnet draws some of its imagery from the *Hérodiade* period, as we can see clearly in various fragments of the *Noces d'Hérodiade*. Mallarmé tried it on his wife and perhaps other early loves before bestowing it finally on the buxom and definitive Méry Laurent.

A magnificent sundown, which provides the theme, is a spectacle—suggesting the death (perhaps suicide) of a hero or god—much favored by Mallarmé. On its lofty stage, the glorious holocaust dramatizes the absurdity of all creation. It brings an honest awareness of death, or the death of meaning, which is both "suicidal" and exalting, "beautiful." Like the paradox of Zeno that "kills" his disciple Valéry (in *Le Cimetière marin*), this eternal drama, *vanitas vanitatum,* is something of both Tragedy—"LA TRAGÉDIE DE LA NATURE," (1169)—and Comedy. The comedy prevails in the sense that the poet leaps forward, having survived or "victoriously fled" once again what is really only an inner suicide (sincere as it is), or awareness of the absurd. The total dilemma is resolved even more securely by the "arational" outburst, the Olympian *rire,* which expresses a sort of victory of health, a sane abdication of pride in a limit-situation. Life goes on. And if he has not won the total struggle of self-expression which he, of all poets, repeatedly confronted—an artistic *coup* to end all *coups*—well, that is bitterly disappointing but it cannot be helped. As an explosion of light, celebrating a victory, there is, not the fireworks of the poet's glory-in-achievement, but the fair hair of his beloved (a humbler version of the constellation-after-defeat of the *Coup de Dés*). At first casually noticed, as a weak substitute for the Real Thing, it suddenly flares up in an expression of enthusiasm for life and love, very much like the exultation of *Quelle soie au baume du temps.*

Victorieusement fui le suicide beau	Victoriously fled the beautiful suicide [sunset]
Tison de gloire, sang par écume, or, tempête!	Firebrand of glory, blood through foam, gold, storm!

133

Ô rire si là-bas une pourpre s'apprête   O laugh if yonder a purple [cloth] is
                                           readied
A ne tendre royal que mon absent   To cover royally nothing but mv ab-
tombeau.   sent tomb.

Victorieusement: is both the glorious sunset and the literal "victory"
of the poet who did not perish in that conflagration. This death-and-
transfiguration myth, of a hero or god, taken direct from nature, is the
central theme of the *Dieux antiques:* "*La Tragédie de la Nature*—la
bataille du Soleil avec les nuages qui se rassemblent autour de lui comme
de mortels ennemis, à son coucher. Comme il s'enfonce, les brumes
ardentes l'étreignent et les vapeurs de pourpre se jettent par le ciel,
ainsi que des ruisseaux de sang qui jaillissent du corps du mythe; tandis
que les *nuages violets* couleur du soir semblent le consoler dans l'agonie
de sa disparition" (1216). The idea of blood and a covering funeral
cloth (*nuages violets*) are directly echoed in the sonnet. The militant
note of "victory" is echoed in the *casque guerrier* below; the woman
symbolizes, and somewhat shares, his special glory.

Compare: "l'agonie du jour sous l'oppression *victorieuse* de la nuit"
(Baudelaire, *Crépuscule du soir*).

In the *Coup de Dés,* Page 4, the *conflagration* is the possibility of a
total victory man sees reflected in a sundown—an *eritis sicut dii*—but
a victory that he foregoes in order to survive as a mere man, as Mallarmé
does also in the sonnet.[1]

fui: the heroic flight untaken by the poet (as in *Le vierge, le vivace);*
suicide avoided; and the fading of the sunset glow.

absent tombeau: is, like the famous "absente de tous bouquets,"
the vivid *idea* of a tomb, glimpsed as a possibility: "pourpre dans la
nue l'universel sacre de l'intrus royal qui n'aura eu qu'à venir" (289).

rire: is double, a victory of health or sanity (survival) and a bitter
laugh at the disappointment of not being a hero.

victorieusement: is a long, elaborate, decoratively baroque word
which suits the lavish pomp of the sunset; sounds of *or* or *ri* (or *rieuse)*
in it are echoed by the *or* and *gloire* and *rire* of the next lines; the flood
of compromised light is emphasized by many bright sounds in the line,
especially in *fui* and *suicide.*

The second line is chock full of magnificent, furiously curdled,
stormy, fiery effects like:

> Crime! bûcher! aurore ancienne! supplice!
> Pourpre d'un ciel! Étang de la pourpre complice!
>   (*Ouverture ancienne*)

suicide: "bûcher [sunset], les jours évaporés en majestueux suspens

. . . ce *suicide"* (402). In the early version of *Ses purs ongles,* the onset of night is described as a *pur Crime,* killing the Phoenix-sun.

sang par écume: the paradisiacal milk of the azure is here whipped up to a creamy foam, reminding us of the milk and blood of Hérodiade's deepest obsessions (and, much farther back, the bloody snow, mirroring Blancheflor's cheeks, which sent Perceval into a religious-erotic swoon).

Quoi! de tout cet éclat pas même le lambeau	What! of all that outburst of light not even a shred
S'attarde, il est minuit, à l'ombre qui nous fête	Remains, it is midnight, in the shadow which fetes us
Excepté qu'un trésor présomptueux de tête	Except that a presumptuous treasure of a head
Verse son caressé nonchaloir sans flambeau,	Spills its caressed nonchalance without a torch,
La tienne si toujours le délice! la tienne	[The head being] Yours [yes, or] if [there is] still the delight! yours
Oui seule qui du ciel évanoui retienne	Yes alone which from the vanished sky retains
Un peu de puéril triomphe en t'en coiffant	A bit of puerile triumph by wearing it [the victorious light as hair]
Avec clarté quand sur les coussins tu la poses	With brightness when you rest it [your head] on the cushions
Comme un casque guerrier d'impératrice enfant	Like a war helmet [her pompadour] on an imperious girl
Dont pour te figurer il tomberait des roses.	Whence to symbolize you [your pink cheeks] roses would fall.

The scene changes in the second quatrain: the poet lies with his mistress at midnight, in the starlit or moonlit shadow—half-light—which fetes them, surrounds their love cosily and touches her hair with discreet illumination.

il est minuit: the calm statement (though the instant is pointed: *i, u),* reflects the end-of-cycle neutrality of that mysterious moment (Chisholm). Debussy uses a similar effect in *Pelléas et Mélisande.*

The use of *fête* for half-light is found in "une fête s'exalte en la feuillée éteinte" *(L'Après-midi d'un faune)* and "matin . . . verse, sur les lointains mourants, ses tristes fêtes" *(Hérodiade).* The neutral sound of *ê* and the Icarian circumflex have much to do with these usages.

lambeau: a similar use is found in *L'Azur:* "Mon âme vide . . . lambeaux."

Excepté: this is like the *Excepté* which introduced the final page of the *Coup de Dés:* from the black night of an apocalypse, a glimmer of light from distant stars promising a possible new life.[2]

présomptueux: the head is "presumptuous" in usurping or taking over the role of that sunset, or the poet's glory.[3] An important element is *somptueux,* the luxuriant hair. The round *o,* swelling *p* and wavy *u*'s are helpful here.

trésor: is illuminated a bit by *or.*

nonchaloir: the caressing *ch* echoes the word *caressé next to it.* Baudelaire slept here: *La Chevelure* is a "parfum chargé de nonchaloir."

si: is ambiguously "yes!," an affirmation against the tentative negative of "What! . . . no shred [is left]"; or "if [there is] still a [some] delight [in the world]." *Si* is a favorite effect of Mallarmé's for a brilliant sharp interjection, as in the lightning-like *SI* (Page 8) of the *Coup de Dés* (C, pp. 305-307) or various Saint Jean fragments (N, pp. 167, 169). The dramatic verticality of this "lightning" is reinforced by the *i* versus *ou* contrast of *si* and *toujours,* like the *boue-rubis* of *Tombeau de Charles Baudelaire* or the corollary *si plonge* of *Petit air I;* the exclamation mark nearby is similarly effective, as it is in the famous *Lys!* of the *Faune.*

La tienne: is "your head," referring to his mistress.[4] The *toujours,* we agree with Chisholm, is gallant.

puéril: the child-woman association is traditional and occurs often in Mallarmé: *Prose:* "L'enfant [his feminine companion] abdique son extase"; Hérodiade is a "froide enfant." (Baudelaire's "Mon enfant, ma soeur," Vigny's "enfant malade," come to mind.) This puerile (virginal, young, somewhat androgynous and militant) quality of Hérodiade persists in the imagery, much of which can be found in the fragments of the *Noces:*

> Ainsi qu'un casque d'impératrice enfant (N, p. 157)
>
> D'où pour te figurer, il tomberait des roses (N, p. 158)
>
> Comme un casque léger d'impératrice enfant
> . . . .
> D'où pour feindre sa joue il tomberait des roses (N, p. 158)

Baudelaire had observed a like quality in his women:

> Tes cheveux, comme un casque bleu,
> Ombrageant ton front de guerrière

Hérodiade was a princess—like the *impératrice enfant* here—descended from warriors; arms decorated her wall, "attirail de siècle belliqueux" *(Ouverture ancienne).*[5]

The idea of putting on one's head a symbol of glory, like a plume—light or a lightning flash—is prominent in the *Coup de Dés,* Page 8: "quiconque / prince amer de l'écueil / s'en coiffe . . . en foudre," which refers to the "plume" (from the top of the Page), the mad ambition, total art.

There is a striking series of *o*'s in the last line: "Dont . . . tomberait des roses." The effect is of the round helmet, something like a horn of plenty (with a slight echo of *dont-don*) spilling forth beauty, and also suggests the round roses and cheeks, as in *Rondel II:* "rose . . . interromps . . . les ronds" (the mouths puckered for a kiss).

NOTES

[1] Variant:

Toujours plus souriant au désastre plus beau,
Soupirs de sang, or meurtrier, pâmoison, fête!
Une millième fois avec ardeur s'apprête
Mon solitaire amour à vaincre le tombeau.

The meaning is ·clear: the poet for a "thousandth" time exults in a sunset glow—as we know not only from his texts but from many anecdotes about him that he did indeed—symbolizing his immortal, tomb-vanquishing, poetic glory, his *solitaire amour* as opposed to the shared love of the next quatrain.

[2] Variant: "Quoi! de tout ce coucher" emphasized the love-death motif, perhaps too heavily.

[3] Variant: "un trésor trop folâtre" emphasized the come-down, apparently too much.

[4] Variant: "La tienne, si toujours frivole" further emphasizes the let-down and supports the partial interpretation of the *si* as "if", though the meaning has shifted considerably.

[5] Variant: "Un peu de désolé combat" referring to the sunset-struggle leads to the helmet image, as "triumph" does in the final version. This whole theme was treated, with remarkably similar imagery, by Ronsard, in his *Sonnets pour Hélène*, I, xi:

Le soleil...
...comme ébloui de ta vive lumière
Ne pouvant la souffrir s'en alla tout honteux
Je ... devins glorieux
D'avoir vaincu ce dieu ...
Quand regardant vers moi tu me dis, ma guerrière:
"Ce soleil est fâcheux, je t'aime beaucoup mieux."

A certain resonance in the name of Augusta Holmès (*heaulme*: helmet) may have been subtly influential here. Augusta, whose first name also smacks of virility, was notoriously masculine in bearing, as well as beautiful (Biog., p. 285).

15. SES PURS ONGLES

A blend of agonizing mystery and geometric precision, somewhat reminiscent of a Redon etching, has puzzled and fascinated many a reader in this much-anthologized sonnet. Though not published before 1887, it is Mallarmé's first truly hermetic poem. The early version, "Sonnet allégorique de lui-même," was written at the time of the well-known major crisis during which Mallarmé had his Vision and projected his lifework. He claimed the sonnet had nothing to do with this, but we can quote, against himself, his later statement "Jamais pensée ne se présente à moi détachée" (883) and insist that the piece reflects some of his main themes and obsessions. It also demonstrates (this he was aware of) his increasingly complex use of language, the famous "réciprocité de feux" (386). Thus a letter to Cazalis (July 18, 1868), informs us:

J'extrais ce sonnet, auquel j'avais songé cet été, d'une étude projetée sur *la Parole*: il est inverse, je veux dire que le sens s'il en a un (mais je me consolerais du contraire grâce à la dose de poésie qu'il renferme, ce me semble) est évoqué par un mirage interne des mots mêmes. En se laissant aller à la murmurer plusieurs fois, on éprouve une sensation assez cabalistique.[1] C'est confesser qu'il est peu "plastique" comme tu me le demandes, mais au moins est-il aussi "blanc et noir" que possible; et il me semble se prêter à une eau-forte pleine de Rêve et de Vide. Par exemple, une fenêtre nocturne ouverte, les deux volets attachés; une chambre, avec personne dedans, malgré l'air stable que présentent les volets attachés, et dans une nuit faite d'absence et d'interrogation, sans meubles, sinon l'ébauche plausible de vagues consoles, un cadre, belliqueux[2] et agonisant, de miroir appendu au fond, avec sa réflexion, stellaire et incomprehénsible, de la grande Ourse, qui relie au ciel seul ce logis abandonné du monde. J'ai pris ce sujet d'un sonnet nul et se réfléchissant de toutes les façons, parce que mon oeuvre est si bien préparée et hiérarchisée, représentant comme il le peut, l'Univers, que je n'aurais su, sans endommager quelqu'une de mes impressions étagées, rien en enlever —et aucun sonnet ne s'y rencontre.

But there can be no doubt that the poem is very close to Mallarmé's central preoccupations: the end of the *Coup de Dés* tells the story of the cosmos after the departure of *Le Maître,* Man (including the Poet), with the same cold distant image of the *Grande Ourse,* standing for the mystery of the eternal laws of Truth and Beauty whence may spring, Phoenix-like, a new life after death (the room gives way to the more impersonal site of the ocean and sky). Even the famous *aboli bibelot* of the sonnet is echoed in the major Poem, by the empty yet haunting *faux manoir,* which is a version of the "Glorious Lie" Mallarmé had early announced (Propos, p. 60) he would build into his great work. In the first line of the sonnet there is another minor prefiguration of the *Coup de Dés,* in the words *ongles . . . dédiant leur onyx.* Now, a somewhat abstruse cluster of associations for Mallarmé revolves around the word *nombre* (see Page 9 of the *Coup de Dés): thus dé* (from Latin *datum)* is associated with *digit (nombre)* which goes back etymologically to *digitum (doigt);* hence the stars, which are the symbol of *nombre* (mathematical number together with its etymological sense of "harmony," recalling Pythagoras' "music of the spheres") are like *ongles,* from Latin *ungula,* root also of the word *onyx.* These complex considerations may help to account for the grouping "ongles . . . dédiant . . . onyx." More important, the poem was deliberately constructed on a rime ending in *x* (see Appendix C) which is the letter representing the cross or, rather, Mallarmé's central epistemological concept which we call "double polarity" (see C, pp. 37-46; also the x-cross in *Le Livre de Mallarmé,* pp. 87-A, 80-B, etc.); this "cross" underlies the four phases of the title-phrase of *Un Coup de Dés,* what Mallarmé refers to as a "symphonic equation" (646). That is, four "crossed" seasons, four times of day, four musical movements, in sum, the quaternary archetype that has haunted the imagination of countless mystics and has been termed the very hallmark of the great C.G. Jung. Suzanne Bernard has recently pointed out, in her *Mallarmé et la Musique* (p. 143), how the revelation of *Le Livre* confirms our own earlier observations in this respect. This *x* is echoed also in the final page of the *Coup de Dés* (C, p. 395) along with some key words of the sonnet: *septentrion, nord, vacante, oubli, peut-être* and the image of the *Grande Ourse,* "x d'un problème et d'un idéal; c'est le grand inconnu" (Villiers, *Isis,* dedication).

Ses purs ongles très haut dédiant leur onyx,	Her pure nails very high up dedicating their onyx,
L'Angoisse, ce minuit, soutient, lampadophore,	Anguish, this midnight, holds up, lamp-bearing [moon-carrying],
Maint rêve vespéral brûlé par le Phénix	Many an evening dream burned by the Phoenix
Que ne recueille pas de cinéraire amphore	That no funeral amphora gathers

The first quatrain is the outdoor setting.[3] Anguish is symbolized by the black night following another disappointing day; the Phoenix-sun

has gone down with his hopes, which are "burned," at whatever level
—metaphysical, creative (the paper of his manuscript?), personal—
yet comes back to life with the morning of each "virgin, hardy and
beautiful today." The "pure nails," as we saw, are the distant cold stars
which seem to be an organic part, a projection, of the universal anguish,
hence "fingernails," and have a sharp feminine "cruelty" about them,
or rather the indifference of the cosmos with its frigid superiority. (The
Great Bear constellation at the end, however, will emerge in a special
way, as promising, beautiful.) Mallarmé favored the image of fingers
(like wing, etc., a penetrating projection of kinetic aspiration, standing
out) as in *Sainte,* and occasionally, as an added refinement, the mere
nail; thus in the *Ouverture ancienne:* "sibylles offrant leur ongle vieil
aux mages."

dédiant: the emergence of the stars seems to be the culmination of
a gigantic dedicatory reaching-up (as in prayer) of the cosmic lucid
Anguish, compare the *"offrant* leur ongle" just quoted. It is a more
static and *suspended* version (closer to his favored *lustre;* 296) of his
occasional fireworks image, a hyperbolic ascension climaxed in a spray
of clustered lights.

L'Angoisse: the night of despair, personified as in Baudelaire's
Spleen (III): "L'Angoisse . . . plante son drapeau noir."

soutient: the fingers of anguish seem to reach up (like the death-
claws of *Tout orgueil)* bearing the dead Dreams.

lampadophore: the black night of anguish also bears the mild lamp-
like glow of the moon, "calme . . . lune" (1297), "lune au-dessus du
temps" *(Igitur,* 433), (see the variant in note 3); compare "lune . . .
une morne lampe" (Leconte de Lisle, *Les Hurleurs).* An actual lamp
in the dark chamber is vaguely possible (see note 2).

The moon is associated with the death of his sister, more or less
consciously, in *Ce que disaient les trois cigognes* (Ayda), where it was
involved in a similar leap from the near and personal (a round cake)
to the remote and macrocosmic form, the moon itself.

Phénix: "Phénix recouvré de sa cendre" (418); "Phoenix, emblème
égyptien de l'immortalité, sous la forme d'un oiseau qui renaît de ses
cendres" (1274); this last passage is from *Les Dieux antiques,* where
almost all myths are traced back to the cycles of the sun. "Quand on
voit chaque soir comme les hirondelles / Une illusion d'or fuir nos
toits" *(Les trois couronnes,* ML). A letter from Lefébure queries: "je
voudrais savoir si l'auteur donne aux transformations du Rituel Égyptien
un sens astronomique" (EL, p. 256).

For a more complete discussion of the sunset theme, see *Victorieusement fui.*

The crisp syntactical or symmetric x-effect is reinforced by the sharp lucid *i*-sound in each rhyme; compare the *i, i, u* of *Igitur:* "an abstract X shape expresses the intellectual element, symmetric, 'classic', as in the chess-like movement of the psychological components in *Cligès, Le Roman de la Rose,* or the medieval concept of the four humors and the four elements. Later, the phoenix (Scève, La Ceppède, Donne), the quincunx (Browne) and the paradox (Du Bartas, Pascal, Donne) will add to the 'X' feeling of the medieval symmetry a sense of cancellation, fall crossing rise." (W, p. 93).

amphore: not only are the dreams burned, the ashes remain scattered, not even collected into a funeral monument. This recalls the *
hopelessness of cosmic fate in *soleil mortel (Toast funèbre).* *

Sur les crédences, au salon vide: nul ptyx,	On the buffets, in the empty salon: no ptyx,
Aboli bibelot d'inanité sonore	Abolished knickknack of sonorous emptiness,
(Car le Maître est allé puiser des pleurs au Styx	(For the Master has gone to dip tears from the Styx
Avec ce seul objet dont le Néant s'honore).	With this sole object through which the Nothingness honors [adorns] itself).

The first quatrain was the outdoor setting: now the indoor, the living room abandoned, in death, which "reflects" (according to the letter to Cazalis) the void night, as one emptiness reflects another (the "luxe, salle d'ébène" of *Quand l'ombre* fuses the two). A further microcosm of emptiness is the *ptyx,* which echoes the hollow amphora of the first quatrain: "me dit-il à moi-même comme il lui manquait un mot en la série en yx, il en avait inventé un, le mot ptyx—auquel il donna le sens de vase, d'urne, et dont il exprima la non-existence par le vers immédiat: 'Aboli bibelot d'inanité sonore'" (Ghil, *Les Dates et les Oeuvres,* p. 222).

But Mallarmé really had not invented the word. Hugo, for example, had used it in his *Satyre.* The strangeness of the term has to do with its occult, ghostly rôle: the *ptyx* is an ultimate or borderline entity, disappearing into and half merged with the original chaos. Compare the *Anastase* of *Prose.*

A variant read: "Insolite vaisseau d'inanité sonore" (1482). The etymology and meaning of *ptyx* have been much discussed: some see it as related to "fold" or "shell." All these meanings, vase, fold, shell, are variants on one elementary meaning: the simplest container of reality (or nothing) a sort of womb developed from the merest bend or concave shape, the fundamental female Rhythm. In *Un Coup de Dés* the womb, a boat-shape, *bâtiment* (Page 3), a vessel of life, was developed from the trough of a wave (C, pp. 133-156). It is related also to the twisting *chimère*, a female line representing art, a bewitching bitch, a deceitful Muse, the dazzling empty container (as in *Toast funèbre*) of the artist's mad dreams, the "Glorious Lie."

The use of *pli*, "fold" (as in *ptyx*) as a fundamental Rhythm of reality—a writhing line of writing—is found in "Rodenbach écrit . . . des phrases absolues . . . les tend par vivants plis" (311) or "Le pli de sombre dentelle [writing] qui retient l'infini" (1565). The disappointing quality of this "womb"—all births lead only to death—is expressed elsewhere in Mallarmé, for example, the "aurait pu naître" of *Une dentelle s'abolit* (note the impact of *dentelle* and *abolit*) and, even perhaps in a subtle way, in the *plis inutiles* of the tapestry of *Ouverture ancienne*. We have compared it to the *faux manoir* of *Un Coup de Dés;* it echoes also the "pur vase d'aucun breuvage / Que l'inexhaustible veuvage / [qui] Agonise mais ne consent" (*Surgi de la croupe et du bond*); the "creux néant musicien" of *Une dentelle s'abolit;* and "nénuphars . . . enveloppant de leur creuse blancheur un rien" (*Le Nénuphar blanc*). The metaphorical sense of the total uselessness or absurdity of life and creative striving overlaps with a more common usage: art as mere play, gratuitous gesture. Knickknacks or gewgaws (for example, Victorian or Second Empire) especially flaunt this frivolous quality, pointless as stars: "où qu'ils expirent en le charme et leur désuétude [compare the final constellation of the *Coup de Dés*, "froide de désuétude"] . . . *les bibelots abolis,* sans usage" (499). The deserted room of the sonnet, abandoned by the dead Master, adorned by the mere ghost of the absent gewgaw which he took with him, reflects, then, the black emptiness (*Néant*) adorned by meaningless stars, the very image of *Hasard:* "l'incohérent manque hautain de signification qui scintille en l'alphabet de la Nuit" (303). The Big Dipper (*Grande Ourse*) is the one seemingly organized form in the sky which reflects the puzzling construction of the trinket (perhaps a shell-like spiral; one thinks of Valéry's *coquille*), man's monument, his "house" (*faux manoir,* a pathetic attempt at a shelter for his spirit like the derelict shell), the little *bâtiment* left behind after Man's (or the Poet's) departure. Mallarmé accordingly refers to his own works as *bibelots* in "un sonnet et une page de prose . . . ces deux bibelots" (6655). But the image of the Big Dipper is only hinted at in the quatrain. It will come into focus, startlingly, in the last line of the poem.[4]

The four *o*'s of *aboli bibelot . . . sonore* are like little round bubbles, or hollow spheres, echoing the empty gewgaw. The three rotund *b*'s abet this effect, as they do in the *bond* of the empty vase of *Surgi de la croupe et du bond* (or in the words *rebondi, bombé,* etc.). The numerous *n*'s reinforce the feeling of negation expressed by *vide, nul, inanité, aboli, Néant,* and others. The omnipresent *i*'s support the lucid quality of the rhymes in *i*-sounds, for example *minuit,* the black-diamond effect of a vigilant midnight of the mind as in *Igitur,* where the word is of key importance. Its brightness, in Mallarmé's idea, is attested by "perversité conférant à *jour* comme à *nuit,* contradictoirement, des timbres obscur ici, là clair" (364).

crédences: A variant reads "des consoles" with similar overtones; we are reminded of the *console* of *Igitur, Tout Orgueil,* or "ornement de consoles, en l'ombre" (377).

inanité sonore: the hollow sound of a fatal clock-chime at midnight in *Igitur* is referred to in similar terms: "sa vacante sonorité . . . son or" (435); the association of *sonore . . . son or,* the "golden" bell-sound, is part of the vibrancy of the sonnet; the gold of the rhyme *sonore* echoes the rhymes in *or* of the first tercet.

Maître: he is Mallarmé's future ghost (reminding us of Valéry's *future fumée*) as the nixie is the remembered ghost of his long-lost youth (including his sister's; Mauron).

Mais proche la croisée au nord vacante, un or	But near the vacant casement [turned] to the north, a gold [something]
Agonise selon peut-être le décor	Agonizes [is dying] according perhaps to [the gold glow is perhaps due to] the decoration [on a mirror-frame]
Des licornes ruant du feu contre une nixe,	Of unicorns kicking fire against a nixie [a sort of nymph],
Elle, défunte nue en le miroir, encor	She, defunctive nude [or cloud, being] in the mirror, while,
Que, dans l'oubli fermé par le cadre, se fixe	In the oblivion [empty mirror] bounded by the frame, is fixed
De scintillations sitôt le septuor.	Of scintillations at once the septet [the Great Bear].

The primary drama is between the empty space and the abandoned room. Within the room there are minor versions of the drama. First, in passing, there is an allusion to the window in which the final vivid image of the Big Dipper will appear. Then, a gleam of gold in the dark —much in Mallarmé depends on this miraculous virgin birth of "une rose dans les ténèbres" *(Surgi)*—is dying or "agonizing," is precarious or ephemeral like all poignant beauty; it is pitted against the dark which will swallow it as it did the Master. The gleam may be a bit of gilt on a mirror frame, as in *Igitur,* perhaps a *licorne* carved there.[5]

There is another little drama between the "male" (unicorn) element, the gold of the frame, and the "female" element, the reflecting, receptacle-like mirror (similar to the maternal *mer* of the *Coup de Dés* which extends and replaces it) or the focus of it, the feminine essence *within* the mirror, the pale naked (or cloud-like) ghost or fantasm, nymph, "nixie," who is ambiguously the reflection of the constellation (see the letter to Cazalis, above) and of the poet's naked being.

selon: it is interesting that this word was retained, though in a different position and use, from the earlier version. It is a favorite preposition of Mallarmé because of its oblique suggestiveness; here there may also be some echo of the word *salon,* in the quatrains.

nixe: the "nixie" is a ghost of Mallarmé's feminine soul (either itself or perhaps the white swan-maiden glimpse in *Hérodiade,* with the echoes of his dead sister and his lost adolescent love, Harriet Smith); how conscious Mallarmé was of this whole phenomenon of self and its projections is made crystal clear in "Qui erre autour d'un type exceptionnel comme Hamlet n'est que lui, Hamlet: . . . Ophélie, vierge enfance objectivée du lamentable seigneur royal" (301). There is a strong erotic (naked) undertone, as is true of most adolescents' ghosts. She is a figure of the naturally somewhat androgynous Mallarmé, either as in *Hérodiade*—the narcissistic mirror in which she appears as a phantom—or as in *Igitur*—where the love-death image of the self again hovers and fades in a mirror as a disappearing ghost. The echo *nu(e)-nue* (cloud)—see *Quelle soie*—extends to *Vénus* as in "O Vénus . . . Qui se baigne en silence, et puis, comme un nuage, s'évanouit" (Villiers, *Hymne à Vénus*).

oubli: the etymology is *obliviscor,* linked with *lividus,* as Chassé has observed. The flat *a*'s of *vacante* are excellent for a window, just as the *a*'s of *matin chaste* are, in *Les Fenêtres.* The *croisée* (cross braces of a casement) reflects, vaguely, the X-pattern of symmetry.

*   *septuor :* the musical term probably refers to the Pythagorean *nombre* (harmony and mathematical number), the "music of the spheres"; compare "l'ensemble des rapports existant dans tout, la Musique" (368). The title poem Mallarmé chose for his *Dieux antiques* is Banville's *Orphée:*

> O Dieux, pendant des nuits sereines, anxieux,
> J'ai longtemps écouté le bruit qui vient des cieux,
> D'où sans cesse le chant des Étoiles s'élance.

There is a curious "cabbalistic" (Mallarmé's term, but not really apt) effect in the last lines: *cadre-quatre, scin-cinq, si-six, sept-sept.* It certainly has something to do with the subliminal poetic impression. Perhaps it also refers to the ticking-off of the stars of the Big Dipper—

the four of the bowl (or is it four in the handle?—an unsure impression many of us have felt in looking at it)—as in the last image of the *Coup de Dés,* the *compte total en formation.*

The final cluster of stars is thus a typical Mallarméan "crowning" image, or halo: circular, static (like the jewel-cluster of *Hérodiade,* the bracelet of *Autre éventail,* the *roue* or fireworks-spray of *M'introduire*), yet—for it is *suspended,* that is, vibrant, alive as well as still—it is fraught with captive voluptuousness, potential dynamic energy, on the brink of melting and flowing (C, p. 407). The potential warmth is, however, more subdued in this particularly taut, self-involved poem (as compared with those poems where the warmth-attracting female figure more fully appears). There are, in Mallarmé, many subtle variations of shading on such fundamental themes.

The four *or* elements in the first line of the tercets echo the eight *or* rimes: the golden gleam in the night, whether the final stars or the ones reflected in the room. The bright *i*'s sharpen the final image.

NOTES

1 A cautionary remark: Mallarmé's sense of humor and personal irony, his extreme modesty, must always be kept in mind. Everything about him indicates that he was a relentless seeker after Meaning—"il y a des lois," he solemnly said to the Rosny brothers—and therefore incapable of surreal, automatic, or "nonsense" verse (other than the most frivolous). Also, nothing indicates a serious interest in the specifics of "facile occultism"; (416). His fraternal sympathy and sense of common goal were tempered by pity: "pauvres kabbalistes ... par inattention et malentendu [ils détachent] d'un Art des opérations qui lui sont intégrales et fondamentales pour les accomplir à tort, isolément, c'est encore une vénération, maladroite" (850); at another point ("Magie") he sees alchemy as leading to finance rather than art.

2 Reminding us of the décor of *Hérodiade,* begun a few years earlier (as well as of *Igitur,* a bit later): "La chambre singulière en un cadre, attirail de siècle belliqueux, orfévrerie éteinte," etc. (*Ouverture ancienne*); the mirror is an important item in the *Scène.* In both parts of *Hérodiade,* the room is notably empty. A phrase in the *Tombeau d'Anatole* (f. 37) alludes to "Temps de la chambre vide—jusqu'à ce qu'on l'ouvre," which implies the death theme and the resurrection motif associated probably with a window, as in *Une dentelle.* "Une nuit ... la lampe de fer ... laissait dans l'obscurité ... les profondeurs de l'appartement ... contempler des firmaments inconnus" (Villiers, *Isis,* p. 121); compare also his *Hymne à Vénus* with its *lampadaire,* etc.

3 Variant:

> La Nuit approbatrice [of the "crime" of light-murder] allume les onyx
> De ses ongles au pur Crime lampadophore,
> [The crime] Du Soir aboli par le vespéral Phoenix [sunset, burning-up day]
> De qui le cendre n'a de cinéraire amphore.

This *pur Crime* is the same as the "Crime, bûcher" of *Ouverture ancienne;* it is the blackness of night, which kills the day (and bears the moon). The softness of the sounds, as in "calme ... lune" (1297), indicates probably a *moon* in *lampadophore* (note, however, "lampe…soleil" (ML, p. 182). In this clearly cloudless night it would certainly be visible. Though it is true Mallarmé usually did not care for the moon, that *fromage*, as he said to Coppée (Biog., pp. 328-329), at times he appreciates its serene glow (*Hérodiade, Dialogue des nymphes*, etc.)

[4] It is possible that the word *puiser*, "to dip," refers to this macro-version of the gewgaw. In *Booz Endormi* there is a similar leap from the personal to the cosmic, from a curved little object to the Big Dipper: "quel moissonneur de l'éternel été, / Avait, en s'en allant, négligemment jeté / Cette faucille d'or dans le champ des étoiles." A comparable leap—or several—is found in *Igitur:* the empty *fiole* is very much like the *ptyx;* it is the pure object that will be left behind when Igitur has drunk the poison from it and departed, like the *Maître*, in a sacrificial gesture to gain purity: "Sur les meubles vacants, le Rêve a agonisé en cette fiole de verre, *pureté*, qui renferme la substance du Néant" (439). It leaps to the blown-up image of the "château de la pureté" (443). Analogously, the blown-out candle leaps to the "lune, au-dessus du temps" (432). Or the clock-face leaps to its "complication stellaire et marine" (LL, p. 24). The central idea of "réflexion (the quoted letter to Cazalis), of the micro by the macro, the inner by the outer, evokes the image of the mirror both in the sonnet and in *Igitur*, as well as the sky-sea reciprocity in *Un Coup de Dés*.

[5] This mythical creature obviously fascinates Mallarmé. He alluded to it in some *Igitur* notes, published by Bonniot, and in the *Noces d'Hérodiade* (f. 128). Its traditional association with virginity is important; his mirrored hero, Igitur (or heroine, Hérodiade), was virginal, alone. The element *corne* is one of the reasons for its fascination. The idea of an outburst of stars, like dice, from this horn (*cornet à dés*) is quite possible, as in the *Coup de Dés* ("issu stellaire," Page 9; C, p. 238, and C, pp. 409-410). Another facet of the word *licorne* is the element *or*, which goes well with its use, in *Igitur* and here, for a gleam of gold from furniture on which it is carved. The variant had: "*dieu* que croit emporter une nixe." Soula sees a possible influence from Heine's *De l'Allemagne* (a battle of unicorns and nixies). There are other minor possibilities (Richard, p. 216).

16. LA CHEVELURE VOL D'UNE FLAMME

◊❖◊❖◊❖◊❖◊❖◊

This late sonnet was published for the first time as part of the prose poem *La Déclaration foraine* (in the August 12, 1887, issue of *L'Art et la Mode*).[1]

The poem is a celebration of a woman whose looks, featuring magnificent hair, need no outer adornment. The earlier prose poem *Le Phénomène futur* was based on a very similar idea (including the sideshow setting, inherited from Banville or Baudelaire): "Je t'apporte . . . une Femme d'autrefois. Quelque folie, originelle et naïve, une extase d'or, je ne sais quoi! par elle nommé sa chevelure," and so on. (269).

In *La Déclaration foraine,* Mallarmé tells, with an air of fantasy, based on some unknown element of fact, how his lady friend (Méry) insisted on their stopping in at a carnival. Seeing an empty stall, Madame impulsively tells an old drummer, seated nearby, to attract a public; whereupon she mounts a table. Mallarmé realizes something must be done for the crowd which has paid admission and might not appreciate, as he does, the mere look at Méry. The poem ostensibly explains to them what they are getting. Actually, the sonnet was, without doubt, written separately and was combined with the prose as an afterthought; its imagery is occasionally inconsistent with the unlikely situation. This view is supported by the fact that Mallarmé published it separately in his *Poésies* and therefore its imagery must be independent of any notion of a crowd-public.

La chevelure vol d'une flamme à l'extrême	The hair flight of a flame at the extreme
Occident de désirs pour la tout déployer	Occident of desires to unfurl it all
Se pose (je dirais mourir un diadème)	Goes down (I'd say a diadem dying)
Vers le front couronné son ancien foyer	Towards the crowned forehead its ancient hearth
Mais sans or soupirer que cette vive nue	But without [deprived of] gold sigh [imperative, addressed to himself, in the hope] that this live cloud
L'ignition du feu toujours intérieur	The ignition of the always internal fire

147

| Originellement la seule continue | Originally the only [cloud] should continue |
| Dans le joyau de l'oeil véridique ou rieur | In the jewel of the eye serious or laughing |

The hair flares up,[2] like the pleasure of the admiring poet; the mistress is undoubtedly combing it out full length in front of her mirror, as in *Quelle soie,* where it is likewise called a "cloud": "la torse et native nue / Que hors de ton miroir tu tends." It is a momentary revelation, a flash of beauty; then it dies down as she arranges it in a braid-crown about her forehead, where it had been "originally."[3] The poet sighs and hopes (or "tells himself"; Noulet) the gift of delight will continue in his sweetheart's eyes.[4] This lover's *soupirer*—compare *Soupir*—is inconsistent with Richard's notion that the eye is the crowd-public's; that would be too much of a leap, and nothing in the sonnet itself announces it.

An association with sunset is clear in the use of the term *occident,* the west (this harmony of fair hair and sunset-glories was the core of *Victorieusement fui* and, partly, *M'Introduire dans ton histoire*). As in *Toast funèbre,* the sun-source of all love is implied; the one original Eros from which this beauty springs is "the internal fire / Originally the only [life-cloud]"; compare "foyer placé au centre de l'univers total" (1192) or "feu . . . le vieux secret d'ardeurs et splendeurs qui s'y tord" (295).

extrême occident de désirs pour la tout déployer: means that the hair is combed out to an extreme point of desire in the watching poet —"desire to unfurl it all"—where it can only fall, or set like the sun having reached the horizon, having run its course of light, as in "la chimère, en la limite de son geste, qui va redescendre" (390). It has also been suggested (by Chadwick and others) that Mallarmé is referring to his declining powers (the poem dates from his forty-fifth year).

pour la tout déployer has a possible meaning of *"in spite of* its all being unfurled (it will fall)"; compare "déroulant ta tresse en flots" (23). It may also imply the spreading fires of sunset (Chisholm).

mourir un diadème: reminds us of the fireworks-hair-Eros of *M'introduire,* "Comme mourir pourpre la roue," a flooding afterglow of dying pleasure, as in Baudelaire's *Jet d'eau:*

L'éclair brûlant des voluptés
S'élance, rapide et hardie,
Vers les vastes cieux enchantés,
Puis, elle s'épanche, mourante
En un flot de triste langueur.

mais sans or: Now that the hair is braided, the golden flash is gone; compare "sans flambeau" (1481), the disappearance of sunset gold; or "Soleil couché . . . Or parti" *(Tombeau d'Anatole,* f. 59); also "Sans or avec le soleil nous partons" (185), an ambiguous idea of leaving moneyless and sunless.

cette vive nue / L'ignition du feu toujours intérieur: the visible "cloud" or flame above the head had arisen from the one inner flame of life or love (the *nue* as "naked" is discussed below). In the same way, the "ors ignorés" were the source of Hérodiade's visible light of eyes and hair: "pierres où mes yeux . . . empruntent leur clarté mélodieuse, et vous / Métaux qui donnez à ma jeune chevelure / Une splendeur"; compare "Tous les rêves émerveillés . . . ne produisent fleur sur la joue / Dans l'oeil diamants impayés" *(Rondel I).*

feu: there is a slight hint of a "dead" *(feu)* flame to be revivified: "l'arrière mais renaissante flamme" (402).

intérieur: "le regard limpide et rieur / Verse . . . / son charmant être *intérieur*" (124); "foyer . . . les intérieurs" (1192); "très à l'intérieur" *(Coup de Dés,* Page 3), the womb-source (C, p. 150).

originellement: "Quelque folie, *originelle* et naïve, une extase d'or je ne sais quoi! par elle nommé sa chevelure" (269).

véridique ou rieur: this is part of the "doubt" of the last line, whether the eye mocks him or favors him with an *authentic* glimpse of the original fire: "véridiques, à même" (385).

Une nudité de héros tendre diffame	A nakedness of tender hero defames
Celle qui ne mouvant astre ni feux au doigt	The one [woman, nakedness] who waving no star or fires on her finger
Rien qu'à simplifier avec gloire la femme	Only to simplify with glory the woman
Accomplit par son chef fulgurante l'exploit	Accomplishes darting lightning with her head the exploit
De semer de rubis le doute qu'elle écorche	Of sowing with rubies the doubt she grazes [skins]
Ainsi qu'une joyeuse et tutélaire torche.	Like a joyous and tutelary torch.

The syntax is ambiguous: "A tender lover's nudity defames the [feminine] Nudity which accomplishes—merely to simplify with glory the woman [object]—the exploit. Or "woman" is in apposition with "The one . . ." and both together constitute the subject of "accomplishes."

In either case, the sense is that a lover (even tender Mallarmé) is *de trop* here, can only "defame," degrade, the feast of pure beauty; she suffices alone, as Hérodiade did. The "nakedness" of his art yields to hers. Another gallant implication is, likely, that Mallarmé's mistress—perhaps anyone's—is defamed if anyone claims she must sleep with a man to bring him joy; she has this other important way. (Richard sees the *nudité* as referring to Mallarmé's sense of exposure before the crowd. But we doubt that he had a crowd in mind when he composed the poem. Her public is her lover.)

héros: has the strong overtone of Eros, as usual in Mallarmé; see under *M'Introduire dans ton histoire.*

Celle: is ambiguous—the woman, the nakedness (the simple unadorned woman's hair, her essence), recalling the similar *native nue* of

*   *Quelle soie* (q.v).

celle qui ne mouvant astre ni feux au doigt: she [or it] needs no external light, such as jewelry (variant: "Celle qui ne mouvant bagues ni feux au doigt," (1461). Compare "deploie avec l'émoi seul de sa robe ma très peu consciente ... inspiratrice" (308). The early *Sonnet à Wyse* had the same idea of sufficiency without trappings: "la chevelure nue / Que loin des bijoux tu détends" (LL, p. 182); "son doigt tremblait, sans améthyste / Et nu" (22); "sans flambeau" *(Victorieusement fui).*[5]

diffame: "on a diffamé l'Art" (569).

simplifier: "simplification apportée par un regard de voyant" (696); "la *nudité* d'une âme *simplifiée* ... redevenir primitif" (Propos, p. 159); recall the *nue* above. The idea of a back-to-the source flash is found in a crudely erotic context in "dégorger cet éclair, vers quelque reddition de comptes *simplificatrice*" (322). A usage closer to the present one, the idea of a superbly direct and "naked" beauty—"la chevelure nue"—combined with conscious art is implied in "elle [la danseuse] te livre à travers le voile dernier, qui toujours reste, la *nudité* de tes *concepts*" (307); or "jet délicat et vierge et une jumelle clairvoyance directe du *simple;* qui, peut-être, avaient à s'accorder encore" (298). The notion, expressed in all these excerpts, of an unconscious, spontaneous, feminine collaborator of his aesthetic is found in the prose poem where the sonnet was imbedded and recited. There, Mallarmé refers to his own poem as a "lieu commun d'une esthétique," and the idea of a stripped *base* for his art runs through the prose as well as the little poem: "la personne qui a eu l'honneur de se soumettre à votre jugement ne requiert pour vous communiquer le sens de son charme, un costume ou aucun accessoire usuel du théâtre ... Ce *naturel* s'accommode de l'allusion parfaite que fournit la toilette [flowers in her hat] toujours à l'un des motifs primordiaux de la femme" (282). This concept of an art that is a synthesis of nature and form is developed more explicitly in "Bucolique" (402):

"Le double adjuvant aux lettres, extériorité et moyen ont, envers un, dans l'ordre absolu, gradué leur influence" and "La première en date, la nature. Idée tangible pour intimer quelque réalité aux sens frustes et, compensation, *directe* . . . au *foyer* subtil [de la musique] je reconnus, sans douter, *l'arrière* (cf. *feu* . . . *intérieur*) mais *renaissante flamme,* où se sacrifièrent les bosquets et les cieux."

That is, the natural sunset is prolonged in the tamed flame of aesthetic joy. In the same passage is found the corollary idea of a distillation (whereby the corruption of the artificial is purified in sacrificial flame), the "ardent, volatile dépouillement en traits."[6] In sum, the *tresse(s)* of the *maîtresse,* as original source and distilled verbal *traits,* will do for poetry.

semer: the "sparks" of light are like the "sown" constellation (C, p. 418) of the *Coup de Dés* versus the dark night of chance or "doubt"; compare "mon doute amas de nuit ancienne" *(Faune:* note the dark *ou);* in the *Sonnet à Wyse* this was expressed as "étincelles d'Être."[7]

doute qu'elle écorche: the light not only touches but *cuts into the substance of* the darkness, a visual effect of sparkling, the light mingling with the dark: "renaissante flamme . . . le manque du rêve [doubt] qu'elle consume" (402); "fulguration . . . consumait l'ombre" (395); "L'Espérance *rebrousse* . . . la Nuit noire" (23). A possible hint of English "scorch" has been noted by others.

rubis: the simple flame sows rubies, as the pure authentic burning of the poet gives off these refined "stars," the "ardent, volatile dépouillement en traits qui se correspondent, maintenant proches la pensée" (402); compare the burning cigar of art in *Toute l'âme résumée.* The image of hair jewels is prominent in the *Faune, M'Introduire* and, somewhat, Baudelaire's *La Chevelure.*

doute: if we accept a link with the prose (even as an afterthought), the doubt could be that of the "crowd," for example, that one described in the prose poem: her hair is a "luminous evidence," like the *astre en fête* of *Quand l'ombre* or the flame of Baudelaire's "tutelary" art in the *Tombeau,* twisted as it was by the winds of public mocking and scepticism; or Villiers' flame in *Tout orgueil,* which is also a *torche,* not only "grazed" but extinguished by the wind of disbelief. Yet, as in the case of Baudelaire or of Villiers, the confrontation with the crowd (cf. "Confrontation") was necessary to literary production: "ceci jaillit, forcé, sous le coup de poing brutal à l'estomac, que cause une impatience de gens" (283). In this sense, the crowd is subtly compared to the merely human aspect of the lady friend who insists on outer results: "Comme vous Madame" (283); compare "La Dame, Notre Patronne . . . la foule" (383); "la foule, délègue ... quelqu'un qui la représente: sa femme" (*Documents iconographiques,* p. 42).

A more important sense of *doute,* independent of the prose, is the overall metaphysical-esthetic misgiving about Beauty or Truth—"le doute du Jeu suprême" (*Une dentelle*)—which is now, once again, miraculously abolished: "irrésistiblement au foyer subtil, je reconnus, *sans douter,* l'arrière mais renaissante flamme" (402). It is the old Phoenix of his artistic faith, as in *Ses purs ongles.*

The doubt is also, secondarily, that of Mallarmé's personal relationship; he wondered, in the quatrains, whether she was serious or mocked him—but the flame of love quells that uneasiness.

NOTES

[1] It is special in the work of Mallamé inasmuch as it follows a Shakespearean sonnet form of three quatrains and a distich. No doubt, for this reason Mallarmé put it by itself, away from the other sonnets, in the edition of the *Poésies* he was preparing when he died.

[2] Perhaps like a comet (the root of "comet" is Greek *komé,* hair): "Je suis heureux, ravi de voir passer cette chevelure blonde dans ton ciel sans comète depuis longtemps" (in C, p. 374).

[3] The flare-up, a kinetic linear flight, gives way to the circular crown, a stasis; compare "on traverse un tunnel ... avant la gare ... qui couronne" (371-372) and C, p. 68.

[4] Antoine Adam has proposed the reading "without sighing any gold except this live cloud" (the verb *continue* would be an indicative). This is a slight possibility; it is contradicted by the fact that the hair as cloud has now disappeared into a crown; moreover, this involves a strained and unprepossessing usage of *soupirer.*

[5] "Et vos longs doigts, cinq rameaux inégaux, / Ne sont pompeux de bagues ni d'anneaux" (Ronsard, *Elégie à Marie Stuart*).

[6] In all this Mallarmé is aiming at an art which will somehow not be alienated from but *be* life; at times, he thought the only way was to become impersonal—put "nothing" between the expression and the reality—by a sort of psychic suicide or total humility or anonymous invisibility: "anonyme et parfait ... art" (367); "Mon théâtre [the world] de plein-pied et le fouler ... dans un congé de tous" (403). Consult C, p. 316. The *nue-nue* ambiguity is constant in Mallarmé, see *Quelle soie* and Gautier's *La Nue* (cloud-woman).

[7] In this early unhappy poem (quoted under *Quelle soie,* note 3), however, the sparks of beauty brought Mallarmé back to a hated reality, "font naître / D'atroces étincelles d'Être / Mon horreur et mes désaveux" (LL, p. 182).

The later poem expresses a more cheerful moment; perhaps Méry helped bring about this change of mood, as various commentators hold.

17. LE TOMBEAU D'EDGAR POE

❖❖❖❖❖❖❖❖❖❖

This famous sonnet was composed for an occasion commemorating Poe, in 1875 or 1876. It appeared in a *Poe Memorial* volume, in Baltimore, on the latter date. Mallarmé sent a translation of it to America, which intriguing item was recently discovered by a scholar, W. T. Bandy; it helps to clarify a point or two.[1]

For Mallarmé, Poe was a princely poet because his daemonic genius, which chanted romantic themes like "the death of a beautiful woman" (and could occasionally refine into the tingling pre-symbolist atmosphere of *The Fall of the House of Usher*), was coupled with extreme critical lucidity, as expressed in *The Poetic Principle.* Consequently Mallarmé translated his poems, a task he said he had inherited from Baudelaire, who had done the prose. Poe is obviously, to us, not so great as either of the Symbolist masters thought. Yet, he just as obviously brought them something. His foreignness and his tragic isolation in raw America, his death from inebriation—such exotic touches had much to do with his appeal, augmenting his other qualities.

These were genuine, despite the well-known adolescent traits: his ragged unevenness, his mawkishness, his Grand Guignol sensationalism, and so forth. For example, *Eureka* was a brilliantly outrageous, "absurdist" meditation, an important source for the cosmogonic vision of the *Coup de Dés,* as well as for Baudelaire's and Valéry's metaphysical notions. There is a probable allusion to it in the sonnet.

The resonance of the name Poe (which Mallarmé occasionally spelled Poë) with its easy overtone, Poet, is featured: "Le Poëte," in line two, is a ringing central word of the poem. And when his name is sounded directly, it is in a line with a series of *o*'s that echo it: "Dont la tombe de Poe . . . s'orne."

Tel qu'en Lui-même enfin l'éternité le change,	Such as into himself eternity at last changes him,
Le Poëte suscite avec un glaive nu	The Poet arouses with a naked sword
Son siècle épouvanté de n'avoir pas connu	His century frightened at not having recognized
Que la mort triomphait dans cette voix étrange!	That death triumphed in that strange voice!

The much-quoted first line tells us the paradoxical truth[2] that man

153

assumes his fixed final identity only with death; or, as a corollary, that the poet "comes into his own" only posthumously, with time proportional to the pioneering quality of his genius.

The second line has the image of a prophetic bard, even Christlike ("not peace but a sword"), who awesomely arouses his era to eternal beauty or truth. His former detractors—the public of his time generally —are frightened when he is finally identified, frightened at the sudden apparition of this Figure and the realization that they were wrong not to have recognized the power of his voice, which reverberates with the organ tones of "death," or naked truth.

Tel has an overtone of "distant" because of Greek *tele;* "Téléphassa, qui veut dire 'celle qui brille de loin'" (1165); compare *Telle loin* in *Salut*.

The icon of the Poet with the sword had been depicted by Mallarmé in an early satiric piece (20):

> Souvent la vision du Poëte me frappe:
> Ange à cuirasse fauve—il a pour volupté
> L'éclair du glaive . . .

We are directly reminded of the angel guarding the gate of paradise, as in "Leur défaite [poets'], c'est par un ange très puissant / Debout à l'horizon dans le nu de son glaive" (*Le Guignon*). The *volupté* of the first quote confirms the feeling that the *glaive nu* of the sonnet vibrates with undertones, as poetry almost always does, especially with Mallarmé. (Of course, poetry exists by virtue of the subdual of the "lower" realms of instinct, like any other civilized expression but, as complex sons of late culture, we are all somewhat *homo duplex,* aware of the dialectic between the "lower" and the "upper," that goes on despite repressions. Moreover, like Mallarmé, we are often aware of both levels *simultaneously.*)

Finally, the image bears a reminiscence, very probably, of Baudelaire's article on Poe: "celui dont le regard est tendu avec la roideur d'une *épée* . . . c'est Poe *lui-même.*"

The bright sounds of *Lui* (with its overtone *lui,* past participle of *luire*) contrast with the dark nasals of *enfin* and *change*. In line two, *suscite* and *nu* are sharp and bright, contrasted with the flat mass-background idea and dry sound of *siècle* with its *è*.

mort echoes its antithesis *triomphait,* which contains all its letters (in reverse order).

Eux, comme un vil sursaut d'hydre	They, like a vile [nervous] start of a
oyant jadis l'ange	hydra hearing of yore the angel

Donner un sens plus pur aux mots de la tribu	Give a purer sense to the words of the tribe
Proclamèrent très haut le sortilège bu	[They] Proclaimed aloud [that] the magic [of his words was] drunk
Dans le flot sans honneur de quelque noir mélange.	In the honorless flood of some black mixture.

The angel is simply "the above said poet," according to Mallarmé's notes that accompanied his translation. There is also a vague feeling of reference to some myth, such as Perseus and the Gorgon, Oedipus and the Sphinx. According to the *Dieux antiques,* every myth is based on a combat of the angelic or heroic sun and the clouds that obscure it at sunset.

Mallarmé commented on the *flot,* not without humor, "in plain prose: charged him with always being drunk."

The second line has become better known since Eliot consciously paraphrased it in *Little Gidding:* "Purify the dialect of the tribe" (Mallarmé is one of the dead masters evoked).

The effect of the hydra is fine: hydra, the many-headed monster is a traditional symbol for the crowd. There is a flat, somewhat disgusting effect of the *eu* in *eux* (cf. *eugh!*) as in the *Coup de Dés:* "rien n'aura eu lieu / que le lieu . . . inférieur."

oyant: is an archaic, vaguely medieval (Villonesque) effect going with *jadis* (echo of *paradis,* befitting *ange*).

Du sol et de la nue hostiles, ô grief!	Of the soil and the cloud [sky, which are] enemies, o struggle!
Si notre idée avec ne sculpte un bas-relief	If with it our [my] idea does not carve a bas-relief
Dont la tombe de Poe éblouissante s'orne,	With which Poe's dazzling tomb [will] be adorned,
Calme bloc ici-bas chu d'un désastre obscur	Calm block fallen down here from a mysterious disaster,
Que ce granit du moins montre à jamais sa borne	Let this granite at least show forever its limit [impose a limit]
Aux noirs vols du Blasphème épars dans le futur.	To the black flights of Blasphemy scattered in the future.

Mallarmé's own translation of *grief* as "struggle" is useful. Actually, the poetic effect is of that *and* "grief" at the poet's tragic life and death, adding a deeply serious flavor appropriate to both Poe and to his admirer. Thus Hamlet, close to both of them in Mallarmé's mind, is described by him in his essay on the same as "Ce promeneur d'un labyrinthe de trouble et de *griefs"* (according to Littré, "grievance," or "struggle," is one possible meaning of the word: Chassé).

Mallarmé translated *nue* as "ether." The idea is a lightning-like op-position (or struggle) and union—a drama—of the two supreme poles of nature, earth and sky, in this baroque flash of grief and beauty, in Mallarmé's memory, appropriate to Poe. These two extremes express for Mallarmé the cosmic, or metaphysical, depth of Poe's art. They remind us of the original and final sea and sky of the *Coup de Dés;* or of *Igitur,* where they are called "réciproques néants" (435). Elsewhere he writes: "Quelque drame d'exception sévit entre eux" (403). See the variant "double grief" in note 1.

The cosmic quality is prolonged in the fall of the tombstone, like a meteorite, from some obscure "disaster," no doubt a reference to the initial cosmogonic explosion of *Eureka* and the *Coup de Dés* (compare "une planète désorbitée" in *Edgar Poe, Baudelaire*). In his essay on Poe, Mallarmé refers to him as "le pur entre les Esprits . . . comme un aérolithe" (531). A similar motif of a hurled-down block of truth is found in the *Koran* and in *Finnegans Wake* (C, p. 122). Rimbaud is

* called a *météore* in Mallarmé's essay on him.

bloc . . . sa borne: "roc . . . qui imposa une borne à l'infini" *(Coup de Dés,* Page 8). in the *Coup de Dés* the self-created monument of the final Poet, depicted in these words, evaporates, like all reality in this total Work, to be reborn again in the constellation at the end, which idea, like the very celebration of the poet's glory, goes back to standard Renaissance themes.

The "black flights of Blasphemy" make one think of bats; such are the nasty carpers shrieking around the aloof and perfect monument. Here is an excellent Renaissance equivalent:

> Malgré ces ignorants de qui la bouche noire
> Blasphème parmi nous contre ta déité.
> (*Aux mânes de Ronsard,* Guillaume Colletet)

A series of *o*'s is prominent in "Dont, tombe, Poe, s'orne, bloc, borne"; the circle is the classic ideogram of monumental self-sufficiency, the pure compactness of the isolated poet and his message, or "tomb"; compare: "vocables . . . mot total . . . isolement de la parole . . . objet nommé" (858); or "Aboli bibelot d'inanité sonore" *(Ses purs ongles).*

NOTES

[1] Here is Mallarmé's translation of a slightly different earlier version of the sonnet, plus his notes:

> Such as into himself at last Eternity changes him,
> The Poet arouses with a naked[1] hymn
> His century overawed not to have known
> That death extolled itself in this[2] strange voice:

But, in a vile writhing of an hydra [they] once hearing the Angel[3]
To give[4] too pure a meaning to the words of the tribe,
They [between themselves] thought [by him] the spell drunk
In the honorless flood of some dark mixture.[5]

Of the soil and the ether [which are] enemies, o struggle!
If with it my idea does not carve a bas-relief
Of which Poe's dazzling tomb[6] be adorned,

[A] Stern block here fallen from a mysterious disaster,
Let this granite at least show forever their bound
To the old flights of Blasphemy [still] spread in the future.[7]

> [1] naked hymn means when the words take in death their absolute value.
> [2] this means his own.
> [3] the Angel means the above-said poet.
> [4] to give means giving.
> [5] in plain prose: charged him with always being drunk.
> [6] dazzling means with the idea of such a bas-relief.
> [7] blasphemy means against poets, such as the charge of Poe being drunk.

Bandy has recently found another, perhaps even earlier, version in *Revue de*   *
Littérature comparée (January-March, 1963). The most significant variant is the line:
"Du sol et de l'éther ô le double grief." Also noteworthy is the title: *Au Tombeau*
d'Edgar Poe, and "Sombre bloc à jamais chu," in line 2.

2 This concept is in the tradition of Hegel, though, as I have opined elsewhere,
Mallarmé is an independent thinker who in some ways either surpassed or bypassed
Hegel. The same highly condensed dialectical truth is developed at length by Sartre
in *L'Être et le Néant,* as well as in his fiction and his plays: we are what we are not
as well as what we are, that is to say, we are largely what we make of ourselves, and
we can be identified "finally" only after death.

18. LE TOMBEAU DE CHARLES BAUDELAIRE

◇❊◇❊◇❊◇❊◇

This is, in our opinion, one of Mallarmé's less successful efforts. It is overwritten, turgid, crammed, loaded in "every rift with ore" and then some, partly, no doubt, because Baudelaire affected him that way but partly, too, one would guess, because Mallarmé couldn't stop himself in this instance. He was apparently too eager to "show" the Shade of the dead master. But when this is said, the poem (which appeared in a special number of *La Plume,* in 1895), is still remarkable in some ways; it is certainly rich in meanings.

Le temple enseveli divulgue par la bouche	The buried temple emits through the
Sépulcrale d'égout bavant boue et rubis	Sepulchral sewer-mouth drooling mud and rubies
Abominablement quelque idole Anubis	Abominably [emits] some Anubis idol
Tout le museau flambé comme un aboi farouche	[With] All its muzzle blazing like a ferocious bark

The buried temple is the hieratic yet "underground" poetry of Baudelaire, symbolizing the same vertical dialectic of extreme opposites as "fleurs-mal" (*boue-rubis,* etc.): "Les *Fleurs du Mal* donnent l'impression d'un temple enseveli . . . les fragments d'une *Divine Comédie*" (Alfred Poizat, *Le Symbolisme*). Temple and sewer, heaven and hell, palace and tomb, it is super- and infra-human: God and dog (Anubis, dogfaced God), mouth and rectum (or pubis, later)—*bouche* and *anus (Anubis).* This last reference was directly invoked in his early prose poem on Baudelaire: "une singulière rougeur . . . odeur enivrante de chevelures secouées [Jeanne Duval's no doubt] . . . Est-ce une avalanche de roses mauvaises ayant le péché pour parfum . . . Ou ce torrent n'est-il qu'un fleuve de larmes empourprées par le feu de bengale du saltimbanque Satan qui se meut par derrière" (263).[1] This is likely, in turn, a reminiscence of Baudelaire's *Le Monstre:* "il [le Diable] pète du souffre . . . Flambeau d'enfer." The fascinatingly muddy and fecal tone has something to do with Jeanne Duval's chocolate skin; she is for Baudelaire a "fangeuse grandeur" ("Tu mettrais l'univers"), hence, for

Mallarmé, a "Vénus . . . Cloacina" and also (in her way) "Purificatrix" (1200). Since death and feces are commonly associated (and both to sexual sin) we are reminded of the perverse delight in Richard Wilbur's "breaching a strangely refreshing tomb," *(Potato)*, or Rimbaud's "latrines . . . [où] il livrait ses narines" *(Les Poètes de sept ans);* compare also Mallarmé's *Plainte d'automne* which has a coppery coprophilic glow in one passage: "décadence . . . chute . . . rayons de. cuivre jaune" (270) and see C, p. 379.

   temple enseveli: "dans une crypte la divinité ainsi d'une majestueuse idée inconsciente" (361), compare "l'homme qui contemple / Qui peut être un cloaque ou qui peut être un temple" (Hugo, *Ce que dit la bouche d'ombre;* note *bouche).*

   divulgue: . . . *aboi:* "ne *divulgue* pas du fait d'un *aboi* indifférent l'ombre ici insinuée dans mon esprit" (288); compare "expirer le gouffre en quelque ferme *aboi* dans les âges" (391); both these "barks" are crude expressions of man's metaphysical depths, the second being the official religious version (from "Catholicisme"); Mallarmé is probably, then, alluding to the somewhat sensational religiosity of certain Baudelaire poems. The vomiting temple image echoes the line: "Tes temples vomissant la prière" of Baudelaire's posthumously published fragment *Aux Parisiens* (1887), which includes a reference to "tes égouts pleins de sang / S'engouffrant dans l'Enfer", as well as the famous "Tu m'as donné ta boue et j'en ai fait de l'or."

   bouche: "cette étrange bouche [vulva]" *(Une négresse).* In ancient Egypt the Pharaoh's mouth was a temple (see *Before History,* Penguin Books, p. 22), as Mallarmé may have learned from his friend, the Egyptologist Lefébure.

   All the *b*'s (there are eighteen in the poem) reflect the *B* of Baudelaire; Mallarmé usually takes his key tone from the name of the celebrated one, in this way.[2] The *b* of *tombeau* is part of this effect; the spilling out of the excessive and muddy richness from a buried tomb (or anus)—"mon tombeau fécond" (ML, p. 182)—is the peculiar fertility of Baudelaire, as it is of the letter *b* for Mallarmé: "B . . . sens divers et cependant liés secrètement tous, de production, ou enfantement, de fécondité, d'amplitude, de bouffissure et de courbure" (929); the belly-like rotundity of the letter (or the buttock-like—as Joyce liked to observe—capital B) has much to do with all this: the cloacal fecundity is echoed in words like "divulgue par la bouche . . . bavant boue et rubis / Abominablement."

   The *ou-i* alternation of the end-rhymes is another version (dark-light) of the overall dialectic; this effect is summed up in the opposition *boue* and *rubis.*

égout: "quelque tempête d'égout qui maintenant s'insurge . . . et
. . . crache" (323); the effect of *dégoût (d'égout)* is certainly intended;
the dark *ou* goes with ten others in this often murky poem.

boue et rubis: Baudelaire had written, and Mallarmé had probably
read, "tu m'as donné ta boue et j'en ai fait de l'or" *(Aux Parisiens);*
this idea of alchemy, beauty distilled from baseness, as in *Une Charogne,*
is more fully implied in the second quatrain below. The *boue,* obviously,
has a disgusting, even nauseating, *arrière-goût* quality, as in "laisse un
bloc boueux du blanc couple nageur" (29) or Eliot's clearly derivative
"garlic and sapphires in the mud."

Anubis: a dogfaced Egyptian god of death: "Anubis est représenté
avec la tête d'un chien ou d'un chacal" (1274); his name appeared in a
poem inscribed in an album of Mallarmé's by Villiers (MI, p. 126);
also in Vigny's *Maison du Berger,* which Mallarmé certainly knew. But
this Egyptianism is typical of the 19th century, ever since Napoleon's
military excursion; one of Mallarmé's closest friends, Lefébure, was an
Egyptologist, who discussed hieroglyphics, and the like, with him in
their correspondence.

museau flambé: associated probably with the fires that are caused by
sewer-gas, or breached tombs; compare the "feu de bengale" cited
above; this leads to the image of the vulgar gas jets which are, nevertheless, crowned in light.

In the second quatrain we have another metaphor ("Or else") like
the sewer-mouth temple; both lead to the metaphor of the tercets;
flaming sewer-mouth or gas jet, either will serve as an appropriate
funeral wreath on Baudelaire's tomb.

Ou que le gaz récent torde la mèche louche	Or else if the recent gas twists the suspicious lock [or wick]
Essuyeuse on le sait des opprobres subis	Receiver [or wiper] as we know of insults undergone
Il allume hagard un immortel pubis	[Nevertheless] It [the gas] lights up haggardly an immortal pubis
Dont le vol selon le réverbère dé-couche	Whose flight sleeps out [wavers away, windblown] in relation to the street lamp.

The *mèche* is human hair, a key Baudelaire image usually related to
his *louche* mistress Jeanne Duval—*La Chevelure* was hers—and ambiguous like her (full of dangerous musky qualities, like the *goudron* of
La Chevelure, as well as the lighter lyric perfumes described in *Cor-
respondances;* she is Muse and Vampire); ambiguously also upper and
lower, as in the *Promesses d'un visage* (one of the forbidden poems
Mallarmé carefully copied, along with the already-mentioned *Monstre):*

"sous un ventre . . . une riche toison qui, vraiment, est la soeur / De cette énorme chevelure." Hence it becomes a *pubis* (pubic hair) in line three. Mallarmé had explored the image in *Mystacis umbraculis:* "son ventre sembla de la neige où serait . . . Tombé le nid moussu d'un gai chardonneret"; also *Une négresse:* "sous le crin, / Avance le palais de cette étrange bouche / Pâle et rose comme un coquillage marin." The hair image is confirmed by the word *tordre* as well as *mèche:* in *La Chevelure,* which is certainly very present here (see under *respirer* below), we find "mèches *tordues,* / Je m'enivre ardemment des senteurs confondues / De l'huile de coco, du musc et du goudron." Mallarmé, too, liked to use *tordre* for hair[3] (partly because of its gold, *or* element); thus, "la torse et native nu / Que hors de ton miroir tu tends" (*Quelle soie*); this is flame-hair, as in *La chevelure vol d'une flamme* (see under *tutélaire* below), and the word *torche* (etym. *torquere,* to twist) is used for the same gnarled gold effect; compare "feu . . . vieux secret d'ardeurs et splendeurs qui s'y tord" (295); compare "d'amour tu te tords" (ML, p. 140). The key link between hair (which Mallarmé admired as maniacally as Baudelaire) and fire is found again in "trésor présomptueux de tête . . . flambeau," from *Victorieusement fui,* of which an early version, *Sonnet à Wyse* exploited the image of tresses as a comet-tail, etymologically from Greek *komē,* hair.[4] The hair-fire image occurs prominently on Page 4 of the *Coup de Dés* (C, p. 170).

The gas, or the wind, twists the flame: *louche* is both twisted and morally "twisted", perverse or base; hence "un certain éclat subtil, extraordinaire et brutal de véracité que contiennent ses becs de gaz mal dissimulés et aussitôt illuminant, dans des attitudes générales, de l'adultère et du vol" (315). The vulgarity of the flame itself is in "gaz . . . langue à nue, vulgaire, dardée sur le carrefour" (377). Mallarmé is remembering Baudelaire's *Crépuscule du soir:*

> A travers les lueurs que tourmente le vent
> La Prostitution s'allume dans les rues

Some commentators have, accordingly, seen the figure of a prostitute running about the sonnet; this is hardly Mallarmé's style, though a suggestion of her is certainly present.

Ou que: the syntax is "Or if the recent gas twist" (subjunctive in both French and English). A somewhat similar construction is: "Prends garde [que] . . . Ou que ce couple qui jouait n'interrompe" (178).

le gaz récent: a newish invention still, in Mallarmé's day; it sounds the note of modernity, urban poetry à la Baudelaire's *Tableaux parisiens,* especially the two *Crépuscules.* The typical jet was covered with a mantle or *manchon (le manchon Auer* was one version which received some insults, we are told), a circular "muff", related to the *pubis.*

gaz: "GAS, notre *gaz,* de GEIST, en flammand, qui signifie *esprit,* comme l'Anglais GHOST" (1036); compare "le gaz ... esprit toujours à nos ordres ... magie" (736); the gas, then, has a dialectic of good and evil spirit (like "daemon") and goes along with all the other ambiguous metaphors; it has the doubleness of a Baudelairian perfume "to be inhaled" for its beauty and truth, though it be poison gas and it kill us *(si nous en périssons).*

tordre: treated earlier; a similar idea of a spirit (music) twisting something by its flow is found in "une musique ... va l'enlever de sa vague de passion ... le *tordre*" (544).

mèche, as we saw, is primarily a lock of hair; secondarily it is a metaphorical wick, that is, jet of flame on a gas lamp. This *mèche louche* may remind us of Villiers' remark in his *Hamlet:* "tout flambeau a une mèche," meaning that the ideal flame is based on a material wick dipped in oil.

Essuyeuse on le sait des opprobres subis: The gas light "wipes out" the dark, as Baudelaire's genius repels the attacks on his book; this can also mean "wipe away" insults (since it lights the streets, the gas protects the women, according to Davies), but at most it is a secondary allusion. A likelier idea is that Baudelaire found consolation for his trials in Jeanne's hair (Combet), compare "une Electre [possibly Jeanne] ... qui essuyait naguère son front baigné de sueur (Baudelaire, preface to "Les Paradis artificiels"); "un visage en pleurs que les brises essuient" *(Crépuscule du matin;* nearby is the "combat de la lampe"). *Essuyer,* in another sense, of "to receive," is found often in Mallarmé: "C'est moi qui ai essuyé les premières colères de Lemerre" (Propos, p. 98); "j'ai essuyé un reste d'influenza" (Lettre à Méry, in *Les Lettres);* "afin qu'elle n'essuie pas les sarcasmes" (Lettre à Cazalis, May 29, 1867); "subit ... essuie le trouble" (367). Some critics have seen a reference to a well-known *(on le sait)* resemblance between a certain kind of gas lamp, *le manchon Auer,* and a sexual organ; in this sense, *essuyeuse ... opprobres* refer to the "insulted" lamp. They probably also imply the humble role of the insulted mistress, Jeanne Duval —"Les stupides mortels t'ont jugée amère" (XXXIX); (Michel Butor has spoken recently of "la beauté insultée de Jeanne"). Jeanne was a lowly, kept woman but equally a beloved creature and muse; (the feminine passive mood of *subis* and *essuyeuse* is appropriate to her supine position, described in various poems). Though she functioned in an air of wickedness and degradation, she gave back the poem-"child" to the man, or light to the renewed genius. As in *La Déclaration foraine,* woman helps man produce. By definition, she, being the Other, brings him out of himself, vulgarizing him a bit but in the name of life. Hence her *pubis* is *immortel* (note the *or* element, gold from this mulatto mud): "la nature . . . De toi se sert, ô femme, ô reine des péchés . . . pour pétrir un génie / O fangeuse grandeur!" (Baudelaire, "Tu mettrais l'univers").

essuyeuse is a fine choice for the "suspicious lock"; etymologically it comes from *ex-succare*," to extract the juice." Perhaps the *suy* has an overtone of *suie* as in "la suie ignoble des quinquets" (*Le Pitre châtié*, q.v.).

hagard: a pallid, drawn, weary, disheveled (confused, haphazard) effect, implying the ordeal of the self-tormenting poet and appropriate to the idea of something scattered publicly to the vulgar, the flames of "hair" of the public gas jet. The disheveled effect is found in "hagard musicien" (a dead bird; *Petit air II);* compare also "nuit hagarde" (*L'Azur*), "bond hagard (*Cantique*) and "abîmes hagards" (var. of the *Cantique);* etymologically, it comes from *haga,* hedge (referring to the untamed hawks that inhabited hedges; Fowlie), which may connect with the hair-foliage cluster and even the wing imagery below.

immortel pubis: this is not only the mistress's but probably also a general image for the sexual "underside" of Baudelaire's art, the indispensable *boue* from which the lotus of his art springs, hence the *immortel* is his troubling genius as in many other uses of the word referring to Poe, Villiers, and others (485, 487); compare "torche . . . immortelle bouffée" of *Tout orgueil,* which is similarly wind-twisted (*bouffée*).

Dont le vol selon le réverbère découche: this recalls Baudelaire's

> Souvent à la clarté rouge d'un réverbère
> Dont le vent bat la flamme et tourmente le verre
> (*Le vin des chiffonniers*)

as well as:

> Et le vent du matin soufflait sur les lanternes
> (*Crépuscule du matin*)

Mallarmé early imitated this:

> Que sur les murs blêmis ébauche leur lanterne
> Dont le matin rougit la flamme
> (*Galanterie macabre*)

It is curious that the rhythm of "Dont le vent" persists, with similar imagery, from the Baudelaire source through the two Mallarmé echoes.

réverbère: associated with the vulgar, the public: "la lueur, à portée, quotidienne du réverbère (391); "le commun des murs réverbère l'écho par des inscriptions ... proclamant l'annonce d'ustensiles, de vêtements, avec les prix" (403). Thibaudet (p. 88) pointed out correctly that for Mallarmé the gas lamp was everything exterior and crass as contrasted to his intimate indoor lamp:

> "le gaz ... Filant dans des verres, il apporte aux séjours d'intimité les réminiscences de lieux publics ... le gaz, lui, a des caractères très-spéciaux: celui, principalement, d'un esprit toujours à nos ordres, invisible et présent. Or, presque tous les appareils qui nous distribuent cette clarté, sont hideux ... Il s'agirait ... de le montrer à même, et je dirais nu, si la nudité n'était l'impalpable: bref, avec tout son effet de magie" (736).

This intimate "naked" light will, accordingly, be abstracted from the *réverbère* of the sonnet, hence "au voile qui la ceint absente," below, saved for poetry.

A street lamp is like a streetwalker, public and pubic, and part of the modern decadent atmosphere Baudelaire was steeped in; for Mallarmé, "maint réverbère attend le crépuscule [cf. *soir* below, the twilight mood of urban decadence] et ravive les visages d'une malheureuse foule, vaincue par la maladie immortelle [cf. *immortel pubis*] et le péché des siècles" (269).

découche: the scattering of the light by the wind goes with the public idea of a street lamp—to "reverberate," means to spread abroad —as well as woman, for Woman incites man to produce (or vulgarize) and hence she is linked with the public in Mallarmé's mind and with the idea of "prostitution" in the sense of lowering oneself by going out to Others, "sleeping out"; an important Other is the mate. Hence texts like: "[vous n'auriez pas compris mon poème] Madame ... si chaque terme ne s'en était répercuté [cf. *réverbère*] jusqu'à vous par de variés tympans, pour charmer un esprit ouvert à la compréhension multiple" (283) or "applaudissements répercutés de la foule" (620) and "la foule—ou notre Dame et Patronne" (383). The word *découche* sums up these ideas of alienation from purity—Baudelaire's message is distorted by the public, the poetry too was *essuyeuse des opprobres subis* —yet the abandonment is a necessary going-out from the self via the impure woman, who is an agent of chance, the eternally feminine capricious flow of life. Hence she is associated with the wind, as in "l'arrière mais renaissante flamme [of natural beauty, reborn in music] ... là, en public, éventée par le manque du rêve qu'elle [the flame] consume" (402). The same idea of wind-*hasard* was expressed in *Toast funèbre* ("irascible vent" q.v.); and it is slightly altered in "le doute qu'elle écorche" referring to the "tutélaire torche," in *La Chevelure vol d'une flamme;* compare the windblown torch of *Tout orgueil.*

A similar scattering, feminine effect—together with some similar language—is rendered by Mallarmé's disciple Rodenbach in *Les Réverbères* (from *Le Miroir du ciel natal,* 1898):

> Où le bouton avec la fleur ouverte attend,
> Selon le caprice du vent,
> Écrasant la flamme ou la relevant
>
> Les réverbères des banlieues
> Sont des cages où des oiseaux déplient leurs queues
> Ils savent la fragilité de leur vol d'or!
> Le vent les tord . . .

vol: the feminine *v* and *o* of *Dont, vol,* and *selon* emphasize the circular effect of the flower-flame, as in *La chevelure vol d'une flamme* (the "front couronné")[5], or the circular conflagration of the *Coup de Dés,* Page 5. One kind of gas lamp was dubbed "papillon."

dont: overtone of *don,* the poet's gift of self; compare the *dont* of the *Coup de Dés,* Page 5, and "une virginité . . . *dont* le *don* exulte vers vous. Scintillation de toute mon intimité" (610).

Quel feuillage séché dans les cités sans soir	What foliage dried in the cities without dusk
Votif pourra bénir comme elle se rasseoir	[What] Votive offering will be able to bless as it [could, the shadow being absent from its shroud, in order] to sit down again
Contre le marbre vainement de Baudelaire	Vainly against the marble of Baudelaire
Au voile qui la ceint absente avec frissons	Absent from the veil [shroud, glass of lamp] which encloses it, with shivers
Celle son Ombre même un poison tutélaire	It [or She] his very Shade, a tutelary poison
Toujours à respirer si nous en périssons.	Always to be breathed [even] if we die of it.

The flaming mouth of the sewer, and so forth, (of strophe 1) and the hagard flower of gaslight *(pubis)* (of strophe 2) now modulate to a funeral wreath (to be appropriately placed against Baudelaire's tomb) with dried leaves, all summing up the modern city, the bizarre woman he made into beauty. Hence the *louche* entity, Jeanne or her *pubis,* is transfigured into splendid light, as was the cadaver of *Une Charogne;* this is the symbol of Baudelaire's art, his very Shade (an ambiguous word itself: death-darkness and its surviving spirit). There is a strong reminiscence of Baudelaire's "Servante au grand coeur" (which Mallarmé copied in a notebook); in this moving confessional fragment, Baudelaire relates how, snuggled in his warm bed, he thinks guiltily of his faithful old servant woman Mariette lying dead in her wintry grave, near other skeletons:

> ... sans qu'amis ni famille
> Remplacent les lambeaux qui pendent à leur grille,
> Lorsque la bûche siffle et chante, si le soir,
> Calme, dans le fauteuil je la voyais s'asseoir,
>
> . . . .
>
> Grave, et venant du fond de son lit éternel ...

This is very close in mood to Mallarmé's *Sonnet, à votre chère morte,* which has the same idea of a returning Shade as a flame in a fireplace, before which the man sits on a cold night regretting, likewise, the absence of flowers on a grave; the *soir-s'asseoir* rime lingers here as in the sonnet we are considering:

> Âme au si clair foyer *tremblante* de m'asseoir,
> Pour revivre il suffit qu'à tes lèvres j'emprunte
> Le souffle de mon nom murmuré tout un soir.

In both of Mallarmé's texts the main idea is of a flame (compare *tremblante* and *frissons*) as a departed Shade returning to be *fixed,* hence "settle" (*rasseoir*) or "sit" (*s'asseoir*), as a presence for the living. And like the flame of the *Tombeau de Charles Baudelaire,* the spiritual *souffle* is enough to replace a floral offering (or wreath) on an imagined tomb. The *voile* from which the specter is absent is the shroud (of Jeanne) and also the glass globe enclosing the flame that is her (and, in a sense, his) ambiguous spirit; the haggard flame-*pubis* would, appropriately, Mallarmé says, desert the globe to be placed, shivering —windblown—against Baudelaire's tombstone.

Quel feuillage séché dans les cités sans soir: the cities are the modern setting of Baudelaire, who occasionally claimed that he abhorred nature; hence the foliage is of "dried" trees in lit cities, "without night"; this goes with the pallid decadent tone of *hagard;* it recalls:

> Quand je contemple, aux feux du gaz qui le colore,
> Ton front pâle, embelli par un morbide attrait,
> Où les torches du soir allument une aurore
> (*L'amour du mensonge,* "Tableaux parisiens")

Quel: an anecdote by Vielé-Griffin (*Esquisse orale*) tells us that Mallarmé was awestruck by the least word, for example, "quel," which he was using in connection with birds, apparently; hence the overtone *aile* and a hint of *queue* may go with the *elle* of the next line as well as the *vol* of the preceding line, flame or flight. See *q* in Appendix C.

feuillage . . . votif: Mallarmé wrote, in a letter praising Baudelaire:

"n'avez-vous pas pu jeter les derniers numéros de notre chère revue sur ma tombe comme on dépose des couronnes mortuaires" (Biog., p. 119); cf. "la pieuse offrande qu'aux jours de fleurs, le génie [Hugo] . . . voua à la mémoire de chers êtres perdus, c'est un livre! Victor Hugo a apporté, sur la double tombe . . . quelques pages justes" (802); "quelques phrases à voix basse que j'ai dites, comme on dépose un feuillage" (Propos, p. 207).

The final image of *Prose* is likewise of complex flowers-of-expression against a tomb.

se rasseoir / Contre le marbre vainement: "j'ai voulu . . . accouder le Songe à l'autel *contre le tombeau*" (391); "mon idée, qui s'accoude à quelque balcon" (293). The "Songe" or "idée" of these quotes is like the flame-specter of "Ombre . . . Ame au si clair foyer tremblante de m'asseoir" *(Sonnet, à votre chère morte),* where the central image is a floral offering (on a tomb), which is replaced by something subtler, the flame-*Ombre.* As in the *Tombeau,* the vivid, volatile and delicate *inner* image is contrasted with a hard external object (tomb, altar), symbolizing triumph over death through an extreme refinement of poetic (imaginative, sensual) spirit.

A curiously similar idea of pubic wreath-flames laid against a tomb was expressed by Robert Musil, in *Le Rêve* (in *"84",* no 12, 1949): "les poils sur le sexe de ce corps abandonné à son impuissance brûlaient comme un feu doré sur un tombeau de marbre."

Contre . . . vainement: a hint of *vanitas vanitatum,* the gratuitousness of any such all-too-human gesture as this one of Mallarmé's. There is also a suggestion of the self-sufficiency of Baudelaire's spirit as opposed to any outer trappings whatsoever: "tombeau . . . ceux du dehors en bénéficient" (502).

The *v*'s of *vol, votif, vainement*[6] are winged, feminine; compare the *con* of *contre* (C, p. 126).

couronne: the "crown" of flame-like hair in *La Chevelure vol d'une flamme* is analogous to the circular *couronne mortuaire* of flame-hair here.

au voile: the veil is a hair covering primarily; also the idea of a shroud from which the Shade has departed: "Du suaire laissant par ses belles guipures / Désespéré monter le vieil éclat voilé" *(Ouverture ancienne,* 42); it is also an allusion to the globe of the street lamp, as in "gaz . . . voile" (736; Mauron).

frissons; dazzling wavy flame-hair was similarly evoked in "le splendide bain de cheveux disparaît / Dans les clartés et les *frissons,"* *(Faune);* compare "Ta chevelure est une rivière tiède / Où noyer sans *frissons" (Tristesse d'été;* the title has an overtone of *tresses,* is very Baudelairian, and likely echoes the "fortes tresses" of *La Chevelure).*

The *ss* in all these—*tresses, frissons*—helps to express wavy hair, as in "ivresse noyer ma tête languissante . . . mes cheveux" *(Hérodiade);* there is a possible overtone of *frisons,* "curls," at work here and, certainly, a reminiscence of Baudelaire's poetry as *frisson nouveau.*

Celle son Ombre même: Mallarmé clearly refers to a Muse with this word in two passages, where she is, as Jeanne was, ambiguously a bitch (or vampire) and a goddess ("la déesse de l'amour pur aussi bien que sensuel," 1199): "Vous sentez donc Celle qui ne lâche pas facilement ses proies anciennes vous aiguilloner. Qu'elle vous blesse, si de vos blessures sortent de la pourpre et des rubis [cf. the *rubis* of the *Tombeau*]. L'homme est fait pour saigner" (Lettre à Lefébure, 1869); also "Celle la Muse" (503). Baudelaire called Jeanne a vampire in more than one poem. She is the "Spectre" . . . C'est Elle! noire et pourtant lumineuse" *(Les Ténèbres);* "la femme est l'être qui projette la plus grande *ombre* ou la plus grande lumière dans nos rêves" (Preface to *Les Paradis artificiels).*

poison: "ton souffle, ô douceur, ô poison" *(Le Balcon).*

tutélaire: the hair of Méry, in *La chevelure vol d'une flamme* was also a tutelary flame, *tutélaire torche* (etymology: *torquere,* to twist, cf. *tordre* above); and, to repeat, it was a *couronne* in one phase, like the windblown, spread light here. Compare "l'arrière mais renaissante flamme" (402), the Phoenix of Mallarmé's artistic faith; for the Shade is the Muse and hence the spirit of the poet himself, as in "L'Ombre tout silence [Poe]." (531).

respirer: the *air* of *tutélaire* and *Baudelaire* echo the *gaz* which is *à respirer;* it is the splendid volatile poison of the Muse and the spirit of Baudelaire, as in *Le Flacon* which combines the idea of Jeanne the Muse, of poetry, of perfume, poison, and flame-like spirit-from-the-grave:

> Parfois on trouve un vieux flacon qui se souvient,
> D'où jaillit toute vive une âme qui revient.
>
> . . . .
>
> Ainsi, quand je serai perdu dans la mémoire
> Des hommes, dans le coin d'une sinistre armoire
> Quand on m'aura jeté, vieux flacon désolé,
> Décrépit, poudreux, sale, abject, visqueux, fêlé,
>
> Je serai ton cercueil, aimable pestilence!
> Le témoin de ta force et de ta virulence,
> Cher poison préparé par les anges! liqueur
> Qui me ronge, ô la vie et la mort de mon coeur!

NOTES

[1] The coupling of Satan and feces is traditional, see Norman Brown, *Life against Death*, chapter on Luther.

[2] "Coppée dont les vers s'amalgament si bien, de loin pour moi, avec la figure de camée, et avec le nom qui s'inscrirait sur une lame d'épée" (*Propos*, p. 75); similar puns on the name Céline (*ciel*) in *Vers de Circonstance* (149), and Voltaire (*vol—taire*) (872). Joyce also enjoyed playing with the mud-overtone (etc.) in Baudelaire which he rendered as "Boudeloire" in *Finnegans Wake*.

[3] Cf. Ronsard: "si fine soie [que ta chevelure] au mestier ne fut torse" (Garnier ed., p. 224); "tordre dans ma bouche / De ces cheveux l'or fin" (228).

[4] "se tordent dans leur mort des guirlandes célèbres" (*Quand l'ombre*); Eliot's *Portrait of a Lady* borrows the hair-flame image; cf. also Milton's "the comet with its horrid hair."

[5] There may be a hint of *vol*, theft, see under *La chevelure vol*.

[6] *Votif* and *vainement* replace *Triste* and *simplement* of a version reproduced in *Mallarmé: Documents iconographiques* (p. LXXXV).

19. TOMBEAU (DE VERLAINE)

The commemorative work, a sonnet, appearing under this simple title, is for a very warm and special friend: Verlaine. It was published on the first anniversary of his death and is correspondingly dated, in an epigraph: "Anniversaire—Janvier 1897"; which wintry time is significant for an understanding of the piece. Much of the color is taken from the name, Verlaine: a tender greenness, which is certainly in tune with the author of *Green,* and a woolly whiteness as of a vagabond cloud symbolizing the free-as-a-cloud poet. Almost all of the affectionate *Vers de circonstance* come about by this irrepressible playing with names; thus:

> Un beau nom est l'essentiel
> Comme dans la glace on s'y mire
> Céline reflète du ciel
> Juste autant qu'il faut pour sourire (149)

or "Monsieur Fraisse n'a la frousse / Que si la mer se courrouce" (174). Voltaire made him think of an arrow *(vol)* released from a bow, Coppée's name set up vibrations of sword *(épée),* and so on. Hence the especially fine line: "Verlaine? il est caché parmi l'herbe, Verlaine" combines grass with its greenness and there is, perhaps, as over a meadow (complete with brook, as we shall see), a fleecy whiteness in *laine.* But this sweetly lyric quality proper to Verlaine's art—the same tone is evoked in Mallarmé's little prose tribute to him—is momentarily hid by the dark winter anniversary day *(noir roc* is partly a storm cloud as well as the darker side of Verlaine's character), just as his genius was momentarily obscured to the crowd by his "somber" or seemingly degraded outer shape. But in time, "tomorrow," he will come into his own as a spring will surely come, and then the thrilling star of his poetry "will silver the crowd."

Le noir roc courroucé que la bise le roule	The black rock [Verlaine, storm cloud, and so on] angered that the north wind rolls it
Ne s'arrêtera ni sous de pieuses mains	Will not stop not even under pious hands [false mourners]
Tâtant sa ressemblance avec les maux humains	Trying [to establish] its resemblance to human ills

Comme pour en bénir quelque fun-	As if to bless some fatal mold [repre-
este moule.	sentative] of them [in a pat formula].

The "black rock" is primarily a storm cloud, angry as Verlaine was in his well-known violent moods that sent him vagabonding, specifically angry now at those who (perhaps attending this celebration as well-wishing but somewhat false mourners) would pin him down with misguided piety (narrow philistine ethics and insufficient understanding), as a type of human pathology, failing to grasp the exceptional nature of Verlaine's genius. Here we are reminded of Mallarmé's decorous attack on Max Nordau for doing just that a few years before the sonnet:

> Ce vulgarisateur a observé un fait. La nature . . . l'abolit, telle faculté, chez celui, à qui elle propose une munificence contraire: ce sont là des arts pieux ou de maternelles perpétrations conjurant une clairvoyance de critique et de juge non exempte de tendresse. Suivez, que se passe-t-il? Tirant une force de sa privation, croît, vers des intentions plenières, l'infirme élu, qui laisse, certes, après lui, comme un innombrable déchet, ses frères; cas étiquetés par la médecine . . . L'erreur du pamphlétaire en question est d'avoir traité tout comme un déchet. Ainsi il ne faut pas que des arcanes subtils de la physiologie, et de la destinée, s'égarent à des *mains* [note this word], grosses pour les manier, de contremaître ou de probe ajusteur (651).

The whole passage is a gem of critical lucidity and irony, as applicable today as ever. A similar attitude was evinced in the Poe sonnet:

> Eux . . .
> Proclamèrent très haut le sortilège bu
> Dans le flot sans honneur de quelque noir mélange.

For *roc* as a rolling cloud, see "brouillard monumental . . . la lumière et le vent ne le roulent" (635; Davies); or the "roc . . . faux manoir . . . évaporé en brumes" of the *Coup de Dés,* Page 8; also the storm cloud of *À la nue:* "basse de basalte." Baudelaire, in *Le Cygne,* had used this abstract-concrete modulation: "mes chers souvenirs sont plus lourds que des rocs." In a perhaps corollary way, rock seems to reflect clouds in "marbres sous le passage des nues" (502).

Secondly, the *roc* (or "Rock"; 552) can be the big bird in the *Arabian Nights,* "rock," which merely reinforces the wandering cloud idea, compare "Noir *vagabond* des nuits hagardes, ce Corbeau" (230).

Another, more important, overtone is Verlaine's tombstone—the title word—which is a "rolling stone" (*roc . . . roule . . . vagabond)* and this aspect is echoed in the word *moule,* that is, the (stone) mold of a degraded Bohemian life to which the crowd would vainly try to reduce the elusive poet.

*

Note the three dark *ou*'s of *courroucé* and *roule* which go with *noir;* the rolled double-*r* of *courroucé* provides an angry effect.

The *tâtant sa ressemblance* is directly echoed in the prose tribute: "Ó plusieurs qui trouverions avec le dehors tel accommodement fastueux ou avantageux" (511); compare "le sens extérieur de notre ami" (511) and *extérieur* below.

Ici presque toujours si le ramier roucoule	Here almost always if the ringdove warbles
Cet immatériel deuil opprime de maints	This immaterial grief [the dark cloud now in winter] oppresses with many
Nubiles plis l'astre mûri des lendemains	Nubile folds the ripened star of to-morrows
Dont un scintillement argentera la foule.	Of which a scintillation will silver the crowd.

The remembered ringdove—who is "almost always" there, except in midwinter—behind the cold scene is Verlaine's lyric poetry. It is hidden, like the star that symbolizes his ascendent reputation, by the oppressive dark cloud (of his deceptively ugly appearance) which further modulates (via an ambiguity of "nubile" as both marriageable and cloudy) to a veil, first funeral then, miraculously, nuptial. The veil conceals the naked *(nu)* virginal art which will be espoused by the public tomorrow, turning this winter into a bridal spring; then, following its "montée lumineuse" (865), the star of his glory will silver them; then they will fully understand "Verlaine, son génie enfui au temps futur" (511):

> La voix vous fut connue (et chère?)
> Mais à présent elle est voilée
> Comme une veuve désolée . . .
> Et dans les longs plis de son voile
> Qui palpite aux brises d'automne
> Cache et montre . . .
> La vérité comme une étoile . . .
> Accueillez la voix qui persiste
> Dans son naïf épithalème.
>
> (*Sagesse,* XVI)

The ringdove is also a symbol of grief, both the plaintive or elegiac quality of many of Verlaine's poems and the general grief of the occasion: "le cri plaintif d'un couple de ramiers" (592). In this we note the *couple,* the love behind the complaint. For the dove is obviously the bird of love, which again is apt for Verlaine's art: "ramiers . . . *amour tendre*" (304). We may remember Baudelaire's *Voyage à Cythère* where the isle of Venus (alas, now hideous) is associated with "le roucoulement éternel d'un ramier." For Mallarmé, the *ramier* is a representative of all the wonderful outdoors as in "[c'est à] regretter qu'Hugo . . habite un froid de crypte; quand avait lieu de renaître pareillement parmi des *ramiers,* ou l'espace" (520); precisely, in our sonnet, Mallarmé is aware that the proper burial site for Verlaine—naively in accord—is outdoor nature (note the Verlainian *parmi,* as in the sonnet).

toujours: is also Mallarmé's belief in Verlaine's prevailing through eternity, like Poe: "un ruisseau mélodieux [Verlaine's verse] qui . . . désaltérera d'onde suave, *éternelle* et française" (510); compare "*toujours* et irrésistiblement Verlaine" (514; remark how much Mallarmé enjoys using his name).

roucoule: "ce n'est pas sans dessein de beauté, tantôt, que le fantôme de Verlaine célébrera le sien [art, de Desbordes-Valmore], à elle, balbutiement, *roucoulement*" (875). In this passage there is a slight condescension toward the woman poet and, indirectly, toward Verlaine's somewhat feminine art, and, of course, a tiny bit is implied in his attitude toward Verlaine altogether, even though the admiration is real.

immatériel deuil: mere clouds as mourning veil; a similar image is "un clair croissant perdu par une blanche nue" *(Las de l'amer).*

opprime de maints / Nubiles plis: compare "ce suprême voile [de vapeur] . . . disparaît comme un nuage idéal, la laissant plus que nue" (603); "obnubilation des tissus" (370) is the same idea of a cloudy "immaterial" stuff obscuring a body; the main sense of *Nubile* is, of course, "marriageable" as in "nubile amant" (550), bringing in the idea of a miraculous conversion from a *deuil* to a bridal veil, as in "nymphe sans linceul" *(Hommage,* à Puvis); see under *toile* in *Salut;* a similar modulation occurs in *Hérodiade:* "le glaive qui trancha ta tête a déchiré mon voile" (N, p. 136), "de l'un et l'autre sein / laissant glisser tout voile" (N, p. 137); "Toute *nubilité* disjointe en la tunique" (N, p. 80).

l'astre mûri des lendemains: this is clear, compare "Verlaine, son génie enfui au temps futur" (511).

scintillement argentera la foule: the *i*'s of *scintillement* contrast with the *ou* of *foule.*

The wedding will be between the crowd—which is the source of genius ("la foule . . . où inclus le génie" 383) and hence a sort of mother-nature—and the wayward poet now returning: "révolte, l'homme se montrant devant sa mère quelle soit et *voilée, foule,* inspiration, vie, le *nu* qu'elle a fait du poète" *(Verlaine,* 511). The *voilée* refers to the mystery of the complex Bride the "naked" poet will eventually please, "la Muse nue et mère" (859).

Verlaine's relations with his mother were remarkably intense; her excessive love led to his attempt to throttle her.

The modulation from storm clouds to cloth is found again in "nuages ansi que d'orageuses étoffes" (624); compare "orages dont la tendresse se dénoue en rubans" *(Desbordes-Valmore, 875)*, which adds the conversion-to-love idea to the cloud-cloth modulation. The emergence of light and hope from cloud is traditional and one of Mallarmé's major themes: *"Tragédie de la nature*—la bataille du soleil avec les nuages qui se rassemblent autour de lui comme de mortels ennemis, à son coucher." (1216). In the *Coup de Dés,* Page 5, the death (or love-death) of the ancestral *Maître* leads paradoxically to a birth and, therewith, to the theme of marriage, "voile d'illusion" (C, p. 216).

Qui cherche, parcourant le solitaire bond	Who seeks, tracing the solitary bound [or bounce]
Tantôt extérieur de notre vagabond—	[Which was] Just now exterior of our vagabond—
Verlaine? Il est caché parmi l'herbe, Verlaine	Verlaine? He's hidden amid the grass, Verlaine
A ne surprendre que naïvement d'accord	To surprise [find] only [with] his lips [being] in naive accord
La lèvre sans y boire ou tarir son haleine	Without drinking from it or drying up his breath
Un peu profond ruisseau calomnié la mort.	[Find] A shallow brook [which has been] calumniated death.

The rhetorical question asks: "Why seek for Verlaine in his (recently disappeared) external shape?" He's really, it goes on to say, a part of nature, appropriately now hidden in the grass so typical of his art. We have noted the coalescence of the green in *"Ver*laine" with the grass: "dans l'herbe verte / Naïf . . . " (88).

Now he has discovered how close—as a pagan, an eternal child—he was to nature. Even death was an expression of his belonging to nature, so that, in his case (and here the gentleness of the lyricism is somewhat opposed to Mallarmé's, and Baudelaire's, deeper art), death turned out to be not so strange, so deep, so frightening. He found that his "lip was naively in accord" with the stream of death, partly because he had drunk of it alive in his ambivalent art, but mainly because he had remained so in touch with the wellsprings of existence, as ar "innocent."

The meaning of *sans y boire* is that he does not really drink of death, since he is immortal (there is an overtone of the mythological Styx or

Lethe), hence the water does not choke off or "dry up" his "breath"; its animation continues, sings on in his poetry.

What better symbol of Verlaine than a brook? "Oui, les *Fêtes galantes,* etc. . . . ne verseraient-ils pas, de géneration en géneration, quand s'ouvrent, pour une heure, les juvéniles lèvres, un ruisseau mélodieux qui les désalterera d'onde suave, éternelle et française—conditions, un peu, à tant de noblesse visible" (511). These last few words indicate that Mallarmé realized there might be some condescension in this tribute and he tries to overcome it, and really does. Verlaine *is* an absolute poet in his generally different way, and Mallarmé knew it.

Verlaine? A similar form of question is found in the essay on Rimbaud, that is, "Verlaine?" (518), but this indicates merely that he liked the name enough to use it more than once by itself, giving it the slight twist of a question. Here it is a way of bringing in the euphonious word twice.

The resonance of *laine*—adding subtle touches of fluffy white clouds emerging with spring—reminds one of the frequent use of the word *moutonner* in Verlaine, and the related image of sheep. For example, in *Sagesse,* which Mallarmé admired exceedingly (we suspect for the properly lyric poems in it like this one) there is the wonderful "L'échelonnement des haies" which goes on:

> Moutonne à l'infini, mer
> Claire dans le brouillard clair
> Qui sent bon les jeunes baies.
>
> Des arbres et des moulins
> Sont légers sur le vert tendre
> Où vient s'ébattre et s'étendre
> L'agilité des poulains.
>
> Dans ce vague d'un Dimanche
> Voici se jouer aussi
> De grandes brebis aussi
> Douces que leur laine blanche . . .

Mallarmé was certainly in a Verlainian mood when he penned:

> Simple, tendre, aux prés se mêlant
> Ce que tout buisson a de laine
> Quand a passé le troupeau blanc
> Semble l'âme de Madeleine.
>
> (107)

parmi l'herbe: parmi is one of Verlaine's favorite words: "parmi les marbres," "parmi les frissons," and so on; compare "Vous laissâtes choir parmi l'herbe / Le fruit" (117).

naïvement d'accord: "l' enfant avec son ingénue audace marchant en l'existence selon sa divinité" *(Verlaine,* 511). This image of harmony with nature, mirroring self in a brook, implies a simple narcissism, as "s'être miré naïvement" (302). This is in tune with the quality of Verlaine's work, "Verlaine, si fluide, revenu à de primitives épellations" (361); "un naturalisme absolu ou naïf" (287). Verlaine himself referred to his poetry as "un frisson d'eau sur de la mousse" *(Sagesse,* XVI). The naïve reflection in the stream is found again in "montrant à l'assistance une image simplifiée d'elle dans les eaux vives de son sentiment naïf" (345); or "source mélodique naïve" (296).

tarir:

> Pret à rentrer sous l'herbe, à tarir, à me taire,
> Comme le filet d'eau qui surgi de la terre,
> Y entre de nouveau par la terre englouti.
>   (Lamartine, *Novissima verba*)

peu profond ruisseau: Verlaine's return to nature, in death, is expressed as a drinking at the source; this traditional idea, akin to the baptismal swimming in *Le Pitre Châtié,* is evoked in the *Hommage* (à Puvis de Chavannes): "conduire le temps boire," that is, in this case, the artist leads others, like sheep, to the original waters; compare "Tout se retrempe au ruisseau primitif: pas jusqu'à la source' (544; this is Mallarmé's admiration-*cum*-reservations for Wagner). The image is likewise found in the translation of Poe's *Pour Annie*—"j'ai bu d'une eau [death] qui étanche toute soif . . . d'une source rien qu'à très peu de pieds sous terre" (209). This likely has a direct bearing on the *peu profond ruisseau.*

It is probable also that an overtone of *ruisseau* is its usage as "gutter," the city "brook" leading underground in which Verlaine often lay after a bout of drunkenness; we recall Anatole France's description of him in *Gestas.*

calomnié: there is a glancing reference here to the calumniation of Verlaine: "l'outrage . . . ne manqua: il importe à un plus rapide dépouillement du malheur inhérent au génie [de Verlaine]" (864).

20. HOMMAGE (À RICHARD WAGNER)

◊░▒░▒░▒░▒◊

Mallarmé uses the title *Hommage* for a dead fellow artist who is not a poet, but a kissin' cousin, as it were; *Tombeau* was reserved for Poe, Baudelaire, Verlaine. The first title of this sonnet was *Hommage à Wagner,* when it appeared in the January 8, 1886, number of the *Revue wagnérienne.*

As Mondor says, "Written after [the essay] 'Richard Wagner rêverie d'un poète français', *Hommage* is somewhat a restatement of it, utilizing a vocabulary often identical; and, like the prose piece, praising the musician for having realized, or at least approached, the ideal drama of which he never ceased dreaming" (1496). Actually, Mallarmé was subtly implying in the essay that Wagner got only *half*way to the ideal summit that he, the poet, knew to exist and hoped to reach. In the poem he speaks admiringly of the recently-deceased German master's authenticity, springing from the original source of beauty and truth, and thereby shaming the cheap clutter of contemporary art. There is a wistful echo, at the end, of his desire to surpass Wagner by means of literature.

The sonnet (excessively complex and not one of his best) is constructed as follows: the first quatrain alludes to the rottenness of contemporary theater, which must fall—"the [theater] trappings that a settling of the main pillar must pull down with the lack of memory" (literally, this last means "un-originality," as well as forgetting its finest tradition). The *moire* is a sort of *housse* or cloth covering laid on the furniture in the empty theater (a *relâche,* because of the death of Wagner, or empty because of the inanity of modern dramatic works). It is also the shroud of Time which will be laid on this decadent institution and, incidentally, the shroud of Richard Wagner, whose recent demise is being commemorated.

The second quatrain turns to an even closer Mallarméan concern, the book. This wonderful old tradition has also been perverted to vulgar uses, cheap sensationalism—*frisson familier!* So let the book—or *that* kind—be shoved into a closet.

The tercets describe Wagner's telling off, or showing up, the literary people with his splendid, fresh art. He has taken over the "stage" (*parvis né pour* . . . [*un*] *simulacre*), which Mallarmé thought ought to be occupied by a modern cult replacing outworn religions. In the last line he decorously refers to the possibilities of a poet, who may not be completely outshone.

Le silence déjà funèbre d'une moire	The silence already funereal of a moire [watered cloth]
Dispose plus qu'un pli seul sur le mobilier	Lays more than just a fold on the furniture
Que doit un tassement du principal pilier	That a subsidence of the principal pillar
Précipiter avec le manque de mémoire.	Must hurl down with the lack of memory.

Le silence déjà funèbre d'une moire: the *moire* is here, as we said, a cloth covering, laid over the furniture of an empty theater. The theater is empty because of the death of its master, Wagner; and it is empty in the sense that the modern theater is generally lacking in substance— "faux temple . . . Odéon . . . culte factice" (331); "flux de banalité charrié par les arts dans le faux semblant de civilisation" (541, "Wagner"); "institution [théâtrale] plutôt vacante" (298).

silence: the hush in the now empty theater. This hush is *déjà funèbre* in the sense that it (already) prefigures another death, that of the sick art that will be swept out.

The scene is, vaguely, a temple[1]—"ton [Wagner's] Temple" (546) —or Theater of a cult, recalling the shift from Old to New Testament upon the death of Christ: "une inquiétude du voile dans le temple avec des plis [note *pli*] significatifs et un peu sa déchirure" (360).

The *moire* is a shroud, image of the death of Wagner and also of the traditional art he has eclipsed.[2] It is *finis* to the useless popular sort of drama Mallarmé consistently decries in his article on the musician, as in the words "nos rêves de sites ou de paradis, qu'engouffre l'antique scène avec une prétention vide à les contenir" (545) and "un théâtre, le seul qu'on peut appeler caduc" (542).

There is in the *moire* a hint of a new text, a "New Testament" of art, laid over an old; *moire,* with its *pli,* is a common Mallarméan expression for text (*textus:* woven); the important rime *grimoire-moire* is part of the reason; another is the overtone *Moire,* the spinner and weaver of fate. Mallarmé thus uses the word for the texture of thought, in *Ouverture ancienne,* where we have the image of an original beauty springing up from under a shroud, as in the *Hommage:*

Par les ... *plis* [cf. *pli*] roidis
Percés selon le rythme et les dentelles pures
Du suaire laissant par ses belles guipures
Désespéré monter le vieil éclat voilé

· ·

Jettera-t-il son or par dernières splendeurs [?]

This last line is the final image of the sonnet; compare [referring to Wagner's music] "Ouïr l'indiscutable rayon ... l'évidence sous le voile" (365), that is to say, radiantly eloquent beneath the garb of non-verbal sounds.

The association with text is further confirmed by "Ce *pli* de sombre dentelle tissé [*textus*] par mille" (1565): see under *dentelle* of *Triptyque*.

dispose plus qu'un pli seul sur le mobilier: the "more than just a fold" means that the cloth is also a text; moreover, it is not *merely* a decorative or protective cloth, but also carries more sinister implications, those of a "funereal" cloth, dooming the cumbersome trappings—a shroud. Thus, in the *Tombeau (de Verlaine)* we have the lines "Cet immatériel deuil opprime de maints / Nubiles plis l'astre mûri des lendemains"; compare "Et nous avons laissé, tous, la foi de nos pères / Au fond des plis de leurs linceuls" (Villiers, *Santa Magdalena*); also "l'espèce de grand suaire qui couvre les choses dans leur état primordial" (*Isis*, p. 88).

mobilier: the furniture in a theater, with a strong suggestion of clutter, old trappings (the very idea of "movables" supports this tone; things that are arbitrary, unnecessary), as in "on ouït craquer jusque dans sa membrure définitive la menuiserie et le cartonnage de la bête [mediocre theater]" (313).

tassement: means "subsidence" (crumbling) as of an edifice, "ruine à demi écroulée sur un sol de foi ... à tout jamais *tassée*" (494)—"théâtre caduc" (542)—brought down by decadence. A second sense is the "packing" of a stagnant substance, with the spirit gone out of it (Richard) as in *Igitur* (436): "se *tassera* en ténèbres."

doit: Mallarmé implies it "must" come down, it cannot survive, this corrupt modern theater.   *

pilier: as of a temple, or a church, is connected with this notion of outmoded cult—"un édifice voué aux fêtes, implique une vision d'avenir ... on a repris à l'église plusieurs traits ... cette songerie restreinte par hasard à quelques *piliers* de paroisse" (397). Wagner, like Mallarmé, would inaugurate a brand new cult. This crisis mood, referring to the death of Christianity and of old-fashioned art, is expressed in "Tout s'interrompt, effectif, dans l'histoire ... L'éternel, ce qui le parut, ne rajeunit, enfonce aux cavernes et se tasse [cf. *tassement,* the packed, stagnant traditional art]: ni rien dorénavant, neuf, ne naîtra que de source. / Oublions / Une magnificence se déploiera, quelconque, analogue à l'Ombre de jadis" (394). Here we have an ambivalent filial attitude of respect and burial.

précipiter: the main idea is the pulling down, the "sweeping out" of uninspired literature by music, as in "La Musique, à sa date, est venue balayer cela ... éclat triomphal ... splendeur définitive simple" (384-385); together with the *tassement ... pilier* and Temple image, we have a mild suggestion of old Samson bringing down the house with his own demise; compare "quelle étrange aventure a *précipité* ainsi cette race?" *(Le Livre,* p. 24A).

manque de mémoire: primarily the inauthenticity of modern art, which has lost its contact with the prime sources of being (as Heidegger would say); "la peur qu'a d'elle-même ... la métaphysique et claustrale éternité" (391: "Catholicisme"); "le vieux sens s'oblitéra" (1164; C, p. 166).

The *manque de mémoire* is thus the lack of original inspiration in the contemporary public theater (contrast the golden voice from the past surging up from under the shroud of *Ouverture ancienne,* previously quoted). The dramatic opposition between a useless present state of creative mind, represented as a stagnant text, *grimoire* (with overtones of *moire,* a *textus,* woven cloth) and, on the other hand, the original spirit of beauty, is the opening situation of *Prose:* "Hyperbole ... Triomphalement ne sais-tu / Te lever" versus "mémoire ... aujourd'hui grimoire / Dans un livre de fer vêtu." The echoes of *triomphal-trompette-trop* (hyperbole) are important in both poems.

Notre si vieil ébat triomphal du grimoire,
Hiéroglyphes dont s'exalte le millier
À propager de l'aile un frisson familier!
Enfouissez-le-moi plutôt dans une armoire.

Our so-old triumphal sporting of the grammarye
Hieroglyphics which delight the crowd
Propagating a familiar shiver of the wing!
Shove it for me rather in a closet.

grimoire: is the old tradition of books, admired *(triomphal),* but outmoded, just as Mallarmé both admired the crowd which reads the books—"la foule ... où inclus le génie" (383), and scorned it: "le chiffre brutal universel" (415). The *grimoire* of *Igitur* is similarly respected and *vieux jeu.*

hiéroglyphes: a vaguely pejorative use, as in his translation of Whistler (575), or as in "Plus l'art voudra être clair, plus il se dégradera et remontera vers l'hiéroglyphe enfantin" (Baudelaire, *L'Art roman-tique*). Mallarmé was somewhat condescending also in his reference to the "hiéroglyphes inviolés des rouleaux de papyrus" (257). The quasi-scientific "heavy" word is naturally unprepossessing and odd to a poetic mind.

millier: is, in its primary sense here, not just the mass but the restricted group of a reading public, as in "Millier . . . en auditoires . . . le chef d'oeuvre convoque" (415); compare "les mille têtes [d'un public]" (390) and "sous le vrai jour des *mille* imaginations latentes . . . elle [la danseuse] te livre à travers le voile dernier qui toujours reste, la nudité de tes concepts" (307). Secondly, the line may refer to the similarly limited mass of signs in a traditional book, as in *Igitur,* or *Les Mots anglais:* "les *milliers* de mots d'une langue sont apparentés *entre eux*" (963).

aile: is any spiritual impulse for Mallarmé. Here it is obviously *too* kinetic, the emotional response of the mass, or thrill ("frisson familier") as in "banal coup d'aile d'un enthousiasme humain" (262), or "le trop d'aile" (859).

frisson familier: this is linked with the *millier* and refers to popular art, as in "aux jeux antiques [grecques] il convenait d'envelopper les gradins de légende, dont le *frisson* restât, certes, aux robes spectatrices . . . la terreur en ce *pli*" (393).

Du souriant fracas originel haï	From the smiling original din [of clarities now usually] hated
Entre elles de clartés maîtresses a jailli	Among them of supreme clarities [the god] has surged up
Jusque vers un parvis né pour leur simulacre,	To a parvis made for their [clarities'] representation,
Trompettes tout haut d'or pâmé sur les vélins,	[The god has surged up as] Trumpets aloud of gold fainted on the vellums,
Le dieu Richard Wagner irradiant un sacre	The god Richard Wagner radiating a sacred rite
Mal tu par l'encre même en sanglots sibyllins.	Ill hushed by ink itself in sibylline sobs.

The syntax is: From the smiling original din (pure Beauty, now hated by false artists) of supreme clarities, among them, has surged up their god—up to the parvis made for their representation—the god Richard Wagner, irradiating a blessing—he being golden trumpets aloud (and not) fainting on vellum paper (unlike literary art which is silent); (but this beauty is) not really silent even in ink, in (subtle) sibylline sobs.

The main idea is found in "La Musique et les Lettres": "de l'orchestre . . . tout à coup l'éruptif multiple [cf. *entre elles*] sursaute-ment de la *clarté*, comme les proches *irradiations* d'un lever de jour; vain si le langage *(encre)* . . . n'y confère un sens" (148). The partiality to language is not so strongly put in the sonnet, but is there, just the same; compare "C'est la même chose que l'orchestre, sauf que littérairement ou silencieusement . . . musique . . . plus divine que dans l'expression publique ou symphonique" (Letter to Gosse).[3] The Wagner essay hints at the same distinction.

The original source of light and beautiful sound ("music" in the broad sense Mallarmé favored: harmony) erupts in Wagner's art which, like the pure source, is now hated by false artists and their followers. His music-drama occupies the stage—the *parvis* is the area in front of a church where Western theater began; and the implication is that both the Church and the traditional theater are now outmoded; as Mallarmé said in "Catholicisme": "Oublions" (393). The radiation of the golden sound, with the awe-inspiring din of Wagnerian brass, echoes the serious original pain underlying life; but the music "tames" it, as Mallarmé describes the process in "De Même," see below. This is the play of meaning between *souriant* and *fracas*. The actual quality of Wagner is rendered in this mixture of golden blare . . . "l'or de leurs trompettes" (630)—or din, and fainting *(pâmé)*, as in the various sweetly swooning or dying falls so typical of the *Meistersinger* prelude, *Tristan, Parsifal.* The gold fainted on the vellums is a modulation from this mood to the literature that must, as Mallarmé said—"vain si le langage n'y confère un sens"—have the last word. The last line mod-estly avers that "this authentic beauty is not badly expressed even in ink," meaning, of course, in his own but partly also in the art to come, for which, as he said to Vielé-Griffin (*Dialogue*) and Verlaine (*Auto-biographie*) he was merely preparing the way.

souriant fracas originel: this is like the explosion at the origin of the cosmos, which is implied on the first page of the *Coup de Dés* (as it is in *Eureka)* or "on peut du reste commencer d'un éclat triomphal trop brusque pour durer . . . Ce procédé . . . notable dans les symphonies, qui le trouvèrent au répertoire de la nature et du ciel" (384-385), that is, the original burst of light (from a cosmic explosion) repeated in each daybreak or in glorious art.

souriant: implies the taming of the original fear (the birth trauma thunder of air on the freshly exposed ear) through the symmetries, the measured rhythms, hence the control, of art. This is, by now, a well-established psychological truth, which Mallarmé formulated in "l'orgue . . . exprime le dehors, un balbutiement de ténèbres énorme, ou leur

exclusion du réfuge, avant se s'y déverser, extasiées et pacifiées . . .
causant aux hôtes une plénitude de fierté et ce sécurité." (396). Compare the *sourire* of *Prose.*

originel: "[Wagner] considère le secret, représenté, des origines" (544); note the *or,* the *o* as womb-source, the bright *igi* springing therefrom, as in *Igitur.*

haï: the authentic source is now "hated," ignored by false artists; the word, incidentally, adds some flavor to the *fracas* of Wagner's music, just as in the *Faune* it contributes to the feeling of deep shadow: *massif [ensoleillé] haï par l'ombrage.*

entre elles: amid the clarities springs up their god, Wagner; the syntax is: "From the smiling din . . . of supreme clarities, amid them, has sprung up their *(de clartés maîtresses . . . Le dieu)* god, Richard Wagner." Also the formula suggests recreated Unity, or harmony, as in "Mots . . . apparentés *entre eux*" (963); *elles* has a suggestion of *ailes,* the rising "wings" of song, see under *irradier* below.

maîtresses: the light is "masterly" in the sense of cosmic truth. Also, Wagner is called "le Maître" (542).

parvis: "dans ton Temple, à mi-côte de la montagne sainte, dont le lever, de vérités, le plus compréhensif encore, trompette la coupole et invite, à perte de vue du *parvis,* les gazons que le pas de tes élus foule, un repos" (546). The ritual quality of the Wagnerian cult is joined with Mallarmé's meditations on the now-outmoded Church (in "Catholicisme," "De Même," etc.) whose *parvis* would give way to a less sectarian, less vulgarly legendary stage, or a modern cult of his own devising.

simulacre: basically, this refers merely to the "representation," that art is, of the original verities—"Livres, théâtres, et simulacres obtenus avec la couleur ou les marbres: l'Art" (718); "un simulacre approprié au besoin immédiat, ou l'art officiel qu'on peut aussi appeler vulgaire" (298); a similar neutral (perhaps slightly condescending) use is found in the Wagner essay: "votre [the public's] raison aux prises avec un simulacre [representation]" (542).

trompettes: like the "trompettes d'or de l'Été *(Prose),* they combine the golden blare of music with the original source, the sun.

tout haut . . . pâmé: "ces pâmoisons, ou l'âme tout haut" (referring to music; 860). Baudelaire's article on Wagner had spoken of "une lumière intense qui réjouit les yeux et l'âme jusqu'à la pâmoison" *(L'Art romantique).*

The modulation to literary expression, which is silent, is implied in this *pâmé* along with *tu* (hushed). Mallarmé discreetly implies that the expression is all the more (subtly) powerful for that; compare his

Musicienne du silence (Sainte) or Keats's "unheard music." Another meaning is that words are silenced, "faint"; they are humbled by Wagner's music. Still a further possibility is an allusion to written music, which Mallarmé had early admired for being closed to a profane public: "Ouvrons ... Wagner ... nous sommes pris d'un religieux étonnement à la vue de ces processions macabres de signes sévères, chastes, inconnus" (257). Something of the "fainting" modesty *(chastes)* of these fetching figures may be left in the sonnet; compare:

> ... Magnificat ruisselant
> Jadis selon vêpre et complie:
>   *(Sainte)*

Le dieu: "l'évidence du dieu" (Wagner, 545).

irradiant: "irradiant, par un jeu direct, du principe" (Wagner, 542); "prompte irradier ainsi qu'aile l'esprit" *(Remémoration);* compare *entre elles* above.

sacre: In *Le Pitre châtié* the word means "true art"; compare, in the *Coup de Dés,* "dernier point qui sacre" (Page 11); it indicates the metaphysical, quasi-religious value of artistic authenticity.

mal tu: a double negative, implying "not badly expressed"; also, the blackness of ink is in the *mal,* like the original sin implied in the word *doute* ("mon doute ... amas de nuit ancienne," *Faune;* "doute ... l'encre apparentée à la nuit," 481); *mal* is used in this way on Page 3 of the *Coup de Dés* (C, p. 146).

tu: "La musique, proprement dite, que nous devons piller, démarquer, si le nôtre propre, *tue,* est insuffisante, suggère ce tel poème [the Great Work]" (Propos, p. 147); compare "singulier défi qu'aux poètes dont il usurpe le devoir ... inflige Richard Wagner" (541).

The sense is mainly the quiet "music" of (Mallarmé's) verse as opposed to the *tout haut* "musique proprement dite" of Wagner, admired, but, after all, a bit vulgar, for "Tout se retrempe au ruisseau primitif: pas jusqu'à la source" (544). The subtlety of letters is further implied in the mysterious *sibyllins.*

sanglots sibyllins: literally, a rapturous but subtle artistic expression. The two words are central to Mallarmé and join in the interesting network of *blancheur sibylline (Don du poème),* referring to milk; *blancs sanglots (Apparition)* referring to music and white flower cups. Thus musical sobs, like the throaty white flower calyxes, are linked with the infantile gulping of milk, the "sibylline whiteness" of which flows from the woman in *Don du poème* or from the "sibylline" nurse in *Hérodiade (Scène:* "ton lait bu jadis"). The *gl* is sobbing exultation, as in the *gloire du long désir* of *Prose;* "G ... une aspiration simple ...

le désir, comme satisfait par *l,* exprime avec la dite liquide, joie, lumière, etc." (938). Note all the *i*'s, which express a brightness and a springing-forth, as in the *jailli,* above.

NOTES

[1] A few critics have seen Hugo in the picture; Hugo's death, just before the appearance of the sonnet, reactivated Mallarmé's life-long meditation on his own relation to the tradition, and the relation between literature and music was often, in his mind, closely corollary to this problem. The stirrings are evident in "Crise de Vers" where he invokes "la mort de Hugo" (360), to whose fatherly example he was very attached, whatever his reservations. The collapse of the mysterous edifice, in the sonnet, would be due to the demise of its "principal pillar," Hugo, in this view. Though Mallarmé undoubtedly had Hugo somewhere in his mind, I doubt if Hugo is directly present in the sonnet. The evidence is too flimsy. It is, then, mainly a common attitude toward dead masters that accounts for the evidence such as the following: "[dans un] faux temple . . . [un] culte factice . . . [essaie de remplacer] le dieu . . . Hugo . . . [et met une] guenille usée plutôt que d'avouer le voile de la Déesse en allé dans une déchirure immense ou le deuil" (331-332).

[2] It may also be a curtain in a theater: the final curtain on Wagner's life as on one of his operas (a *Götterdämmerung*). The ambiguity is exploited in "le rideau, dr: p mortuaire . . . la pièce est la tragédie L'Homme" (196, tr. of Poe); compare *Une dentelle s'abolit:* "flotte plus qu'il n'ensevelit" refers to a shroud-curtain.

[3] Published in *Revue de Littérature comparée,* no. 25 (1951), pp. 355-362.

21. HOMMAGE (À PUVIS DE CHAVANNES)

◆❂◆❂◆❂◆❂◆

An album presented to the painter Puvis de Chavannes, a friend of Mallarmé's, included this poem.[1] Puvis was a dreamy idealist, somewhat neoclassic (shades of Poussin), whose vaguely Pre-Raphaelite or *art-nouveau* manner, akin to that of Maurice Denis or Serusier, is hardly admired today. Nevertheless, he was a sincere and often pleasing artist. His style is pale, broad, mat in color, serene, two-dimensional or flat, and pastoral, typically depicting shepherds and nymphs on open meadows; hence the key words *pâtre* (with its broad flat *â*) and *ample*. As we establish in detail in our chapter on *Prose*, Mallarmé uses the word *ample* for sweeping and simple art, such as Tolstoy's (as opposed to his own). To this effect we must add the unusual deployment of three tiny words consisting exclusively of the letter *a (A)*; also *frappant, pas, par avance* and, above all, it is the name of the celebrated one, Chavannes, which, as practically always in Mallarmé, sounds the tone of his poem. The word *Hommage* is perhaps in line with this; the similar use in *Hommage (à Richard Wagner)*—even though Wagner was dead —very likely has to do with the fact that Wagner was not (really) a poet or that he was in Mallarmé's eyes only a demi-god, halfway up the slope, so to speak.

The subdued (early-dawn) quality of Puvis' tones are emphasized by the image of the "numb" fist drowsily clutching the trumpet, plus the dark tones *(ou)* of *sourde* ("dull") and *gourde* ("numb") and the eight or nine other *ou*'s, the direct meaning of the word *obscur,* the many somber nasals relieved by extremely few bright sounds.

As Richard observes, the Dawn symbolizes the artist's hope for a better world; even a dull morning *(même gourde)* has this hope, subdued. But this is a secondary meaning, since the hope is symbolized most clearly by water, not hidden light.

The classic image of Dawn's fingers had been used by Mallarmé in *Hérodiade* and in *Don du Poème*. Here the fingers are "numb," sleepy and clumsy, as if reluctant to give off the musical light of day *(clairons d'azur.)*

The Puvis-like landscape setting of the first strophe is followed by the figure of the second: he is a typical Puvis-creature, a solitary pastor in search of "water" for his flock, with the image of his divining rod hitting always just ahead of his step (striking out, as the artist does, but not too far, in Chavannes' case) and "hitting hard," that is to say, with firm precision and authority. He is ahead of his time—the *temps* of the last tercet, the masses of his era being compared, as often, to a flock of sheep which he leads to drink at the eternal, maternal Muse-source, a "nymph without shroud"—pure, naked, immortal.

Toute Aurore même gourde	Every Dawn even [or however] numb
À crisper un poing obscur	In clenching an obscure fist
Contre des clairons d'azur	Against [or on] bugles of azure [light, blaring out in the sky]
Embouchés par cette sourde	[Which are] Blown by this dullard [the Dawn].

This quatrain is all a muted Puvis landscape, a background for the figure of the next quatrain.

gourde: "un public plus curieux des jeux de la Muse que celui qui allait s'engourdissant . . ." (Baudelaire, "Théophile Gautier").

Contre: helps indicate the inept nature of the gesture, perhaps it also implies the use of the fist as a musical mute.

A le pâtre avec la gourde	[Each dawn] Has the shepherd with the gourd
Jointe au bâton frappant dur	Joined to the stick [a water-divining rod] hitting hard
Le long de son pas futur	Along his future step [hitting just ahead of each step]
Tant que la source ample sourde	So that [or as long as] the ample spring wells up

pas futur: "Vous allez superbement dans votre chemin, ou, mieux, l'ouvrez devant vos pas" (Propos, p. 170).

The stick-image is found in a very early poem, *Éclat de rire* (ML, pp. 214-215): "t'achète un bâton / Pour diriger tes pas au bord de l'insondable," which is pretty close to the idea here.

The image of the sheep led to an eternal source is found in a passage of Villiers' prose that Mallarmé quotes in his lecture on him: "le pâtre ne prend garde aux vagissements du troupeau qu'il dirige vers le lieu tranquille de la mort ou du sommeil" (482); compare "l'instinct simple de l'artiste . . . de s'abreuver à un jaillissement voulu par sa soif" (324).

Par avance ainsi tu vis	Thus ahead you live
O solitaire Puvis	O solitary Puvis
De Chavannes	De Chavannes
jamais seul	[but] never alone [i.e., you are admired]

De conduire le temps boire	[You live] To lead the time [people, like sheep] to drink
À la nymphe sans linceul	At the [fountain] nymph without a shroud [the immortal muse, source of art]
Que lui découvre ta Gloire.	That your Glory uncovers to it [to your time, the public].

le temps: this can mean infinite Time in the apocalyptic sense of "we few artists are the last heirs of all time," developed by Mallarmé's most serious texts; it can also be just "the time," that is, "our time." *le temps* is used in this complex way on Page 8 of the *Coup de Dés* (C, pp. 327-329).

The naked *nymphe* is confused with the water, as in classic myth (we may recall the *naïades* of the *Faune;* an early version of the *Faune* expressed the commingling in "l'eau qui va nu en sa promenade")— hence the overlapping ideas of sexual union and baptismal swimming in *Le Pitre Châtié.* Here a similar idea of renewing dull life by "drinking" at the source is expressed, as in "tu rajeunis la source / Où va boire ton pied" (in this little *vers de circonstance—LL, hors texte—* the water is renewed by its woman-sister, but the reverse is also implied).

sans linceul: recalls the *nubiles plis* of *Tombeau* (de Verlaine).

Gloire: the effect of this word is sure; it is the high point of various poems, for example, the "Gloire du long désir" of *Prose,* the "cri des Gloires qu'il étouffe" of *Quelle soie;* part of the reason for its power is described in Appendix C, under *g*.

NOTE

[1] It was published in a special number of *La Plume* (1895).

22. TOUTE L'ÂME RÉSUMÉE

This succinct sonnet was not included by Mallarmé in the edition of the *Poésies* he prepared shortly before his death, though it had been published in 1895. It is a playful-serious little *art poétique,* as undefinitive as Verlaine's equally famous one in verse, not to be relied on for rounded poetic doctrine, however often it is quoted by hurried simplifiers.

By its very modesty it tells us something of Mallarmé's aesthetic. It is discreet, almost inaudible, extremely precise (despite the negative reference to the "sens trop précis," used in a special sense) yet gracefully supple. It is airy as "smoke," yet sensual as a "kiss," or a bright red glow. The humble, everyday bourgeois-artistic reality ("cigar") once again belies the myth of Mallarmé as the blankly cold, starry-eyed neo-Parnassian turning away from us all.

The first line, *Toute l'âme résumée,* reminds us that Mallarmé— who said of his friend Manet that he hurled himself at the canvas each day afresh, as if it were his last chance—gave his all, *toute l'âme,* each time, *summed it up (résumée)* in each of his serious productions. There is even a hint of the small death-in-life implied in any authentic work, in the word *expirons.* Certainly there is a tiny "death" implied in self-criticism that mercilessly does away with our enthusiastic first outbursts: initial "rings" are "abolished" and give way to "other [new] rings." The separation of the bright "kiss of fire" from the ash is the distillation of innocent beauty he seeks to achieve as avidly as any alchemist in quest of philosopher's gold (but with a fuller awareness of the odds). The *romances* that spring to the poet's lips are crude art needing purification by exclusion of the "real," that is, the lumpish unrefined stuff of experience not made over into art (just as the dense "intrinsic wood" is opposed to the airy "thunder in the leaves" he spoke of in "Crise de vers," 365-366). Although the modern esthetician is quick to object here that we need that "intrinsic wood," the ruggedness and rawness of life, in lively art, he is merely in so objecting uttering a dialectical truism of which Mallarmé was himself well aware (C, p. 20); what Mallarmé is saying here remains *a* truth, not all truth at once, especially in so limited a medium as this modest verse. In sum, if we put the question "Is art ordinary life?" one might answer for Mallarmé, "Yes, but it is even more *art*."

In a similar way, it can hardly be held that Mallarmé is against precision because of the *sens trop précis* (opposed to his *vague littéraire*). The word *trop* is important here, and the word *précis* is obviously being used in a special way, that is, it indicates a cold literalism, or misplaced "scientific" accuracy such as mars much Parnassian work.[1]

Toute l'âme résumée	The whole soul summed up
Quand lente nous l'expirons	When we slowly exhale it
Dans plusieurs ronds de fumeé	In several rings of smoke
Abolis en autres ronds	Abolished in other rings

Toute l'âme résumée: "le texte . . . résumé de toute l'âme, la communiquant au passant" (529-530). Note the progress from dark *ou,* the site, through a middling broad *â,* to bright *u* and *é.* This is the stasis-kinesis-stasis pattern which is so important in the *Coup de Dés:* for example, Page 3, under *résume* (C, p. 150); compare "Surgi de la croupe et du bond."

lentement: this reflects his doctrine of artistic *patience,* the keynote of *Prose.*

expirons: probably hints at the sacrificial giving of self in art, the little *suicide (beau)* and transfiguration of the soul that beauty requires; compare: "Expirer . . . Le cri des Gloires qu'il étouffe" (*Quelle soie*) or:

> L'oiseau qu'on n'ouït jamais
> Une autre fois en la vie
>
> Le hagard musicien
> Cela dans le doute expire . . .
>   (*Petit air II*)

The sterile vase of *Surgi* was incapable of this total act: "rien expirer."

fumée: "tout est fumée, Tabac d'Espagne et vers français" (19). The nature of smoke, an airy almost illusory (fictive) distillation, makes it an apt metaphor; like incense, it seems to be offered up, as in "le tabac sans parler roule les oraisons." (*Aumône*); compare "la prière . . . parmi les flots d'encens" (10) and "l'odorant nuage / De ton amour céleste image / Qui s'exhale au pied de l'autel" (3); see Page 6 of the *Coup de Dés,* under *enroulée.*

Note the series of *o*'s for smoke rings: "ronds . . . abolis . . . autres ronds." The *b* and the element *bol* are part of this (C, pp. 222-223).

The rounded lips funnel the smoke, "muet muet entre les ronds" (a kiss, *Rondel II*); the *o* is prominent there too, as in the word *interromps;* compare *Surgi.*

Atteste quelque cigare	Attests some cigar
Brûlant savamment pour peu	Burning cannily if
Que la cendre se sépare	The ash separates at all
De son clair baiser de feu	From its bright kiss of fire

atteste: has a nice hint of savoring (Old French *taster*) the cigar.

cigare: "s'exprimer, ainsi que d'un cigare, par jeux circonvolutoires, dont le vague, à tout le moins, se traçat sur le jour électrique et cru" (371). The indirect quality of subtle art *(circonvolutoire, vague)* is implied in this cigar-smoke. Note the *ar* transparent effect, as in *clair, sépare;* compare the use of this word in *Prose.*

clair baiser de feu: delightful overtones of *braise, fraise* (rhymed by Baudelaire, CXV). Ronsard used exactly this cluster *(baiser-braise-fraise)* in his *Baiser* (ed. Garnier, p. 237): compare "le baiser de feu" (Lamartine, *Novissima verba*).

Ainsi le choeur des romances	Thus if the chorus of romances
A la lèvre vole-t-il	Flies to your lips
Exclus-en si tu commences	Exclude therefrom if you begin [to compose]
Le réel parce que vil	The real because [it's] abject
Le sens trop précis rature	A too precise meaning erases [or crosses out]
Ta vague littérature.	Your [poet's, smoke's] vague literature.

romances: refers to the crude stuff of art, springing directly ("pornographically," Joyce would say) from love, like a sentimental ballad: "air suranné, banal . . . ballade *romantique*" (271). The *a,* and the *an,* have something to do with the banality: "Quoi de moins essorant et fluide que ce mot *flat*." (921).

rature: compare:

> A ce papier fol et sa
> Morose littérature
> Pardonne s'il caressa
> Ton front vierge de rature
> (109).

NOTE

[1] Or the drily exact statement of business, the matter-of-fact term of ordinary communication. These may add crispness occasionally to modern verse, and some genuine gains have been registered in this direction. Too often, unfortunately, at a steep cost: the loss of total artistic drive.

23. AU SEUL SOUCI DE VOYAGER

A late poem, not included by Mallarmé in any edition of his *Poésies, Au seul souci* first appeared in a collection honoring the memory of Vasco da Gama.[1] It is a greeting (or "health"), like *Salut* —*ce salut* occurs on line 3—addressed to young artists by the declining old Master, who is going down with his ship, as it were.[2] He incites them to the lonely creative voyage, gratuitous, disinterested, "for the sole sake of traveling" *beyond (outre)* the metaphorical "India"—a land of fascinating but material commerce (jewel and spice trade), facile art.

Let this greeting be the messenger of time itself (beyond the limited Indias of space), the Eternal Way (which I represent, in the great tradition)—such is the real journey you must make, the cape you (like the historical Vasco going around the Cape of Good Hope) are rounding as you rise to artistic maturity.

The messenger from all time is then compared to the voice of a bird from pure space settled on the boat, like an angel guiding the poet. The bird announces a new discovery, over and over it reminds him of the "treasure" he must stubbornly seek, without changing course . . . a "useless treasure" (unlike those meretricious splendors he goes high-headed past); the dark night of the despairing soul, the perfect jewels of ideal beauty, that is his fate and his reward (like the final remote constellation emerging from the apocalyptic Night of the *Coup de Dés*).

These, the last couplet says, are reflected through the voice of the angelic bird to the stoically "smiling," grimly "pale" (but, we are to feel, happy in his depths) Vasco.

Au seul souci de voyager	To the sole concern of voyaging
Outre une Inde splendide et trouble	Beyond a splendid and uneasy India
—Ce salut soit le messager	—Let this greeting be the messenger
Du temps, cap que ta poupe double	Of time, cape that your stern rounds

The syntax is ambiguous: "Here's to the sole, and so forth"; or "Let this greeting be the messenger to (you, sharing, or you, bearing) the sole concern of voyaging."

We are forcefully reminded of Baudelaire's "Les vrais voyageurs sont ceux-là seuls qui partent pour partir" (*Le Voyage*).

souci: "Le blanc souci de notre toile" (*Salut*) has the same fascinating combination of somber concern and bright quest; compare the *blanche agonie* of *Le vierge, le vivace.*

splendide et trouble: "splendid" for its fabled jewels (cf. his friend Villiers' *Akaëdysséril*), *trouble* or "uneasy" because it is also supposed to be a land of dark mystery and danger for the traveler from the West. It represents a special risk for the artist, tempting him with its exotic earthly treasure; he must sail on. Note the bright *i* and hard *d*'s of *splendide* contrasting with the dark *ou* of *trouble.* The darkness of the voyage is reflected in the many *ou*'s, as in *souci, outre, trouble, poupe, double.*

Ce salut soit: originally read *Ce salut va, le messager . . . .*

Time, eternity is the true field of the creator's striving, the chaos he must mold ("conduire le temps," 72), the true current he must sail on or "beat against" (as Scott Fitzgerald said); compare "Tel qu'en Lui-même enfin l'éternité le change" (*Tombeau d'Edgar Poe*). Time is also the source of the ideal message, Truth or Beauty. The Time-voyage is that of the rising to manhood of the young, filial poets.

Temps, cap que ta poupe double: The passive backdrop—land and water—for the voyager is mainly in flat vowels; the various round consonants (*p, b*) and vowels (*o*) may have something to do with the "rounding" idea. The cacophony of the line is harder to explain. It is rare in Mallarmé. Perhaps it is one of the reasons he did not include the poem in his collection. (The poem is successful anyway.)

Comme sur quelque vergue bas	As on some yard-arm lowly
Plongeante avec la caravelle	Plunging with the caravelle
Écumait toujours en ébats	Foamed always fluttering
Un oiseau d'annonce nouvelle	A bird of new tidings
Qui criait monotonement	Who cried monotonously
Sans que la barre ne varie	Without the tiller's changing
Un inutile gisement	[About] A useless lode [pure art]
Nuit, désespoir et pierrerie	Night, despair and jewels
Par son chant reflété jusqu'au	By its song reflected to
Sourire du pâle Vasco.	The smile of pale Vasco.

In the second quatrain it is clear that Baudelaire, who is in the august lineage Mallarmé speaks for here, had helped steer him toward some apt imagery:

> Mon coeur, comme un oiseau voltigeait tout joyeux
> Et planait librement à l'entour des cordages,
> Le navire roulait sous un ciel sans nuages.
> (*Voyage à Cythère*)

*

> ... vaisseau
> Qui roule bord sur bord et plonge
> Ses vergues dans l'eau ...
> (*Le Serpent qui danse*)

vergue ... *avec* ... *caravelle:* the series of cutting *v*'s remind us of "vous l'avant fastueux qui coupe le flot" of *Salut;* compare "Le vierge, le vivace et le bel aujourd'hui."

Écumait: the white bird merges with foam at each down-movement.

annonce: originally, *ivresse.*

monotonement: as in the "solo long" and "monotone" of the *Faune,* the three *o*'s are part of the effect; the four *a*'s of the next line are comparably flat, steady, calm.

barre: may have, ambiguously, an overtone of "shoal" or "sandbank": danger (cf. the *écueil* of *Salut*). The *barre* held by the old Master of *Un Coup de Dés* (Page 4) was likewise double in meaning.

As a symbol of virile steadfastness, the *barre* supports the notion that the hero heads straight for his goal.

inutile gisement / Nuit, désespoir et pierrerie: compare the *Solitude, récif, étoile* of that other credo and greeting, *Salut; nuit* is the total setting, double in mood (*désespoir et pierrerie,* in apposition to *nuit,* as Cellier says). These lines are studded with bright acute effects (*i, u, é*), the constellation jewels. These are not the "pierres précieuses de l'Inde" (263) but reflect them in their ideal way,[3] as "pierreries d'une couronne [art]" (531). *gisement* may also mean "landfall" (Cellier), in which case it is again the "ideal beyond."

Vasco: he symbolizes the old poet and also, potentially, his spiritual sons. As the historical figure, he contains, in a sense, these future types of Man (see note 2).

NOTES

[1] See the chapter "Le Vaisseau fantôme" in Cellier for an account of the poem's origin, a deflation of A. Gill's remarks on it, and a host of parallels from Poe, through Wagner, to Hugo.

[2] This may remind us of Vigny's *Bouteille à la mer.* Although we cannot be certain to whom the message is addressed, this idea of a greeting to the young seems to be the most likely and characteristic of Mallarmé. It is possible, as some have seen it, that he is addressing Vasco, who has successfully navigated "time" by his glory; Mallarmé might then be the bird chirping his "useless" poet's message to the great ancestor, a hardy extrovert like the *Maître* of the *Coup de Dés,* who merely smiles and keeps on his active course; *monotonement* would be Mallarmé's ironic awareness that his repeated puristic doctrine generally goes unheeded by the world's doers; *reflété* would mean that such men receive their spiritual message only indirectly, through poets. Symbolized by the bird on his boat, the ideal seems to have already haunted Vasco,

if only potentially (just as the *Maître* was Man and contained the germ of the future poet), so that there could be a theme of reconciliation between these eternallly opposed types, as in "Conflit" and "Confrontation" (C, p. 159). Whether the greeting goes backward or forward, the theme of mystic male succession remains basically the same; perhaps both interpretations were intended. We note that Mallarmé, who took up sailing in his later years, became increasingly aware that he bore within himself, dialectically, an earlier type of Man (see *Salut* and "Le Livre" as well as the *Coup de Dés*).

[3] Hérédia's *Conquérants* has similar imagery:

> Ils allaient conquérir le fabuleux métal
> Que Cipango mûrit dans ses mines lointaines
> . . . .
> Ou penchés à l'avant des blanches caravelles,
> Ils regardaient monter en un ciel ignoré
> Du fond de l'Océan des étoiles nouvelles.

24. TRIPTYQUE

◊◝◟◝◟◝◟◝◟◝◟◊

These three sonnets, labelled simply I, II, III, form a conscious unity around one main theme: the inexorability of death. From dead center of the total despair, there emerges, miraculously, a faint glimmer of hope. This distant possibility is related to the remote constellation appearing in the dark night of an apocalypse, in the *Coup de Dés*. In a sense, the words sprinkled on the page are finally seen to form a star-cluster of promise. As in the Gospels, all has been lost, symbolically, and, symbolically, the hint of a total redemption at last appears in artistic space.

The linkage between the three sonnets is not very strong beyond this one point, and should not be forced in regard to details. I suspect they were written separately over a longish period (they were published in 1887), not in a single *élan*. After all, it is enough to execute one solid poem at a time, and Mallarmé's genius is synthetic, self-involved, "circular." As we have described in detail elsewhere (C, pp. 89-116), his words cluster and evolve internally, slowly forming those "stalactites" of which Thibaudet wrote; his talent is not at all schematic, suited to the construction of a sequence or any such strung-out purpose. Either he was busy crystallizing his entire poetic vision of reality, which eventually became the *Coup de Dés,* or else he worked microcosmically on a unit-piece, the individual poem that reflected the whole; nothing important in-between. The grouping, then, is probably an afterthought, as often happens in such cases. Aside from the room setting and the time sequence, the only direct link of detail—probably also a retouch,[1] —is the capitalization of one word in the middle of each: *Orgueil, Chimère, Jeu,* all symbolizing a supreme expressive act menaced, or annihilated, by *hasard;* these impersonal entities are the little "hero(es)" of this trilogy, the hero being reduced, as Mallarmé theorized in "Solennité" (334), to a mere *trait,* like the one on Page 8 of the *Coup de Dés* (C, p. 293).

The first poem, *Tout orgueil,* evokes a dead poet figure, one close to him like Villiers—whose subsequent disappearance evoked similar imagery in Mallarmé's lecture on him—potentially Mallarmé himself. The torch of life is extinguished and his room is left unwarmed. The

piece ends in despair; yet something survives in the last word, *console*
—after all, this image hovers in the dark like a ghostly star. The setting
of this sonnet is evening passing into night *(soir)*, in a solitary room
reminiscent of Poe and various *décors* of Mallarmé *(Sonnet, à votre
chère morte;* Hérodiade's chamber; or *Igitur*, where the furniture,
chimère, gleams in the dark when all has been reduced to zero in the
hero's consciousness).

Number II is the same setting, but now become fully night
(veillée); the nocturnal chamber is dimly lit, with a vague light fixture
visible in the gloom. There is still no hope, no progression of hope
through the sonnet sequence. All that shifts really is the time of night
as we spin through the darker hours. But in the last sonnet, number III,
the implied physical advent of dawn does bring some buoyancy, furthered by other themes in the poem. Whereas the theme was first an
unlit torch (I), then an ungiven "kiss" (II), here a universal sexual
union or act of creative Eros *(Jeu suprême)* overlaps with a general
Dawn theme; all this is a little stronger (the poem is richer, more cen-
trally Mallarméan, complexer), and this strength of texture, together
with the Dawn motif, adds something to the *quand même* note of hope.
Despite the predominant recurrence of the unremitting idea of loss, the
last word is *naître*, a word hard to deprive of all promise, even in the
past conditional tense with which he has muted and all but swamped it.

I: TOUT ORGUEIL FUME-T-IL DU SOIR

Tout Orgueil fume-t-il du soir,	Does all Pride [turn to] smoke in the evening,
Torche dans un branle étouffée	A torch snuffed out in a shake
Sans que l'immortelle bouffée	Without the immortal puff's [spirit's]
Ne puisse à l'abandon surseoir!	Being able to defer the abandonment [nothingness]!

Orgueil: during "une méditation [about the death of Villiers]
commencée dans une chambre [Villiers'] où le mal, quelque mois
auparavant, s'était abattu, et le foyer éteint, ensemble" (498), Mallarmé
speaks of "chacun de nos *orgueils,* les susciter" (481), this *orgueil* being his pious re-creation of his friend, an ephemerally flaring-up flame—
"une bouffée unique de joie et une exaltation suprême" (Villiers' memory, 510)—in the fireplace that he thought of as the theater of his mind

(l'âtre . . . un théâtre . . . minuscule," 295); compare the *Sonnet, à votre chère morte,* or "exaltations . . . jaillissant, avec *orgie* d'immémorialité" (389). (We may sense, in passing, some minor overtones of *orgueil: orgie-orgasme-organe*).

The drama is echoed in the eternal "tragedy of nature" *(Dieux antiques)* that Mallarmé saw behind every myth: the birth and death (and rebirth?) of light. Thus the stars of *Quand l'ombre* are an *orgueil menti par les ténèbres,* cancelled by the dark, as here. There is possibly some reminiscence of a poem by Leconte de Lisle that he chose as an epigraph for *Les Dieux Antiques:* "les grands astres . . . triomphants d'orgueil."

torche: this *orgueil*—recalling the Elizabethan overtones of the word "pride" (e.g., in Shakespeare) or, in Mallarmé, the faun's *vanité . . . flamme*—is broadly speaking a flame of Eros, and there is thus a gentle sexual connotation in *branle,* the snuffing action of smothering death (like the murderous *Mère²* of *Les Fleurs*) that extinguishes this joyous flare; thus, also, the word *étouffée* may echo the feminine word *touffe,* the hair of *Quelle soie; torche . . . orgueil* is like the *cri des gloires* that expires in the *considérable touffe* of Méry, the faun's *rire* in the *touffe échevelée* of the nymphs.

branle: Chisholm alludes to the spinning of the earth which has extinguished the sunset-torch. Perhaps.

étouffée: the dark *ou* is as effective as in the cited *considérable touffe* (in which the poet's eyes are darkened, *enfouir mes yeux*). The golden *or* of *torche* is in striking contrast.

The suggestion of "blown out by a wind" in *branle* is supported by the breezy *ff,* also in *bouffée:* "soufflé [Baudelaire] comme une bougie par la froide haleine qui nous éteindra tous" (Gautier, *in* Cellier). In *Claire Lenoir,* Villiers wrote: "Quelle serait la gloire des torches s'il n'y avait pas les ténèbres?"

bouffée: "gloire, ou autres *bouffées* infinies" (389); "une *bouffée* unique de joie et une exaltation suprême" (a memory of Villiers, evoked in his talk; 510).

abandon: "*Affres* . . . révulsif ébat . . . par surcroît / L'ordinaire *abandon* sans produire de trace / . . . vers l'infini vorace" (1446).

La chambre ancienne de l'hoir	The old chamber of the heir
De maint riche mais chu trophée	Of many a rich but fallen trophy
Ne serait pas même chauffée	Wouldn't even be warmed
S'il survenait par le couloir.	If he [the hero] came back through the corridor.

The dead Villiers' unwarmed room is described by Mallarmé with the inherited cultural objects this aristocratic, final heir of a long tradition had revivified. Now, alas, they are fallen *(chu)* into disuse with his death: "luxurieux logis et mémorable à cause d'un trés vaste et suranné piano . . . Le Wagner s'y était tu et aussi maint accompagnement essayé à ceux des vers qu'aimait le maître" (498). We are also reminded of Hérodiade's tradition-rich chamber, lined with trophies. She too is a lonely fateful heir.

There is also a strong reminiscence here of *Ses purs ongles,* of 1868, the décor of which Mallarmé himself described as "une chambre avec personne dedans . . . de vagues *consoles* . . . ce logis abandonné du monde" (Propos, pp. 83-84). This has a later cosmic equivalent in the deserted *lieu* of the *Coup de Dés,* with the Maître gone for good (Man, rather than just the poet, but including him).

The desolation of the "unwarmed" room hardly needs comment: life, even his own intimate setting, have rejected the poet, would no longer greet him. There is the minor suggestion also that even if he came, as a ghost, he would bear no vital warmth.

The spectre of the corridor recalls *Toast funèbre: l'espoir du corridor,* (q.v.); a poem of Longfellow, well-known to Mallarmé since it was cited in Poe's *Poetic Principle,* had the lines: "the bards sublime / Whose distant footsteps echo / Down the corridors of time," perhaps echoed anew in *Igitur:* "le bruit dans le corridor du temps de la porte de mon sépulcre" (439), referring, precisely, to his dead spiritual ancestors. All this converges toward the one meaning in the sonnet: the death of a revered poet-master representing a true tradition (C, pp. 197-203).

trophée: the element *trop* is important, reinforcing the note of *orgueil* in the word, which is in the major cluster of *Prose: troptriomphe-trompette,* (q.v.); the *or* of *orgueil* and *trophée* is also effective; the round *o* and swollen *p* are dominant.

Affres du passé nécessaires	Necessary death-anguish of the past
Agrippant comme avec des serres	Gripping as if with claws
Le sépulcre de désaveu,	The sepulchre of disavowal [tombstone that denies life]
Sous un marbre lourd qu'elle isole	Under a heavy marble [tablet, table top] it isolates
Ne s'allume pas d'autre feu	There is lit no other fire
Que la fulgurante console.	Than the flaming buffet.

The buffet or console has "claws" (perhaps clasps, or carvings) that (seem to) hold the marble top; they are claws of "necessary" fatality *(affres du passé:* death-agony of the deceased).[3] They are perhaps like the fingers of a hand of a buried corpse that tries futilely to push the oppressive tombstone. The "anguish"—the hopeless revolt of the "living" memory of a beloved friend (himself in *le passé*) against the present death-state—is "necessary" to the piety and prolonged grief of true friendship and to future life, the poem. Another possibility, suggested by Chisholm, is the idea of fated death sorrows (*passé*: tradition). Chisholm also sees in the claws a reminiscence of Poe's raven, perched on the marble bust; compare "un rêve m'étreint sous sa griffe" (155).

Mallarmé remarked on an image of his Poe sonnet, in the *Bibliographie* of the *Poésies:* "un bloc de basalte que l'Amérique appuya sur l'ombre légère du poète, pour sa sécurité qu'il n'en ressortît jamais" (1487). This reinforces the feeling that it is the uncompromising finality of death (as in *Toast funèbre*) that gives the fullest meaning to a poet's life. Mallarmé expressed a similar idea in his *Tombeau d'Anatole* (f., 67; f., 111). Compare also, "ce sépulcre . . . la pierre que mon doigt / Soulève avec l'ennui d'une force défunte" (*Sonnet,* 69), which emphasizes the powerlessness of the deceased.

affres: referring to Villiers' death, Mallarmé wrote: "craignant qu'il n'y ait impiété à changer les *affres* en gloire prompte" (502). As in the *Tombeau d'Anatole* (f. 43), he rejected a too-easy consolation (dialectic); compare *"affres* que jusqu'à leur lividité hérisse / Un révulsif ébat" (1446), referring to the fright of the nurse over the decapitation of Saint John and the horror of the act itself; compare "affres . . . éclat" (393). AFFRE (in capitals) occurs prominently in Villiers' *Clair Lenoir*.

passé: an apt word for the Villiers mood, compare *hoir*: Villiers was haunted by tradition; "des heures que ne fréquentera peut-être pas même *le Passé*" (letter to Villiers, September 24, 1867); in this phrase Mallarmé seems to be communing with, or paying homage to, his friend's favorite mood (see note 3). Communion with the past, with tradition, "necessarily" involves communion with death.

serres: the "necessary" hold of death on life, of gravity on lightness: "aile tendue [vs.] . . . *serres* enracinées" (653); "le coeur comprimé par la griffe du souvenir" (Baudelaire, *Un Mangeur d'opium*).

sous un marbre lourd qu'elle isole:

isole: by contrast, surrounding or framing it with its claws, the body of the console makes the tablet top stand out singly. Like the *pâle mausolée,* the swan, Hérodiade herself, and the *bassin* of *Ouverture ancienne,* or the *froid glacier* (89), the *marbre* is an image of sterility transfigured into pure beauty (death into poetic life), just as Gautier's tomb, indifferent, hard and cold, is a *beau monument.* (Experienced readers of poetry know that images that play a negative role in the "story" can, nonetheless, be imbued with strange attraction, can participate in the total harmony, as Boileau and Joyce, among others, have observed.)

The resemblance of the *console,* with its marble top, to a mantelpiece is part of the vibrant atmosphere of presence-absence.

la fulgurante console: "notre bahut est très vieux: contemple comme ce feu rougit son triste bois" (271); the sterile yet fascinatingly, even maddeningly lively effect of mere reddish wood as an absent fire—like the "absente de tous bouquets"—the defunct fire of the poet's life, came perhaps directly from this old chest in the room at Tournon in which Mallarmé began the long meditation which led to *Hérodiade, Igitur, Ses purs ongles* and the entire dead-poet lineage, including this poem. (Of course the dead poet most prominent in Mallarmé's mind was his future self, of which all the other poet figures are more or less remote projections. Recent commentators, discovering various relatively external causes for his imagery, tend to ignore this simple fact of creative life.)

The possibility of a vestigial sunset glow, as the source of this evening light, has been mentioned by Chisholm. Richard sees a *veilleuse* (p. 258).

console: "sur des consoles en le noir Salon: nul ptyx . . . Car le Maître est allé puiser," and so forth *(Sonnet allégorique de lui-même,* 1482). The slight pun of "consolation" gleaming in the dark is found again in "consoles, en l'ombre" (377) "de vagues consoles . . . .. logis abandonné" (Propos, pp. 83-84).

II. SURGI DE LA CROUPE ET DU BOND

Ronsard, a prime influence on Mallarmé (he celebrated him, *en passant,* in his *Symphonie littéraire)* had used a conceit similar to the central theme of this sonnet, in a little poem entitled *Le Baiser de Cassandre:*

> Baiser fils de deus lèvres closes,
> Filles [the lips] de deus boutons de roses

Another Renaissance poet, Jean Second, indulges the same conceit in a Latin sonnet. Mallarmé liked the vein enough to work it again in *Rondel II:*

> Si tu veux nous nous aimerons
> Avec tes lèvres sans le dire
> Cette rose [the kiss] ne l'interromps
> Qu'à verser un silence pire

further symbolizing the abstract entity as a "sylphe":

> Muet muet entre les ronds
> Sylphe dans la pourpre d'empire [the red lips]
> Un baiser flambant . . .

Here in the sonnet sequence, the "sylphe" is an event that does *not* occur; it is light not lit (no encounter of the light-source and the air of the room); a potion not poured; love seed not given; even ink not spilled fecundatingly on a page (the seed of the unborn perfect poem). In sum, the poem, a mere ghost of itself, is a tense, limit-situation drama of Expression.

The drama is essentially the same as the one depicted on Page 4 of the *Coup de Dés:* the "fist" that shakes the dice will also fail to make its throw. The image of the fist is remarkably close to that of the vase-rump, and with similar undertones (C, p. 172).

As Mauron surmised, the vase, or *verrerie éphémère,* is probably a glass light fixture typical of the era; it may well have resembled the "veilleuse [cf. *veillée*] de verre de Bohême, en forme d'urne [cf. *breuvage*] suspendue au plafond par des chaînettes," which Proust describes in the opening pages of *À la Recherche.*

Surgi de la croupe et du bond	Having surged up from the rump and the [round] bounce
D'une verrerie éphémère	Of an ephemeral glassware [vase or lamp base]
Sans fleurir la veillée amère	Without adorning with a flower the bitter waking hours
Le col ignoré s'interrompt.	The unknown [ignored] neck [of the vessel] is interrupted [by empty air, no act].
Je crois bien que deux bouches n'ont	I well believe that two mouths haven't drunk,
Bu, ni son amant ni ma mère,	Neither my mother [air] nor her lover [vase-neck],
Jamais à la même Chimère,	Ever at the same Illusion [a Kiss],
Moi, sylphe de ce froid plafond!	[I believe this], I, sylph [unborn being] on this cold ceiling!
Le pur vase d'aucun breuvage	The pure vase of no potion [love-pouring]
Que l'inexhaustible veuvage	Except the endless emptiness
Agonise mais ne consent,	Agonizes but doesn't consent [to "exhale"],

Naïf baiser des plus funèbres!	—Naïve kiss [the Expression] most funereal!—
À rien expirer annonçant	[Consent] To exhale anything announcing [leading to]
Une rose dans les ténèbres.	A rose in the darkness [the flowering product of the union, the beautiful kiss, the poem-child, the embodiment of the sad, waiting-in-limbo sylph].

Surgi de la croupe et du bond: we are offered a graphic, almost Braque-like, image of the "vase," with round bottom (rump) and linear neck. The effect of *croupe* and *bond* is like that in the common expression *croupe rebondie* (e.g., "quelque croupe rebondie," of a struggling horse, in *Boule de suif);* the dark *ou* and sensual *our (amour-lourd-velours-nourrir-pourpre)* in *croupe* and the round *o* and *b* of *bond* are part of the poetic reason for the expression. Verlaine's earthy career is a series of *bonds (Tombeau);* Saint John's head bounces humbly on the ground in *quelque bond hagard.* A possible overtone of *bond* is "boundedness," limitation (as in *bonds).*

The *surgi* effect of linear up-thrust is based on the bright virile acute *i,* with the *u* perhaps as the tense container, as in "urnes . . . croupe" (670), see *u* in the Letter Table; caressing *g* and liquid *r* are active, and the whole line is memorable.[4]

verrerie éphémère: "le Rêve a *agonisé* en cette *fiole de verre,* pureté, qui renferme la substance du *Néant"* (439).

veillée amère: "sans écouter minuit qui jeta son *vain* nombre, / Une *veille* t'exalte à ne pas fermer l'oeil" *(Sonnet,* 67).

col: it is rather like that of the hopeless sterile swan in *Le vierge, le vivace et le bel aujourd'hui* and is similarly agonized: "Tout son *col* secouera cette blanche *agonie . . . Mais non . . .";* compare *"Agonise mais ne* consent" here. The *col . . . s'interrompt* also recalls the decapitation theme of *Hérodiade,* that is, the desperate encounter with the murderous nothing which stops our aspiration: "Un révulsif ébat vieil horrifié droit . . . par surcroît / L'ordinaire abandon sans produire de trace . . . vers l'infini vorace" (1446). The complex aura of meaning around this excerpt (and the *col* of the sonnet) is discussed in note 11 of *Hérodiade.*

ignoré: a complex sense of an unknown or ignored object abandoned useless in a darkened room—the mood of the objects in *Ses purs ongles, Igitur,* and the final stars on the *Coup de Dés,* like the pure work of art, "hors l'intérêt" and "froide d'oubli et de désuétude" (Page 11); compare "où qu'ils expirent [cf. *expirer* below] en le charme et leur *désuétude . . .* des bibelots abolis, sans usage . . . une appropriation à son décor, et l'on se meuble de *chimères"* (499). The "chimère" is a closely associated idea, both in *Igitur* and in this sonnet. Its hopelessness is evoked by the Icarus-curve of the rising and falling outline of the *col,* as in: "chimère, en la limite de son geste, qui va redescendre" (370) or "contour coupé là où il cesse d'être" (Corr., p. 234).

A second sense is that the neck is not "known" in the Biblical sense or, as a corollary, is simply "ignored" by the dark air with which it will not mate. A comparable idea of deserted beauty is the *ors ignorés* and the *splendeur ignorée* of Hérodiade, the *mystère vain de [son] être.*

s'interrompt: the *o* here and in *col* are suggestive of a round rim of the neck of a vase, and so on; the overtone of *rond* is part of this effect, as in "Cette rose ne l'interromps . . . entre les ronds" *(Rondel I).* For a fuller use, see under *sylphe,* below.

deux bouches n'ont / Bu: "nous ne serons jamais une seule momie [cf. *sylphe*]" (37).

ma mère: like the *aucun climat, son aïeul (Prose),* the original air of the empty *lieu,* the nature-womb to which all returns in the *Coup de Dés;* compare "par surcroît / L'ordinaire abandon [air] . . . vers l'infini vorace"* (1446); "la Mère qui nous pense et nous conçoit [quitte à nous] renier" (391) or "O Mère qui créas . . . avec la . . . mort" *(Les Fleurs);* "de maternelles perpétrations" (651). The mother and father of the dubious Act are the *anima* and *animus* of the creator (or of life generally).

Chimère: the Illusion, the Life Lie or "Glorieux Mensonge" of the early letters; Mallarmé uses the term frequently in *Igitur* and in *La Musique et les Lettres,* and so on, as the mirage of meaning in an absurd universe where all is subject to one fatal, forever promising, law. Here, too, it is that illusion of a total *coup,* something Solid and the be-all-and-end-all, which all reality eternally seeks, in the *Coup de Dés,* as, for example, in the true act of love, or in the hope of immortality through a child, or through a Work. The drinking of the same "chimère" emphasizes the human-love aspect, as in the *Tristan et Iseut* love potion *(breuvage),* suggested in fragments of *Hérodiade* (N, p. 169) and in "Le Livre" (p. 169 A). The *Chimère* may be figured on the vase: "urnes . . . à leur croupe deux chimères" (670).

Chassé observes the etymology, according to Littré, of *chimère* from Greek "goat," hence the possible reference to milk in *bu.* He exaggerates the importance of this. The idea of a kiss as mutual drinking is traditional (particularly in the baroque era); compare "Les délices cherchés au nuptial repas / Quand l'âpre faim muée en pâmoison / Les entrelace bouche à bouche puis les vautre / Le mets supérieur qu'on goûte l'un à l'autre" (N, p. 169).

sylphe de ce froid plafond: "Ce cri de pierre [cathedral of Poetry] s'unifie vers le ciel en les piliers *interrompus* [*col . . . s'interrompt*] . . . enfin quelque immobilité [the empty air]. J'attends que, chauve-souris éblouissante . . . le fol, adamantin, colère, tourbillonant génie heurte la ruine; s'en délivre, dans la voltige qu'il est, seul. Théodore Banville devient parfois ce *sylphe* suprême." (521). This miracle, this mad breaking away to creative autonomy and freedom, is like the final stars of the *Coup de Dés,* or those bursting in the severed head of Saint John (C, pp. 314-316).

The sylph is partly like the perfect-poem-which-cannot-be, that he claimed for Banville, not too convincingly, and despaired of for himself and which, in a sense, by his despairing, won. It is the unborn child of an unconsummated (spiritual) union, as in "nous ne serons jamais une seule momie" (37). In the *Tombeau d'Anatole* (f. 1) Mallarmé refers to such a failure: "père et mère . . . mal associés" and ascribes momentarily to this the death of his son. But it is, no doubt, mainly a subconscious memory here: the father and mother principles have become generalized.

plafond: the flatness of the element *pla,* the *a,* emphasize the cold emptiness of this *lieu,* as in *L'Azur:* "un grand plafond silencieux." It is the place par excellence of coldly blocked aspiration for the meditative, perhaps sadly horizontal, man.

Le pur vase: the broad emptiness of the air is echoed, microcosmically, in the bounded void of the "pure" vase with "no" potion; just so, the empty room (or the *ptyx*) echoed the dead outdoor space in *Ses purs ongles;* again in *Igitur,* the empty, or death-containing, *fiole,* was a "pureté, qui renferme la substance du Néant" (439). It is the male "womb" of (despairing) spiritual creativity recalling the virgin "birth" of *Don du poème* as well as the projected work Mallarmé mentioned to George Moore (*Avowals,* pp. 276-280), involving a dialogue between a man and the seed in him of a dubious future birth. Compare also the womb-window of the final sonnet, with its *nul ventre,* whence a (virgin-male) birth might occur. The womb idea is emphasized by the *v*'s of *veuvage* and *vase* (cf. *ventre*).

agonise: "le Rêve a *agonisé* en cette fiole de verre" (439).

naïf baiser des plus funèbres: a pure (naive) love-death would be literally "funereal." But the failure to bring off a true gesture is likewise implied.

rien expirer: "expirer: expulser de la poitrine par une contraction" (*Petit Larousse*). The ambiguity of love-death is in this act, which is its own death (*expirer:* to die). *Cela dans le doute expire* (*Petit Air II*), involves a similar double use of the verb: the bird exhaled its life in its song. That is why, Hamlet-like, the act is untaken.[5] Eliot alludes obliquely to this drama of expression in "Every poem is an epitaph," as does Dylan Thomas in "Poems are statements made on the way to the grave." All that is offered is the ghostly *possibility* of a meaningful, non-self-cancelling, poetic act.

rien (from Latin *res,* "thing") is part of the ambiguity, as in *Salut: Rien cette écume vierge vers;* a nothing-something.

The numerous *n*'s help create an atmosphere of negation, the darkness from which the "rose" might flower, *aurait pu naître (Une dentelle).*

une rose dans les ténèbres:[6] "Dans l'ombre on trouve encor des fleurs" (Villiers, *Premières poésies;* p. 134); the wistful final image is of the forlorn possibility of a "Joyau intact sous le désastre" (302).

III. UNE DENTELLE S'ABOLIT

The central network of sensibility in this unusually intricate poem is: milky dawn—white lace curtains—window—belly (birth)—mandolin (music of love-hunger, lullaby). The lyricism of all this, merely potential in the quatrains, emerges fully with the tercets. In the first part of the sonnet, the mood is one of ambiguous discouragement, the defeated hope of a dawn. Dawn ought to mean victory; but, alas, there remains the old problem of finite life standing in the way of the infinite. Yet, as we read on to the end, the mood subtly lifts. Is there, after all, some promise?

The central image running throughout the poem is the window with its curtains. This decor of the room prolongs the setting of the preceding sonnets. But this main motif is the point of departure for several prominent secondary motifs, as we shall see.

The window is very close to the one of *Les Fenêtres:*

> La bouche fiévreuse et d'azur bleu vorace,
> Telle jeune, elle alla respirer son trésor,
> Une peau virginale et de jadis! encrasse
> D'un long baiser amer les tièdes carreaux d'or.
>
> . . . .
>
> Je fuis et je m'accroche à toutes les croisées
> D'où l'on tourne l'épaule à la vie, et, béni,
> Dans leur verre, lavé d'éternelles rosées,
> Que dore le matin chaste de l'Infini . . .

The feeling here again is of morning-birth, milky whiteness, washed (and caressed) baby, early musical sweetness and light.

To this same important cluster of associations we may add the stirring milk-music-morning-birth group of *Don du poème* and the *paradis ... ton lait bu jadis* of the *Scène* of *Hérodiade;* also, secondarily, the "carreaux bombés par les rêves" (Propos, p. 74) which belong to the eidetic (or hyperbolic) imagery we discuss elsewhere (under *Prose*).

The window of the sonnet is a potential womb, the site of a possible renewal, as in *Le Pitre Châtié,* wherein the clown punches a *fenêtre* through the wall of his tent in order to *renaître* ("be reborn" through baptismal swimming or sexual love); the rime is very important to Mallarmé. The window is a womb-entrance not only because of the occasional *bombé,* or convex, effect (which similarly fascinated Eliot, "slotted window bellied like the fig's fruit," and may haunt us in Flemish painting like that of the Van Eycks), but rather because, like Keats's "magic casements," it is a porthole onto the eternal life, of nature or the heavens—"que la vitre soit l'art soit la mysticité" (*Les Fenêtres*). Windows are, accordingly, passages to the tomb-womb of Eternal Return (like the *sépulcres* of *Le Pitre Châtié),* but in a conditional, tentative and, so to speak, vibrant, way. This return to the All is only potential. Windows are favored motifs for poetry or painting, not only because they are attractive objects in themselves but also because they are only partially exits, unlike doors, and are so only visually or spiritually. Windows keep us in physically while allowing us to *see through.*

The window opens onto the pure Nothing to which man will always aspire as long as he is a mere Something, and through which lies his only hope of having or being the All (the longing for omnipotence we are supposed to leave behind with babyhood). This childish, God-like, miraculous innocence is symbolized by the transparency of the glass of the window, like the ecstatically empty air of *L'Azur* or *Le vierge* or *Surgi* or the limpid water of *Le Pitre Châtié.*

The *dentelle* of the sonnet is largely the white lace of this Birth: a new day, a new self, or new baby, a new poem (as in *Don du poème)*— successive levels of the spiral evolution of all reality, as described more fully in the *Coup de Dés.* The main window-motif and the overtones may be given as follows: a) As a window-curtain it disappears either because the tentative morning light is suddenly disappointingly overcast or else because the white fabric is invisible against the milky sky of the dawn; *s'abolit dans le doute du Jeu suprême* means that in the troubled or dubious half-light of the supreme Play of light versus dark, the curtain fades. Then,

b) As curtains to a bed, inviting one to a supreme Game of love, they are fingered timorously aside—but there is no real or solid basis for it inside, no *lit;* these are not the lost-paradisiacal "rideaux inconnus du remords" he dreamed of in *Angoisse.*

c) As the lace dress of a woman (and the feminine essence inside the dress) the drama is similar: "dentelles d'une jupe . . . dans une flottaison [cf. *flotte* below] . . . cette initiative par quoi la marche s'ouvre [cf. *entr'ouvrir*], tout au bas et les plis rejetés en traîne, une echappée, de sa double flèche [cf. the two *guirlandes*] savante" (285). To this we may add: "virginité [la page blanche] . . . elle-même s'est comme divisée en ses fragments de candeur, l'un et l'autre, preuves nuptiales de l'Idée" (387). The feminine essence is, as we shall see, associated with the white body of a page (see e., below), opened up or "violated" by the male act of writing.[7] The lace curtains of the sonnet symbolize the potential opening of the virginal into the maturely womanly as in the just-cited phrase; this is one of the loveliest aspects of the poem, the ecstatic *invitation* and promise between two white curtains—portals to the womb (rather like those "floating" or oscillating twin panels of the dark tomb-chamber of spiritual Rebirth in *Igitur*)—white curtains billowing apart in a fresh dawn wind: *conflit . . . flotte.* The two *guirlandes* are like the "deux ailes" of a woman's hair (in Richard, p. 91), and are also very much like the "lys à jamais renversé de l'une et l'autre jambe" of Hérodiade (N, p. 78) dreaming of the noble intervention of Saint John (upon which nuptials the virgin princess would become the mature queen), "Pour que je m'entr'ouvrisse et reine triomphasse" (N, p. 79). Compare the *entr'ouvrir comme un blasphème* below, the impulsive act in which heads (maiden and saintly) are lost.

d) As a baby's veil (see the *naître* below) it is put aside *(s'abolit),* half-opened, as we peek in at the delicate new life; compare "entr'ouvrir . . . les dentelles," a passage from a letter to his friend Rodenbach *(Corr. avec Rodenbach,* p. 65), describing such a stolen look at a neonate.

e) As a white page, it is abolished, annihilated by writing, any line of which divides it into a pair of white garlands, half-opening (expressing) a Reality but getting in its own way (as Montaigne said any human gesture does at the end of his *Apologie,* cf. under *bras,* C, p. 183), like the "omniprésente Ligne" (648) of the "jeu" (647) of *La Musique et les Lettres,* the "jeu insensé d'écrire" of the Villiers lecture (481). Here, too, there was a *doute:* "un doute . . . la goutte d'encre apparentée à la nuit sublime" (481), see under *doute* in the *Faune,* also the *crime . . . avoir divisé la touffe.*

The *Jeu* is the drama or Play of love at various levels. It is the universal emergence of joy which is the milky matinal light of the sun rising from darkness at dawn; the human equivalent in procreation; the artist's version of the supreme Game, a creative act (see Appendix A). The word, like the whole poem, is certainly ambiguous, for it oscillates between the *free creativity* of play and its vain *frivolity,* and carries all the Olympian disenchanted-ecstatic implications it has in Heraclitus, Nietzsche, Camus.

Une dentelle s'abolit	A lace [curtain, etc.] abolishes it-self [disappears]
Dans le doute du Jeu suprême	In the doubt of the supreme Game
A n'entr' ouvrir comme un blasphème	To half-open like a blasphemy
Qu'absence éternelle de lit.	Only an eternal absence of bed.

It is morning. In the dubious light the white curtain fades *(s'abolit).* Hope rises with the light, as in *Le vierge, le vivace, et le bel aujourd'hui,* but is immediately tempered by the old "doubt," for either the light is sadly overcast *(blême,* below) or, in any event, morning will be followed by night; that is the supreme Game of nature, "lutte de la lumière et de l'ombre" (1169). The ambivalence is quite like the modern existential mood. Sartre called our poet an "absurdiste avant la lettre" (in his *Genet).* We had likewise pointed out (C, p. 21) that the central term of *Igitur* was *l'absurde:* "Bref dans un acte où le hasard est en jeu [note the *jeu*] . . . Devant son existence la négation et l'affirmation viennent échouer. Il contient l'Absurde [the *jeu* unresolved]" *(Igitur;* 441). This *Jeu* is the core of the *Coup de Dés,* the paradoxically dialectical "symphonique équation propre aux saisons, habitude de rayon et nuée" (646). (See C, p. 36 *et seq.).*

An overcast Dawn is the theme of *Hommage:* "Toute Aurore même gourde."   *

The half-opening of "hope" (the originally overlapping curtains gently lifting apart, inviting in) are like the paradoxical panels of Igitur's tomb-chamber promising access to a Future but immediately closing again (C, p. 453 and *passim).* The *doute,* at this level, is the tentative mood of opening, symbolized by the relative darkness between the white curtains. Here the curtains are not only access to the infinite space outside the window—"l'absolu existera en dehors . . . il soulèvera les rideaux" *(Igitur,* 433)—they are also, as we said, the entrance to a "bed," ("dentelles à flot torses sur le linon," *Hérodiade,* 1446), the hopefully solid site of metaphysical repose, of love, of creation on a page blank as sheets, as in "le lit aux pages de vélin" *(Ouverture ancienne).*

The *dentelle,* at this last level, is mildly associated with the fabric of writing, as in "le pli de sombre dentelle qui retient l'infini, tissé par mille, chacun selon le fil [cf. *filial* below] ou prolongement ignoré de signe" (1565; see Letter Table under *x);* compare "une langue, loin

de livrer au hasard sa formation, est composée à l'égal d'un merveilleux
ouvrage de . . . *dentelle: pas un fil* [cf. *filial*] de l'idée qui se perde . . .
[grâce à] l'instinct de harmonie que, grand ou jeune, on a en soi [cf.
below, *creux néant musicien*]" (828). In the sonnet, the image of
dentelle as writing is modified; it is probably rather the white page made
into lace by authorship.[8] Mallarmé was often bemused by the fact that
"l'homme poursuit noir sur blanc" (370) since white ink would have
been more appropriate to the *Jeu suprême*.

The main sense of *s'abolit dans le doute du Jeu suprême* emerges
from a number of similar remarks: "dans le *doute* ici d'une réalisation"
(491) refers to Mallarmé's renewed, by the death of Villiers, scepticism
about the possibility of any meaningful success here on earth. Elsewhere
in the Villiers talk he speaks in the same bitterly questioning metaphysical vein about his art: "ce jeu insensé d'écrire, s'arroger en vertu d'un
doute—la goutte d'encre apparentée à la nuit sublime—le devoir de
tout recréer" (481). It will be noted that various of the images of the
sonnet come together in this one phrase. The doubt (symbolized by
black ink), like the very dark one of the *Faune—mon doute, amas de
nuit ancienne* (q.v.)—is generally the Hegelian phase of negation that,
dialectically, makes affirmation possible, as in "le blanc revient, tout
à l'heure gratuit, certain maintenant" (387).

The *Jeu* is further illuminated by usages such as: "par une super-
cherie, on projette . . . le conscient manque chez nous de ce qui là-haut
éclate . . . un jeu" (647) or "ce jeu qui reste transmission de rêveries"
(643) or "le Livre . . . le jeu littéraire par excellence" (663).

suprême: the circumflex is graphic, a little crest of a wave like the
one of Page 4 of the *Coup de Dés,* with erotic undertones, or "la mouvante écume demeurée et suprême" (337), the "Si blanc cheveu" of
A la nue.

entr'ouvrir: at the level of window curtain, a half-opening and
peering into nature, the All; as bed curtains, an analogous peeking; as
a lace dress of a woman (or her essential femininity) a tentative intervention, as in "ta gorge *entr'ouvrant* son corsage" (18), "entr'ouvrant
un baiser" (N, p. 119), or the already-cited "Pour que je m'*entr'ouvrisse*
et reine triomphasse" (N, p. 79); as a baby's veil, "[Bébé, quand]
s'entrouvre cette dentelle, . . . Le *filial* [see below] instinct vous prit"
(177); as the two garlands of white paper created by the act of writing
—"*entr'ouvrir* la scène intérieure" (328)—they half-open before the
potential Promethean penetration of the secrets of life. The floating or
hovering feather-pen of Page 6 of the *Coup de Dés* ("voltige autour du
gouffre / sans le joncher / ni fuir / et en berce le vierge indice"), represented this same potentiality. The feather was ambiguously "in a cap"

(ideal) or the down-pointing pen, engaged in a human act, writing (with an undertone of an erotic deed).

blasphème: implies the hubris act of the profound penetrator of universal mysteries, going back no doubt to the original child's curiosity about the supreme "parental" Game, at overlapping metaphysical and sexual levels; *O sûr châtiment . . . du blasphème* is the inevitable expiation of such Promethean heaven-storming *(Faune),* or its erotic equivalent, the ravishing of the goddess, Venus.

This sort of glancing through a window at infinite secrets was subtly foreshadowed also in the faun's staring at light through the transparent grapeskins.

At the level of human love, the *blasphème* is further illuminated by the multi-faceted *Faune* passage: "mon *crime* c'est d'avoir divisé la touffe . . . que les dieux gardait si bien mêlée," in conjunction with "virginité . . . s'est divisée" (387) and "Le reploiement vierge du livre . . . prête à un sacrifice . . . l'introduction d'une arme ou coupe-papier, pour établir la prise de possession" (381), also "Solennités tout intimes, l'une: de placer le couteau d'ivoire dans l'ombre que font *deux* pages jointes d'un volume" (718). See Appendix B.

This mutates to the level of artistic creation: the "brutality" of spoiling a virgin page with an ink stroke. Mallarmé, like most sensitive men, is occasionally appalled by the implication of any Act which, in a sense (as the existentialists recently reminded us) involves everything, every time—we might, for all we know, upset the whole "deal," and yet we blindly proceed, such being faith and its daughter, impulse.

lit: the site of the wished-for Deed, nonexistent though dreamed-of. It is the universal site of the final sowing of the constellation-seed (cf. Hugo's *Semeur)* in the *Coup de Dés* (C, p. 407): "quelque surface vacante et supérieure"; or the love bed to which the curtains give access, as in various fragments of *Hérodiade,* as in "dentelles à flot torses sur le linon" (N, p. 60); the early grouping of the elements "fenêtre, naître, mandoline, ventre, drap maternel du vieux lit / Vierge" are in one short fragment (N, pp. 159-160).

The transition to art is made in "le lit aux pages de vélin" *(Ouverture Ancienne d'Hérodiade),* compare "du papier, un lit blanc aussi" (515).

Cet unanime blanc conflit	This unanimous white conflict
D'une guirlande avec la même,	Of a garland with the same,
Enfui contre la vitre blême	Fled against the pale pane
Flotte plus qu'il n'ensevelit.	Floats more than it buries.

The "conflict" of two—dialectically related *(la même)*—opposites in a supreme dilemma or *doute* (the Absurdity of the *Jeu)* is a mediocre oscillation—(*flotte*) like the final *indifféremment* . . . LE HASARD of Page 9 of the *Coup de Dés,* not a final "burial" as long as we are thinking of it or are merely alive. This restless paradox was evoked earlier in the *Coup de Dés* in the artist-nature relation, on Page 6, symbolized as a white feather or feather-pen *floating* with the rhythm of writing (there is an etymological connection; the Sanscrit root of *plume* being *plu,* "to float") over the raw reality waiting to be expressed, molded, or formed, which is, in turn, symbolized as the original chaotic ocean, or, again, as the white passive page.[9]

A general abstract statement of this dialectical *conflit* is found in "quelle divergence que creuse le *conflit* furieux des citoyens, tous, au regard souverain, font une *unanimité*" (652). In the sonnet it occurs at all the previously indicated levels:

a) The hope of a new day in the universe as a final summer Beauty, recalling the "white conflict" of the swan versus the snow in *Le vierge, le vivace et le bel aujourd'hui: la blanche agonie;* there a winter day opened with just such a Promise.

b) The desperate hope of total joy in love: we are reminded of the lace bed-curtains, half-hiding the bed of Hérodiade (and half-keeping her, so to speak, from consummation): "panache / De dentelles . . . taciturne vacille [cf. *flotte*] en le signe que non" (1446). A likely source of the feeling of wavering in curtains is Poe's *Raven:* "the silken sad *uncertain* rustling of each purple *curtain* / Thrilled me" [note the echo "uncertain" - "curtain"]. Compare "rideaux vagues . . . du vide les vagues" (*Alternative,* NNRF, January, 1954). Here the conflict has an overtone of sexual act, as in "blanc couple nageur" (*Le Guignon,* 29); remember also the white couple of nymphs in the *Faune,* symbolizing the duality of the faun's hesitation (and a feminine essence) as well as a sexual pairing. This last is brought out more directly in an early poem describing a taut sexual dialectic, a tension or "conflict" of opposites, "lutteuse . . . nous ne serons jamais une seule momie" (37). The failure to attain total consummation, the love-death of *momie,* is exactly our *flotte plus qu'il n'ensevelit.*

c) As a woman's dress, and its contents: "dentelles d'une jupe . . . dans une *flottaison* . . . double flèche [the two halves of her train]" (285). Compare the vibrant suspension of "tourbillon de mousseline ou / Fureur éparses en écumes" (65); or "voile . . . *flotte* . . . hésite et disparaît, la laissant plus que nue" (603). The theme of the nuptial veil has been treated at length under *Tombeau (de Verlaine).*

d) The conflict of hope and despair of survival through progeny recalls the analogous, somewhat Schopenhauerian passage of the *Coup de Dés,* Page 5: "le voile d'illusion rejailli leur hantise" (C, p. 216).

"Voile de tulle illusion" (764) indicates the material basis for the "pun."

e) As writing, the conflict is the poet's creative hesitation, which we have already discussed, based on a central total doubt; an overtone is the opposing garlands of whiteness above and below the "omniprésente Ligne" of his act; compare "Poésies . . . guirlandes" (503).   *

même: "identical," as in "Un rossignol . . . jette sa folle et *même* perle" (149); the paradox of identity is fully implied (C, pp. 46-48).

contre la vitre: "contre la vitre" (360) describes the poet peering anxiously at the sky, as if for an augury, in a crisis; "contre une vitre" (636) evokes this same familiar (banal but hopeful) *décor.* Some of the levels are lost or subdued here.   *

flotte plus qu'il n'ensevelit: mediocre (in relation to the absolute) yet surviving *Ewig-weibliche* principle; no total doom or victory; compare "rideaux vagues . . . du vide les vagues" *(Alternative)* and C, p. 154; compare also "la blancheur banale des rideaux" *(Les Fenêtres).* The etymological echo of *plu* "to float" is, as we said, at work here; compare Mallarmé's highly significant remarks on *w;* "Les sens d'*osciller* (celui-ci semblerait dû au *dédoublement vague* de la lettre, puis de *flotter,* etc.; d'eau et d'humidité; d'évanouissement et de *caprice;* alors de *faiblesse,* de charme et d'imagination)" (932). Recall our earlier remarks on the feminine duality *(Faune)* and consult our table of letters under *w*; compare also "toujours une banalité flotte" (308); "flotte l'illusion" (564).

There is a passing allusion to a shroud in *n'ensevelit* but it is rather *no*-shroud; compare "le rideau drap mortuaire" (196, Poe tr.). The lace curtains wavering in the dawn wind are spectral, a mere shadow of something real as in "flotte l'illusion" (564) or "la subtilité *flottant* entre les lignes" (565); the ghost of martyred Saint John similarly emerges from the wavering curtains of certain *Hérodiade* fragments (1446, etc.) as in Poe's *Ligeia* (Cellier), or *The Raven,* and no doubt there is a lingering desire here for union with his various dead loved ones (though we must caution against too personal an interpretation).   *
The meaning thus is suspended, in the sonnet, between a no-death (mediocrity) and a death of our hope for something permanent. But there is finally a promise in that *flotte,* despite the defeat.

Mais, chez qui du rêve se dore	But in whoever gilds himself with dream
Tristement dort une mandore	Sadly sleeps a mandolin
Au creux néant musicien	With hollow musical nothingness
Telle que vers quelque fenêtre	Such that towards some window

Selon nul ventre que le sien,   According to [depending on] no belly but
                                     its [own],
Filial on aurait pu naître.   Filial one could have been born.

The act of the *Jeu* is a failure in terms of the highest hopes; the defeat, the catastrophe of the Absurd, is followed by a miraculous leap as in *Igitur* (C, p. 39) and in the *Coup de Dés:* the constellation *ex nihilo*. But, in all these cases, it is an extremely tentative, wistful, barest possibility of a glow: *aurait pu naître* (in the *Coup de Dés* it was *peut-être* and *aussi loin qu'un endroit fusionne avec au-delà*).

The poet, renouncing the clumsy kinetic act, is rewarded by a mere gleam, but a pure one; by subtle trickery, vaguely resembling Abraham's substitute sacrifice, he records it somehow.

The mandolin is glimpsed in some early pages of *Hérodiade* (N, pp. 159-160).

> Non! nul jour—de la belle fenêtre
> Elle n'a pas aimé, cette princesse, naître
> Et cette mandoline au ventre [space] dit
> Pourquoi que sur le drap maternel du vieux lit . . ,

Here, too, we see how the element *nêtre* in *fenêtre,* with its direct hint of *n'être (pas)*—see the variant "naître . . .n'être" (1475)—leads to the idea of an extremely conditional birth, the sort of not-birth of the three sonnets, reinforced by the negating *n* in the word *naître* itself: the "n'a pas aimé naître" leads to the emptiness of the mandolin, a beautiful "sterility" (in a special sense of that last word).

rêve: "j'ai toujours rêvé et tenté autre chose" (662); "suggérer voilà le rêve" (869); the word is almost always very positive in
*   Mallarmé, referring to pure art.

dore: "verre . . . Que *dore* le matin chaste de l'infini" is this same morning light. *Don du poème:* "Par le verre brûlé d'aromates et d'or."

The mandolin is glimpsed again in *Sainte* (later in Eliot's *Ash Wednesday),* with its alluring belly, linking music with desire, or thirst for childhood purity. In *Don du poème* the music of a *clavecin* is similarly linked with desire, the desire-hunger of the infant for the paradisiacal milk (as in *Kubla Khan)* and, beyond that, the heavenly womb, so the morning music takes on the dulcet strain of a lullaby *(O la berceuse).* The window panes, "bombés par le rêve" (Propos, p. 74) —which helps account for our partiality to bay windows, suggesting womb-snugness (cf. the playful term "bay-window" for stomach)— are the milky promise of union and the birth of self.[10] The rime *naître-fenêtre,* as we observed, form an irresistible pair for Mallarmé, as in *Le Pitre châtié:* "ivresse de renaître . . . troué . . . une fenêtre (a sort

of re-entry of the womb in a simplifying act of love, or baptismal swimming) "je me mire [*dans la fenêtre*] et me vois ange! et je meurs, et
j'aime / —Que la vitre soit l'art, soit la mysticité— / À renaître." (*Les
Fenêtres*).

tristement: makes explicit the wistful quality of this whole revery
... as in the "baiser amer" against the pane of *Les Fenêtres*—and recalling *Tristesse d'été* with its "nous ne serons jamais une seule momie"
or the "incertain et *triste* bruissement en chaque rideau" (tr. of *The
Raven,* 190).   *

dort: echoes the absent *lit* sought outside; the more promising
"sleep" is inside (Richard).

The inner harmony of the *creux néant musicien* (emphasized by the
golden melodious *dort . . . dort . . . dore* sequence) is as in "chiffration
mélodique tue, de ces motifs qui composent une logique, avec nos fibres
[cf. *filial* below]. Quelle agonie . . . la Chimère versant par ses blessures
d'or [cf. *dore;* this splendor is the tragically-beautiful truth of the absurd fact that nothing obviates the merely human Line]...l'omniprésente
Ligne espacée de tout point à tout autre pour instituer l'idée; sinon sous
le visage humain, mystérieuse, en tant qu'une Harmonie est pure"(648).
Compare "instruments de musique, tendus des fibres mêmes de coeurs
aimants . . . le bonheur qui est muet." (605); "Musicienne du silence"
(*Sainte*); "musicalement se lève l'absente de tous bouquets" (857);
Keats's "unheard melodies"—all this is an aristocratic perfection of
presence through absence. In fragments of *Hérodiade* (N, p. 155), we
find a very similar grouping: "la viole . . . un ventre chaste et creux /
sur un lit vierge et froid d'une horreur maternelle."

vers quelque fenêtre: the *vers-verre* harmony is exploited frequently
by Mallarmé, as in "vers une fenêtre" (N, p. 105); compare *l'hiver
lucide (Renouveau).*

quelque: leaves open the multiple possibilities of meaning.

fenêtre: includes, as we observed, the negation of being, for a rebirth: "vers une fenêtre / au point de n'être plus" (N, p. 105), found
again in the subtle pun of *Autre éventail, naître pour personne* (originally *n'être;* 1475).

The "glass-purity-beyond" association recurs in "la pure verrière.
Je sais celle qui vous occupe, Tailhade." (527).

nul ventre: "je fis des pas dans la rue et reconnus dans le son *nul*
la corde tendue de l'instrument de musique" (*Le Démon de l'analogie*),
see Appendix C under *u.* The tension between the acute sound and the
feminine form of *u* give it this taut potential-birth feeling and link it
with the tight-stretched cord over the belly of a mandolin. Note all the
u's in the above-quoted sentence and in the whole prose poem. Also *nul*

has the element *nu* in it, one of Mallarmé's favorite words (the tension
of the *u* is augmented by the negative *n*); *ventre-naître* is an obvious
association of ideas; compare "par le ventre . . . Renaître" *(Chansons
bas, II)*.

filial: (a) as window or bed curtain, as in "dentelles à flot torses sur
le linon . . . Selon la guimpe puis la coiffe par surcroît . . . Sursautant à la
fois en maint épars *filet* / Jadis, d'un blanc, [space] et maléfique lait"
(1446); the white curtains are made of such milky threads. In the
fragment just quoted, we are not sure whether the curtains are on a
window or of a bed, probably both; (b) as woman's dress or feminine
essence: the threads implied in the quoted passage are also those of the
nurse's headdress, *guimpe* or *coiffe,* and modulate further to the stream
of milk from the old nurse's now withered breasts. The old nurse is
called "sybilline" in various passages of *Hérodiade;* compare "Avec le
doigt fâné presseras-tu le sein / Par qui coule en blancheur sibylline la
femme" *(Don du poème)*. So the association of *filial,* "of a child," and
fil, "thread," is prominent here; compare the ambiguous *fils du travail*
of Rimbaud's *Mémoire;* (c) as baby: *Pour un baptême:*

> "Que s'entrouvre cette dentelle,
> Le filial instinct vous prit" (177)

Note the *instinct* here (see below). Also the *baptême*. We may surmise
that the tragedy of the loss of his son, Anatole, is indirectly reflected
here with the wistful desire for a more permanent birth of all sorts.
The window of the sonnet, as Richard says, may be present in a
feuillet of the *Tombeau d'Anatole:* "Temps de la chambre vide—jusqu'à
ce qu'on l'ouvre" (f. 37); (d) as art:" les *fils* de ces rapports qui forment
les vers" (871); "pas un *fil* de l'idée qui se perde . . . [grâce à] l'*instinct*
de harmonie que, grand ou jeune, on a en soi" (828). This is the *inner*
harmony Mallarmé refers to in the quoted passage of *La Musique et les
lettres:* "en tant qu'une harmonie est pure" and so forth; here the term
"fibres" stands for the sheer threads of relationship, like the spider web
of Being at the center of which he saw himself installed—"araignée
sacrée, sur les principaux *fils* déjà sortis de mon esprit . . . je tisserai
aux points de rencontre [Mallarmé's italics] de merveilleuses *dentelles.*"
See the Letter Table under *x*. Since spider webs are made of threads
that are a milk-like secretion, there are some subdued associations in
Mallarmé between the idea of creation and the male procreative substance, see Appendix A. We recall, in this connection, the dialogue with
the male seed reported in George Moore's *Avowals,* and the "semence"
of the *Tombeau d'Anatole* (f. 16).

on aurait pu: "la merveille [a poem which Rimbaud *might* have

written and that could be discovered posthumously] on y songe comme
à quelque chose qui eût pu être" (518); compare the elaborate condi-
tionals of Page 9 of the *Coup de Dés,* representing a limit-situation of
poetic possibility.

NOTES

1 Four words were capitalized as an afterthought, on the proofs of the Lahure edition
of the *Coup de Dés,* in the same way. The triadic arrangement here may have something to do with the birth theme.

2 The ambivalent *Mère* who gave us life only to remove it: *renier* (391-392).

3 *le passé* as "the dead man" would involve an unusual usage, but a possible one, especially since "the past" clearly refers to the poet's past existence, as in "Que sommes-
nous dans *le passé?* Tel rêve . . .". (Villiers, *Axël,* quoted by Mallarmé, 501).

4 Ravel has set the poem to music, with an effect of painful and exquisite loneliness.

5 The act *described* in the poem is untaken but, of course, the act of the poem is taken.
Paradoxically, behind the poet's back, so to speak, despair has led to victory, death
to life. There is an interesting distinction we ought to note between the ordinary
man's yielding, through a death of the will to omnipotence, to life ("pitching in")
and the creator's provisional rejection of both the total striving and the ordinary
life in favor of a sublimated "pitching in" which is closer to the infantile aim, and
partially enacts it. The ordinary man tends to relegate more of this daemonic drive to
the non-vocational realms.

6 Maeterlinck uses this same image in *Pelléas et Mélisande.*

7 Mallarmé often uses the "l'un et l'autre" formula for the feminine principle, e.g.,
"l'une et l'autre jambe" (N, p. 206), "deux moitiés d'une troupe de femmes . . . tendent
les bras d'une part et d'autre" (*Le Livre,* pp. 17-18); "se penche-t-elle d'un côté—
de l'autre—montrant un sein—l'autre—" (N, p. 113); compare "penché de l'un ou
l'autre bord," the boat-womb of Page 3 of the *Coup de Dés* (C, pp. 156-157);
"Hérodiade au clair sein double" (N, p. 164).

8 At this level (of literary creation), the *doute* may also refer in a minor way to the
dubious or tentative recording of a line that is only thought of or is subsequently
erased: *s'abolit.* The page is then only "half-opened," by a ghostly or merely possible
line, as in "virginité [la page] . . . s'est divisée" or "mon crime c'est d'avoir divisé la
touffe," the timorous gesture of the faun, like the hesitant poet's, who knows no
gesture will prevail: N'ABOLIRA LE HASARD (*Coup de Dés*): "je connais des
instants où quoi que ce soit, au nom d'une disposition secrète, ne doit satisfaire"
(647).

9 Richard (p. 262) sees the "sameness" as the principle of defeat, banality. He believes
that for Mallarmé only a *synthesis of opposites* would constitute a fertile dialectic.
But actually there is a rich "same-other" dialectic in the *guirlandes;* it is rather in
spite of it that the defeat occurs. There *is* no solution, however dialectical, here on
earth. But . . .

10 Later, of course, we settle for the survival of a modified version of our self in progeny.

25. QUELLE SOIE AUX BAUMES DE TEMPS

❖❖❖❖❖❖❖❖❖❖

Here is another of the poems conceived under the spell of Woman, originally Madame Mallarmé.[1] Méry Laurent is probably involved in the final version (published in 1885).

In the first quatrain, the natural (*native*) hair is exalted above preciously ancient but artificially woven and embroidered silks. In the second quatrain, the silk modulates to a flag. Mallarmé is the tender wooer, not the tough conquering hero of an earlier era; he has no use for the victory banners flapping outside on this public holiday. *His* flag is his mistress' silken tresses. Nay, the poet goes even further, he stifles all personal glory whatsoever (*le cri des Gloires qu'il étouffe*), as he does in *Petit air I:* "regard que j'abdiquai / Ici de la gloriole." In favor of this joy of loving, he snuffs out his art in his lady's hair. The sonnet is in a sense a paean to life's victory over art, very much as in *Victorieusement fui.*[2]

The conceit of the hair as flag goes back far, to a finished little piece of juvenilia called the *Château de l'espérance* (23):

> Ta pâle chevelure ondoie
> Parmi les parfums de ta peau
> Comme folâtre un blanc drapeau
> Dont la soie au soleil blondoie . . .

A later, and closer, precedent is the *Sonnet à Wyse:*[3]

> De l'orient passé des Temps
> Nulle étoffe jadis venue
> Ne vaut la chevelure nue,
> Que loin des bijoux tu détends

Much later, in a prose poem entitled *La Gloire,* Mallarmé will deeply inhale the sufficiency of being alone on the earth, under a magnificent sunset. He is thinking, of course, of the sacrificial splendors of his aristocratic art. And this is part of the sonnet too, that behind its back, so to speak, the disinterest and humility lead to a special triumph which shines through its lines.

Quelle soie aux baumes de temps	What silk with balms of time
Où la Chimère s'exténue	Where the chimera writhes
Vaut la torse et native nue	Is worth the twisted and native cloud [of hair]
Que, hors de ton miroir, tu tends!	That you stretch forth beyond [or from] your mirror!
Les trous de drapeaux méditants	The holes of meditative flags
S'exaltent dans notre avenue:	Exalt themselves in our avenue:
Moi, j'ai ta chevelure nue	Me, I have your naked hair
Pour enfouir mes yeux contents.	To bury my contented eyes in
Non! La bouche ne sera sûre	No! The [lover's] mouth will not be sure
De rien goûter à sa morsure,	Of tasting anything in his bite,
S'il ne fait, ton princier amant,	If he doesn't make, your princely lover,
Dans la considérable touffe	In the considerable tuft
Expirer, comme un diamant,	Expire, like a diamond,
Le cri des Gloires qu'il étouffe.	The cry of Glories he stifles.

First quatrain: A precious antique silk (from the Orient), bearing a chimera motif, is nothing to his mistress' hair. The hair-*étoffe* association is found in "sa chevelure se ploie avec la grâce des étoffes" (269), as well as in *Igitur* (435). Ronsard had expressed a similar idea: "Si fine soye [que ta chevelure] au mestier ne fut torse" (Garnier edition, p. 224). The Oriental quality (see the earlier written version cited above) is present in the typically Asiatic *chimère;* compare "chimères . . . les morceaux d'étoffes d'Orient" (499).

temps: depth and preciousness are added by time; an obvious overtone is "weathering"; compare the expression "couleur du temps." A very similar grouping of perfume, time, and weather is "baume antique le temps" (*Remémoration d'Amis belges*). There may be an over tone of *tempe.*

native nue: the echo "naked" is obvious from the direct rime *nue,* "naked." The *native* is etymologically associated with *naïve,* as in "Quelque folie, originelle et *naïve,* une extase d'or, je ne sais quoi! par elle nommé sa chevelure, se ploie avec la grâce des étoffes" (269). Hence, there are subtle harmonies of *native—naître* (the nakedness of birth)—*naïve.* An early version was entitled *Alternative* and featured the word *naître* (cf. the fecund *alternative,* on Page 3 of the *Coup de Dés,* C, p. 154).

torse: echoes the twisting *chimère* that retains a faint hint of the contorted agonizing *chimères* of *Igitur* and *Toast funèbre* (q.v.) (*monstre d'or*). The full overtone, *torse* as "torso," may go with the nakedness group.

hors de ton miroir: a startling leap from mirrored image to reality, one Mallarmé delighted in, for example, "maint subtil rameau ... demeuré les vrais bois" *(Faune).* It brings a "stereoscopic" or Alice-in-Wonderland quality of depth to the mirror, an eidetic effect of extended third dimension. The mirror of Hérodiade became likewise, suddenly, a frozen block of ice, a pond with leaves caught in its transparent depth; or, again, its flat hardness could turn into a gushing fountain.

hors, together with *torse,* because of the *or* in them, may remind us that Méry's hair like his wife's was golden. The *Sonnet à Wyse* had "cheveux / Lumineux". The *Château de l'Espérance* sang of blond hair too ((blondoie"). It is just possible that the *t*'s provide a crisp effect of a (German) lady's fingers snappily braiding her hair.

Second quatrain: The *trous* in the flags are from bullets, and some military victory is being celebrated: "Un drapeau ... Vous n'y trouverez que des trous" (Villiers, *Premières poésies,* p. 127).

méditants: the grave nodding or waving of flags in the wind, compare the twinkling stars of the *Coup de Dés*—"roulant brillant et méditant" (Page 11) or "mainte vibration de certitude et de ténèbres jointe en un *méditatif* unisson" (390). The chief allusion is to the meditation over the "piously dead for the fatherland" (Du Bellay) proper to a commemorative holiday. (The reference to a specific occasion proposed by Austin is unconvincing.)

notre avenue: how agreeable, this perspective of a Parisian street! One can almost see Mallarmé's faun-like decorous amused head thrust from a window near a diagonal flagstaff.

Tercets: The "sureness" expressed here, the pure taste in the mouth, is the *authenticity* of the poet who can sacrifice his vanity and, occasionally, just live; be reborn, be baptized in existence: "un comique y éclatera strident et comme retrempé, parmi les vagues, au rire de nature" (338).

morsure: a play on *mort sure,* see under *expirer.*

princier amant: the elect lover, lordly. Mallarmé's clever gallantry is the weapon that leads to victory.

considérable: there is an active element *sidér,* as in *sidéré (sidéralement, Coup de Dés,* Page 11), "thunderstruck" (etymologically from the Latin word for "star"), echoing the *diamant.* In the *Sonnet à Wyse,* the hair was *étincelles* in the dark; compare Villiers' "femme sidéralement belle" *(Premiéres poèsies,* p. 50).

expirer: he snuffs out his personal vanity, Glory, in the hair. But the *Gloire* is twofold: it is that of the love he savors, "expirer [exhale] ... le cri des Gloires," as well as the art he sacrifices; "expirer" (to die), as in, "Cela dans le doute expire" (death of a bird, *Petit Air II*); compare *Toute l'âme résumée:* The two readings are: "If he does not cause to exhale the cry of Glory" and "If he does not suppress (make to die) the cry of Glory." In the second case, the thought of all he is losing seems to flash through the back of his mind as he exults. He exults only for the moment, we must add, for we note that the sonnet, *Mes bouquins refermés,* which tells just the opposite story (ordinary life sacrificed to art), comes last in the collection.

There is a contrast between the flash *(i)* of joy, as in *expirer-cri-diamant,* and the darkness*(ou),* in which the poet's eyes are buried, as in *enfouir-touffe-étouffe,* see Appendix B. The *ff* is a snuffing effect as in the popular expression *ouf;* compare *Tout orgueil,* "Torche dans un branle étouffé." The *gl* is a favorite effect of Mallarmé: "G . . . une aspiration [cf. *expirer,* the opposite] simple . . . le désir, comme satisfait par *l,* exprime avec la dite liquide, joie, lumière, etc." (938).

NOTES

[1] The closely related *Sonnet à Wyse* was dated July 2, 1868, long before Méry.

[2] A related theme is that of *Le Pitre Châtié* where, however, the escape into sexuality is seen as disastrous to his art. Various fragments of the *Noces d'Hérodiade,* from the early (Tournon, Avignon, Besançon) years, reflect these preoccupations and images, see under *Victorieusement fui.*

[3] Eileen Souffrin, who first published the *Sonnet à Wyse (Fontaine,* no. 56) commented on the relation of the Sonnet to *Igitur:* "l'image de la chevelure s'associe aux images de tentures et de linceuls, à celle du Néant et de la Mort" (quoted in B. Fleuriot, "La chevelure vol d'une flamme," article in *Les Lettres:* "Stéphane Mallarmé," p. 183). Fleuriot mentions Baudelaire and Poe as predecessors here. We suspect also that the echo *chevelure-velours-velu* (this last word is frequent in *Igitur,* like *velours*) has something to do with all this.

The rest of the *Sonnet,* which is a mere sketch, goes:

> Moi qui vis parmi les tentures
> Pour ne pas voir le Néant seul,
> Aimeraient ce divin linceul,
> Mes yeux, las de ces sépultures, [sic]

> Mais tandis que les rideaux vagues
> Cachent des ténèbres les vagues
> Mortes, hélas! ces beaux cheveux

> Lumineux en l'esprit font naître
> D'atroces étincelles d'Être,
> Mon horreur et mes désaveux.

Still another version, *Alternative,* was published in the *NNRF,* January, 1954. It seems to date from around 1870, according to Mondor.

De l'oubli magique, venue,
Nulle étoffe, musique et temps,
Ne vaut la chevelure nue
Que, loin des bijoux, tu détends.

En mon rêve, antique avenue
De tentures, seul, si j'entends
Le Néant, cette chère nue
Enfouira mes yeux contents!

Non. Comme par les rideaux vagues
Se heurtent du vide les vagues
Pour un fantôme, les cheveux

Font luxueusement renaître
La lueur parjure de l'Etre,
Son horreur et ses désaveux.

The "rêve, antique avenue de tentures" is like the *Igitur* chamber, with curtains shutting off all inessential reality as this *fantôme* concentratedly confronts the *Néant* to wrest from it a deep meaning. The individual curtains are like "waves" of the nothing-abyss, compare *Une dentelle* and Page 3 of the *Coup de Dés*.

26. M'INTRODUIRE DANS TON HISTOIRE

◊❖◊❖◊❖◊❖◊

This love poem, addressed no doubt to Méry, was first published in 1886, in *La Vogue,* under the title *Sonnet.* The piece has achieved a certain fame because Proust quotes it in one of the later volumes of *À la Recherche du temps perdu,* and T. S. Eliot echoes it, mingled with a line from the *Tombeau de Charles Baudelaire,* in his *Ash Wednesday.* *M'introduire dans ton histoire* is, despite some initial dubiety, one of Mallarmé's most joyful poems. The dazzling *roue* is the supreme delight of a love climax, with overtones of fireworks—*roue à feu*—peacock's tail—*faire la roue* (he fondly called Méry his *Paon,* with her magnificently deployed blonde hair in mind)—and the blazing wheel of the sun-chariot.

The poet seems to be answering a request on the part of his lady friend to write a story for her, perhaps about herself as heroine, with himself as hero. We know that he wrote, or rewrote, the amorous *Contes indiens* at her behest, and in one of them there is a passage containing much of the imagery of the sonnet (although the *Contes* were written in the 'nineties, he may have considered the task, or something like it, earlier):

> Sûr de regagner son *royaume,* quand il voudra, le *char vole* et, le lende-main, à l'heure dite, entre dans la cour du palais, avec les roulements de *tonnerre.* La foule accourt enthousiasmée; il n'est pas jusqu'aux paons perchés sur les tuiles incendiées par le *soir,* qui n'imitent, avec leur queue éblouissante, chaque *roue* du char véloce" (628-629).

If I do enter your story, he seems to answer, it is as a very particular kind of hero, a frightened poet-lover, quite unlike this fierce Hindu warrior on his chariot. *My* only chariot wheel is the sunburst of love.

M'introduire dans ton histoire	Introduce myself into your story
C'est en héros effarouché	It's as a frightened hero
S'il a du talon nu touché	If he has touched with his naked heel
Quelque gazon de territoire	Some turf of territory

"Introduce myself into your story [affair]" is, as has been recognized by exegetes such as Mauron, ambiguous: *histoire* is not only "story," but can refer crudely to a sexual organ. The line accordingly vibrates, like the whole poem (and much of Mallarmé altogether) between extreme opposites of ideal beauty and sensual pleasure. The superbly reserved, civilized Mallarmé is usually as careful about committing himself to an act of any sort (certainly a love act) as he is to putting pen to paper, whence the emphasis on the tactful or tacit as in *O si chère* ("Tout bas") or *Rondel II* ("sans le dire") or the "entr'ouvrir comme un blasphème" of *Une dentelle s'abolit* or "mon crime c'est d'avoir divisé la touffe" of the *Faune*. Yet, he also expresses the most drastic sensuality underneath (or at other times). For example, *L'Après-midi d'un faune* modulates between the purity of "unwrinkled sky" and "the eternal swarm of desire" in the animal blood. On another occasion, Mallarmé dreamed of the *absent* breast of an Amazon, as opposed to the perfumed and swelling real breast, yet even here we sense that, like the virginal Hérodiade, he is hovering on the brink of the eruptive lower life, which makes for a rare cake-and-eat-it delight.

One of his finest prose poems, *Le nénuphar blanc,* tells of the possible contact with a flower-lady, an *absente de tous bouquets,* whose pure unglimpsed barely-guessed-at presence exhales an almost maddening beauty. Rowing meditatively in his little boat, on the Seine near Valvins, he pulls into some inlet or little stream tributary to the river and arrives, inadvertently, at the edge of the property of a neighbor he has never met. He hears soft footsteps behind foliage, but he cannot decide to make a move to meet the lady in the flesh. At last he prefers to shove off and row away with his dream of her intact. The whole prose poem is alive with this presence-absence of a woman, unsure between an airy lightness of sublimation and fierce eroticism:

> une haie clôturant des pelouses. Je me rendis compte. Simplement
> le parc de Madame, . . . l'inconnue à saluer.

Note, in passing, that the "pelouses-parc" of the prose poem is close kin to the *gazon* of the sonnet, as we shall see; the *histoire* of the sonnet is exactly equivalent to the meditative isolation, the *intimité* of the lady he imagines in the *Nénuphar:*

> Sûr, elle avait fait de ce cristal [water] son miroir intérieur . . . *Ombre* [cf. *ombre* below] enfouie en . . . [une] jupe . . . la marche s'ouvre, tout au bas . . . une échappée ["space between two bodies," Larousse] de sa *double* flèche savante . . . chose installée ici par le bruissement d'une venue, oui! ce charme instinctif d'en dessous que ne défend pas contre l'explorateur la plus authentiquement nouée, avec une boucle, en diamant, des ceintures . . . Séparés, on est ensemble; je m'immisce à de sa confuse *intimité* . . . un de ces magiques nénuphars clos qui . . . surgissent tout à coup, enveloppant de leur creuse blancheur un rien, fait de songes intacts . . . rapt de mon idéale fleur." (284-286). See Appendix B.

The use of the word *introduire* in this context is found in "Solennités tout *intimes,* l'une: de placer le couteau d'ivoire dans *l'ombre* [cf. the *ombre* just cited] que font deux pages jointes d'un volume" (718) compared with "Le reploiement vierge du livre, encore, prêt à un sacrifice dont saigne la tranche rouge des anciens tomes; l'introduction d'une arme, ou coupe-papier, pour établir la prise de possession" (381).

Richard confirms these associations (which we had previously worked out in detail in our *L'Oeuvre de Mallarmé: Un Coup de Dés):* "la touffe contient aussi en elle l'espace troublant d'une ombre, d'un secret ... l'image la plus sexuelle de l'accueil" (p. 104). See also *L'Après-midi d'un faune,* under *ombre* and *mal d'être deux.*

M'introduire dans ton histoire no doubt emphasizes primarily the gentler sense of playfully entering a story made up for his mistress or perhaps just the idea of entering the dream of his loved-one, or her life story, as in the literal level of the just-quoted "je m'immisce à de sa confuse intimité" or "je commence à entrer dans sa [Marie, his future bride's] vie" (Corr., p. 45). Mallarmé, as poet and gallant editor of *La Dernière mode,* clearly delighted in penetrating the lives of his lady readers via the dream, as a particularly "tender hero": "la dame [d'un salon] ... ressent ... jusqu'à l'âme ... la revendication [du rêve] ... Voyez l'usage d'un livre, si par lui se propage le rêve" (500) "toutes les femmes aiment les vers ... leur plaire donc ou mériter cela: je ne sais pas d'ambition, changée en triomphe si l'on réussit, qui aille mieux à un ouvrage" (716); "le Poète (dont l'autorité en matière de vision n'est pas moindre que celle d'un prince absolu) dispose avec la pensée seule de toutes les dames terrestres" (803).

héros: the hero-Eros association (going back to Plato's *Cratylus)* has been discussed in our *Hérodiade* chapter in connection with the title. Here Mallarmé is the timid, courageous hero of a love story, as in *La chevelure vol:* "héros tendre." This conceit of a love conquest as a substitute for a military deed was the core of *Quelle soie* and its early version, *Le Château de l'espérance.* Compare "le *héros,* que résume, en soi, maintenant le poète" (letter to Verlaine).

effarouché: he is "frightened away" from the lady's "lawn," as in the cited *Nénuphar blanc,* for to enter a life (etc.) is a fearful responsibility.

talon nu: like the wing or finger or hand or toe of many Mallarmé poems, the *talon* expresses a kinetic projection, impulse, or act. Thus "un besoin de talons nus" in *Chansons bas I* expresses a desire to be a pagan ("suckled," like Wordsworth, "in a creed outworn") and thus the "pur orteil du séraphin" makes the feminine Dawn blush *(Les Fleurs).* In the *Faune,* the naked heel of Venus caused Mount Etna to spout. A suggestive comparison may be made with the hand of the soldier whom he met while strolling one day with Méry: "gants blancs encore d'un enfantin tourlourou qui les rêvait dégourdir à l'estimation d'une jarretière hautaine" (283). The nakedness evokes the classic Greek hero, perhaps Achilles with vulnerable heel; compare "une *nudité* de héros tendre" (*La chevelure vol*).

   gazon: "touffe d'herbe du Tendre" (Biog., p. 55)—it has the general idea of a pleasure site, as in "les gazons que le pas de tes élus foule" (Wagnerian haunts, 546) or, more pertinently, the site where the poet seeks the "rapt de mon idéale fleur" of *Le Nénuphar blanc*. Mallarmé who knew well, and properly worshipped, his Shakespeare, may have recalled *Venus and Adonis:* "I'll be a park, and thou shalt be my deer; ... within this limit is relief enough, / Sweet bottom-grass, and high delightful plain," as well as Baudelaire's *Géante:* "Parcourir à loisir ses magnifiques formes; / Ramper sur le versant de ses genoux énormes," and so forth.

A des glaciers attentatoire	Assaulting [subject: the "sin"] glaciers [the cold woman]
Je ne sais le naïf péché	I don't know what [undefinable] naïve sin it is
Que tu n'auras pas empêché	That you won't have prevented
De rire très haut sa victoire	From laughing aloud in its triumph

The syntax is ambiguous: "I don't know what (undefinable) sin it is / That you won't have prevented," that is to say, the woman was immediately indulgent to some desire of the poet; then, "I know no sin however naive (or innocent) / That you won't have prevented," in other words, the poet complains at her stopping even the most harmless physical expression of affection.

   In the first case, the erotic assault, in spite (or because) of the earlier timidity, has the pagan directness of Mallarmé's *Faune,* hence *naïf,* not guilty. The woman consents. In the second case, she demurs, though perhaps only momentarily. So, in either case, it is possible that she who was initially indifferent, chilly as a glacier, finally melts and joins in the dazzlement, as in "Cette frigidité se fond / En du rire de fleurir ivre" (59, addressed to Méry). On the other hand, the poet's triumph may be as solitary as the faun's—"Je tiens la reine!" And, further, it may only be a substitute gratification, aesthetic pleasure in mere contemplation of the beloved's hair and/or the sunset. But, we suspect the fuller meaning, for various reasons (some to be stated): sensual as well as ideal delight in an ambiguous suspension such as the cluster of jewels in *Hérodiade*.

   rire: is often clearly, though complexly, erotic for Mallarmé: "cacher un rire ardent sous les replis heureux" (*Faune*); "Cette frigidité se fond / En du rire de fleurir ivre" (59); "[rose] ouverte au rire qui l'arrose" (145).

naïf: associated etymologically with, and directly recalling, *natif* and therewith the born-naked cluster discussed under *nativement* in *Hérodiade,* or *naître* in *Une dentelle s'abolit.*

victoire: recalls "victorieusement fui . . . O rire," the highly refined version of a heroic deed of the sort Mallarmé describes in various myths of *Les Dieux antiques,* a victory of light over darkness, symbolized by his heroine's fair head of hair versus the shadow of love-doubt and the general blackness of night: "un peu de puéril triomphe." Here the exploding light is of his love act, equally childish and superb. Perhaps, as we said, the act is merely the kiss bestowed on Méry's hair (which, however, does not silence it or prevent it from "laughing aloud" as in *Quelle soie:* "dans la considérable touffle / Expirer . . . Le cri des Gloires qu'il [the lover] étouffe") but, from the letter we quote later on, we may feel a wider resonance than this.

Dis si je ne suis pas joyeux	Say if I am not happy
Tonnerre et rubis aux moyeux	Thunder and rubies at the hubs
De voir en l'air que ce feu troue	To see in the air this fire holes through
Avec des royaumes épars	With scattered realms
Comme mourir pourpre la roue	As if dying purple the wheel
Du seul vespéral de mes chars.	Of my only chariot of evening.

The passage of the amorous *Contes indiens* addressed to Méry, which we quoted previously, is helpful here: "Sûr de regagner son royaume, quand il voudra, le *char* vole et, le lendemain, à l'heure dite, entre dans la cour du palais, avec les roulements de *tonnerre.* La foule accourt enthousiasmée, il n'est pas jusqu'aux paons perchés sur les tuiles incendiées par le soir, qui n'imitent, avec leur queue éblouissante, chaque *roue* du char véloce" (628-629). In sum, the only triumph for *this* hero is the lover's triumph mingled with the sunset glow, just as in *Victorieusement fui* the only ("evening") triumph is the "puerile" one of her shining hair.

The association of peacocks' tails—*faire la roue*—together with Méry's blond hair, and fireworks—*roue à feu,* Catherine's wheel, or the fireworks of sunset in the evening sky—and the erotic equivalent is found in a letter, precisely, to Méry, whom he called his Peacock, *Paon:*
"Voilà que je croyais t'envoyer un baiser à l'heure des feux d'artifice (tu te rappelles, Paon dont la queue les défie, où nous vîmes ensemble le dernier)" (MI, p. 242).[1] Compare "vertige d'une âme comme mise à l'air par un artifice" (308).

Perhaps in the *roue* there is a reminiscence of the "roues" (279) of the carriage in which he and Méry are taking an evening ride in *La Déclaration foraine*. The *roue* is a circular constellar effect of joy-burst as in "un vol circulaire, supérieur de pierrerie ou d'âme" (615), or like the *bracelet* of *Autre éventail*, or "éclata en pierreries d'une couronne" (531); a possible indication is the "en tête la tiare papale, dômale et . . . blanche, ceinte des trois couronnes gemmées de toutes pierreries . . . symbolisation Phallique" which Mallarmé described to René Ghil [C, p. 94]; compare the cluster of melting jewels—ideal or sensual?—at the end of *Hérodiade: Scène* (and the "mourir un diadème" of *La chevelure vol*).[2]

The dark *ou*, with the melting and spilling-over *r* is very prominent in the deeply amorous cluster, sweetly dying light, of *mourir-pourpre-roue* (*amour-velours-lourd*, "mourir . . . de l'amour," 610; see C, p. 97 and Appendix C). This is also very effective in the *Faune*, as in "Tu sais, ma passion, que, pourpre," and so on, or *Toast funèbre*, "pourpre ivre." Baudelaire uses the same effect magnificently in *Le Jet d'eau*: "Puis elle s'épanche, mourante, / En un flot de triste langueur." The *mourir* of our sonnet is very much like the one in *mourir un diadème* of *La chevelure vol d'une flamme*.

Seul vespéral de mes chars: the main sense is the playful idea that this experience is the only "ride" or triumph he has in the evenings (or Evening?) of his life.

NOTES

[1] "un beau feu d'artifice . . . paon [Méry], je l'ai considéré en ton honneur" (letter, in Richard, p. 513). The fireworks-Eros association is similarly exploited in Joyce's *Ulysses*, in the Gerty Macdowell episode. Mallarmé planned using *feu d'artifice* as an important image from the modern world for his Great Work (*Le Livre de Mallarmé*, pp. 80(B), 81(B), etc.). Incidentally, Eliot took the line "Say if I am not happy" for a minor poem, *Lines for an Old Man*: "Say if I am not glad!." The line of *Ash Wednesday* which echoes the sonnet is "Garlic and sapphires in the mud / Which clots the bedded axle-tree" (together with the "bavant boue et rubis" of *Le Tombeau de Charles Baudelaire*).

[2] This dying-alive, static-dynamic circle (of hair, etc.) recalls a similar, but more complex one in *Igitur*, which expresses a suspended moment between the intimate centrifugal and centripetal impulses of the psyche: "frémissement de pensée, lumineuse brisure du retour de ses ondes et de leur élargissement premier . . . frémissement amorti . . . comme une chevelure languissante autour du visage . . ." (435). This is like the circular wave around a shock in water (or air), momentarily caught: "la mouvante écume demeurée et suprême" (337).

27. À LA NUE ACCABLANTE TU

◇❀◇❀◇❀◇❀◇

This late sonnet appeared in the Berlin review *Pan,* in 1895. It is a stormy seascape *sub specie aeternitatis.* What has happened? Has there been a shipwreck? Or, for the lack of anything so grandiose, has the abyss merely "stingily" drowned a siren, the mirage of whose infant flank appears out there in a wisp of foam? The real question here is: Is man's fate tragic (implying a certain dignity), or is he just a rumor in the meaningless movement of water, so that nothing has really happened at his demise?

The shipwreck theme is total, as at the outset of the *Coup de Dés:* man's Fall, which reverberates throughout the major Poem in countless emanated versions, through universal analogy, the network of Being. And, as in the *Coup de Dés,* it is all in a perfectly sensuous lyric form, akin to the mood of the last movement of Debussy's *La Mer* (or the piano prelude "Ce qu'a vu le vent d'Ouest"), or perhaps a foam-flecked storm painted by Vlaminck.

Henri Charpentier has rightly observed that the dislocated syntax adds to the feeling of scattered wreckage, dispersal amid the elements of nature.

À la nue accablante tu	Hushed to [or beneath] the overwhelming [storm] cloud
Basse de basalte et de laves	[Which is like a] Base [shoal] of basalt and lava
À même les échos esclaves	[Hushed] Down even with the enslaved echoes [mere slapping of water]
Par une trompe sans vertu	[Kept silent] By a virtueless [ineffectual] horn
Quel sépulcral naufrage (tu	What sepulcral shipwreck (you
Le sais, écume, mais y baves)	Know, foam, but [just] drool there)
Suprême une entre les épaves	[Abolished as a] Supreme one [example] among the bits of floating wreckage
Abolit le mât dévêtu	Abolished the stripped mast
Ou cela que furibond faute	Or [is it] that for furious lack
De quelque perdition haute	Of some exalted perdition
Tout l'abîme vain éployé	All the vain abyss outspread

229

Dans le si blanc cheveu qui traîne	In the so white thread which drags
Avarement aura noyé	Will have [probably] drowned stingily
Le flanc enfant d'une sirène.	The childish flank of a siren.

The closer sense is: What sepulcral [cosmic] shipwreck, silenced [now] beneath the lowering storm cloud, abolished the stripped mast [the naked being, at death]. The *abîme,* ambiguously total space and ocean, [through its storm-cloud and stirred-up water] did it accomplish something dramatic: an "exalted perdition"? Or just close over a quickly-forgotten insignificant, now dream-like or mythical, creature, a mere trace, wake, or foam-wisp in the water?

À la nue accablante tu: This recalls the stormy scene at the opening of the *Coup de Dés,* with the "slack-tide" sea, "furious," seething, as if with resentment at its defeated aspirations (waves)—[*coupés*] *au ras les bonds* (Page 3).[1]

nue: a *nakedly* "feminine" revenge of nature over man, its master, may be implied in this word, with which Mallarmé loved to play (*Quelle soie:* 817; etc.). Chassé has proposed a more personal interpretation, which seems to me out of place.

accablante: the three *a's* (five, with *à la*) have the flattening effect of "Quand l'ombre menaça de la fatale loi."

tu: the compressed, acute sound of *u* expresses something of the tense drama (this is furthered by the tension between the sound and the trough shape, C, pp. 251-252). There are four rimes in *u* and many *u*'s running through the sonnet. The effect is similar to that of *si* below.

Basse de basalte et de laves: The heavy black storm cloud, which remains as witness to the event, is like basalt—a crushing ceiling clamped on man's highest aspirations or dreams (or even his desire to survive), as in "bloc de basalte que l'Amérique appuya sur l'ombre légère du Poète [the monument to Poe], pour sa sécurité qu'elle ne ressortît jamais." (78); "contenir par le voile basaltique du banal" (298); "massif arrêt de toute réalité, ténèbres, basalte" (329). It is really the cloud of death, a black smothering murderer-principle. Compare the "brouillards . . . grand plafond silencieux" which cuts off the poet's haunting vision of perfection (helpfully) in *L'Azur.* Note all the flattening *a*'s, as in *Quand l'ombre menaça,* where a crushing weight likewise descended from the sky.

Basse: implies the solid quality of the storm cloud, like the *noir roc* which is the brooding cloud of *Tombeau (de Verlaine);* compare "brouillard monumental" (653) and the "roc . . . faux manoir . . . évaporé en brumes" of the *Coup de Dés,* Page 8. *Basse* also means "bank under water" which, together with the sense of "low," implies the murderous descent, reaching right down into the level of life, to the extent that cloud and water are mingled, as in *A même les échos esclaves*. There may be a musical overtone, sort of heavy "bass" notes to go with the *trompe*.

basalte: the meaning is "black igneous rock"; it is a limit-case, a kind of congelation of black terror into a block: "massive arrestment of reality" (329); "tréfonds ... basalte ... lieu du plus noir secret" (N, pp. 191-192); the overtones are *bas* with, possibly, a defeated aspiration in *alte* or *salte* (*saute*). In this particular context we might also suspect a Latin vibration in its *sal* ("salt").

laves: overtone of *laver*, the flowing, as in the *Coup de Dés: lavée par la mer* (Page 5).

À même les échos esclaves: "des élans abattus de prière—au ras" (391), and "coupant au ras les bonds" (*Coup de Dés,* Page 3) imply the cutting-down action ascribed here to the murderous shipwreck-causer (partially represented by the storm cloud): *tu ... à même les échos esclaves,* meaning "silenced (the human event, life itself) down to the slapping of waves, those mere slaves of physical law"; the *trompe* (below) is related to this idea; compare *clapotis inférieur quelconque (Coup de Dés,* Page 10), the empty place—*rien n'aura en lieu que le lieu* (see *n'aura* below)—which is all that is left after man's departure.

The *a*'s are, again, flattening, like *ras;* the neutral *e*'s, likewise*; m* hints at the returned-to maternal site as in "Mère qui créas *(Les Fleurs);* compare *au même principe qui m'élut (Cantique);* "véridiques, à même" (385).

esclaves: some of the *clapotis quelconque* effect (see *c* in Table) is here; the *laver* overtone functions as in its rime, *laves.* Perhaps the down-pointing feminine *v* accentuates the humbleness.

trompe sans vertu: the horn that could signal distress, or that could at least protest, is silent, ineffectual, drowned with the rest; even art goes down, eventually, as in the first part of *Toast funèbre.* The sense of *trompe,* "deceives," is operative. The *trompettes tout haut* of *Hommage (à Richard Wagner)* sounded quite another note; compare the "tient debout" versus "sans vertu" of "La Cour" (415). There is a suggestion of fallen man *(virtus-vir),* as in the "stripped mast" image, below.

trompe: the roundness of the horn is in the *o,* its pomp in the *p;* compare "pompeux mensonge" (N, p. 184).

sépulcral naufrage: the total shipwreck (Fall) at the cosmic origin, as on Page 2 of the *Coup de Dés: du fond d'un naufrage* (cf. Jasper's *Schiffbruch*). As in that passage, the "feminine" quality of this watery "grave" is emphasized by *sépulcral;* compare "j'innovais dans l'onde / Mille sépulcres pour y vierge disparaître" of *Le Pitre châtié.* The element *nau (navis)* and the *Abolit* (*Coup de Dés:* N'ABOLIRA, Page 5, at the bottom of the Page, in the trough position, like the *naufrage cela direct de l'homme* of Page 4; C, pp. 125, 130, 222), and the *u* of *sépulcral* all go with this effect; note the association of a feminine principle of beauty, *Pulchérie,* with *sépulcre* in *Prose.*

The *naufrage cela direct de l'homme* is a modulation between the total event of individual death and the derivative *act* of love (-death). Here too, in the "stripped mast," the double nakedness, for burial or for love, is implied.

The shipwreck theme runs, in one form or another, throughout Mallarmé. In *Brise marine* the desire for adventure is sobered by the thought:

> . . . peut-être, les mâts, invitant les orages
> Sont-ils de ceux qu'un vent penche sur les naufrages
> Perdus, sans mâts, sans mâts . . .

The haunted repetition of "sans mâts, sans mâts" emphasizes the importance of the theme that life brings down death, hubris leads to punishment as, secondarily, sexual aspiration leads to possible castration. This latter theme is discussed under the *Cantique de Saint Jean.* This despairing tone of Mallarmé—not only late, as some think, but in his early writing as well—informs most of his work. For example, the "shipwreck" of his dreams is the core of *Triptyque.* But in all these poems, miraculously—"behind his back," as Hegel would say—a constellation blooms beyond all care, born transfigured from the death (of hope) itself: the poem.

écume: part of an important whiteness-cluster (see Appendix A) along with *baves* and *si blanc cheveu;* its splash of brightness (helped by *é* and *u)* reminds us of that effect in *Brise marine:* "ivres d'être parmi l'écume." See *Salut: écume.*

Suprême une entre les épaves: even the highest effort goes down; the bit of floating wreckage that was the *mât dévêtu* is like the supreme effort of a final artist—"une oeuvre suprême à venir" (Biog., p. 779)— who tried to prevail over fate on behalf of all humanity but went under eventually like the rest; this is described on Page 8 and 9 of the *Coup de Dés* (the "roc . . . faux manoir / tout de suite / évaporé").

suprême has a little Icarus curve in its circumflex recalling the one on *Maître* of the *Coup de Dés,* Page 4; compare "la mouvante écume demeurée et suprême" (337); (*suprême* is in a subtle cluster with *crème,* etc.; see Appendix A).

Abolit: a frequent Mallarméan term for death, it is used in a similar sense in *Une dentelle s'abolit,* and in *Un Coup de Dés* (Page 5): the *t,* as in *mât dévêtu,* provides a mast effect, like that on *bâtiment,* in the *Coup de Dés* (C, p. 156).

mât dévêtu: contains a suggestion of the spiritually or physically naked man; also a hint of the *pure* art whose final defeat Mallarmé envisages, as "ardent, volatile *dépouillement"* (403); *mât* has an overtone of defeat, *mat (échec et mat).*

Ou cela: meaning "Or (is it) that?" A second possibility suggested by someone is "Or (what sepulcral shipwreck) hid" *(cela,* the past definite of *celer,* to hide).

que: the *q* here and in *quelque* help slightly to give the wave-slapping effect, as in *Quelconque une solitude (Petit air I)* or *clapotis quelconque (Coup de Dés,* Page 10).

furibond: the defeated waves of aspiration (on Page 3 of the *Coup de Dés)* were *furieux* and *bonds.*

faute: a hint of the original Fault or *mal* which defeats us in the end; compare the *mal (originel)* on Page 3 of the *Coup de Dés: mal à dresser le vol* (C, p. 145); "le vieux mal de vivre" *(Tombeau d'Anatole,* f. 168).

perdition haute: the "high tragedy" that may have occurred may be nothing at all, mere foam; recalls the *perdition* of the *Coup de Dés* (Page 8), which was the disaster a God-rivalling creation would have brought down; hence it too did not take place, perhaps.

Tout l'abîme vain éployé: The *abîme* is chaos of stormy sea and sky, like the original chaos; its metaphysically "feminine" *gouffre* quality is brought out by the *éployé,* a wing-spread effect which goes with a vast network of symbols based on the one-two, male-female dialectic "comme une aile . . . bifurque" (393), "l'allure habituelle du vol" (305) (see C, pp. 144 *et seq.).* The swallowing of the "stripped mast" by this dark gulf recalls the expression "dans l'amour s'abîmant" (15), or, more importantly, the *Abîme* of Page 3 of the *Coup de Dés* in which the *Maître* will drown after wrestling with Her: *la mer par l'aïeul tentant ou l'aïeul contre la mer;* it is the "Mère qui créas, en ton sein juste et fort, . . . la balsamique mort" *(Les Fleurs).* The *ou* of *tout* adds a color of darkness; note the circumflex, like the little wave of foam.

vain: "vain" because it is brute nature; the meaningless stars, *feux vils,* of *Quand l'ombre* were contrasted, in this sense, with the light of man's genius. Pascal similarly meditated about the superiority of man over the rock that could crush him. The feeling is one of Shakespearean *(King Lear)* irony at all the effort put forth to destroy this puny creature, man. This implies a certain Promethean bitterness, as in Hugo's *A Villequiers;* what an unequal contest! The same note was sounded in the passage describing the shipwreck-drowning of Man *(le Maître),* on Page 4 of the *Coup de Dés,* by *où vaine.*

éployé: the immense spread of the seascape all in vain, drowning a pathetically helpless mortal, a mere "child," "une larme noyée au sein d'un flot géant" (ML, p. 182).

si blanc: echoes *sirène* (the *si*) in its thyrsus effect of sinuous *s* and virile *i,* like the twist of the alluring creature with the brightness of the flash of white foam. The closely-related *sirène* of the *Coup de Dés* (C, p. 324) had this double quality expressly: "stature mignonne téné- breuse debout / en sa torsion de sirène"; compare *blancheur sybilline (Don du Poème)* that similarly exploits the (milky) whiteness of the *i* sound, as do "blanchit l'étoile sibylline" (258); "si ce très blanc" (76); "blanche si" (61), "blanc souci" (27).

cheveu: the thread of white foam refers to several levels of meaning: the mere trace (or *Wake,* as Joyce has it) that a man's career represents in the sea of life ("written in water"); the sexual "wake" or jet of life through which he procreates and passes life on to his son;[2] a modulation to the white thread of lace standing for writing, or art, as in *Une dentelle s'abolit,* (q.v.)—thus in *Salut* the "virgin verse" is compared to (cham- pagne) "foam," and, further, to a "drowning" troop of "sirens"—then to the white hair of an old man who is about to go under, and who in this late meditation contemplates his death and the "splash" he will (not?) have made. This is all exactly parallel, in its various meanings, to the death of the *Maître,* on Page 4 of the *Coup de Dés: maniaque chenu . . . coule en barbe soumise.* From this death there emerges an ambiguous son, who is either the son he procreated physically (his death includes the derivative manifestation of the sex act) or the son of his spirit, a work of art (C, pp. 158-200).

The old-man idea fits with the *enfant,* below, in the sense that in the face of death we are all children (of God); or in "second childhood" there is a sort of return to innocence. No doubt Mallarmé also had (in both the *Coup de Dés* and this little sonnet which reflects some of its main themes) his actual son Anatole, who died at the age of eight, somewhere in his mind (C, p. 214). But, as in the *Coup de Dés,* the father and the son, *son ombre puérile,* coalesce mysteriously; it is hard to say where one begins and the other ends. The "child" or the "siren" is, rather, a generic figure of man, father or son, faced with the eternal; for, after all—and particularly this is true for the artist—where does the Self end? Are our children (or dead children) in our own minds not ourself, *quelqu'un ambigu?* (C, p. 200).

avarement: continues the bitter note of reproach (cf. the *avare silence* of the tomb in *Toast funèbre*). Literally, it refers to the little "catch" of the mere child-siren as opposed to the putative dramatic major Wreck. There is an overtone of *avarie*, "damage to ships": "Comme un yacht princier Marie / Magnier va sans *avarie*" (171).

aura . . . noyé: reinforces the meaning of his own death contemplated in the future; secondly, it means "probably drowned" (future perfect). *aura* has a slight overtone of the second meaning of the word: "aura," that is, a feeling announcing a crisis.

noyé: establishes that *abîme* refers to water (as well as Space); note the plunging *y*, see under *sirène* (the *bifurcation*); compare "Telle loin se noie une troupe / De sirènes" *(Salut).*

flanc enfant: the "stature mignonne ténébreuse debout" of Page 8 of the *Coup de Dés* had this same idea of a vulnerable, sweetly innocent (but serious, "dark") child-figure,[3] like a siren flashing out of the water of the infinite only to twist back down into the deep and disappear forever. To repeat, no doubt all the sacrificial children Mallarmé grieved for (e.g., his sister; Harriet Smith; Anatole) are somewhere in the picture; but all are summed up in the One figure, mainly himself, the childlike poet who grieves. As Hopkins says, "it is Margaret you [Margaret] mourn for."

The suggestion of whiteness in a swimming flank (cf. "blanc enfant" somewhere, and "blanche créature," his dead sister, 270) goes with the *si blanc,* and a hint of *oie* in *noye,* as in *Château de l'espérance* (recall the "blancheur animale" of the naïad-swans in the *Faune*).

enfant: etymologically *in-fans,* "not speaking," may echo distantly the *tu,* "silent," above.

d'une: hint of *dune,* a bright hump?

sirène: one of Mallarmé's richest words; "she" is a key figure in the *Coup de Dés,* representing the ultimate, somewhat androgynous, angelic poet, or, ambiguously (like the son mentioned earlier), his final Work, disappearing back into the all-sea. She sings a dangerous song, luring humanity back in with her. "She" is half-human (or divine), half-animal; moreover the "child" adds another dimension of ambiguity to her feminine dangerousness. In the *Coup de Dés* her epicene nature was directly evoked, as we saw *("stature* mignonne ténébreuse *debout"* versus "torsion de sirène"). On the whole, she is Mallarmé's image of himself as the representative of mankind, reminding us of Shakespeare's "poor forked creature" *(King Lear, III),* who is born to die. Or, more promisingly "une image de soi qu'il y garde intacte autant qu'une Ophélie jamais noyée . . . Joyau intact sous le désastre." (30). In the *Coup de Dés* the siren, as she went down, slapped with her "bifurcated" tail *(squames ultimes bifurquées)* a monument, the Work the poet left behind; it too "evaporated in mist," like the "cloud-capped towers and gorgeous palaces" of *The Tempest.*

NOTES

[1] Gardner Davies draws on this image, the storm-cloud, to prove that the *aile* of Page 3, *Coup de Dés* is a cloud; this is no doubt suggested, since *Abîme* is both sky and sea, but it is certainly also water; the chief image of the *aile* is the ocean waves, rising and falling, archetypes of all doomed aspiration in the Poem: *mal à dresser le vol.* Here too, in the sonnet, the *abîme* is ocean as well as sky; *Tout l'abîme vain éployé . . . aura noyé* certainly implies *drowning* action by water, which is stirred up angrily, *furibond* (as well as cloud). If all the action in the scene were concentrated above, it would be a strange poem, lacking in this depth of oceanic beauty; the same holds for the *Coup de Dés.*

[2] The network is complex: a good example of the modulation from milky thread to emission of a secretion is in a fragment of *Hérodiade* (1446), see Appendix A. The *ch* here is the sound of issuing, as in *blanchi,* Page 3 of the *Coup de Dés;* "*sh* donne . . . avec netteté, jet lointain" (947).

[3] Among the numerous examples of this poignant image in world literature (*Macbeth, Boris Goudunov, Doctor Faustus*) we are particularly reminded of little Rudy in *Ulysses.*

28. MES BOUQUINS REFERMÉS

❖❖❖❖❖❖❖❖❖

Published in 1887 in *La Revue indépendante,* under the title *Autre sonnet,* this was chosen to be the last in order of the *Poésies.* For the most part, it is quite clear and direct and, in its quiet way, is very fine.

Mes bouquins refermés sur le nom de Paphos,
Il m'amuse d'élire avec le seul génie

Une ruine, par mille écumes bénie

Sous l'hyacinthe, au loin, de ses jours triomphaux.

Coure le froid avec ses silences de faux,
Je n'y hululerai pas de vide nénie

Si ce très blanc ébat au ras du sol dénie
A tout site l'honneur du paysage faux.

Ma faim qui d'aucuns fruits ici ne se régale
Trouve en leur docte manque une saveur égale:

Qu'un éclate de chair humain et parfumant!

Le pied sur quelque guivre où notre amour tisonne,

Je pense plus longtemps peut-être éperdument
A l'autre, au sein brûlé d'une antique amazone.

Having closed my books on the name of Paphos,
It amuses me to elect [summons up] with nothing but genius
A ruin, blessed by a thousand foams [waves]
Under the hyacinth [purplish-blue, sky], far off, of its triumphal days.

Let the cold run with its silences of a scythe ['s strokes],
I won't howl out to it [its accompaniment] any empty [Greek] funeral chant
[Even] If this very white sporting at the ground level denies
To any site the honor [summer beauty] of the false [fictitious: dreamed of] landscape.

My hunger which regales itself with no fruits here [tangible beauty]
Finds in this knowing [cannily turned into presence by poetic gift] lack an equal savor:
Though one of them [fruits, i.e. breasts] bursts with human perfumed flesh!

With a foot on some wivern where our [nostalgic meditation of] love [usually] stirs the ashes
I think longer [and] perhaps desperately
Of the other [breast], the burned breast of an ancient Amazon.

This preference for the ideal (a very sensual one: the ideal cruelly drives him to a peak of exasperation on the other side of which lies exquisiteness), is typical Mallarmé, recalling "l'absente de tous bouquets" and the like. His *plus longtemps* and *éperdument* in the sonnet may remind us of Laforgue's succinct statement that "L'art, c'est le désir perpétué."

The first quatrain vaunts the power of the artist to evoke a summer with mere talent: "Sous un hiver qui neige, neige / *Rêvant d'Edens"* (118); far from hampering, the winter—*saison de l'art serein (Renouveau)*—may even help, or as Baudelaire said:

> Et quand viendra l'hiver aux neiges monotones
> . . . je serai plongé dans cette volupté
> D'évoquer le Printemps avec ma volonté
> (*Paysage*)

or Gautier:

> Sans prendre garde à l'ouragan
> Qui fouettait mes vitres fermées,
> Moi, j'ai fait *Emaux et Camées.*
> (*Préface*)

This poem of Gautier's, incidentally, is followed directly by *Affinités secrètes:* "un temple antique . . . sur le fond bleu du ciel attique."

According to Mondor, Paphos is a Greek city founded by the Amazons. The mood of the place recalls perhaps: "Hélène . . . Par des mers désespérées . . . ta chevelure *hyacinthe,* ton classique visage . . . m'ont ramené . . . à la gloire qui fut la Grèce" (tr. of Poe, 193). Wais thinks the "book" was Keats's *Sleep and Poetry,* and observes that Keats's *Fancy* develops the same theme.

The name, as in Proust's "Noms de lieu," conjures up a fancied scene, especially when the too-literal book is closed: "le sens trop précis" *(Toute l'âme)* hobbles the flight of dream. This ruin-by-the-sea, under a blue blue sky, is, indeed, very ideally Greek.

mille écumes bénie: the *i, é, u, é, i* add touches of foamy crest, as in Valéry's "maint diamant d'imperceptible écume." Noulet detects here a reference to the birth of Venus, from the foam that is famous (or, as Joyce would say, "foamous"), in this spot, near Paphos.

In the second quatrain, we note the sharp effect of "hululerai . . . vide nénie . . . si . . . dénie," the keening howl of the wind that Mallarmé will not imitate. In the epic project he confided to George Moore *(Avowals),* the rising wind made the *i* sound in *oui.* Here it contrasts rather with the flat land; *blanc . . . ébat . . . au ras* (repeated *a*'s).

ébat: as Noulet says, this movement banishes *(dénie)* the quiet vision. The repeated *n's* of *n'y . . . nénie* are notably negative (see Appendix C).

aucuns fruits: these are very much like the ones described in a *Vers de circonstance*:

> Ces vils fruits ne sont que mensonge
> Pour un oeil ravi d'épier
> Tout l'éclatant jardin du songe
> (117)

docte: this knowing conversion of a lack into a poetic presence is similar to that of *Prose*:

> L'enfant [patience] abdique son extase [trop directe]
> Et docte déjà . . .
> Elle dit le mot . . .
> Né pour d'éternels parchemins

which again hints at the hesitations and prolongations (or the resultant staying power) of art.

guivre: "wivern," a heraldic monster, rather like a cockatrice. Such twisting creatures represent the squirm of Mallarmé's meditative agony in the dark (or near-dark) of a room, as in *Igitur* (440); compare "un rivage de guivres dédorées" (271).

notre amour tisonne: a general "we" or "our," that is, where we, usually, nostalgically stir up the ashes of our past loves in meditation. But Mallarmé is here stirring up his love of poetic beauty, rather than the memory of Méry.[1] The *brûlé* of the *sein* obliquely echoes the fire and emphasizes that remote but hot—*éperdument*—passion (acute *u* and *é in brûlé* heighten this fierceness), even while referring to the well-known fact that the terrifying ladies burnt off one breast in order to facilitate the launching of arrows against hapless males. Under the embers Mallarmé's quiet sense of humor about his relation to Woman is also stirring: "Je ne suis . . . qu'un passant qui se gare [contre] l'éblouissement [féminine qui] me renverse et me darde" (881).

NOTE

[1] Cellier thinks Méry is nearby (hence the *notre*) and that the concrete *fruit* is hers. This is quite possible.

29. PROSE (POUR DES ESSEINTES)

◊❖◊❖◊❖◊❖◊

> There appeared to me a miraculous vision in
> which I saw things that resolve me to say no more
> about the blessed one [Beatrice: Beauty or Truth]
> until I should be capable of writing about her in a
> more worthy fashion. And to achieve this, I am
> striving as hard as I can, and this she truly knows
> (Dante, *Vita Nuova,* XLII, tr. Musa).

Prose is Mallarmé's most daring poem before *Un Coup de Dés.*
First published in 1885, it marks an attempt to utilize, or try out, some
of the poetic vocabulary Mallarmé had amassed for the Great Work
of which he had laid the visionary groundwork in his famous crisis, or
series of crises,[1] from 1866 to 1869. It also seeks to explain to an
admirer[2]—des Esseintes, the decadent dilettante hero of Huysman's
A Rebours (which had just appeared, in 1884, and had boosted
Mallarmé's reputation considerably with enthusiastic praise)—the true
nature of the crisis and its vision, and the reason why the Great Work
was not yet forthcoming.

In our *Mallarmé's Un Coup de Dés* (1949), we wrote as follows:
"*Prose* later recounts to a sympathetic listener the story of how Mallarmé
really attained a perfect vision and how his wiser, more patient self
abandoned the attempt to capture that perfection which also threatened
madness or the *néant*" (116); ... [it] recounts ... that which caused
Mallarmé to delay until his means, patiently developed, could match his
vision" (130).

Gérard de Nerval, in his *Aurélia,* has recorded a very similar experience, often using the same terms. Though it provides striking con-
firmation of the true meaning of *Prose,* the passage is fairly long and we
must therefore, with some reluctance, relegate it to the notes for this
chapter.[3]

In 1952 Charles Mauron (*Introduction à la Psychanalyse de
Mallarmé*) came to the same conclusion (I do not know whether he
had read my study or not), but did no more than mention this prime
source of *Prose.* Some other commentators have meanwhile clarified a
few minor obscurities.

Mallarmé's adventure, at the culmination of his youth, into unprecedented realms of beauty and truth, has become in *Prose* a voyage
to a mysterious enchanted island, with a comparably mysterious and

240

lovely feminine companion. We are reminded of other such islands, classic Cytherea or the medieval Avalon, Parny's "île fortunée" in his *Elégie* ("Projet de Solitude") Baudelaire's *Invitation au voyage*[4] and *Parfum exotique* (in the last three, as in Venus' isle, the woman associate is of the essence).[5] The poet is mad with desire to have it all—as eager as Macbeth, "but here upon this bank and shoal of time"—is *hors de lui,* ecstatic. His companion, beneath her feminine splendor, is wise as women are, speaks in the name of patience, perpetuation of life. And so, as we reluctantly "leave this little island," we know that this beauty will not be lost, it will be captured for us all, but in good time.

The title has caused considerable speculation. The notion that it refers to "proses chrétiennes," the simple Latin hymns of the Byzantine period referred to in *Plainte d'automne,* is possible and would confirm a notion of race-memory underlying the personal experience.[6] Mauron's contention that the title is ironic is even more to the point. The rimes are lavishly rich ("millionaire," in the French phrase.) More important, we think, is the oblique reference to Mallarmé's high ideal. The title *Prose,* like the self-deprecatory *Divagations,* would point ironically and modestly to the failure to write a Poem (we note that the attempt at his Great Work, the *Coup de Dés,* is proudly entitled "Poème"). Finally, the title is a curiously good one for a poem. The whole feeling of the word, with its prominent *P,* the round *o* and the harmonious *r,* is in the tonality of the poem, sets into motion its main flow of poetic "music." All three letters are found in the following words: *Prose, pour, trop, triomphalement, promenions, approfondit, trompette, porte* (used, surprisingly and instructively, three times) *porta, trop, pour, porter,* and finally again, *trop,* the key word of the poem—the last phrase is *"trop grand glaïeul."*

The early version published by Mondor in his *Autres précisions sur Mallarmé et inédits* presents a number of interesting variants to which we will refer in each instance, after the symbol "Pr. I."

Hyperbole! de ma mémoire	Hyperbole! from my memory
Triomphalement ne sais-tu	Triumphantly can't you
Te lever, aujourd'hui grimoire	Rise, today old gramarye [occult science]
Dans un livre de fer vêtu:	Cloaked in a book of iron:

Mallarmé summons the old and beautiful, but excessive and dangerous vision to rise up out of his memory or race-memory (as in *Igitur,* 438). Through disuse, the vision has become unclear, like a dusty old book of occult science left in an attic. Such texts were often bound with clasps of iron (as in Poe's *Silence:* Cellier) that become a symbol for its congealed or hardened inaccessibility. In *Las de l'amer repos,* the "sterile" poet speaks of "le terrain avare et froid de ma cervelle"; in

Renouveau it is "mon crâne qu'un cercle de fer enserre." The best parallel is "de la pensée . . . les plis roidis . . . Du suaire laissant . . . Désespéré monter le vieil éclat voilé" *(Ouverture ancienne)*.

Hyperbole!: is an essential aspect of deep art; the epiphany of the perfect poetic flowers, representing his vision here, *stands out* exaggeratively, like any such glowing Appearance (the meaning of the word Epiphany, initially used for the Christ child), is "bigger than life." For a fuller discussion of the phenomenon, we refer the reader to *Toast funèbre.* The vision may swell *too* big and threaten to destroy the mind —as it actually did in Nerval's case—of the megalomaniac poet, with his God-rivaling "juvenile" drive to omnipotence, or hubris. But Mallarmé, precisely, learned his lesson from the crisis he now recounts.

An overlapping secondary meaning is the youthful exuberant lyricism Mallarmé outgrew (historically and individually), as expressed by "l'homme hyperbolique . . . lyrique . . . s'élance en l'air par *trop* de légereté et de dilatation, comme pour atteindre une région plus haute" (Baudelaire, "Théodore de Banville"); compare Mallarmé's remarks on Banville: "la fontaine de lyrisme . . . il marche à travers l'enchantement édenéen désignant . . . l'éclatante blancheur du *lys enfant* . . . lyriquement comme la foudre" (521-522). See C, p. 263-291.

The *p* of *Hyperbole* is an important effect throughout the poem. The exclamation mark is corollary, like the one after *Lys(!),* in the *Faune.*

Triomphalement: a subtle *trop* is woven in, a *p,* a *mort,* and a *phal.* There is a magnificent effect of a proud, stubborn rise in the length of the word; *triomphalement . . . te lever* recalls "musicalement se lève . . . l'absente de tous bouquets," (857).[7] (In note 7 there is a lengthy discussion of the flower hyperbole.)

aujourd'hui: see the Montégut passage under *patience,* below. We are reminded of the *aujourd'hui* in *Le vierge, le vivace.*

grimoire: the compelling rhyme with *mémoire* adds a depth of time and mystery; the cluster *moire-grimoire-mémoire* (as in the *Hommage à Richard Wagner*) joins with a vast network of associations: writing as a tissue *(tissere, textus,* "text"), web, lace, linen, folds, and so forth, running throughout his work (e.g., *Ouverture ancienne, Une dentelle*). All of these associations came together in the *grimoire* of *Igitur* (433), which contained, now obfuscated, one grand old Idea to be revivified by this ultimate son of humanity.

Pr. I (the early version) read:

> Indéfinissable, ô Mémoire,
> Par ce midi, ne rêves-tu
> L'Hyperbole, aujourd'hui grimoire
> Dans un livre de fer vêtu?

This confirms the sense of a recurring "high noon" of Vision, and the rest of our interpretation. (Richard sees in the *midi* a reference to the rise of lucidity in the Renaissance; this seems farfetched).

Car j'installe, par la science,	For I install, through science [or knowledge]
L'hymne des coeurs spirituels	The hymn of spiritual hearts
En l'oeuvre de ma patience,	In the work of my patience,
Atlas, herbiers et rituels.	Atlases, herbals, and rituals.

The sense is that now, today, as a mature, patient, wiser man—or a son of late civilization—through steady practice of my craft, I embody the essential beauty I (or the Christians) once envisioned, in various (literary) creations. "Atlases" probably refers to his intellectual or critical writings, "herbals" to his lyric poems, "rituals" to his contemplated dramas, or dramatic poetry à la *Hérodiade* (the *Faune* too was originally planned for the stage. At times he also thought of his Great Work as theatrical, a ritual to replace official religion, see "Catholicisme"). At varying points in his life, as we follow in his correspondence, Mallarmé plotted his future career according to these several genres. Later, he invested his hopes in the one new genre of the *Coup de Dés*. Mme. Noulet has pointed out that the three terms form a progression from the site of art through its means (vocabulary) to a total cult. She compares *atlas* and *rituels* to the "contrée" and "doctrine" of *La Musique et les Lettres* (646). See also C, pp. 227-228.

science: "knowledge," but in the rather special sense closer to our word "science." Mallarmé often uses it this way (849, 851), confirming his *historical* usage.

hymne: the Oeuvre was to be "l'hymne . . . des relations entre tout" (378). Embodied, it is the "spiritual instrument" (378), for instance, the book joining a man to the All, and one to the many, as religious hymns do. There is a probable allusion here to Mallarmé's modern, complex, and critical substitute for an outmoded, vestigial religious cult (cf. his "Catholicisme" and the race-perspective of *Igitur*). His views here, as recent commentators have demonstrated (see Richard, p. 455), were no doubt stimulated by E. Montégut, in an article that elicited the poet's enthusiasm. *hymne* has a strong echo of *hymen,* a joining in love.   *

patience: a key word of the poem, later echoed by the lines describing the "sensible" woman who restrained his mad impulse and set him to steady work: "as if heeding her / I exercise my old concern." Patience is a female virtue par excellence, and a product of late culture. Montégut wrote: "Ce n'est que par des greffes habiles et *patientes* que nous pourrons faire reverdir ces puissances *aujourd'hui* languissantes de l'imagination et de la passion" (in Richard, p. 455). Note the contrasting qualities of the acute *y*-sound in *hymne,* the broad *a*-sound in *patience.*

herbiers: "désinences ... détachées prudemment et méthodique-ment classées ... dans l'*herbier* du botaniste [grammairien]" (964). This confirms the sense of *patient* and *scientific* production.

Now there occurs a break, represented by the asterisks in the first edition, published in the *Revue indépendante,* which later were removed, though the reason for them is clear enough: the first two strophes form an introductory section from the viewpoint of the present, after which comes the account of the original experience, as it occurred in the past.

Nous promenions notre visage	We were promenading our glance
(Nous fûmes deux, je le maintiens)	(We were two, I maintain)
Sur maints charmes de paysage,	Over many a landscape charm,
O soeur, y comparant les tiens.	O sister, comparing them to yours.

Who is the *soeur?* Mauron sees her as the actual sister, Maria, who died at age thirteen, when Stéphane was fifteen, whom he certainly loved and who haunted his memory (witness his correspondence to Cazalis where he speaks of this openly) along with his dead mother. He alludes to Maria directly in *Plainte d'Automne.* But this is a hobby-horse that Mauron drives to death, "discovering" subconscious mani-festations that are perfectly obvious and first of all, to Mallarmé him-self. No, the evidence is all against Mauron here. *Soeur* is used as tra-ditionally—for example, the "my sister, my spouse" of *The Song of Songs*—by poets:

> Mon coeur qui dans les nuits parfois cherche à s'entendre
> Ou de quel dernier mot t'appeler le plus tendre
> S'exalte en celui rien que chuchoté de soeur.
>
> (*Sonnet,* 61)

The woman addressed in the *Sonnet* is his mistress, Méry Laurent, just as Baudelaire's "Mon enfant ma soeur" refers to Marie Daubrun.[8] In sum, *soeur* is a favorite poet's term, largely because of its rime with *douceur,* expressing keen tenderness and also because of the hint of chaste remoteness which goes well with the transcendental necessities of art: "elle [his fiancée] était ma soeur et ma femme" (Corr., p. 82). She is *above,* an idealized flower-woman, like Ronsard's unreal (trans-figured in death) rose-lady, Marie; the term *soeur* also provides a hint of the compensatory *below* of art, a slight taint of delightful perversity. As an ideal woman she tends to be no individual woman but a spectral creature taken, so to speak, from the poet's own ribs, like Chateau-briand's *sylphides* or Nerval's chain of beloveds stemming from his mother—all of them certainly present in the one prodigious figure of "la dame qui me guidait" of the passage from *Aurélia* we quote (note 3). Mallarmé's mother and his sister Maria (closely linked in a letter to Cazalis as objects of a sublime love, a cult; Corr., pp. 73-75), Harriet Smyth, Poe's dead women, Ophelia and his mistress Méry, and others, are each a dream-woman who corresponds to, or is, the poet's own "better half," his feminine soul, his *anima:* "mon âme . . . une si exquise dame" (293).

The *soeur,* then, is the woman principle in the poet's self and cosmos. Like Hérodiade, she is the youthful being of beauty his male persona courted and continued to court. But she is also the poem-nursing mother, his wife (Marie), of *Don du poème,* the maternal muse, "celle, la Muse" (503) and even feminine divinity: "O Mère qui créas" (*Les Fleurs*). As the *Ewig-Weibliche,* that which prolongs life, she represents "patience," common sense, and mild tenderness (*cette soeur sensée et tendre*); her sanity is further evidenced by the wise *sourire.* She refuses to go off the deep end with regard to the madly ambitious vision the poet confronts.

Woman is "generally closer to nature" (W, p. 123), and Mallarmé plays on this obvious truth in his "maints charme de paysage / O soeur y comparant les tiens," which may remind us of Vigny's Eva (*La Maison du berger*) who is a comparably complex companion, *compagne* and *campagne.*

The eternal feminine is often recognized by Mallarmé as an immanent aspect of his own being," as in "O mon âme . . . une si exquise dame anormale: car ce n'est pas elle, sûr! s'il y faut voir une âme, ou bien notre idée (à savoir la divinité présente à l'esprit de l'homme) qui despotiquement proposa: 'Viens' [au théâtre]. Mais un habituel manque inconsidéré chez moi de prévoyance . . . etc." (Here, the *anima* as *soeur sensée* is clearly evoked, 293); "Celle, la Muse, pas autre que notre âme, divinisée!" (503); "à travers une allée titanique de cyprès j'errais avec mon âme . . . avec Psyché, mon âme" (196, tr. of Poe). From all this we may see that the ideal woman's charms (*les tiens*) are ambiguously his own, those of his art.

nous fûmes deux, je le maintiens: this may imply, as Chisholm notes, a perpetuation (*maintiens*) of a lost youthful love in himself (*je*); however, at most, this is a remote echo.[9] More important, we believe, is the idea that at the present time Mallarmé is carrying on as he really (or potentially) had been all along: the *patience* was latent in him, and had saved him then.

The *promenions notre visage* is a pleasant, mildly "hyperbolic" effect, vibrant with a unity-in-duality; the hyperbole is in the *p* the *pro,* and the face-image; compare "plongea la volupté de son visage dans l'eau" (602).

The r's of *soeur, charmes, comparant* are tender and the *ar*'s are the clear transparent light of the summery isle, to be more fully appreciated later.

Pr. I: the last line read "Aurais-je su dire: les siens!" This indicates that the later version was modified to imply an at least oblique address of the woman (as overhearer, at his elbow):

L'ère d'autorité se trouble	The era of authority is troubled
Lorsque, sans nul motif, on dit	When, without cause, it is said [by us?]
De ce midi que notre double	Of this southland [or "noon"] that our paired
Inconscience approfondit	Unconscious mind explores
Que, sol des cent iris, son site,	That, soil of the countless irises, its [the southland's] site,
Ils savent s'il a bien été,	*They* [ironic tone] know if it really existed,
Ne porte pas de nom que cite	Carries no name cited
L'or de la trompette d'Été.	By the gold of Summer's trumpet.

The carpers . . . the "Spirit of litigation," below—are bothered when of this southern landscape (or possibly "high noon" of the spirit) —either "on no true grounds" (if an objective commentator is implied) or "gratuitously (if Mallarmé is implied)—it is said that this ideal scene has no name under ("announced by") real summer sun. Later they will insist "que ce pays n'exista pas," that is to say, *they* know if it exists or not (the tone of Mallarmé is sarcastic here in describing the know-it-all attitude of the debunking, dull-spirited, rationalistic carpers). In the next strophe Mallarmé will claim that it really did exist, though not in the way the carpers understand the word real, but in the "realer than real" sense in which Proust, for example, speaks of artistic phenomena (it is better, we think, to speak of "artistic imagination" here rather than "Platonic ideas"). "They" may be also the traditional theologians or religionists whose vision Mallarmé aims to replace.

The region, the island, is the object of an imaginary voyage, in a long mystic and artistic tradition, to which we might add the "jardin des délices" of Chrétien de Troyes and other medievals, Mignon's southern paradise ("Connais-tu le pays?"), Lamartine's *Novissima verba,* Nerval's "petit parc" in *Aurélia* (or the chateau-grounds *in Sylvie),* Baudelaire's *Invitation au voyage*—where the anchored boats quiver with anticipatory voluptuousness no true voyage can bring—or des Esseintes' dreamed-of trips that he never took (cf. Rimbaud's "on ne part pas"). It is the marvelous world on the other side of the looking glass, as in "pays prestigieux par lui [Villiers] habité et maintenant surtout [qu'il est mort] car ce pays n'est pas" (510). Compare also:

Et des fleurs qu'au ciel seul fit germer la Nature,
Des fleurs qu'on ne voit pas dans l'Été des humains
Comme une large pluie abondaient sous leurs mains.
(Vigny, *Eloa*)

L'ère d'autorité: ironic, like the *ère d'infinité* of Pr. I. We do not see how this can refer to the Middle Ages, recent commentators notwithstanding, though it may refer to official religionists who would monopolize Truth; they uphold the simple vestigial Christian myth to which Mallarmé opposes his maturely critical and complex vision, art, "sans acolyte": "Le vieil éclat voilé . . . sans acolyte, / Jettera-t-il son or par dernières splendeurs [?]" *(Ouverture ancienne).* Mallarmé, in a Catholic country, courageously becomes his own prophet after his famous "lutte" with God.

trouble: the dark *ou* contrasts vividly with the *i*'s of *midi.*

double inconscience: the doubleness of *animus* and *anima,* mentioned earlier, runs throughout Mallarmé *(Hérodiade, A la Nue, Un Coup de Dés),* whose thought is complexly dialectical: "Moi, c'est moi et toi" (Corr., p. 86). The examples are too numerous to cite; they are discussed at length in *L'Oeuvre de Mallarmé,* for instance on pp. 330-336. For Mallarmé, as for Baudelaire, man, particularly modern man, is a *homo duplex.* Baudelaire's prose poem, *L'Invitation au voyage,* seems to have exerted a particular influence in this respect (see note 4).

iris: they grow near water. Later, this word will modulate into that of the invented species, *iridées; iris* is both bright and melting *(i, r);* cluster: *iris-désir-iridées-iridescent-rire-délire-lyre* (C, p. 369).

Ils savent s'il a bien été: the ironic effect of *bien* is confirmed by the variant *certe;* it is the same as in "Il s'agit bien vraiment de pittoresque . . . Il s'agit bien de poésie. Ce qui compte c'est la vérite" (Camus *Noces,* "Le Désert"). It is also possible that, by a wilful ambiguity, the line means that *"they,* the irises, know the site was real (in the ideal sense)."

L'or de la trompette d'Été: this recalls the "trompettes tout haut d'or" of *Hommage à Richard Wagner*—both are synesthetic—and depends on a rich cluster: *or-trop-trophée-triomphe-trompette,* involved in the original sunburst coup of the *Coup de Dés* (C, pp. 120-120). Pr. I.: "Entre tous ses fastes, l'Été."

Été: as bright as *midi,* for similar reasons *(é).* See the Vigny fragment just quoted.

Oui, dans une île que l'air charge	Yes, on an isle that the air fills
De vue et non de visions	With view and not visions
Toute fleur s'étalait plus large	Each of the flowers spread wider [one than the other]
Sans que nous en devisions	Without our talking of them

The poet proudly affirms it *did* exist, a *real* spectacle (cf. *ordinaire-ment,* below), not just empty imagination: "La voix divine . . . en pluie de fleurs . . . prodige . . . calices véritables" (631), and (cf. Rimbaud's "j'ai vu ce que les hommes ont cru voir," *Bateau ivre*) every flower spread out spontaneously, without our talking them into existence; or, more simply, we kept silent, as in "pourquoi s'exprimer plus que ces lotus, ces roses, ces jasmins tus, incueillis: ne s'étaient-ils pas tout dit? Ils trempèrent, l'un et l'autre, pour renouveler leur être; en le silence lustral" (631). See note 4 and Baudelaire's "dans le haschisch rien de miraculeux, absolument rien que le naturel excessif" (Théâtre de Séraphin," *Paradis artificiels).*

Nerval's similar experience in *Aurélia* caused him to declare "Je ne pouvais douter de ce que j'avais vu si distinctement."

The *île* reminds us of the *fertiles îlots* of *Brise marine;* also of "tout ce vers quoi mon âme languissait—une île verte en mer" (199, tr. of Poe).

s'étalait plus large: broad effect of *a*'s; transparent *ar*'s in *air, charge, large* (see next strophe); echo of *étale-pétale.*

Telles, immenses, que chacune	Such, immense, that each one
Ordinairement se para	Ordinarily was adorned
D'un lucide contour, lacune	With a lucid contour, lacuna
Qui des jardins la sépara.	Which separated it from the garden.

In *Les Fleurs* we have the same stunning effect of huge flowers: *les grands calices, grandes fleurs.*

We have spoken previously of the "epiphany"—and its halo of glory —"eidetic vision," and their connection with the artistic *hyperbole;* compare "cernés d'un contour précis et soigné" (the effect of drugs on the appearance of objects; Baudelaire, "Théâtre de Séraphin").

The *ar* cluster is very prominent here: *(air-charge-large)—ordinaire-ment-se para-jardins-sépara.* The *para* and the whole cluster has echoes of *transparent, paradis, parfum,* as well as of *art, clarté, clair* and others.

ordinairement: emphasizes the almost casual realness of the flowers; compare the "songe ordinaire de dos" of the *Faune,* meaning the usual (natural) body. *ordinairement* is parallel to the *vue et non de visions* of the preceding stanza; these are *real* visions. The effect is to anchor the poetry, so to speak, give it a depth and body, as in "maint rameau subtil . . . demeuré les vrais bois" *(Faune).* This play between the ficti-tious and the real is featured in "Bucolique": "ce site . . . arrivât-elle, l'écriture [à la décrire] sur le sol où je mets le pied, plus évidemment leur mirage, *ordinaire,* demeure" (404). The *air* in *ordinairement* goes with the *ar*-group; compare "L'ordinaire abandon sans produire de trace" (1446).

jardins: recall those of *Toast funèbre* where Mallarmé admired his master, Gautier, for going to the pagan sources of life, *seeing* directly, and bypassing official religion. Pr. I read: *jour pur,* the sheer air of the garden against which the flowers appeared.

The capital *T* in *Telles* helps the "broad," "immense," calyx-effect; the *o*'s of *contour* and the *o* of *ordinairement* are active; *u* and *i* are bright in *lucide.*

The ambiguous nature of these flowers—flowers of vision, even of speech—may recall "le Vers!—fleur rapide, sur quelque transparence comme d'éther" (333). The purity or *claritas* (Aquinas, Joyce) in which all true poetry swims is certainly present in both texts.

Gloire du long désir, Idées	Glory of long desire, Ideas
Tout en moi s'exaltait de voir	Everything in me was excited to see
La famille des iridées	The family of *iridées*
Surgir à ce nouveau devoir,	Spring up at this new duty,

The poet's ambition rises to a mad thirst for glory to *possess* all this beauty, to be *the* creator, nay Creator! (As Malraux put it simply "Tout homme rêve d'être Dieu," in *La Condition humaine;* Baudelaire reveals the vision of the "Homme-Dieu" in his *Paradis artificiels).* At this peak—and in all of Mallarmé's better moments of art—Ideas and desire are inseparable, as they had been (music and mathematics) for the Pythagoreans; "je crois que pour être bien l'homme, la nature en pensant, il faut penser de tout son corps, ce qui donne une pensée pleine et à l'unisson comme ces cordes de violon vibrant immediatement avec sa boîte de bois creux . . . il faut cela pour avoir une vue très—une de l'Univers." (EL, p. 352).

Gloire du long désir: "l'enfant près de finir jette un éblouissement" (406); compare the end of *Hérodiade (Scène).* The long *désir* may refer to the *patience* he already had (hence *nous fûmes deux* [déjà] and *mon antique soin)* and indeed must have had to reach this point of desire. In the experience he will re-learn patience.

The effect of *g,* followed by the release of the *l* in a sort of *glousse-ment* or *sanglot,* the broadening expression of the *oi* and the harmonious *r,* all this makes the word *Gloire* especially apt for an outburst of delight after a protracted pent-up desire, as Mallarmé foresaw in *Les Mots Anglais:* "G . . . une aspiration simple . . . le désir, comme satisfait par l, exprime avec la dite liquide, joie, lumière, etc." (938); compare "jaillir le sanglot" (66), "le cri des Gloires" (75), "sanglots glissants" *(Apparition).* Pr. I read "Obsession, Désir, idées."

The bright *i* and the liquid *r* form the essence of *iridée* (an invented term for a species of ideal flower—analogous to *orchidée*—to rhyme with *désir, Idées*), a sort of glistening tear quality like that of the flowers of *Toast funèbre: pluie et diamant,* compare the melting jewel of *Dame, sans trop: ouïr . . . pleurer le diamant.*

famille: emphasizes the oneness of the vision; element *mille* (the harmonized multiplicity).

Surgir: the receptacle *u* is followed by a brimming-over *r* (like the *source en pleurs* of the *Faune);* the caressing *g* is the same as in the reverse movement of *plonge;* the *i* is bright, rising. Pr. I read "Connaître le nouveau devoir," which has basically the same sense of "rising to meet" [his need].

Mais cette soeur sensée et tendre	But that sensible and tender sister
Ne porta son regard plus loin	Carried her look no further
Que sourire et, comme à l'entendre	Than a smile and, as if heeding [or understanding] her
J'occupe mon antique soin.	I exercize my old concern [craft].

The gracious lady, companion or *anima,* stops the dangerous impulse with a merely human smile, and "I carry on my old concern"—"le devoir idéal que nous font les jardins de cet astre" *(Toast funèbre)*— "as if under her guidance." As Cellier observes, *entendre* may refer to Mallarmé's effort to *interpret* (and combine) naive natural beauty with the critical intellect of an advanced civilization; this idea was influenced by the article by E. Montégut (see his letter to Lefébure, Corr., p. 246).

The sinuous feminine *s*'s in *soeur, sensée, sourire* help oppose the madly direct brightness of *iridées.* The whole strophe is in mainly gentle, subdued tones.

The *souriant* of *Hommage* marked a similar taming.

The variants are important here:

> Mais cette soeur, sensée et tendre,
> Ne porta ses regards plus loin
> Que moi-même: et, tels, les lui rendre
> Devenait mon unique soin.

The idea here was that the poet gave up his vision for her love, and thenceforth spent all his time looking back into her eyes, life (as in *Victorieusement fui*).

Oh! sache l'Esprit de litige,	Oh! know, Spirit of litigation,
A cette heure où nous nous taisons,	At this hour when we are silent,
Que de lis multiples la tige	That with multiple lilies the stalk
Grandissait trop pour nos raisons	Grew too much for our reasons.

Know, carpers, that if at present we are silent—not yet uttering the Great Work—that the stalk *grew too much for our reasons* (mine and my lady's) *to handle,* with multiple lilies (contrary to your belief that there were *no* real flowers) . . . The *lis* are no doubt simply meant to be the equivalent of the *iridées*. They recall "il [Banville] marche en roi à travers l'enchantement édenéen célébrant . . . l'éclatante blancheur du *lys enfant*" (265). As we said earlier, this image is related to the lyric hyperbole of youth. The *Lys!* of the *Faune* is a perfect example of the adolescent hubris.

We note that *taisons* is in the present tense, a parenthesis amid the account of the past. Mallarmé addresses his era to explain why the Great Work is not yet apparent. In the veiled prose of his critical pieces he was often doing just this—the examples are too numerous to cite.

The experience was recorded in his early letters. At first Mallarmé wrote confidently of his vision: "Tu vois que j'imite la loi naturelle" (Propos, p. 69); then came the breakdown and "la nature, elle est trop faussée en moi, et monstrueuse, pour que je me laisse aller à ses voies" and "Ma pensée, occupée par la plénitude de l'Univers et distendue perdait sa fonction normale . . . le *trop*-plein de [ma] pensée" (note *trop;* Propos, p. 86). Finally, "je redeviens un littérateur pur et simple . . . Contes . . . Poésie . . . Critique [recall *Atlas, herbiers, rituels*]. En somme les matinées de vingt ans." (93). This is the toning down and prolongation essential to survival, *patience!* After having yielded to the "voie pécheresse et hâtive, satanique et facile, de la Destruction de moi" (Corr., p. 246), he sought the "fameuse patience" he admired in his friend Lefébure (Corr., p. 299). For, "ce n'est qu'à travers . . . des ans d'étude et point dès l'éclair révélateur qu'on peut le [the Great Work] traiter définitivement" (letter to Ghil, in *Les Dates et les Oeuvres*, p. 92).

Esprit: was not capitalized in the first version. The capital may indicate a reference to official religion, the Church.

tige: "fleur . . . ta majestueuse tige, imagination" (526) is a very direct comment on the image; compare also "les rimes dardées sur de brèves tiges" (327).

Grandissait: recalls an article by Baudelaire on Poe which Mallarmé certainly had read: "celui dont le regard est tendu avec la roideur d'une épée sur des objets qui grandissaient à mesure qu'il les regarde—c'est Poe lui-même." (The sword image occurs in the *Tombeau d'Edgar Poe,* q.v.).

In the Nerval passage that we cite in the notes, we read: "La dame . . . entoura . . . une longue tige . . . elle se mit à grandir . . . semblait s'évanouir dans sa propre grandeur."

The "L'interdire au rêve ennemi de sa charge" of *Toast funèbre* is a similar caveat against spontaneous vision, though rather of a sentimental sort, "revery."

Et non comme pleure la rive,	And not as the shore weeps,
Quand son jeu monotone ment	When its monotonous game lies
A vouloir que l'ampleur arrive	In wishing that [the] amplitude should arrive
Parmi mon jeune étonnement	Amid my young astonishment
D'ouïr tout le ciel et la carte	At hearing all the sky and the map
Sans fin attestés sur mes pas,	Endlessly attested as I walked,
Par le flot même qui s'écarte,	By the very wave that draws back,
Que ce pays n'exista pas.	That this land did not exist.

The first line of these two strophes is followed by a six-line paren-
thetic remark introduced by "Quand," and is then completed by the last
line, "Que ce pays n'exista pas."

The sense is: And it is not as the dry-land carpers (inferior artists
or critics whom I left behind on shore when I voyaged) tearfully pro-
claim: that this land did not exist when (also) they would have it, according to their dreary and lying aesthetic, that a prolix production
(immediate results), should have come from (the experience I had as a
young man, that is) my astonishment at having all nature (or Nature)
made available to me, as I went, by the very receding flood (of chaotic
ordinary life which I traversed to reach this shining island-vision).

An overlapping sense is that the critics believe the "ample" vision
occurred *only* in his unreliable youthful imagination, and did not really
exist in any valid sense.

jeune étonnement: is in the main sense a direct reference to the fact
that Mallarmé was young when he had the vision, and that he is looking
back on it from the viewpoint of wiser maturity taught by his patient
"feminine" self. This has been consistently misinterpreted. Secondly,
jeune here means "fresh, original." Both senses are implied in the *jeune*
paysage of *Las de l'amer repos.*

ampleur: this, too, has been missed in various ways. Most or all have
seen it as referring to the *trop grands glaïeuls,* which it partly (ambiguously) does. But *ampleur* refers primarily to spontaneous, facile, prolix
production and is elsewhere so used by Mallarmé—partly because of its
rather limp and flaccid sound, its broad (though nasalized) *a*—in a
context of slight condescension, as in "sens divers et cependant liés ...
de fécondité, d'*amplitude,* de bouffissure" (929). A good example is in
his reply to an inquiry about Tolstoy, who had attacked his own complex
art. Mallarmé wrote with gentle irony: "Les appréciations de Tolstoy ...
me semblent celles-là même qu'il faut accepter de lui, génie *ample* et
simple, direct dans l'expression de l'idée" (873); or, again, "Naturelle
ampleur ... bonhomme et très grand dans la nature ... l'aboutissement
par excellence de la pièce populaire" (344-345) or "moins *ample*(s) ...

intense" *(Les Gossips,* no. 4); or "le romancier . . . avec une sereine *ampleur"* (399);[10] and "efforts qui sont d'un vigoureux carton. Malice un peu *ample"* (331). Although we must allow that breadth, or copiousness, "may have its own poetry, its own infinite" (W, p. 154), and occasionally so for Mallarmé, it usually implies for him a loss of concentration. Almost all the other examples of the use of *ampleur,* and cognate terms, given by Richard (pp. 332-333) have a slightly condescending tone and refer to the works of more easily lyrical poets, like Régnier.

rive: the dry land as contrasted to the island-vision; compare: "Je reste en la rumeur d'un rivage par le flot tourmenté et tiens dans la main des grains de sable d'or—O Dieu! ne puis-je en sauver un de ta vague impitoyable?" (199, tr. of Poe).

pleure la rive and *monotone:* form an image of waves repetitively "weeping" running to the shore, the *jeu monotone* is like the recurrent rhythm of nature implied in the *Jeu suprême* of *Une dentelle* (Noulet). All this is mainly a symbol of the dry land (left behind), as the habitat of the carpers.

jeu is a frequent term for art, in Mallarmé, for example, "ce jeu insensé d'écrire" (481), "le jeu littéraire" (663).

The *flot même qui s'écarte* implies a spontaneous yielding of nature, somewhat like the Hebrew crossing of the Red Sea (C, p. 180). The sea is obviously the infinite source of the organic beauty envisioned here, floral or feminine. In a minor way, the *flot* may connect back with the *pleure* (Noulet).

The rime *carte-s'écarte* emphasizes the secondary idea that the chaotic sea, like the overall *HASARD*-ocean of the *Coup de Dés,* reveals the "map"—the chart of beauty and truth, a Work—by receding, as in Proust's "sentant au fond de moi des terres reconquises sur l'oubli [cf. *de ma mémoire*] qui s'assèchent et se rebâtissent" (Vol. I, p. 67). The variants are useful here:

> Et, non comme en pleure la rive!—
> Car le jeu monotone ment
> Pour qui l'ampleur de l'île arrive
> Seul, en mon jeune étonnement
>
> D'entendre le Ciel et la carte
> Sans fin attestés sur nos pas
> Par l'onde même qui s'écarte,
> Que ce pays n'exista pas!

The first and last lines are basically the same as in the final version: "And it is not as the mainland weeps [that] this [fairy] land did not exist!" The intervening lines also confirm our interpretation:

For the monotonous game [of mediocre artists] lies
For which alone the ampleness [prolix production] of the island arrives

That is to say, as contrasted to my sparse production. (The *en mon
jeune étonnement* is the site of the *pays* of the last line, in this version).
The capital C, indicating, again, the depth of the vision, was probably
too rhetorical and was removed.

There is another break implied here before the last two strophes,
which return to the present tense.

L'enfant abdique son extase	The child gives up her ecstasy
Et docte déjà par chemins	And already learned through ways [of life]
Elle dit le mot: Anastase!	She says the word: Anastase!
Né pour d'éternels parchemins,	Born for eternal parchments.

The patient *anima* or muse-companion is referred to as a child (cf.
Hérodiade: "notre reine enfant,"; N, p. 169), in the same convention
as *soeur;* compare Baudelaire's "Mon enfant, ma soeur" of his *Invitation au voyage,* or Vigny's "la femme, enfant malade" *(La Colère de
Samson).* She is a child, too, in the sense that she is learning; perhaps
the implication is that her natural wisdom prevails over the male, "a little
child shall lead them," that is, "she" is the first to understand what must
be done. She tells the man, by gently pronouncing for him his Word
(Logos)—echoing the original "Hyperbole!"—how to "stand up"
(etymology of *Anastase)* or, at the least, she utters whatever mysterious
sesame Word opens the door to the living future, to "eternal parch-
ments" or immortal, effective, or recorded art, that bespeaks "Woman's
power to make a man act and live . . . whether to create at the level of
society or to procreate at the level of the flesh . . ." (W, p. 346).

The rhythm of the experience—the voyage to a distant island and
the return to normal life—is duplicated in reverse in "Bucolique,"
where the poet first speaks of "un lieu adonné à la foule ou hasard" and
adds "Que, cependant, nécessaire d'y être venu et même d'avoir tenu
bon; pour s'en retourner *docte"* (401). The canny conversion of a loss
(through "abdication" or renunciation) of the too-direct is similar
to the *docte manque* of *Mes bouquins,* when the real fruit (breast) is
surpassed by the ideal. Books are elsewhere referred to as existing in a
"docte sépulture," or library (417).

enfant: is probably used with an awareness of the etymology *in-fans,*
"not speaking"; the speechless ecstasy gives way to the "word" *(le mot)*
or Logos. The word is "born" *(né),* a new life arises and for good.

The childish or *original* freshness of a new Word may be sought in
the semichaotic *Anastase;* compare, at the other end of life, merged with
death, *ptyx* (M. Szykowski helped here).

The many *d*'s may help indicate a new firmness of purpose.

Avant qu'un sépulcre ne rie	Before [lest] a tomb laugh
Sous aucun climat, son aïeul	Under any clime, its ancestor
De porter ce nom: Pulchérie!	At carrying this name: Pulchérie!
Caché par le trop grand glaïeul.	Hid by the too-great gladiolus.

Pulchérie: is close to the Latin word for beauty, *pulcheria,* and no doubt refers to the natural beauty that is menaced with never being recorded.[11] The expression *porter ce nom: Pulchérie* is parallel to the expression *ne porte pas de nom que cite / L'or de la trompette d'Été* in an earlier stanza; both examples refer to unrecorded realities, on a map or in a work. The *trop grand glaïeul* is spontaneous vision, which threatens by its very power to mask, to defeat, the effective art, or cause it to remain buried in a "tomb" of unaccomplishment just as in *Le Pitre châtié* the too-pure experience, the immediate or unmediated, swept away the calculated techniques which were all his effective art *(tout mon sacre);* compare "Ainsi je pacifiai Psyché et la baisai . . . et nous allâmes à la fin de l'allée où nous fûmes arrêtés par la porte d'une tombe; par la porte, avec sa légende, d'une tombe, et je dis 'Qu'y a-t-il d'écrit, douce soeur, sur la porte, avec une légende, de cette tombe? Elle répliqua: 'Ulalume! Ulalume! C'est le caveau de la morte Ulalume!'" (198, tr. of Poe). This too-natural vision of perfection has as its obverse, death; and Mallarmé, having followed his master Poe to this limit-situation, this edge of the precipice, warned by his "sister"—"Psyché, élevant son doigt,[12] dit: ' . . . je me défie' (197)—became healthily frightened just in time (perhaps the example of Nerval helped somewhat, cf. *Le Guignon*). So that when he did die, "Sans pleurs, je dormirai dans mon tombeau fécond" (ML, p. 182).

There is some reminiscence, as we said, of his sister Maria in all this, but joined with other feminine figures (his mother, his friend Harriet), and literary ones like Ophelia and Ulalume (Poe's ideal being the death of a beautiful woman), and finally, most important, his own "Psyché," as various quotes attest.

Avant qu'un sépulcre ne rie: the tomb is a mouth as in the *Tombeau de Charles Baudelaire*—"bouche sépulcrale"—and can laugh ironically at all-too-human attempts to defeat it; compare Hugo's *bouche d'ombre.* The depth of this *rire* contrasts with the gentle *sourire* of life *(soeur).*

Sous aucun climat, son aïeul: means the unlocated (however real) cosmic site of the drama of consciousness, the background preceding ancestrally, so to speak, the drama, as the act of total creation precedes any individual creation (and this climate will swallow it eventually as it gives it birth, eternal maternal womb-tomb, like the metaphysical *lieu* of the *Coup de Dés,* which is its source and its grave: "des tombes béantes bâillent au niveau des lumineuses vagues" (tr. of Poe, 212).

trop: we have earlier indicated some of the reasons for the effectiveness of this word, which has overtones of *héliotrope, tropical, trope* (flower of style) as well as *trompette-trophée-triomphe;* we also noted the round calyx and halo-effect of the *o*, the "hyperbolic" swelling *p.*

glaïeul: the *gl* has much the same impact as in *gloire;* the etymon, "sword," may be connected with the hubris implied, as in the *Coup de Dés* (see note 7, especially the quotation "STEM, tige . . . STAB").

NOTES

1 Actually these crises are in one continuum with all the others, major and minor, of his whole life, but we, like himself, are forced to simplify in order to maintain some sense of direction.

2 The adventurous uninhibited aestheticism of des Esseintes helped make him a good listener to this story. But he was really an afterthought; the admirer Mallarmé thought of when he originally began the poem (long before Huysmans' book) was undoubtedly the theoretical ideal reader, "tel autre" (153).

3 The following passages are from *Aurélia* (page references are to the edition of Mercure de France, 1907): "Alors l'une d'elles se leva et se dirigea vers le jardin.

Chacun sait que dans les rêves . . . Les objets et les corps sont lumineux par eux-mêmes. Je me vis dans un petit parc . . . à mesure que la dame qui me guidait s'avançait sous ces berceaux, l'ombre des treillis croisés variait pour mes yeux ses formes et ses vêtements. Elle en sortit enfin, et nous nous trouvâmes dans un espace découvert. On y apercevait à peine la trace d'anciennes allées qui l'avaient jadis coupé en croix . . . des arbres d'une croissance vigoureuse . . . la dame . . . entoura . . . une longue tige . . elle se mit à grandir . . . semblait s'évanouir dans sa propre grandeur . . . je vis que le jardin avait pris l'aspect d'un cimetière." (329).

". . . je ne pouvais douter de ce que j'avais si distinctement vu" (339).

". . . la chaîne infinie des choses créées; c'est un réseau transparent qui couvre le monde, et dont les fils déliés se communiquent de proche en proche aux planètes et aux étoiles" (367).

4 In his prose poem *L'Invitation au voyage* the woman is invited to a:

Pays singulier supérieur aux autres, comme l'Art est à la Nature, où celle-ci est réformée par le rêve, où elle est corrigée, embellie, refondue . . . [là] j'ai trouvé ma *tulipe noire,* et mon *dahlia bleu!*

Fleur incomparable, tulipe retrouvée, allégorique dahlia, c'est là, n'est-ce pas, dans ce beau pays si calme et rêveur, qu'il faudrait aller vivre et fleurir? Ne serais-tu pas encadrée [la compagne] dans ton analogie, et ne pourrais-tu pas te mirer, pour parler comme les mystiques, dans ta propre *correspondance?*" (italics Baudelaire's).

The doubleness of Mallarmé's vision (*double inconscience; Anastase* and *Pulchérie*) is duplicated here, in the two flowers as well as the Art-Nature dialectic to which Mallarmé will frequently refer in his critical writings. We note also that Mallarmé has, in *Prose*, further defined the nature of the *rêve;* "vue et non . . . visions," that is, more real than real. Baudelaire would undoubtedly agree.

5 We may speculate that there is a biological source for the fantasy of the magic island, within the mother, the ultimate goddess of the isle. Robert Graves would call her the "white goddess" (and "the source of all poetry"; he exaggerates, of course, in this).

[6] Especially since Anastase and Pulchérie have a vaguely Byzantine quality, perhaps influenced by Huysmans' reference to the same decadent mood. The Huysmans influence is possible here since the last two strophes seem to have been composed much later than the preceding ones. But Pulchérie occurs in the early parody, *Prose pour Cazalis.*

[7] Huysmans had written Mallarmé asking him for examples of his work "vers ou prose"; but it is unlikely that this is reflected in his title, as the parody of the poem, *Prose pour Cazalis,* seems to have been written around 1868.

The passage in *Plainte d'automne* reads: "la littérature à laquelle mon esprit demande une volupté sera la poésie agonisante des derniers moments de Rome, tant, cependant, qu'elle ne respire aucunement l'approche rajeunissante des Barbares et ne bégaie point le latin enfantin des premières proses chrétiennes"; this confirms the impression that the title *Prose* is apologetic. It also indicates a possible philogenetic parallel to his own growth from naive youth to critical maturity (from Christian myth to visionary art; we note that the young Stéphane had been an ardent believer, until the famous struggle with God in the late 1860's).

Mallarmé uses the word *Prose* satirically in the subtitle of a scabrous little poem called *Mystacis umbraculis;* the title perhaps suggests the notion of Latin hymn. Also in *Prose des fous* (22), the word is used in a loose, mildly pretentious way, again possibly referring to the Latin tradition or, more probably, giving the ironic and self-deprecatory twist Mallarmé often sought in his titles, short of a major work.

The best indication is that Mallarmé rhymes *prose* with *rose* at least four times (18, 20, 134, 140), in all cases with the literal sense, for example, "ce poème devenu prose" (apologetically; 134). In other words, the title is chosen primarily for the two suggested reasons: the flower-overtones and other poetic qualities of the word; its modesty, apologizing for this "interim report" still far short of the promised poetic *Oeuvre.*

As we noted, *Prose* already contains a hint of the subject of the poem, poetic flowers. The *glaïeuls* or *iridées* (or *iris*) here are cousins of the *Lys* and *Rose* surging up from the *Eden* of *Toast funèbre.* The flower symbol or motif is most important throughout the writings of Mallarmé. With the first word of *Prose: Hyperbole!,* we think of "Je dis une fleur! et musicalement se lève ... l'absente de tous bouquets" (857), echoing the exclamation mark (as in the *Lys!* of the *Faune*) and the *te lever* of the first stanza of *Prose.* The flower-woman association is traditional, and strong in Mallarmé (*Hérodiade la rose,* etc.) Now, the "hyperbolic" quality of the flower, the rising, upward-thrusting, bigger-than-life monumental epiphany can also be the woman's, the stunning stature of a beautiful creature. All this is brought together in the early *Phénomène futur:*

"J'apporte vivante ... une Femme d'autrefois. Quelque folie, originelle et naïve, une extase d'or ... sa chevelure, un visage qu'éclaire la nudité sanglante de ses lèvres. A la place du vêtement vain, elle a un corps; et les yeux, semblables aux pierres rares, ne valent pas ce regard qui sort de sa chair heureuse: des seins levés comme s'ils étaient pleins d'un lait éternel, la pointe vers le ciel ... " (269).

The *levés* and the *pointe vers le ciel* underscore the "monumental" or "hyperbolic" quality, just as the flower of young womanhood, Hérodiade, is also a "reptile inviolé" (*Scène*). Dr. René Laforgue, in his *Echec de Baudelaire,* has commented on this phallic aspect of the female body, breast, or leg, and so forth, in Baudelaire's *femme-serpent* images. Freud was, as so often, the pioneer here.

Mallarmé himself often spoke, in his critical writings, of these underlying obsessions and motivations of art, and also often consciously integrated them into his complex, dialectically evolved poems. It is hard to say, of course, just what is conscious and what is not in a poem like *Hérodiade*, written in the poet's early years. But the critic can hardly be blamed for trying to do what the poets themselves, sooner or later, themselves do. Incidentally, Richard fully confirms our analysis here (pp. 125-126).

Apparition, dedicated to the fiancée of Cazalis, has these lines:

> Quand avec du soleil aux cheveux, dans la rue
> Et dans le soir, tu m'es en riant apparue

The self-parodying *Prose pour Cazalis* echoes this:

> Et dans son extase
> Le soleil riant
> Fulgore Anastase
> C'est tout l'Orient

and part of the following quatrain reads:

> Fleuris Pulchérie
> Au bord de la mer

Now, if we remember that the etymology of Orient is *orior*, "to rise" and that of Anastase is "I stand up" or approximately; if we recall the cluster of standing or rising flower-woman, in *Le Phénomène futur* (noting the impact of *Phénomène*), her *ecstatic* (etym: "to stand out") hair, like a rising sun, and join all this with the same effects in the phenomenal "apparition" (epiphany) like a sunburst of the blond woman in *Apparition*, and, finally, the *extase* of the sun plus the up-thrusting flower-woman, *Pulchérie*, standing out against the sea (her source), in the *Prose pour Cazalis*, we get some sense of connexus here, of direction.

Gautier, in his *À la femme*, wrote:

> En Venus Anadyomène
> Poser nue au bord de la mer

(Mallarmé notes in *Les Dieux antiques*: "Anadyomène ... (celle qui si lève"; 1198). Gautier's woman dies at the end of the poem, and the poet goes to pray at her tomb. Is such a transfiguration (Beauty-from-death) implied in *Prose*? There may be a hint of such a Poe-like motif in the image of *Pulchérie* written on the tomb. A bitter hint of mortality may be added to the youthful vision of the so-alive woman, as in the ambivalent image of the siren on Page 8 of the *Coup de Dés* (with the corollary ambivalent "male" image of the Work as monumental rock and tombstone, nearby). But let us be wary of following Mauron in his biographical simplifications. Here there may be a hint of the woman's death-and-transfiguration (as in Goethe's Gretchen, as well as Poe's Lenore), but the work, it is implied, will survive. Only in the *Coup de Dés* itself will a more purely ambivalent mood prevail (C, pp. 320-346).

Banville, who was at times for Mallarmé *the* poet (see 257), published *Une Femme de Rubens* in his *Exilés* of 1859; we line up some verses and phrases of Mallarmé with some of its strophes:

Une Femme de Rubens	*Prose pour Cazalis*
Pour la race future,	Et dans son extase
En ta haute stature	Le soleil riant
Sous le baiser riant	Fulgore Anastase
De l'orient;	C'est tout l'orient

Comme une fleur d'Asie
Epandant l'ambroisie
D'un buisson de rosiers
Extasiés;

Magnifique, vêtu
Ainsi qu'une statue
De la seule fraîcheur
De ta blancheur,

Alors quand nos idoles
Mourantes et frivoles,
Aux yeux irrésolus,
Ne seront plus

Que des chimères vaines
Toi, le sang de tes veines
Montera, vif et prompt,
Jusqu'à ton front.

On verra luire encore
Ton sein...

De tes formes parfaites,
On verra les poètes
Tourmentés par le mal
De l'idéal,

Attester par leurs larmes
Le pouvoir de tes charmes
Et l'immortalité
De ta beauté.

Fleuris Pulchérie, etc.

Le Phénomène futur
"A la place du vêtement vain, elle
a un corps

"Se rappelent leurs pauvres
épouses, chauves, morbides...".

"Quand tous auront contemplé
la noble créature"

"seins levés"

"les poètes de ce temps, sentant
se rallumer leurs yeux éteints"

"la paupière humide de larmes"
(les hommes qui regardent)

In *Le Forgeron* of Banville are the lines: "de l'écume jaillit une divinité... Elle
était droite ainsi qu'un chaste lys éclos... Et [les fleurs] soupiraient d'extase et
s'écriaient: C'est elle! / C'est la Beauté!"

To these indications of association between a beauteous flower-woman, her stature
(like a statue), and the Anastase-hyperbole of *Prose*, we must add the important
word *trop* of the final phrase of *Prose*: *le trop grand glaïeul*.

It has echoes of *tropical* and *héliotrope* as well as *trope*, flower of language. The
swelling *p* (see our Letter Table, Appendix C) and the round *o* which contributes
also the halo-effect described in the poem, are part of the reason it was chosen for a
prominent role in the *Coup de Dés*, where it expresses, as in *Prose* (it recounts the
same poetic crisis in both) a monumental hubris (with mushroom—as in the now-
famous cloud-shape—or phallic overtones), "cette blancheur rigide / en opposition
au ciel / trop / pour ne pas marquer."

Mallarmé, who was a professor of English and whose poetic use of language often
reflects the fact, was undoubtedly influenced here by the word "proud" (which in
Shakespeare's time had a decided phallic overtone, as in "print their proud hoofs i'
the receiving earth," *Henry V*). In *Les Mots Anglais* he speaks of *p* as follows:
"l'intention très nette d'entassement, de richesse acquise... que contient cette lettre"
(933) and lists among the words containing it "PROP, soutenir, Lat. propago;
PROUD, orgueilleux, et PRIDE, orgueil."

Another revealing passage from *Les Mots Anglais* (948) is: "*St* est l'une des
combinaisons qui, dans beaucoup de langues, désigne stabilité et franchise, trempe,
dureté et masse..." As examples he gives in one group: "STAFF, baton; STEM,
tige (Latin sto); TO STAB, blesser; STARK, franc et (adv.) totalement; STARCH,

empèse; TO STARVE, mouirir d'inanition ou roide de froid" (*sic*—this solicitation of an old usage is instructive). Compare *Anastase.*

[8] In *Soupir* his beloved is addressed: "ô calme soeur."

[9] The *deux* may refer, as Cellier thinks, to the modern critical spirit (cf. *double inconscience*, later). But this must be in passing, since at this stage of the poem the poet is young, uncritical.

[10] At the death of Villiers, Mallarmé imposed silence upon himself, "aucune intervention littéraire," whereas "elle occupe, unanimement, les journaux, comme les blanches feuilles de l'oeuvre interrompu ressaisiraient leur *ampleur* et s'envolent porter le cri d'une disparition vers la brume et le public" (510). There may be a slight rebuke to Villiers' prolixity, but mainly the word *ampleur* refers to vulgar journalism.

[11] Why *Anastase* and *Pulchérie*, with their murkily Byzantine sound (no convincing historical reason has been found, and Mallarmé is not at all apt to draw on the historically specific in his poems) for the notions of effective artistic action ("Stand up!)" and natural beauty, which are the best guesses so far proffered? I do not know. The parallel of the just-cited "Ulalume" seems to be part of the reason (see also note 12). We do not much like them, partly because of exegetic frustration (*mea culpa*) but also because proper nouns are almost always too limited or determinate—or else "unearned"—for good poetry.

Support for the notion that *Anastase* implies a vigorous rise is found in "Anadyomène (celle qui se lève)" (1198).

Some minor light is shed by the early self-parody *Prose pour Cazalis* (170); though in the notes to the Pléiade edition (1504) Mondor says nothing that helps one to date the little poem, in his *Vie de Mallarmé* (271) he sees it as possibly connected with a letter from Mallarmé to Cazalis (of July 21, 1868), in which Mallarmé wonders what has happened to his invited guest. The line "que tu passasses ... l'autre portion [de tes vacances] au bord de la mer" seems to echo the "Fleuris Pulchérie au bord de la mer" of the letter-like *Prose pour Cazalis* (a letter of August 27, 1868, has "Et te voilà désenchanté de la Méditerranée").

A letter to Wyse (in LL, p. 26) of 1868 has similar *Prose*-like language: "félicitations ... heureux voyageur, après celles des fleurs, du ciel, des paysages."

In *Prose pour Cazalis*, the Barroil is undoubtedly Fernand Barroil to whom Cazalis dedicated in part his early collection of poems *L'Orient*, and the *orient* of the parody is thus partly a reference to Cazalis' poetic world. But we note that there is no reference to the Orient in *Prose pour des Esseintes*.

[12] This gesture, recalling the traditional raised finger of the annunciatory angel (as in *Sainte* and *Ouverture ancienne*), stands for the monumental upthrust, or transcendent movement, of duty. And since the hand is the source of effective, realistic creativity on earth (cf. *la main* of the *Coup de Dés*, Page 5; C, p. 197) its gesture through the raised finger is an excellent symbol of dutiful, transcendent but *sane* artistic work: the male *Anastase* is pronounced by a female, just as it is the "feminine" Psyche who elevates her finger in the quotation from Poe; the result is a balanced flight, a classic-romantic combination.

The echo *doigt-doit* (C, p. 399) may have some bearing here. In a letter to Cazalis (Corr., p. 74), Mallarmé sees his future life, married to the sensible Marie Gerhard, as one of balanced duty: "je *dois* m'y plonger ... je *dois* le faire ... *devoir*. Je le dois et le ferai. Et serai fier ... une chose noble" (Mallarmé's italics).

APPENDIX A:

A Translated Extract from *L'Oeuvre de Mallarmé:*
Un Coup de Dés, Slightly Modified

blanchi

The paradoxical becoming emerges from the metaphysical level (of Pages 1 and 2) and enters the level of physical reality. Thus it begins with a concretion of the positive pole, crest, light, and extends from Eros or Hindu *soma* (universal substance similar to milk), to sea foam. As a projection of the depths of *l'Abîme*—compare *écumes originelles;* (Page 9), Eros—it is a sort of universalized milk (or *soma*): woman's milk properly speaking, *jaillissement* of stars as in the milky way, or thought, male expression such as poetry, or seed, and so forth. Through all the work of Mallarmé, we find a constant play between these divers modes. For example, in *Don du poème,* woman's milk is a key image, but since a *don* is essentially something we give forth from ourselves,[1] the notion of gift is attached to the birth (and the nourishing) of the poem itself. It is the poet who is the author of this *naissance;* compare "une virginité qui se révèle, que je sens tressaillir en mon sein; et dont le don exulte vers vous. Scintillation de toute mon intimité" (610). Having "failed" as an author, he calls on the woman to nourish his poor offspring: "presseras-tu le sein / Par qui coule en blancheur sibylline la femme." In other words, variously, the love-stuff of which the poem is made can be the poet's *don . . . intimité* or the milk. In several fragments of *Hérodiade* the image of milk is important, and in *Scène* it evokes the lost paradise of the child:

> Si tu me vois les yeux perdus au paradis,
> C'est quand je me souviens de ton lait bu jadis.

Analogous to milk, blood, which also runs through the *Hérodiade* framents, is identified with poetic expression in "l'éternelle blessure glorieuse qu'a la poésie, ou mystère, de se trouver exprimée déjà . . . oui il en presse les authentiques lèvres pour un jaillissement nouveau" (860). Another passage combines *voie lactée*[2] and sperm: "les pertes nocturnes d'un poète ne devraient être que des voies lactées" (Letter to Cazalis, October, 1864) and there is a further association with foam in "pourquoi prendre pour éternel modèle de l'Art l'inconsciente nature et dire 'Soyons sales!' parce que l'Océan écume?"[3] (Propos, pp. 37-38). The passage from the idea of foam to that of thought[4] is well illustrated by *Igitur:* "arrête un vague frémissement de pensée, lumineuse brisure du retour de ses ondes et de leur élargissement premier" (435).[5] Compare "cette écume, vierge vers" *(Salut)*.

In sum, the *blanchi* refers to something like the birth of Love in Hesoid's *Theogony:* from the sperm-foam of Zeus floating on the waves is born Aphrodite.[6] A pure springing of beauty, as a snowfall delights the heart of a child, it will spread through universal analogy to all the possible springings of light or whiteness[7] or Form such as wing, sail, *cheveux chenus,* goose feather, plume on Hamlet's bonnet, lightning flash, stars in the milky way, and again, thought. And since, as Hermes Trismegistus has it, "that which is above is below," if the whiteness is the angelic light of ideas or the stars—"blanchit l'étoile sibylline" (258)—it is also the "blancheur animale" (51) or the "fragments de candeur" (387) which are for Mallarmé the essence of a feminine body. In sum: "la déesse de l'amour pur aussi bien que sensuel" (1199). [C, pp. 137-139].

NOTES

[1] Freud has shown that the child considers its feces to be a gift made to the mother.

[2] "qu'un astre pâle jaillisse / La nuit noire" (23). Mallarmé undoubtedly knew the myth that tells of the origin of the milky way in the breasts of Juno. In *Les Dieux antiques* he cites: "Et la Vache céleste en ce temps était née! / ... la vie immortelle aux mamelles sacrées! / ... Les astres, des éclairs..." (Leconte de Lisle, *Poèmes barbares*).

[3] Cf. "ivre(s) ... écume," *Brise marine* (38) and "des seins levés comme s'ils étaient pleins d'un lait éternel, la pointe vers le ciel" (269); cf. "vers l'infini vorace / Sursautant à la fois en maint épars filet / Jadis d'un blanc ... et maléfique lait (*Hérodiade*; 1446); also, "un blanc jet d'eau soupire vers l'Azur" (39); note "Sève" (Biog., p. 369), "les ivresses de la sève" (first *Faune*) and the "sève immense" of spring (*Renouveau*).

[4] "Je me refais aussi mes fonds et blanchis, en buvant du lait, ma cellule intérieure" (Letter to Régnier, September 25, 1893).

[5] Thought is foam, on the crest between the ascending and descending wave movements, like the ballet dancer: "la mouvante écume demeurée et suprême" (337).

[6] "Cependant le membre mutilé dès que Cronos l'eut coupé avec l'acier et que, du continent il l'eut jeté dans la mer, fut longtemps traîné au large; tout autour une blanche écume se dégageait dans laquelle une jeune fille prit forme ... Les dieux et les hommes l'appellent Aphrodite, parce qu' elle fut formée de l'écume" (trad. Bergougnan); compare "la blanche écume fut mère de Vénus" (ML, p. 141).

[7] "Elle ... neige, hermine, plume de cygne, toutes les blancheurs" (Letter to Cazalis, September, 1862); cf. "fromage mou, déjà la neige des cimes, le lys ou autre blancheur constitutive d'ailes" (278). Mallarmé, especially in his early writings, is haunted by white, for example in *Sa fosse est fermée*: "maison blanche," "couronne blanche," "cheveux blancs," "l'algue blanche de l'écume," "l'étoile laisse une blanche lueur," and others. (7-10). Gautier's *Symphonie en blanc majeur* was very likely a major inspiration here.

APPENDIX B:

A Translated Extract from *L'Oeuvre de Mallarmé:*
Un Coup de Dés, Slightly Modified

The element *con* is very important in *Un Coup de Dés;* it is a common prefix, signifying "with" in French and in other Western languages and suggesting, secondarily, another common use of the word. The circularity of its vowel *o* confirms the general tone of *con* which Mallarmé uses very often to describe Woman, or that which is feminine in a general epistemological sense; for example: "Avec sa *contraire* (double) précaution, la Mère qui nous pense et nous *conçoit*"[1] (*Catholicisme,* 391). This quotation closely comments upon the use of *con* in *circonstances;* here, too, the word signifies womb, receptacle or site for creation. The most striking example is found in *Le Nénuphar blanc* with its exquisite suggestive musicality. Here the element (and related forms) is found at least ten times in connection with "l'*inconnue* à saluer": "ce charme instinctif . . . que ne défend pas *contre* l'explorateur la plus authentiquement nouée, avec une boucle en diamant, des ceintures. Si vague *concept* se suffit . . . je m'immisce à de sa *confuse* intimité", and so on. (285). Here, the ideal image, inviolate, finds its counterpart in the image most typical of the erotic reveries of men. It is with this image also that the poet leaves the place "en mémoire d'un *site,* l'un de ces magiques nénuphars clos qui y surgissent tout à coup, enveloppant de leur creuse blancheur un rien" (286).[2] Since for Mallarmé the passive crowd is a Woman, a site for the hero-poet, the following passages are discovered: "ce que de latent *contient* et d'à jamais *abscons* la présence d'une foule" (507), or "quelque chose d'occulte au fond de tous . . . quelque chose d'*abscons* . . . cette masse . . . [plusieurs individus] agissent peu délicatement, en précipitant à pareil accès la Foule. . . exposant notre Dame et Patronne à montrer sa déhiscence ou sa *lacune*" (383).

The combination of duality and circularity in the two lines that describe the womb-source (Page 2) is an important scheme which is renewed on Page 3 where we will return to it in detail; let us note merely that in *Le Nénuphar blanc* we find:

> Subtil secret des pieds qui vont, viennent, conduisent l'esprit où le veut la chère ombre [cf. *Mystacis umbraculis*] enfouie en de la batiste et les dentelles d'une jupe affluant sur le sol comme pour circonvenir du talon à l'orteil, dans une flottaison, cette initiative par quoi la marche s'ouvre, tout au bas et les plis rejetés en traîne, une échappée,[3] de sa double flèche savante. (285).

This closely recalls a strophe of Baudelaire's *Beau navire:*

Tes nobles jambes sous les volants qu'elles chassent,
Tourmentent les désirs obscurs et les agacent
Comme deux sorcières qui font
Tourner un philtre noir dans un vase profond.

These texts are to be compared with: "Virginité . . . elle-même s'est comme divisée en ses fragments de candeur, l'un et l'autre, preuves nuptiales de l'Idée" (387). The "l'un et l'autre" is a Mallarméan formula for the feminine principle (duality) which is found in many of his works. See *Triptyque,* note 7.

l'ombre enfouie dans la profondeur par cette voile alternative. The principal meaning of this line has been sketched out in our introduction to the Page, where we also noted the secondary sense (a concrete one) of a wave-trough as a container of shadow, *ombre enfouie,* like the "en un puits . . ." of *Igitur* (437), or Hugo's "bouche d'ombre." We noted the combination of duality *(alternative)* and circularity, whose evident concretion is the feminine organ (or womb) which is specifically developed here as an application of eternal metaphysical law. Thus in the following passage, to which we referred previously, Mallarmé associates these two feminine attributes, duality and circularity, with a third, the one we have just indicated, *l'ombre (enfouie):* "*ombre* enfouie en . . . jupe . . . *circonvenir* . . . *double* flèche savante." *(Le Nénuphar blanc).*

The "shadow" of *Mystacis umbraculis* (22) refers unequivocally to these "feminine secrets."

A subtler reference is the "Solennités tout *intimes,* l'une: de placer le couteau d'ivoire dans l'*ombre* que font *deux* pages jointes d'un volume" (718). But there can be no doubt of the undertones when we juxtapose this with "Le reploiement *vierge* du livre, encore, prête à un sacrifice dont saigna la tranche rouge des anciens tomes; l'introduction d'une arme, ou coupe-papier, pour établir la prise de possession." (381). And we recall again the *"Virginité* qui . . . elle-même s'est comme divisée en ses fragments de candeur" (387).

NOTES

[1] The juxtaposition of *pense* and *conçoit* suggests a masculine-feminine ambiguity which is important in this part of the *Coup de Dés.*

[2] This *site,* as in the *Coup de Dés,* signifies total Circle or womb; the image of the diamond (clasp) is found in various poems to Méry; cf. the *rejet* of *éternelles* on Page 2, also "le palais de cette étrange bouche [vulve]" (*Une négresse*), and "le nid moussu d'un gai chardonneret" [sexe féminin] (*Mystacis umbraculis*). The "chardonneret," or finch, has red plumage.

[3] *échappée*: "espace entre deux corps," (Larousse). We note, in passing, the *circonvenir* and *conduisent* and, immediately following this passage, "*Connaît*-elle un motif à sa station?" (285).

APPENDIX C: LETTER TABLE

Significance of Letters: Symbolism in Sound and Shape

The following table of letters is as they struck Mallarmé, not any-one else; it is, in short, empirical.[1] Other French writers, roughly to the degree of their purity and importance, use letters, however uncon-sciously, to much the same effect (as in Grammont's *Le Vers Français* and several of Jean Royère's analyses), but they obviously cannot come up for consideration here. The examples below are usually from the *Coup de Dés,* but some interesting cases are adduced from Mallarmé's other writings.

Les Mots Anglais is of comparatively little usefulness here because of the difference between French and English with regard to usage and sound of letters. But, taking this into account and without trying to force any point, one can find cases where the letters are enough alike in the two languages so that Mallarmé's comments on the English language are of at least secondary interest.

Once again, it is clear that Mallarmé's use of letters is not and can-not be consistent since he had to work with an already-formed medium and there is a limit to what can be accomplished in the way of purifi-cation by mere elimination. However, again, probability and not absolute consistency is the stuff of all laws for the twentieth century.

The significance of the sound of words is, for Mallarmé, primordial: "Ces mots comptent également par leur son et pour leur signification qui sont intimement liés d'après tout ce que nous savons sur les origines du langage . . . (Mallarmé, freely quoted by C. Mauclair in *L'Art en silence,* p. 93). The sounds of words are direct functions of the com-ponent letters, which act on the reader both aurally and visually, for "Le lecteur peut être considéré comme auditeur, puisqu'il entend tout bas, pour ainsi dire, en lisant . . .". (Mallarmé, freely quoted by C. Mauclair in *Les princes de l'esprit,* p. 114). The letters are presented be-low in this light, in their combined effect, with little attempt to isolate the sound or sight factor in each, in order to set some limit on the present undertaking.

a—flat (middling, broad, ample, etc.): *plat, vacant, blafard, mat, vaste, banal, ras, hasard. Les Mots Anglais:* "quoi de moins essorant et fluide que ce mot *flat,* plat." (921). In French, *a* is situated in the center of the vowel-scale and is thus, according to the acoustical law, the flattest (most placid) sound. Examples: "ras" (Page 3); "banale et vaste place" (391); "Quand l'ombre menaça de la fatale loi" (67); six *a* sounds support the idea of the flat line of death; "Hasard" (Page 9); "étaler la banalité" (384); "blafard" (15); "pâleurs mates" (45); a beautiful effect for the flat or mat surface of sky and window: "matin chaste" (33); "Las" (32, 35); "hélas" (38); the nasal *an* retains a little of the quality of *a,* visually, as in "romance," "Fiançailles," in part because of an association with *an,* "year," in "air suranné, banal . . . ballade romantique" (271).

b—somewhat rounded effect: *bol, bassin, bouffi, bond, courbure, boule.* *Les Mots Anglais:* "sens, divers et cependant liés secrètement tous, de production ou enfantement, de fécondité, d'amplitude, de bouffissure et de courbure . . ." (929); *Le Tombeau de Baudelaire* is a classic example: eighteen *b*'s echo with those of the poet's name and of "tombeau," in order to express, precisely, an artistic "fécondité" with a nuance of "bouffissure": "bouche . . . bavant boue et rubis / Abominablement . . . etc." (70); "bord enchâssant l'oubli" (1540); for the important case of "aboli," see "n'abolira," Page 5; "le cygne / Inoubliable" (41), profits by the form of a swan suggested by the printed *b* (with the *o,* a delicate allusion to the lake or basin); Mallarmé has, not fortuitously, copied from Baudelaire "caressant les fruits mûrs de leur nubilité" (M.I., 60), and has himself employed the word "nubile" with this usage in *Le Guignon* ". . . orne à point un sein fané / Par une rose qui nubile le rallume" (29), and "bouton de la nubilité" (537); "BHAR, porter" (962), is found among several important Sanscrit roots, grouped in a page of *Les Mots Anglais.*

c (hard)—slapping or sharp sound, of waves, for example: *clapotis, claquer, conque, quelconque. Les Mots Anglais:* "actes vifs" (940); "AC ou AÇ, vif ou aigu," Sanscrit roots (962). One finds a classic example of sounds of waves in "Quelconque une solitude / Sans . . . le quai . . . etc." (65); F. Rauhut has indicated this effect, but has falsely envisioned it as "musical" and influenced by Wagner, even though *Les Mots Anglais,* which dates from 1877, precedes by a long time Mallarmé's knowledge of Wagner, and though music is only one among many other qualities that converge in the letter; other examples: "coupant . . . couvrant" (Page 3); "Coup" (Page 1). Placed at the end of a word, *c (k)* may express, as the other gutteral *g,* a receptive value, of swallowing, and so on.

d—hardness: *dé, dur, diamant, décisif, démon, dentale.* Examples: "durs os perdus entre les ais" (Page 5); "dur sou à sortir à seule fin de se dépenser" (280); "Dans la considérable touffe / Expirer, comme un diamant" (75); "déchirée ... délace ... diamant" (60). In *Les Mots Anglais* the effect is rather different: "Seul, il exprime une action suivie et sans éclat, profonde, comme plonger, creuser, ou tomber par goutte, ainsi que la stagnation, la lourdeur morale et l'obscurité; avec *r,* c'est l'effort prolongé dans un sens ou dans l'autre, ou pousser ou tirer." (950).

é—brightness and ascent: *pensée, idée, dé, été.* "A côté d'*ombre,* opaque, *ténèbres* se fonce peu" (364). Placed high on the vowel scale in French, this sound is very close to *i* in its pronunciation. Examples: "rit sur la haie et l'éveil / ... au soleil." (34); "Eté ... Idées ... iridées" *(Prose,* 56); "la cloche éveille sa voix claire" (36).

è—mediocrity, placidity, descent: *tiède, mère (mer), sèche,* and phonetically: *blême.* This sound is situated a little below the centre on the vowel scale, and is, hence, rather low. Examples: "ta chevelure est une rivière tiède" (37); "teintes quelque peu mates et sèches" (686); "sèche" (922); "blême" (54). In *Un Coup de Dés:* "jamais" (phonetically, Page 2); "énumère" (Page 11), expressing an ascent (by means of the *accent aigu)* and a relaxation (with the *accent grave);* "évènement" (Page 10: Mallarmé's spelling expresses, in part graphically, an ascent and a descent).

e—neutral: *que le lieu* (Page 10). An unobtrusive letter, neutral by default. It is near the center of the vowel scale.

f—breeze, laughter, undulation, shiver: *esclaffement, frisson, effleure. Les Mots Anglais:* "forme avec *l* la plupart des vocables représentant l'acte de voler ou battre l'espace" (935). This combination *fl* is itself important (in particular the derivatives of Latin words in *fl,* as *flatus).* Examples: "rafales ... Fureur ... Foudroyer" (65); "gonfler sa flûte" (111); "vent ... flagellait de froid" (28); "Fuir! là-bas fuir!" *(Brise Marine,* 38); "flûte ... souffle artificiel" *(Faune,* 50); "éventail frais" (60); "fraîcheur ... battement" (58). A classic example is found in Hugo *(Booz endormi):* "Un frais parfum sortait des touffes d'asphodèle / Les souffles de la nuit flottaient sur Galgala." Plato noted the same effect of the Greek *f* in his *Cratylus*. The form of the letter as a curved feather decorating a hat is developed especially on Page 7.

The *f* is part of a rich grouping of explosive and active sounds, therefore masculine, to which also belong *ph* and *p*. K. Burke, a critic of the first order, following here the linguist R. Paget, maintains that there exists a link between the group *papa, father, Vater*, and so forth, and that other, all as striking, of *poo! faugh! foo! pouah!* and so on. (Perhaps the fable of Jack-the-giant-killer, where the giant sings "fee fi fo fum" is a good example of the Oedipus complex). The group seems to include the root *fusis* and flower, feather, plume, phallus: "feather, plume, Lat. penna; fish, poisson, Lat. piscis" (936).

The sound of *v* (not its form) has some rapport with *f;* see under *v*.

g (soft)—caressing: *plonge, longe, linge*. Similar to *ch*. Examples: "langoureusement longe / Comme de blanc linge ôté" (66); "Gorgée à gorgée" (131).

g (hard)—glottal, greed: *gouffre, glotte, sanglot, goulu, goinfre*. Examples: "gouffre" (Page 9); "goûter . . . goinfre" *(Une Négresse . . . ,* 31); "Gorgée à gorgée" (131). *Les Mots Anglais:* "G . . . une aspiration simple . . . le désir, comme satisfait par *l*, exprime avec la dite liquide, joie, lumière, etc. . . . Avec *r*, enfin, il y aurait comme saisie de l'objet désiré avec *l*, ou besoin de l'écraser et le moudre" (938). An excellent example of the *gl* thus described is "Gloire du long désir"[2] in *Prose* (56); similarly, "sanglots glissant" (30); "jailli le sanglot" (66); "le cri des Gloires" (75).

h—(when pronounced, as it is occasionally) exclamatory, violent, wind-like: *hurlé, hilarité, horreur, hululer, hé! ha!* etc. Examples: "hurlé . . . hilarité . . . horreui ' (Page 6); "haut comme va le cri" (396); "hululerai" (76); "to howl, hurler; to yell, hurler, Lat. ululo" (955). *Les Mots Anglais:* "H . . . le coeur ou la tête, ce qui *se cache derrière*, oui, mais ce qui *s'élève* très haut" (955). The group "he, il: HEAD, tête . . . hood, chaperon" (954) is perhaps significant for the male-tower symbolism of Page 7 and "tendre trop haut la tête" (285).

i—male principal, hero, light, centripetal: *rigide, rire, brille, luit, Igitur*,[3] *si. Larousse:* "Droit comme un I." The examples are innumerable: all *Le vierge, le vivace . . .* (67-68); "Midi brille" (180); and others.

j—similar to *i: jonc, jaillir. Les Mots Anglais:* "*J*, placé rien que devant une voyelle ou une diphtongue, y montre une tendance à exprimer ainsi quelque action vive, directe" (939). Examples: "joncher" (Page 6); "Le jonc vaste et jumeau dont vers l'azur on joue" *(Faune); "*injonc-tions (-flèches) . . . directes" (391).

l—languor, liquidity, *(l* is a "liquid"), languid wing or wave: *lente, long, langueur, aile, elle. Les Mots Anglais:* "Cette lettre semblerait parfois impuissante à exprimer par elle-même autre chose qu'une appé-tition point suivie de résultat, la lenteur, la stagnation de ce qui traîne ou gît ou même dure; elle retrouve, cependant, de la spontanéité dans des sens comme sauter et tout son pouvoir d'aspiration avec ceux d'écouter et d'aimer, satisfait par le groupe de *loaf* à *lord*" (957-8). Examples: "belle indolemment" (37); "De ce blanc flamboiement l'immuable accalmie" (37); "langoureusement longe / Comme de blanc linge" (66); "ployé son aile" (67). The group "l -aile - elle" is to be noted: "comme la mouette, aux flots qu'elle a rasé / Jette un écho joyeux, une plume de l'aile, / Elle donna partout un doux souvenir d'elle!" (8). The "lenteur" in the passage cited from *Les Mots Anglais* goes well with the languid wave, condemned in advance, in *Un Coup de Dés;* compare "banal coup d'aile" (262). The "aspiration" is sus-tained by the slender aspect of the letter and this is manifest in all the *Coup de Dés,* in particular in the element *al,* very frequently used. The "groupe de *loaf* à *lord*" is: *"loaf,* pain entier, *Lammas,* fête (ou masse) des primeurs; *lord,* seigneur, qui fournit le pain. Latin libum" (957). This, with the previously-quoted passage, has significant bearing on the imagery of Page 8 of the *Coup de Dés,* where the sacrificial rite of male fertility is evoked.

m—maternal, womb: *mère, mer, molle, matrice,* and others. *Les Mots Anglais:* "M traduit le pouvoir de faire, donc la joie, mâle et maternelle; puis, selon une signification venue de très loin dans le passé, la mesure et le devoir, le nombre, la rencontre, la fusion et le terme moyen; par un revirement enfin, moins brusque qu'il ne paraît, l'infériorité, la faiblesse ou la colère" (960). This is particularly useful, as this letter, "venue de très loin dans le passé," is connected with two Sanscrit roots "MA, mesurer (metron, metior, to mete)" and "MAN, penser (menos, mens, mind)", both figuring among several important roots innumerated separately in *Les Mots Anglais* (962-963); compare "Manu. C'est le même que le Minos grec; et son nom vient d'une racine commune aux mots *mens* et *homo*: l'homme tirant son nom de ce qu'il est 'celui qui mesure', soit le penseur" (1174). But if *m* includes these different as-pects, all important for the Poem, it especially sets off poetically the aspect of matrix (womb) or maternal (in a very general sense) even of a male creator or a male source. This letter being the common denominator of the word "mère" in almost all the principal languages, strikes us by its essentially maternal quality (certain linguists, like Sir Richard Paget, take this phenomenon back to the position of lips while suckling) and this is accentuated by the graphic suggestion of breasts, and by the appeasing sound. Examples: "la mer (mère)" (Page 5); "le Maître (homme-source)" (Page 4); l'Abîme (chaos-source)" (Page 3); "la main (source du coup de dés)" (Page 5); "enfant d'une nuit d'Idumée" and "coule en blancheur sibylline la femme ... affame" (40); "femme allaitant" (38); "temple ... divulgue ... Abominablement" (70).

The "rencontre, la fusion et le terme moyen" quoted above is illustrated by the following examples: "match, pareil ... to meet, rencontrer; mate, compagnon ... to melt, fondre ... mid, moyen ... milk, lait ... meal, repas, Lat. molo ... to mingle, mêler" (959-960). This rich group is of a particularly revelatory value for the bearing of the word "mêler," on Page 4: the preliminary oscillation between two poles, which results in the spurting forth of the dice as "terme moyen" or resulting child, "joie mâle et maternelle."

n—negation: *nie, ironie, non.* Examples: "vide nénie ... dénie" (76); "n' ... néant ... nul" (74); "ignoré ... n' ... ni ... ni ... aucun ... Agonise mais ne consent / Naïf ... funèbres ... rien" (74); "naufrage" (Page 2; 76); "n'abolira" (Page 5). *Les Mots Anglais:* "plutôt incisive et nette" but *"near ... et new ...* où semblerait se révéler l'intention même de la lettre" (961). This would be true also for "nouveau" and "neuf" in French; nevertheless, the only definite effect is that of negation, particularly in *Un Coup de Dés.*

o—stasis, circularity: *bol, rond, roc.* Examples: "ronds de fumée / Abolis en autres ronds" (73); "O miroir!" (45); "dort une mandore" (74); "bassin, aboli" (41); "Aboli bibelot d'inanité sonore" (68). The archetype conception of a word as "isolement" is tied to a group of Mallarméan words in *o:* "vocables ... mot total ... isolement de la parole ... objet nommé" (858); "un mot, son nom" (492). *"Prose ...* Hyperbole" (55); "symbole" *(passim).* In *Un Coup de Dés:* "roc" (Page 8); "toque" (Page 7); "coque," "bond" (Page 3).

A corollary of the circularity is evidently the feminine principle: at least a dozen elements "con" in *Le Nénuphar blanc,* all to describe "l'inconnue à saluer"; see *circonstances,* Page 2, for a more detailed development. (See Appendix B.)

p—male, plosive: *père, perce, pénètre, plume, explosion, pouffer*. *Les Mots Anglais:* "l'intention très nette d'entassement, de richesse acquise ou de stagnation que contient cette lettre (laquelle s'affine et précise parfois sa signification pour exprimer tel acte ou objet vif et net)" (933).

The mushroom form (opening out; "richesse acquise" above) of the letter is important in the preceding passage as well as in the *Coup de Dés*. Examples: "épanouie, pétale et papillon géants" (308). The classic case is found in *Prose,* where the letter is the germ of the entire poem, with its flower value-hubris-excessive vision-phallus: *"Prose . . . pour . . . Hyperbole . . . Triomphalement . . . promenions . . . approfondit . . . porte . . . trompette . . . plus . . . se para . . . sépara . . . lis multiples . . . trop pour . . . ampleur . . . porter . . . Pulchérie . . . trop"* (55-57) (See *trop,* Page 7, for a more detailed development). Other examples: "trop pour" (hubris; Page 7); "plume . . . éperdue" (Page 7); "poign" (Page 4); "durs os perdus entre les ais" (Page 5). Phonetically, *p* is classed as "plosive," which gives a good indication of its value, similar to that of *f* (q.v.). The group: *pouah! pan! explosion, expostuler, pousser* is parallel to *foo! faugh! foutu, fichu,* and others.

q—similar to *c (k);* also a group "queue": *quelconque, quel, queue. Les Mots Anglais:* "le Q . . . équivaut . . . à *cw* ou *kw* . . . La vivacité, la violence du mouvement, voilà (avec un détail très particulier et très divers) la signification que comporte habituellement ce digramme" (942). The "détail très particulier" disengages itself from examples that accompany this passage: "to quake, trembler; qualm, étouffement avec nausée . . . quag (mire), fondrière; quaggy, marécageux; squeamish, dégoûté; queasy, ayant la nausée; wench, donzelle (Gr. guné)." This reinforces my impression that Mallarmé employs this letter in a group "queue" in French, influenced by the little tail on the letter and the phonetic resemblance between *q* and *cul*. A striking example is found in *Un Coup de Dés:* "squames ultimes bifurquées" (Page 8). In the dialogue with Griffin, Mallarmé says: "Comme un vol posé de corbeaux et en un tourbillon, la myriade des idées noires qui accablaient ce papier: lisez, un mot: QUEL." *(Dialogue avec Vielé-Griffin, p. 28).* This association "vol-QUEL" recalls the other, of "aile" and "quel" or "que" ("Aile quels," 107; "Aile que," 109) see under *l).* In the *Tombeau de Baudelaire* (70), a poem remarkably "construit," the group "bouche sépulcrale d'égout bavant boue . . . pubis . . . Quel feuillage" appears to us to indicate such a use of *q,* but this is evidently difficult to prove.

Examples: "quiconque / prince amer de [suggérant: "à merde"] l'écueil" (Page 7); "que le lieu (cf. "les absolus lieux"—W.C., 63) inférieur clapotis quelconque comme pour disperser l'acte vide" (Page 10); "que" suggests "queue" and an element of *cloaque*.

The "cw" in the quoted passage indicates an association with the feminine letter *w* (water, woman, etc., q.v.), and the "wench, donzelle (guné)," which is evidently included here only by a willed detour, accentuating this double notion of woman and of "dégoût." The value *c(k)* of the letter, noise of waves as in "clapotis quelconque,".completes this complex knot by a feminine association—water; compare "hors d'anciens calculs" (Page 4).

r—musical, liquid: *mandore, dore, or, sonore, harmonie*. Many other beautiful affinitive effects are carried out in *Hérodiade*, in particular. With certain consonants the effect becomes harsh: *cri, fracas, craquer*. Examples: *Les Fleurs:* "avalanches d'or du vieil azur, au jour / Premier" (33); "pur orteil du séraphin" (33); "pudeur des aurores" (33); "claire / A l'air pur" (36); "Vers l'Azur attendri d'Octobre pale et pur / Qui mire aux grands bassins sa langueur" (39); "dédore . . . mandore" (53); and many others. *Les Mots Anglais:* "L'élévation, le but atteint même au prix d'un rapt, la plénitude" (959). This indicates an entirely different effect, the pronunciation of the English *r* not being at all the same.

s—"analytique" (All the plurals and second persons), sinuous, sibilant, hissing: *issu, éparse, disséminer*. "un rapport, oui, mystérieux . . . entre cet *s* du pluriel et celui qui s'ajoute à la seconde personne du singulier dans les verbes, exprimant lui aussi, non moins que celui causé par le nombre une altération . . . quant à qui parle . . . / S, dis-je, est la lettre analytique; dissolvante et disséminante par excellence" (855). *Les Mots Anglais:* "s (représente) le jet indéfini" (953); "des lueurs que jettent à ce sujet des écrivains magnifiques: oui, SNEER est un *mauvais sourire* et SNAKE un animal pervers, le *serpent, SN* impressionne donc un lecteur de l'Anglais comme un sinistre digramme" (921). The visual sinuosity of *s* (as well as the negation of *n*) is without doubt part of the effect here. *S* is classified phonetically as a sibilant and evokes a hissing sound.

Examples: Sinuosity: "une insinuation simple / au silence enroulée" (Page 6); "torsion de sirène" (Page 8). Sibilance: "comme siffle le rire" (532). Dissimination or spurt: "surgi" (Page 4); "issu stellaire," "éparse," "profusion," "sursauta" (Page 9); "se dissout" (Page 10); "le heurt successif / sidéralement"(Page 11).

t—staccato, sharp: *total, être, arrête, net*. *Les Mots Anglais:* "fixité et . . . stationnement" (953); "cette lettre, qui représente, entre toutes, l'arrêt (comme *s* le jet indéfini)" (953). Examples: "compte total . . . s'arrêter (Page 11); "cette blancheur rigide" (Page 7); "aigrette de vertige" (Page 8); "une stature mignonne ténébreuse debout" (Page 8). The height and the form of a hat (with perhaps the plume) of the upper part of the letter are included in the "toque" of the *Coup de Dés,* as in "tendre trop haut la tête, pour ces joncs à ne dépasser" (285), compare "mainte aigrette luit divinatoire" (390). This is in accord with the huge flower that this letter represents, particularly the capital: "Toute fleur s'étalait plus large . . . Telles immenses." *(Prose;* 56).

u—clarity (of the sound, similar in this to *i*); concavity or inversion (from the shape): *lucide, luit, incurve, creux, s'ouvre.* As the case is difficult to prove, and as the vowels are not described in detail in *Les Mots Anglais,* we shall appeal to two exterior sources: "Pas d'autre mot qui sonne comme cruche. Grace à cet *U* qui s'ouvre en son milieu" (Francis Ponge, *Cinq Sapates); "Exultatrice* (un grand mot incurvé qui fait jaillir des gerbes d'eau) . . ." (A. Thibaudet, *La Poésie de Stéphane Mallarmé,* p. 53). Examples: "squames ultimes bifurquées" (Page 8); "guné" (963): this Greek *u,* closely linked with the woman-birth cluster of associations, is an important source for the effect of the letter (accentuated by the *g,* q.v.); "au rebut d'une illustre vaisselle" *(Hérodiade,* LL, p. 18); with the *v,* of a similar effect (see that letter), the four *u*'s express the receptacle; nine *u*'s signify "trou" in "auprès du trou par quelqu'un creusé depuis l'aube" (409); "Verse un salut" *(St. Jean,* LL, p. 20); in "source en pleurs" (50); the *r* adds a very beautiful effect of spilling water; "Quel sépulcrale naufrage (tu . . . " (76); "surgi" (Page 4), compare the "Exultatrice" that Thibaudet cites from *Quelconque une solitude;* "du fond d'un naufrage" (Page 2); "envergure . . . coque / d'un bâtiment" (Page 3). And here is an example, among many others, of the value of the sound of the letter: "altitudes lucides" (Biog., p. 211).

The contrast between the sound and the shape of the *u* produces a masculin-feminine tension that enters into play in "résume" (Page 3), "plume" (Page 7), and so on, from *Un Coup de Dés.* This subtle value is the most important element of the linguistic and literary net which haunts Mallarmé in *Le Démon de l'Analogie* (272-273): " 'La Pénultième est morte' . . . Je fis des pas dans la rue et reconnus en le son *nul* la corde tendue de l'instrument de musique." The word *plume* ("La phrase revint, virtuelle, dégagée d'une chute antérieure de plume ou de rameau") is included in the word *Pénultième,* as well as the well-known Latin ambiguity *penna-penis:* "Pénultième . . . pénible jouissance"; the "corde cassée" ("la corde de l'instrument, si tendue en l'oubli sur le son *nul,* cassait sans doute et j'ajoutais en manière d'oraison: 'Est morte' ") brings to light the inversion or the "chute". (See: "j'ai aimé tout ce qui se résume en ce mot: chute," *Plainte d'Automne,* 270). The piece ends with another series of *u:* "la boutique d'un luthier vendeur de vieux instruments pendus au mur." The grouping of *instrument-plume-musique* will be once again exploited in *Sainte:* "le plumage instrumental, / Musicienne du silence" (54).

Here the main effect is the silent tension-and-release of musical "milk" from a maternal Muse *(musique-muse-suce-jus-écume),* or the corollary tension between rounded source (or lips) and kinetic flow. In *Le Démon* thus there is considerable infantile nostalgia.

The tone that emanates from the *Démon* is without a doubt that of one of Poe's stories, and *La Chute* (!) *de la Maison Usher*—particularly the poem-epigraph—that Mallarmé calls a masterpiece, is a source of certain of his associations, together with *Ulalume;* compare "Ce nom d'Eulalie ne me semble demandé à aucune figure existante de l'entourage de Poe; je l'attribue à l'exquise euphonie qu'il a dans l'anglais" (233). The English *u* is, it is true, different from the French, but resembles it enough to present some interest here.

v—feminine: *Vierge, Vénus, Eve, volupté, vulve, bivalve, veuve, vallée, vagin, bas-ventre.* It is graphically, as well as linguistically, a corollary of the *w* (q.v.), with a nuance of statuesque purity. The triangle with the point toward the bottom, the lower part of Solomon's seal, is a traditional symbol of the feminine principle, largely exploited in *Finnegans Wake.* It goes without saying that the value of the letter is seen more justly in a group of associations that is both vague and vast. Mallarmé's classic example is found in *Hérodiade:*

> Vers lui nativement la femme se dévoile,
> Me voit dans ma pudeur grelottante d'étoile,
> Je meurs!
> J'aime l'horreur d'être vierge et je veux
> Vivre parmi l'effroi que me font mes cheveux
> Pour, le soir, retirée en ma couche, reptile
> Inviolé . . .

It is significant that the verse of the earlier version "En lequel par instants la femme se dévoile" (1443) became "Vers lui nativement la femme se dévoile." This word *native* is one of Mallarmé's favorites, as in "native nue" (75), "naïve" (47), "alternative" (the concavity formed by two waves, Page 3). Another example is the beautiful word *Venus:* "Vénus, vêtue de l'azur qui sort de sa chevelure, lui verse l'ambroisie"

(265) and Mallarmé exploits it often (52, 251, 262, 265, 270, etc.).

In the following case, the effect of *v* is sustained by auxiliary elements, *u, con, cun,* and the image: "verrerie . . . Le pur vase d'aucun breuvage / Que l'inexhaustible veuvage / Agonise mais ne consent" (74); compare *"Widow,* veuve, (Lat.) vidua" (932). A direct example of the effect of the letter is *Mysticis Umbraculis:* "Elle dormait . . . / Il s'arrêta, levant au nombril la batiste / Et son ventre sembla de la neige" (22). Just as direct is the word "s'ouvre" as in: "La terre s'ouvre vieille à qui crève la faim" (40). The *v* contributes to the power of the element *vulg(ue),* as in "divulgue par la bouche" (70) or "divulgue . . . vomis" (288). A slightly different effect is brought to light in "intervalle vif entre ses végétations . . . d'un . . . ruisseau" (284), or in "creuser par veillée une fosse nouvelle / Dans le terrain avare et froid de ma cervelle" (35). This combination *creuser-v* is found often, as in *L'Azur:* "ma cervelle, vidée" (38); in *Angoisse* (35) and in *Renouveau* (34). Also, "quand s'ouvrent . . . les juvéniles lèvres" (511), "verveux" (754). A definitely corollary effect, as in "glaive" (70) is manifested in *Le vierge, le vivace . . . ,* where the *v*'s help to express the wintry, glacial air and suggest a cutting winter wind; compare *f.* Thus: "vents" (Page 4).

A long time after having made our remarks on the letter *v* we found the following passage in the work of Charles Baudoin, *De l'Instinct à l'esprit* (p. 234): "le symbolisme spontané de cette lettre: outre le symbole bien connu du receptacle (vase, vagin), symbole statique, il faut certainement attribuer au *v* le symbole dynamique du vertige et du tourbillon aspirant, où se rejoignent le dessin de la lettre et son sifflement prêt à 'vrombir' . . . ".

w—rare and, in itself, unimportant in French, but very important with regard to *v,* as follows: "Les sens d'osciller (celui-ci semblerait dû au dédoublement vague de la lettre, puis de flotter, etc.; d'eau et d'humidité; d'évanouissement et de caprice; alors, de faiblesse, de charme et d'imagination) se fondent en une étonnante diversité; peut-on, par exemple, dire que *wr* authentiquement, désigne la torsion . . . ?" (932). This "dédoublement vague" is without doubt related to the perspective of Mallarmé in: "Virginité [la page] qui solitairement, devant une transparence du regard adéquat, elle-même s'est comme divisée en ses fragments de candeur, l'un et l'autre, preuves nuptiales de l'Idée" (387), and "Cet unanime blanc conflit / D'une guirlande avec la même" (the duality caused by violation—"n'entr'ouvrir comme un blasphème" —of the pure page in the "Jeu suprême" (74); and to duality as a feminine principle on Page 3 of the *Coup de Dés:* "cette vague alternative / . . . en tant que la coque / d'un bâtiment / penché de l'un ou l'autre bord"; compare the ambiguous "Mon crime, c'est d'avoir . . . divisé la touffe" of *L'Après-midi d'un faune* (52).

Many of the examples of *w* that Mallarmé gives in *Les Mots Anglais* are of a great interest for *Un Coup de Dés: "to wave,* ondoyer, et *to waver,* vaciller, puis *to weave,* tisser; *to waft,* flotter; *web,* toile; *weft,* trame . . . *to warp,* ourdir; *water,* eau" (929-930). These examples illustrate the development of the feminine principle from duality.

In English, *w* is a powerful element in the group *woman-womb-wife-wench-wrench,* with this corollary aspect: *cow-sow-ewe.*

x—double polarity, cross: *Fixe, crucifix, croix, texte* (Lat. *texere: tisser), syntaxe, paradoxe.*

The central importance of the cross in the epistemology of Mallarmé has been shown in detail. The sonnet *Ses purs ongles* . . . , manifesting a by-product of the period of the crisis of *Igitur* and significative of his effort then, presents the classical example: Mallarmé applied himself to the difficult task of finding six rimes in *x*—and never in his poetry did he play lightly with words. See under *Constellation,* Page 11, for a more detailed development. In a letter in which he describes his crisis we read: "araignée sacrée, sur les principaux fils déjà sortis de mon esprit . . . je tisserai *aux points de rencontre* de merveilleuses dentelles" (Propos, p. 71): the nature (involving a double polarity) of the process of weaving gives a particular force to the word "texte," coming from the Latin *textus,* the past participle of the Latin root of the word "to weave"; and thus we find again "dentelle," 'toile," and others, as important themes in all the writings of Mallarmé.

The meaning of this archetype can be traced from the beginnings of literature (and of occult thought), beginning with "l'araignée sacrée" of the Hindu *Vedas* (which perhaps influenced the above letter), the golden thread of Hephaistos, the first artist, in the *Odyssey,* as well as the lyre of the blind musician weaving melodies from the vertical-horizontal disposition of a stringed instrument ("D'une main la lyre, pareille à la trame tendue sur le métier, et de son autre main / Elle [Euterpe] applique le plectrum comme une navette" (Claudel, *Cinq Grandes Odes).* This image of a web or cross, passing through the "rose-croix" of Dante, leads to Keats, the English poet of the nineteenth century nearest in spirit to Mallarmé: "the wreathed trellis of a working brain" *(Ode to Psyche);* compare: "Cette poésie . . . trellis délicat et net tendu sur un azur connu . . . longues fleurs sortant de l'enlacement" (Letter to Albert Mérat, May 6, 1866, two months before the letter on the spider's web). This archetype is the basis of the plunging vision of Nerval in the first chapter of the sixth part of *Aurélia,* where the image of the cross is given in the form of a trellis, of two roads that cross, and so on, and where, later on, the universe is described as "immense réseau." Among the modern representatives, besides Mallarmé, we find, in Joyce, the theme of the cross ("Cross," *Finnegans Wake,* p. 262, *x* as a letter, as a symbol for kisses, as a sign of multiplication richly ambiguous, etc.) is found throughout *Finnegans Wake;* T. S. Eliot: "In the brief transit where the dreams cross / The dream-crossed twilight between birth and dying" *(Ash Wednesday,* VI) and the Dantesque theme of the "rose-croix" in *Four Quartets,* where the quadripolar scheme predominates in the architecture, the four elements, and so forth.

In a letter of July 18, 1868, Mallarmé describes the décor of his "sonnet en *x,*" that includes "une chambre avec personne dedans . . . un cadre, belliqueux et agonisant, de miroir appendu au fond, avec sa réflexion, stellaire et incompréhensible, de la grande Ourse, qui relie au ciel seul ce logis abandonné du monde . . . ce sujet d'un sonnet nul et se réflechissant de toutes les façons . . ." (Propos, pp. 83-84); note "belliqueux [*x*], "cadre" [*carré*]). It is easy to connect the key word "réflexion" (the repetition "réflexion . . . se réflechissant" is significant), with its *x,* to its direct use as a résumé of double polarity in *Igitur* (438):

> Elle ("la conscience de soi") se présente également dans l'une et dans l'autre face des parois luisantes . . . Tandis que devant et derrière se prolonge le mensonge exploré de l'infini . . . Dans cette inquiétante et belle symétrie de la construction de mon rêve, laquelle des deux ouvertures (i.e., "dimensions" de la chambre quadripolaire) prendre . . . Ne sont-elles pas toutes deux, à jamais équivalentes, ma réflexion?

To repeat, "ma réflexion" is the résumé of the symmetry in a cross. An analogous use of *x* is found in *Igitur* (442): "l'Infini est enfin *fixé*" (Mallarmé's italics).

Other examples: "Syntaxe" (385); "paradoxe" (377); "extases équilibrantes" (Biog., p. 259); "Génuflexion" (before the cross) with "glorieux" *(Hérodiade,* LL, p. 18); "expiatoire" (Page 8), the sacrificial role of the "crucified" poet; "crucifix" (32); "excepté . . . feux" (Page 11), the theme of the Great Bear, emblem of cold symmetry, with its cross formed by four stars and its tail formed by three; compare "dans l'oubli fermé par le cadre, se fixe / De scintillations sîtot le septuor" *(Ses purs ongles . . . , 69)* with its suggestion of four, five, six, seven in "cadre," "scin . . . ," "si . . . ," "sept . . . ."

The image is found in the prose poem *Frisson d'Hiver* (271-272), written before Mallarmé had fully developed his use of the letters through the "étude projetée sur la *Parole*" (Propos., p. 83) of which, as he says, "J'extrais ce sonnet" *(Ses purs ongles . . .)*; the images of "toiles d'araignées" and of "croisées" are clearly associated in the refrain, and repeated three times: "Ces toiles d'araignées grelottent au haut des grandes croisées."

y—similar to *i;* bifurcation or convergence: *type, ptyx.* Its penultimate position in the alphabet is noteworthy. Examples: "Un cygne d'autrefois se souvient que c'est lui / Magnifique" (68); the "cygne" has that clear (white) and monumental quality that we have mentioned in regard to *i;* "ptyx" (68); "Type" (545). The aspect bifurcation-convergence is emphasised on several occasions in *Un Coup de Dés:* "reployer la division" (Page 4); "ayant . . . induit / le vieillard vers cette conjonction" (Page 5); "mystère" (— "insinuation . . . au silence enroulée") (Page 6); "rythmique suspens . . . s'ensevelir / aux écumes originelles" (Page 9). Compare the form in *y* of the ideogram on Page 8. The effect is similar to the one for *v,* as is evidenced in the word "nymphe" (50).

z—unimportant in itself, but included in the word "Hasard" (phonetically and etymologically, and Mallarmé, in fact, wrote it "hazard" often) where it expresses finality, befitting its position in the alphabet. It is implied phonetically in "hésite," a kind of tacking, compare *zigzag,* indecision. Example: "horizon" (Page 4).

Among the various combinations of letters we can point out the following as being particularly interesting:

ch—caressing, noise of water, jet: *chuchoter, choyer, chuintement. Les Mots Anglais:* "*sh* donne encore, avec netteté, jet lointain (947). Compare *g* (soft). Examples: "blanchi" (Page 3); "joncher" (Page 6); "proche et blanche, si / Délicieusement toi" (61).

eu—neutral, mediocre: *neutre, inférieur, peu.* Examples: "fond neutre et d'erreur" (562); "peu" (Page 9); "rien . . . n'aura eu lieu . . . que le lieu / inférieur clapotis quelconque" (Page 10); "oiseuse" (Page 5). However, in combination with *r,* the effect of *eu* (or *oeu*) can be very beautiful: *fleur, pleur, douceur, soeur.*

ou—dark, emotional, love-death: *doute, gouffre, mourir, amour, pourpre, nourrir,* and others. *Les Mots Anglais:* "I, éclaircissement . . . iou, assombrissement" (983); *our* is an extension or variation of it. It has already been fully treated in our general remarks on the letters, but here are some other examples: "Assoupi de sommeils touffus" (50);

"noir roc courroucé que la bise le roule" (71); "ou trou / Grand
ouvert" (in a very carefully arranged fragment; 1445); velours" (Page
7); "le lourd sommeil" (35); "la lourdeur triste de l'ours" (276):
"langoureux . . . amoureux" (36).

om, on—somber: *ombre, sombre, foncer.* "A coté d'*ombre,* opaque,
ténèbres se fonce peu" (364). Examples: "fond" (Page 2); "retombée,"
"ombre," "profondeur" (Page 3). *Les Mots Anglais:* "AN et ON . . .
deux des plus beaux sons de notre langue" (980-981).

an, en—somewhat somber: "temps . . . tentures" (in the somber chamber of *Igitur,* 435).

st—station, standing. *Les Mots Anglais:* "La signification fondamentale
de fixité et de stationnement, exprimée admirablement par la combinai-
son *st . . .* " (953). The meaning is easily established with the help of
the Latin roots grouped around *sto, stare.* Examples: "constellation"
(Page 11); "stature . . . debout" (Page 8).

Marks of Punctuation and Orthography:

grave accent and *acute accent:* treated under *è* and *é*.

circumflex accent: effect of waves: *crête, arrête.* Examples: "suprême"
(Page 5, a crest of foam); "se déplièrent des tentes de fête" (278).

dot (on the *i*): shape of a rock, sign of finality. Examples: "folie" (Page
5); the etymology of the word is *follis,* a balloon, and the dot on the *i*
symbolizes an artistic creation thrown into the air in an effort of libera-
tion; "scintille . . . roc . . . borne à l'infini" (Page 8) is a final version
of the "folie."

!—similar to *i:* treated in the general remarks. But here are other examples: "Droit et seul . . . / Lys!" (51); "un blanc jet d'eau soupire
vers l'Azur!" (39).

NOTES

[1] It is necessary to reconstruct the table, because for Mallarmé, different from Ghil,
there were there some "lois par maints avoués à soi seul" (857, *Avant-dire* to the
Traité du Verbe by René Ghil). But the "lois" of Mallarmé are for the most part
disseminated in *Les Mots Anglais,* published in 1877, eight years before the rudimen-
tary system of Ghil in the *Traité.* Ghil is therefore doubly guilty when he accuses
Mallarmé of having made some borrowings from his *Traité* for *Le Vierge, le vivace,*

et le bel aujourd'hui.

[2] With the "gloire" is associated the word "glaïeul" and the form of the corolla, compare "blancs sanglots...corolles" (30) and "blancheur sanglotante des lys" (34).

[3] A possible, and unnoted, source for Mallarmé's use of the name is a page of Villiers' *Elen* (Chamuel, p. 58): students are singing the traditional *Gaudeamus igitur* and there is a reference to the river *Elbe*, as in *Elbehnon*. Mallarmé seems to be locating his drama in the same suspended, vaguely Franco-German legendary region as Villiers in his metaphysical plays and stories, or Maeterlinck in *Pelléas et Mélisande* ("Allemonde"). Renéville's well-known explanation seems far-fetched.

NEW TEXT

1. MORE POEMS

I: APPARITION

Apparition is an early poem, transparently tender and intimate. Mallarmé wrote it in London, in 1863, to celebrate the English fiancée of his close friend Cazalis, Ettie Yapp. The poem was published only much later, in 1883, in *Lutèce* and then in Verlaine's *Poètes maudits*. Why Mallarmé didn't think enough of it to include it among the poems presented by the *Parnasse contemporain* is puzzling. Debussy set it to music; it is a favorite of many discriminating readers.

La lune s'attristait. Des séraphins en pleurs	The moon saddened. Seraphim in tears
Rêvant, l'archet aux doigts, dans le calme des fleurs	Dreaming, bow in fingers, in the calm of vaporous
Vaporeuses, tiraient de mourantes violes	Flowers, drew from dying violas
De blancs sanglots glissant sur l'azur des corolles.	White sobs slipping over the blue of corollas.
—C'était le jour béni de ton premier baiser.	—It was the blessed day of your first kiss.
Ma songerie aimant à me martyriser	My revery pleased to torment me
S'enivrait savamment du parfum de tristesse	Intoxicated itself cannily with the perfume of sadness
Que même sans regret et sans déboire laisse	Which even without regret or disappointment
La cueillaison d'un Rêve au coeur qui l'a cueilli.	The culling of a Dream leaves in the heart that plucked it.
J'errais donc, l'oeil rivé sur le pavé veilli	So, I wandered, eyes fixed on the old pavement
Quand avec du soleil aux cheveux, dans la rue	When with sun in hair, in the street
Et dans le soir, tu m'es en riant apparue	And evening, you appeared to me laughing
Et j'ai cru voir la fée au chapeau de clarté	And I thought I saw the fairy with hat of brightness
Qui jadis sur mes beaux sommeils d'enfant gâté	Who once over my beautiful sleeps of a spoiled child
Passait, laissant toujours de ses mains mal fermées	Passed, letting always from her weakly closed hands
Neiger de blancs bouquets d'étoiles parfumées.	Snow white bouquets of perfumed stars.

Apparition's title puts it in an august lineage.[1] The archetypal ancestor here is the appearance of the Christ Child to the Magi—*the* Epiphany —and if that sounds remote from this poem of a modern non-Christian, it nonetheless can't help color it with a nuance of immemorial spirituality, suggested, at the very least, in the *chapeau de clarté*, a hinted halo. Of course there is also the aura of faëry's pagan cult, but these two forms of spirituality have always overlapped with one another and with the other strain of deep piety which is the wellspring of the main flow of feeling in the poem: the nostalgia for the lost-paradisial mother, clearly sung in the final lines.

In a letter to Cazalis (30 Jan. 1863), near the time of the poem, Mallarmé recalls his mother in conjunction with his adored sister—he lost the first at age 5, the second at age 15, when she was 13—in a patent attempt to bolster his sense of obligation to marry Marie, his fiancée. The network of associations in the poem involves all of these: Ettie, Marie, and "ma mère, ma soeur—qui voient les choses de haut." Here a traditional romantic-religious spirit is being refined into the impressionistic or symbolist mode of delicacy, vibrancy, nuance, suggestion, understatement, gentle-yet-fierce *tendresse*, diamond precision, and intimacy, as it passes through miraculous filters of the new art. But the Victorian earnestness of the day has its effect, however subdued, along with a certain Pre-Raphaelite mood in the first seraphic verse-lines, characteristic of Mallarmé's adolescent manner, early Debussy (*La Damoiselle élue*) and the whole transitional aesthetic era.

Another letter (1 July 1862, to Cazalis) sounds the note of the poem: "Je ne veux pas faire cela d'inspiration: la turbulence du lyrisme serait indigne de cette chaste apparition que tu aimes. Il faut méditer longtemps: l'art seul, limpide et impeccable, est assez chaste pour la sculpter religieusement." Here we have the symbolist process of refinement Mallarmé was working out, along with the vestigial religiosity which was metamorphosing into something like a sacred art: something purer, more aspiring, more perfect than anything the world had seen on a page, as Valéry would claim, together with an unspoken faith which surpassed his art at times, in family matters for example. Ettie, Marie, his sister Maria, his mother, were the complexly combined Muse of this metamorphosis: "elle [Ettie] se rangera dans mes rêves à côté de toutes les Chimènes, les Béatrices, les Juliettes, les Reginas, et, qui mieux est, dans mon coeur à côté de ce pauvre jeune fantôme qui fut treize ans ma soeur, et qui fut la seule personne que j'adorasse . . ." (I July 1862).

How much Marie is entangled with all this is evident in the following: "je suis heureux de vous voir, même de loin; il me semble, quand

vous tournez la rue, que je vois un fantôme de lumière et tout rayonne"
("sans date," July 1862). The *fantôme*—recalling his sister's above—
is part of the distance—"même de loin"—which is the essence of the
"sublime" relation with the mother, particularly a deceased one, as well
as a sister for similar reasons of incest-prohibition (entwined with forbidden death-wish, as Mauron surmised); all of which seeps like a
ghostly palimpsest into the late-romantic vision of the fiancée of Cazalis (with whom he closely identified),[2] as happens readily enough in life,
given the usual replacement of mother by wife; literature is rife with
this transfiguration.[3] In the poem the distance is, in time, the nostalgia,
the sense of lost paradise which will be developed in great poems such as
Hérodiade.

  La lune s'attristait: the moon has a sad face, as we know from popular representations. But moonlight is in the wistful mood of the poem,
"quasi-triste" as Verlaine puts it in his *Claire de lune*, with the gentle
melancholy of (late) romanticism. The moon may be appropriately
waning. Mallarmé, incidentally, tended to be diffident of the moon-
image, but not always.

  séraphins en pleurs: sad angels were standard images of Mallarmé's
juvenile poems and prose lamenting his beloved dead. The musical
angel recalls the iconography of Saint Cecilia (which influenced his
Sainte); the bowing angel may be out of Matthias Grünewald's Eisen-
heim altar.

  fleurs vaporeuses: Baudelaire's *Harmonie du soir* featured this image of flowers, like censers, evaporating in the evening air.

  mourantes violes: a "dying fall" (*Merchant of Venice*) the "swoon"
of sweet music, cf. the *pâmé* of *Hommage* (*à Wagner*); *ou* is appropriately dark and *r* adds a liquid touch, putting it in a sensual cluster Mallarmé enjoyed: *mourir-amour-pourpre*, etc., e.g. "mourir pourpre la roue"
(*M'Introduire . . .*), see Appendix C. *Violes* is in a sweet-flower cluster
with *violets* including a hint of *violer* echoing the feminine shape of the
instrument, as in the *viole* of *Sainte* (accompanied by *flûte*), cf. the feminine belly of the mandolin of *Une dentelle s'abolit*.

  blancs sanglots glissant: in *Les Mots anglais* Mallarmé wrote: "G . . .
une aspiration simple . . . le désir, comme satisfait par *l*, exprime avec
la dite liquide, joie, lumière, etc." (938)

  An excellent example of the *g* thus described is "Glorie du long désir"
(*Prose*); also "jailli le sanglot" (66); "le cri des Gloires" (75). See
Petit air II in this volume for a total love-death *sanglot*; also "sanglots
sybyllins" (71).

  As in the *glaïeuls* of *Prose*, there is a poetic connection between the throaty effect of sob and the shape of the calyx, very much a part of our delight in these angelic flowers, and that is the case with the *corolles* here.

azur des corolles: the *azur*, heavenly blue, typical of early Mallarmé, is part of the chaste love lyricism, of which flowers—with their openly receptive shape, so feminine—are a classic expression. In a letter to Marie (no date, July 1862), Mallarmé writes: "Ce rayon [from his love-letter] devait ouvrir en votre coeur la fleur bleue mystérieuse." One recalls the mysterious 'blue Dahlia' of Baudelaire's prose *Invitation au voyage* (stemming in turn from Novalis). Marie's eyes were blue as were Ettie's, ethereally English or Germanic—flowers and eyes, feminine, are traditionally associated. As Edmund Wilson noted in *Axël's Castle*, *Apparition* is partly colored white and blue. These are colors of cloud and sky, fresh and airy. The white connects with the snow-flower-star (manna-milk) imagery below and is linked generally with the theme of nostalgic light and joy which, despite the sadness of loss, dominates the poem.

La cueillaison d'un Rêve au coeur qui l'a cuelli: the diphthongs are woeful, Greek-wailing, like a knife-twist in a wound, cf. Verlaine's "coeur qui s'écoeure . . . deuil" (*Il pleure . . .*). The vestigial regret is the "eternal note of sorrow" (Arnold) or "Aye, in the very temple of Delight/Veiled Melancholy has her sovran shrine" (Keats)—the pain arising (and never totally subdued) from the first separation from the mother, or beyond her the mysterious Source: "The yearning a beautiful woman sets up in us can only be satisfied by God" (Valéry). At times the lost young, or departed, mother is primary, deified sufficiently herself—the distant princess she becomes for us, as the fairy stories fantasy her—so beautiful as we were streamed upon by her powerful love when we first emerged from her womb (Theodore Reik, in *Of Love and Lust*, tells of the terrible trial of separation, at varying levels, mankind goes through).

J'errais donc: lost in his puzzled regret, the poet wanders alone through the city, looking at the old paving stones—the *v*'s help to give them their savory precision. A wandering in a city, often a strange one, is *the* locus of this nameless yearning.

dans la rue/Et dans le soir: a stirring effect of "taking off" from the horizontal street up to the vertical of evening sky, from concrete and limited this-worldly to diffuse, expansive and even total Reality; the conversion from one infinite dimension or "set" of knowing to another is subtle and startling. As Kafka said, and demonstrated, "Miracles are in the street." Apparitions, Mallarmé's modern art generally, are such miracles.

en riant: a laugh is essentially a triumph of life and, in its feminine aspect, of health—i.e the good river-flowing temper of spirit and body that goes on and can help us to go on, maternally.

apparue: an apparition is a birth of a phenomenon, as we note in the Epilogue. At times, the greatest grace of a mother is just to be there, as Claudel hymns her in his poem, *La Vierge à Midi*, "Parce que vous êtes là." The epiphany of a born baby has to do with a paradox of maternity: our mothers are born unto us, in a sense *of* us (certainly in our homesick memory, as here). Cf. Wordsworth's "the child is the father of the man"—there is a deep circular mystery here which we treat in *Modes of Art*, Ch. I. The dead beauty (or woman) is reborn to us in the young one at the street corner; life goes on, laughing.

Apparition (the title), *apparue, clarté, parfumées, riant*, are part of the *ar*-cluster, transparent, tenderly bright (liquid *r*), clear: *art, paradis,* (*perdu*, cf. *jadis*) are overtones from this compelling cluster which we discuss in the chapter on the *Faune*.

chapeau de clarté: the loved-one is a blond, echoing a lost fair-haired lady, undoubtedly maternal.

jadis: always has the overtone of *paradis perdu* in Mallarmé, most tellingly in "Si tu me vois les yeux perdus au paradis,/C'est quand je me souviens de ton lait bu jadis" (*Hérodiade, Scène*). The primal milk theme is sounded here which is close to the core of Mallarmé's poetic universe (see the Epilogue). In *Apparition*, it appears in the imagery of the white flowers ("white sobs," above), snow, (manna), stars as in the image of the Milky Way which ends the *Coup de Dés*. This network of *blancheur* is treated at length in Appendix A (also *L'Oeuvre de Mallarmé* under *blanchi*); Derrida comments on this in *La Dissémination*, Part II.

mains mal fermées: Mallarmé seems to have owed this expression to Hugo: Mondor in his notes to the *Pléiade* edition quotes:

> . . . marche avec l'or qu'on voit
> Luire à travers les doigts de tes mains mal fermées
> Tous le biens de ce monde en grappes parfumées
> Pendent sur ton chemin . . .
>   (*A l'homme qui a livré une femme,*
>   *Chants du crépuscule*).

The image is of a grace so divinely natural, so total, that it is as if by inadvertance or a slight weakness that her bounty descends upon us and overwhelms us, mere mortals, her spoiled children.

étoiles parfumées: flowers, stars, snowflakes, bread-manna flakes are kindred crystallized images of beauty descending to a child—as in Rimbaud's *Mystique*—with more than a hint of mother-milk (cf. "milky way," etc.). The distant yet procreative stars at the end of the *Coup de Dés* are subtly linked to this ultimate Edenic delight, promise of life.

NOTES

[1] It may well have influenced James Joyce's classic notion and definition of that literary concept (he owned a copy of *Les Poètes maudits*, where it was republished). See David Hayman, *Joyce et Mallarmé*, Vol. I, p. 26.

[2] The Eros is even more complex: we have here a clear case of the male-male affection and rivalry expressing itself through common or fused object(s).

[3] Rousseau's Mme de Warens, Balzac's Mme de Mortsauf, Stendhal's Mme de Rênal, Flaubert's Mme Schlésinger, Proust's Oriane de Guermantes.

II: BRISE MARINE

Freshness and reality: Mallarmé's sea breeze blows away the obfuscations of subtle enemies like Claudel who try to push him into a corner of nineteenth-century bloodless idealism. A heady, much-quoted poem, *Brise marine* was written in 1865 and first published in the *Parnasse contemporain* the following year. A letter to a lady friend (8 Feb. 1899)[1] speaks of its theme: "ce désir inexpliqué qui vous prend parfois de quitter ceux qui nous sont chers, et de *partir*." This refers clearly to his wife and his newborn child, Geneviève. Mallarmé was a loving and dutiful husband and father, but Geneviève yelled a lot as an infant, while he was composing *Hérodiade*, and he was human and had his moments. Besides, his master Poe had given him an example of the "imp of the perverse" which overtakes the best of us. And all he did was dream, unlike his friend Gauguin of whom he would say later: "On n'a pas le droit d'abandonner ses enfants même pour fonder une religion."

Baudelaire in his *Parfum exotique*, as Mondor noted, had provided the model for the ocean departure, the exotic clime, the siren sailor song. But the *topos* is an old one, going back through Parny and Watteau in the 18th century, all the way to the *Odyssey*.

Mallarmé, with his *steamer* "makes it new" and contemporary in substance even as the liveliness and intimate precision of the texture, the unity of tone or color, mark the poem as fully his.

La chair est triste, hélas! et j'ai lu tous les livres.
Fuir! là-bas fuir! Je sens que des oiseaux sont ivres
D'être parmi l'écume inconnue et les cieux!
Rien, ni les vieux jardins reflétés par les yeux
Ne retiendra ce coeur qui dans la mer se trempe
O nuits! ni la clarté déserte de ma lampe

Sur le vide papier que la blancheur défend
Et ni la jeune femme allaitant son enfant.
Je partirai! Steamer balançant ta mâture,
Lève l'ancre pour une exotique nature!

Un Ennui, désolé par les cruels espoirs,
Croit encore à l'adieu suprême des mouchoirs!
Et, peut-être, les mâts, invitant les orages
Sont-ils de ceux qu'un vent penche sur les naufrages
Perdus, sans mâts, sans mâts, ni fertiles îlots . . .
Mais, ô mon coeur, entends le chant des matelots!

The flesh is sad, alas! and I've read all the books.
Flee! yonder flee! I sense that birds are drunk
At being amid the unknown foam and the skies!
Nothing, even old gardens reflected by eyes
Will hold back this heart which dips in the sea
O nights! nor the desert brightness of my lamp
On the empty paper which its whiteness defends
Nor the young wife giving suck to her child.
I'll leave! Steamer swaying your masts,

Raise anchor for an exotic nature!

A boredom, desolated by cruel hopes,
Still believes in the supreme wave of handkerchiefs!
And, perhaps, the masts, inviting storms
Are of those a wind leans over shipwrecks
Lost without masts, without masts, nor fertile isles . . .
But, oh my heart, hear the sailor song!

The "color" white—purity, freshness, a *tabula rasa* like a page of a clean new start, the whiteness of ocean foam and sea birds, mingled in an orgy of delight, the *originality* of his favorite milk-theme, redolent of rebirth, the white hanky waving goodbye—runs through the poem and gives it an intoxicating unity of tone rather reminiscent of Gautier's *Symphonie en blanc majeur.* I have treated this *blancheur* in Mallarmé's universe in Appendix A and *L'Oeuvre de Mallarmé: Un Coup de Dés,* under *blanchi.* One thinks of Vlaminck's white-splashed stormscapes or Mallarmé's own *A la nue,* Debussy's sea-windy *Ce qu'a vu le vent de l'ouest.*

La chair: a famous line expressing first, a general world-weariness. Also, Mallarmé, like Shakespeare (Sonnet 129) thought of the expression of the flesh as an "expense of spirit in a waste of shame"; thus "la sottise . . . pressée de dégorger cet éclair . . . la prostitution . . . fait sournois et brutal de sa présence parmi d'incomprises merveilles" (322). His early letters to Cazalis frequently exhibit this very human view, typical of aspiring youth as it used to be in more promising times, *passons*. But *la chair* may be less specifically sexual in intent here—just ordinary mortal fleshly life.

"Ce lui semble avoir lu tout" he says in "Crise de vers" (360). This ennui is a constant theme of the early correspondence and of *Igitur*, undoubtedly influenced by Baudelaire or the romantic *mal du siècle* generally, but all this is mentioned rather dutifully here: who doesn't get bored with books (and bourgeois-civilized life) in any period, from time to time, and want to get away from "Words words words words words" (*Hamlet*)?

Fuir! *là-bas fuir*: the breezy effect of *f* was noted by Plato in his *Cratylus*. Mallarmé uses it nicely in his fan poems, flute poems, etc. (*Faune*: "instrument des fuites"). The flat *a* in *là-bas* brings out the horizontal perspective of flight by sea-voyage, *way out yonder*[2]—and sets up the next *fuir* with its acute *i* and *u*, bright as the foam, intense as the yearning; the *r* is helpfully liquid. Great word, *fuir*, hence repeated.

Je sens: this whole poem, like most of his, is solidly anchored in the senses.

oiseaux ivres/D'être parmi l'écume inconnue et les cieux!: these intoxicated birds may remind us of the drunken wing-beat of the dreamed-of ecstatically free swan in *Le vierge, le vivace*—in both cases *ivre* is all tied up with *vivre* or just *être*, the ontological purity of our life-poet: simply *être parmi*, etc.; as in *La Glorie*, all he wanted was to be "l'intrus royal qui n'aura eu qu'à venir . . . pour l'être" (289) or "se percevoir, simple, infiniment sur la terre" (405). In this sense the mobile Eden we speak of in our Epilogue is paradoxically always here and now wherever we are, though we restlessly run off toward it *là-bas* in the exotic distance or, temporally, future, or else dream back to it all the way in the past. The same vibrant paradox mingles the Edenic between sky and earth here: the pure sky, the earthy sensuality of the foam[3] with the milky whiteness and other undertones as in *suprême* below (see Appendix A); *écume*, with its bright *é*, ambiguous *u*, and maternal *m*, in rife with this lively paradox of being (see *u* in Letter Table). The *nue* in *inconnue* accentuates the lusty mingled with the heavenly Eros: *nue* as cloud or nakedness, one of Mallarmé's favorite ambiguities (see *Hérodiade, Scène*). Cf. the orgiastic whipping-together of *sang par écume* in *Victorieusement fui* (68) and the blood-milk universal Dionysiac substances of *Hérodiade* (p. 135).

vieux jardins: though potentially rejected, their obvious attraction—especially reflected by eyes, which raises them, makes them airier and deeper, aesthetically (aside from the fact that the eyes are beloved-familial)

—adds poetically to the whole tone of the piece, its *transparent* quality (the *ar* cluster is part of this coloration: *marine, parmi, jardins, clarté*). The domestic beauty can pall, though it remains remembered and promising for a *nostos*, return.

O nuits: the nights of cruel creative struggle he describes in *Don du poème*, etc., with the familiar lamp (and that desert-like plot under it: "clarté déserte"—ah!). The series of *a*'s abets the flat sterility here—and the empty sheet staring at him reproachfully and forbiddingly with its unsullied perfection (this is central Mallarmé, of course).

la blancheur: *the* tone, joining with the milk image in the next line. In *Don du poème* the milk-giving mother was a natural creator, in harmony with all outdoors that came to mock his artificial creativity, a powerful theme linked with the Promethean idea of man dwarfed by God's creation, only maternal in accent. Mallarmé is caught between the natural mother and awe of the nature-God who will overwhelm him (or "castrate" his mast) if he ventures forth too far. When totally defeated by both these perspectives he will "scream" out his great poems, just before going under as in *A la nue*: his drowning hoot of protest rising over the waves, like foam. What total sensitive honesty about the odds, the powers that be!

adieu suprême: there are subtle undertones from the whiteness-cluster here (*crème-sperme*), which Derrida, after myself, has treated at length. The waving handkerchiefs and sea-journey link with imagery of the prose poem *La Pipe* and the coeval correspondence.

The rest of the poem goes on to hope he can escape and "make it," but the timidity or awe, together with a hint of repeated disillusionment in "cruels espoirs," gives the hope a wistful, childish, lovable quality. At the end, Mallarmé's "timid courage" (Joyce) lifts his heart and ours. This discreet little man was as indomitable as Proust and a very few others. In *Salut* he sets sail, as if in his little Valvins boat, on a cosmic ocean he will return to in the *Coup de Dés*, stormy with the death-threats of old age and creative risks, ready to face "N'importe ce qui valut/Le blanc souci de notre toile." He repeats this dauntless theme in *Au seul souci*. Was there ever a greater bravery for the *inner* voyage?

The last line is correspondingly impenitent, faithful, childishly eager to set forth. The song of the sailors, facing the worst, stirs him as virile venture has ever stirred the homebound little boys we all were and ever will be vis-à-vis some eternally inspiring image beyond us. Rimbaud's quest for a father to follow sounds this note very often, most poignantly in *Mémoire* and *Génie*. Mallarmé will set forth for us all, the Master himself, in the *Coup de Dés*, when a spiritual maturity and responsibility has reached its prime. In *Brise marine* the adventure is still a wispy, distant possibility, like the ghostly *ohé ohé* from the storm-tossed ship in the descending night of *Pelléas et Mélisande.*

NOTES

[1] Presented by Mondor in his notes to the poem in the Pléiade edition.

[2] The miraculous *la mer* mat tone of Debussy at the end of Geneviève's letter aria, in *Pelléas et Mélisande.*

[3] " 'Soyons sales!' parce que l'Océan écume." (Corr., V.I, 25 April 1864).

III: PETIT AIR II

This little poem is almost unbearably poignant. All Mallarmé says of it in the *Bibliographie* is that "it belongs to the album of Daudet." A modest mention for a piece which is modest in appearance—brief, slender—but explosive in exactly the sense that Richard Wilbur describes birds as "exploding with joy" (*Wedding of the Puppets*). The little unseen bird in this sonnet gave its all, as Mallarmé felt he hadn't really done—the theme of his swan sonnet—hence his awe before this humble God's creature. Rimbaud had felt the same way in *Enfance*: "Au bois il y a un oiseau, son chant vous arrête et vous fait rougir."

Indomptablement a dû	Indomitably must have
Comme mon espoir s'y lance	[—]As my hope is flung after it[—]
Eclater là-haut perdu	Burst forth up there[,] lost[,]
Avec furie et silence,	With fury and silence
Voix étrangère au bosquet	[A] Voice stranger to the grove
Ou par nul écho suivie,	Or followed by no echo
L'oiseau qu'on n'ouït jamais	The bird one never hears
Une autre fois en la vie,	Another time in one's life
Le hagard musicien,	The hagard musician
Cela dans le doute expire	It [the question] expires in doubt
Si de mon sein pas du sien	Whether from my breast or his
A jailli le sanglot pire	The worse sob spurted
Déchiré va-t-il entier	Torn, will he whole
Rester sur quelque sentier!	Remain on some path! [?]

In the quatrains, at some unsure distance a bird hidden in a forest grove sings its "heart out," furiously, followed by an ominous silence. The poet, in the tercets, speculates that it must have died, its tiny body "torn" with the effort, yet *entier*, implying a *total* explosion, total gift of self. And he is not sure whether the bird's sob of beauty is not surpassed in pain by his own—so great is his identification, his sympathy.

Indomptablement a dû: the long word followed by the short and acute one (*u* in *dû*) gives an effect of a final brief climax to a gradual working up of song and energy.

Comme mon espoir: the poet is immediately entangled, fully involved; his hope, ambiguously, follows the aspiration of the song and the anxiety of its aftermath.

furie et silence: acute effects (*u, i, et, i*; followed by descending nasal); the *f* is effective for bird *sifflet* or *souffle*. Mallarmé uses *furieux* for the crest of a desperate wave of aspiration in the *Coup de Dés*.

étrangère: the voice is a "stranger" in the sense of extraordinary and even extra-terrestrial; perhaps it is an unusual bird-call, hence surprising, unexpected, suddenly arrived as a stranger would be; its solitude is emphasized by the fact that no other bird replies: *par nul écho suivie [la voix]*.

jamais/une autre fois: he describes the voice of Villiers in comparable moments of existential uniqueness, "des moments de foudre [qu'on] expie de sa durée" (495).

hagard: good for a bird, from *haga* hedge, referring to hawks caught in a hedge, hence roughed up, ruffled by an ordeal. The flat *a*'s seem right for this effect of being flattened by the ordeal, just as the *u, i, i* of *musicien* are apt for the acute song which led to it.

expire: the doubt—whether the bird's or the poet's sob was worse and, ambiguously, whether the bird would be found dead—is deeply colored by this *expire*, referring to the song. One feels the tone of "dies" refers ahead to the poor lifeless body on the path.

Si de mon sein pas du sien: the identification is made concretely present through the anagrammatic entanglement of *sein* and *sien*.

jailli . . . pire: stabbing *j*, woeful *aill{e}*, acute *i*'s are effective here.

sanglot: "G . . . une aspiration simple . . . le désir, comme satisfait par *l*, exprime avec la dite liquide, joie, lumière, etc." (938) cf. "Gloire du long désir" (*Prose*), "le cri des Gloires" (75), and "sanglots glissants" of *Apparition* (Mallarmé's own mysterious death from a glottal or laryngeal convulsion comes irresistibly to mind).

Déchiré: again, the sounds are most appropriate.

entier: the creature's integrity is fully implied, as well as the whole little body one might find torn, exploded for his total gift.

IV: REMÉMORATION D'AMIS BELGES

In his Bibliography of the *Poésies*, Mallarmé notes:

> J'éprouve un plaisir à envoyer ce sonnet au livre d'Or du Cercle Excelsior
> où j'avais fait une conférence et connu des amis.[1]

He had gone to Belgium in 1890 to give his lecture on Villiers de
l'Isle-Adam and been warmly received by a group of local poets. Mallarmé, always grateful for friendship, warmed back and wrote this commemorative piece, one of his finest sonnets, not particularly difficult.

It is a poem of evanescence at varying levels, ending on a note of
some spiritual buoyancy typical of his homage to authentic poets or artists generally.

The dissolution through time of all seeming-solid existence is put
here in terms of evaporating stone, an effect he caught from the foggy
old northern city of Bruges. This fundamental meaning spirals in layers
—*pli selon pli*, to use a term from the sonnet itself, which we will discuss below—from eternity through the tradition of Bruges to the specific span of time involved in his meditative memory of a bygone cher-
ished event. The visibility of the layers of time in the fog—*pli selon pli*
—adds up to something paradoxically solid, a reversal of usual reality.
This is what happens, with comparably exciting poetic impact in *Le
vierge, le vivace*: the airy block of the "transparent glacier des vols qui
n'ont pas fui" on which I commented: "these [are] frozen layers of his
past history, deep, crystallized dream-memories."

This was one of Mallarmé's favorite images; in the introductory pages
of *La Musique et les Lettres* (635) he sees London in the same atmosphere:

> Son brouillard monumental—il ne faudra le séparer de la ville, en esprit;
> pas plus que la lumière et le vent ne le roulent et le lèvent des assises de
> matériaux bruts jusque par-dessus les édifices, sauf pour le laisser retomber
> closement, superbement, immensément . . .

The play between the solidity of the fog and the obscured buildings emphasizes the dubiousness of reality, which he refers to elsewhere (276)
in these disabused terms:

> Artifice que la *réalité*, bon à fixer l'intellect moyen entre les mirages d'un
> fait . . .

or again: "la fiction . . . semble être le procédé même de l'esprit" (851).

Thus in the *Coup de Dés* the *manoir* which sums up all mankind's
futile attempts to build something enduring on this earth is at last seen

as a "roc évaporé en brumes." And the impermanent external tomb-stone of Verlaine, in the sonnet of that name, is associated with a cloud whose "folds" are very like the *plis* of this poem.

Behind all this lies a long tradition of elegiac meditation: the end of Montaigne's *Apologie de Raymond Sebond* (after Plutarch), Shake-speare's "we are such stuff as dreams are made of," Calderón's *La Vida es sueño*, the whole baroque *desengaño* climate of illusion and disillu-sionment. Richard Wilbur in our time seems particularly close to Mal-larmé's image in his "cloudy cloudy is the stuff of stones" (*Epistemology*).

A des heures et sans que tel souffle l'émeuve	At odd times, and without some breath [of air] stirring it
Toute la vétusté presque couleur encens	All the ancientness, almost incense-colored,
Comme furtive d'elle et visible je sens	As furtive from it [the ancientness] and visible I feel
Que se dévêt pli selon pli la pierre veuve.	That the widowed stone strips itself fold according to fold.

Note: the main verb is yet to come: *Flotte*, "all the ancientness floats."

A des heures refers to his recurring remembrance at odd, spontaneous times and sets the tone of fleeting time for the whole.

sans que tel souffle l'émeuve: unlike windy London in the passage above, this is an unstirred atmosphere apparently characteristic of Bruges, at least as he saw it. The feeling of quiet provincial stagnancy which we further appreciate from Rodenbach's "Bruges-la-morte" and which is brought out in the *défunt* below is enhanced by this stillness of the air. The object here is the *vétusté*: no breath troubles it.

vétusté: the worn, ancient surface which is gradually stripped off.

encens: the still evaporation is underlined by this image which also adds a sacramental touch, life returning to its source as in *Toast funèbre*, the *Faune*.

furtive: secretly, in the narrow or darkened streets, the stripping of the "widow"—the bereft city of stone—goes on without notice.

d'elle: the *vétusté*: a minor echo of the *aile* below; the rising "spirit" of the stone is parallel to all the winged returns to heaven in poetry (or Plato's *Phaedrus*).

se dévêt: figuratively, the wearing away and evaporation of the stone in the air of time is seen (*visible*, in the fog) as this "stripping."

pli selon pli: the involutions of fog, curling on itself, are those folds, one after another or arising spirally one from the other, as in organic development. The unusual *selon* here—"according to"—brings out a certain sameness in the folds, i.e., each reflects the preceding, which is characteristic of Mallarmé's vision: "La totale arabesque . . . similitude avec elle-même . . . évidence de tout l'être pareil" (648). And all the reality of the *Coup de Dés* is variations on an original *Coup,* as in Kierke-gaard's "repetition." In "Une dentelle s'abolit," the meaningless *flotte-ment* of life is seen as a "unanime blanc conflict / D'une guirlande avec la même."

In the *Tombeau* (*de Verlaine*), the wandering cloud which reflects the evanescent tombstone has such *plis.* Much has been made of this image in general by Derrida and Boulez: Derrida rightly sees a basic two-in-one paradox in the idea of the fold in Mallarmé; I had developed this same idea in *L'Oeuvre de Mallarmé* at length and in my discussion of *Ses purs ongles.* But I do not see the present image as bringing out this epistemological depth—the image is rather direct here. Why Boulez chose it for an overall title of his works inspired by Mallarmé I fail to understand. He is wrong to think of it as referring to an *unfolding,* re-lated to his musical exfoliation of parallel themes and figures; no, the image here is of a *folding* rather, a curling as in fog or smoke. Butor's comment on it is comparably dubious.[2]

la pierre veuve: widowed, or "empty" (the etymon) of permanence or of its once-lively past. The absence of meaning implied in *veuve* is paralleled in *Surgi de la croupe*: the empty vase. The connections be-tween *pli* and vase (*ptyx,* etc.) are made in our comment on *Ses purs ongles*; but I don't think they shed much light here. The image is rather clear: the stone is being stripped of its past, visibly, leaving it barren like a widow.

Flotte ou semble par soi n'apporter une preuve	Floats or seems in itself to bring no proof
Sinon d'épandre pour baume antique le temps	Except to spread time as ancient balm
Nous immémoriaux quelques-uns si contents	[—] We immemorial few [being] so happy
Sur la soudaineté de notre amitié neuve	About the suddenness of our new friendship

Flotte: the verb complement of *vétusté* above: "all the ancientness floats."

ou semble par soi n'apporter une preuve: carries on the disabused or existential tone of meaninglessness, except *soi* may have a minor overtone of "silk" (*soie*), see below.

Sinon d'épandre pour baume antique le temps: there is an excep-tion here, in the tone of the *excepté* of the last page of the *Coup de Dés* (and other poems). The word *baume*—in the *Tombeau d'Anatole* he refers to the "balm in Gilead" of Poe's *Raven* in his grief over the death of his son, hoping for some consolation—has a note of buoyancy, furthered in the final tercets.

The sonnet *Quelle soie aux baumes de temps*, uses the same image of consolation in the aura of time, there associated with hair reminding him of old silk. The *soi* above may vaguely echo this.

Nous immémoriaux quelques-uns si contents: this is a dangling construction. The *immémoriaux* picks up the idea of consolation in total time, the feeling of cosmic rootedness that poets may enjoy together. The *quelques-uns* is dialectically proud-modest, as authentic poets should be. He uses *quelqu'un* in just this sense of a mysterious Somebody for Wagner and others.

la soudaineté: the new friendship is an eruptive event, brilliantly original, reflecting totality. As I note in the Epilogue (and *Modes of Art*), the two infinite dimensions—vertical-instantaneous and horizontal-eternal—meet in a zero-infinite, micro or macro.

O très chers rencontrés en le jamais banal	O very dear people met in the never banal
Bruges multipliant l'aube au défunt canal	Bruges multiplying dawn[s] in the dead canal
Avec la promenade éparse de maint cygne	With the scattered promenade[s] of many a swan

banal: though it denies (provincial) banality, it gives a flavor of it (with those flat *a*'s).

Bruges: "Bruges que c'est miraculeux" (letter of 18 February, 1890). The word is savory, with its vibrant *Br*, liquid *r*, keen *u* and caressing *ges*. The overtone *brumes* is undoubtedly hovering in the air.

multipliant: seems to reflect the *plis* above: time in its many "folds" brings dawn after dawn, the same—yet deeply rooted, we now feel. Also there is a multiplication of the sky in the water, space added to time.

défunt canal: still night-shadowy or dull; no longer used in commerce.

maint cygne: there were real swans in the town's canals; the swan adds a touch of ancient lost power with its hint of divinity now earthbound in this animal form, as in *Le vierge, le vivace*. In this sense, its failed wings offer a contrast to the spiritual "wing" of poetry, below.

Quand solennellement cette cité m'apprit	When solemnly this town taught me
Lesquels entre ses fils un autre vol désigne	Which of its sons another flight designates
A prompte irradier ainsi qu'aile l'esprit.	To irradiate spirit like a prompt wing.

fils: the poets are the city's "sons," with a possible echo of "threads" (of spirit) as in *Une dentelle s'abolit*, "filial" ("fils . . . sortis de mon esprit," *Corr.* v. I, p. 225).

un autre vol: "other" than the real swan's flight, this one is the spiritual flight of poetry.

prompte: the impulsive flight, or "irradiation" of spirit in inspired poetry, cf. the *soudaineté* above.

NOTES

[1] The *or* of *livre d'Or* and Excelsior—in his "golden" memory—still seems to glow in the title word *Remémoration*; as Mallarmé wrote to a friend "on cherche l'idée devant le titre qui le [poème] résume."

[2] The Boulez *Pli selon pli*, though interesting, seems to me to display the one-sided Byzantine emphasis on complexity (without the complementary necessity, harmony, inevitability which would alone make it worth following), sophistication, openness which is typical of contemporary French avant-garde art and thought and is falsely thought to be Mallarméan. Mallarmé, I repeat tirelessly, was as naive as he was sophisticated (cf. Baudelaire on Delacroix); I have treated this at length in *Modes of Art*. Mallarme's approving references to simplicity, naivete, ingenuousness and the like would fill a small volume; e.g., see under *La Chevelure vol* ("simplifier").

From this viewpoint, the test of the enduring value of Boulez' music would be to feel as one does of classical masterpieces when they become unshakeable—to the extent that a single false or slightly "off" note grates. Why anyone—including Butor—would settle for less, in their judgment of contemporaries, beats me.

2. EPILOGUE: MALLARMÉS POETIC VISION

◊♋◊♋◊♋◊♋◊

In the Introduction there is a brief allusion to Mallarmé's vision: "All of his favorite symbols, flower, window, feather, siren, bird, star, hair, and so on, are at a crossroads of cognate polarities—up-down, static-kinetic, light-dark, male-female, cold-hot, past-future—that emanate from a parent pair, Being and Nothingness."

"Vision" is a more incarnate, artistic expression of the "epistemology" which Blanchot, Barthes, Foucault, among others, see as Mallarmé's signal contribution to twentieth-century thought. I have treated this subject *in extenso* not only in *L'Oeuvre de Mallarmé*[1] (the first version[2] of which goes back to 1949) but, more recently and theoretically, in *Modes of Art*.[3] Mallarmé's philosophy was a rather underground activity, as befits a poet,[4] and I have had to reconstruct it in large part from scattered or posthumous fragments or through sheer intuition. The pithiest statement of the tragic, radically ambivalent, absurdist, paradoxical nature of this epistemological vision is in *Notes*:[5] "La fiction lui semble être le procédé même de l'esprit humain." As is detailed in the theoretical discussions, the basic paradox underlying fiction-as-the-ground-of-knowing develops through multiple dimensions—is squared, raised to the third power, etc.—in what I term, successively, "bipolarity," "tetrapolarity" and so on through "polypolarity." This was shown to be the armature of the *Coup de Dés*, parallel, in its "tetrapolar" phase, to the formula "la symphonique équation propre aux saisons" which Mallarmé said, in *La Musique et les Lettres*, would be the structural principle of his future Great Work.

---

[1] *L'Oeuvre de Mallarmé: Un Coup de Dés*, Librairie Les Lettres, Paris, 1951, pp. 31–72.

[2] *Mallarmé's Un Coup de Dés: an Exegesis*, A Yale French Studies Publication, New Haven, 1949.

[3] *Modes of Art*, Anma Libri, Saratoga, Ca., 1975, pp. 23–48.

[4] "Je révère l'opinion de Poe, nul vestige d'une philosophie, l'éthique ou la métaphysique ne transparaitra; j'ajoute qu'il la faut, incluse et latente" (*Sur Poe*).

[5] P. 851 in the *Oeuvres Complètes*.

In this "polypolar" sense, in *Modes of Art* (p. 39), I spoke of the mobility of Eden throughout our tradition: is it all the way up, as in "heaven" ("paradise" in that locus)? Mallarmé's *azur* points in that direction—or maybe it is all the way down, at the core of things, as Bachelard showed it can be in his studies of the oniric imagery of earth (e.g., in Novalis), "sweet and low," at the fountainhead where life gushes forth; this is the telluric region of Mallarmé's "savants abîmes éblouis" in *Hérodiade, Scène,* for example (which could, incidentally, serve as a motto for Freud and Lacan on the paradox of the articulate unconscious). Perhaps it is all the way back as in Platonic "reminiscence" (*Meno*) and its avatars in Wordsworth, Kierkegaard *et al.*—Mallarmé's "ciel antérieur où fleurit la Beauté" (*Les Fenêtres*) and also his ambiguous "Eden" (*Toast funèbre, La Musique et les Lettres,* and the crucial remark "On ne peut se passer d'Eden" reported by René Ghil).[6] Or, again, Eden can be all the way forward, perhaps near the New Jerusalem, in our tradition (including, prominently, Dante). Poems of ecstatically promising departure, such as Baudelaire's *Invitation au voyage,* point in this future direction; as does Mallarmé's *Brise marine*: "Je partirai!"

In provisional sum, past-future forms one Edenic dimension—the time dimension which we usually schematize as horizontal—and up-down forms a spatial Edenic dimension which is obviously vertical. The "tetrapolar" paradoxical or vibrant relation between these two axes which is the core of Mallarmé's "symphonic equation," the armature of his creative vision, can be clearly seen in these "Edenic" terms. A third dimension can be added in the form of a horizontal axis of space, the *exotic* axis—the "là-bas" of *Brise marine*—but for our present purposes this much exploration of pure theory is sufficient.

My aim in marshalling these bare ideas here is simply to prepare the ground for understanding better, despite the complexity of his ambiguous and absurdist vision in which we can easily lose our way and miss the fuller truth, the tremendous power of nostalgia in Mallarmé and, potentially, the rest of us. Although he does not usually state it very explicitly, beauty is often for him, as for Proust,[7] Baudelaire, Dante, Wordsworth, the Rimbaud of *Mémoire,* agonizingly "way back there," in a lost paradise. The haunting quality of this cosmic homesickness is excruciatingly put in the *Ouverture ancienne d'Hérodiade*:

---

[6] In *Les Dates et les Oeuvres,* Paris, Crès, 1923, p. 114.

[7] The connections with Proustian memory are obvious; we made some further connections in "Proust and Mallarmé," *French Studies,* vol. XXIV, no. 3.

Une voix, du passé longue évocation

. . . .

Désespéré . . . le vieil éclat voilé
S'élève (ô quel lointain en ces appels celé!)

. . . .

Jettera-t-il son or par dernières splendeurs?

This strain is equally important in that other swan-song, *Le vierge,
le vivace et le bel aujourd'hui*: the "cygne d'autrefois se souvient" of that
sonnet is in this lost-paradisiacal vein; the variant "l'antique fuite du
cygne" echoes the similar image at the beginning of the *Ouverture*
"fui[e] un bel oiseau . . . le cygne inoubliable" (*flown* in an ambiguous
sense: in space to impossible, divine heights of beauty where we cannot
follow; in time, gone with our childhood, "sweet bird of youth," in the
exquisite lost life before).

As is the case with all deep experience of beauty, nostalgia of this
intensity is dangerously entangled with death; we have to die to reach
paradise, and even to approach it in memory is risky: as T. S. Eliot remarked, glimpsing the hidden rose garden of childhood, in the *Four
Quartets*, the cost "is not less than everything." Hence it is not surprising
that we approach the vision gingerly, through mediators. Every poetic
image is a mediator in this sense, with more or less of that plunging return to the Source. If the mediator is a woman, as Victor Hugo noted in
Les Misérables and Valéry in an aphorism, "The yearning a beautiful
woman sets up in us can only be satisfied by God." We may move through
her palimpsestically to the deep image of the mother, as Mallarmé did in
Apparition, and further back through maternal milk (*Hérodiade*: "paradis . . . ton lait bu jadis") to the milky *azur* (*Don du poème*: "presseras-
tu le sein . . . Pour les lèvres que l'air du vierge azur affame", cf. "le ciel
comme du lait," Verlaine, *Sagesse*, XIII) and ultimately the milky way
of those distant stars in the *Coup de Dés*. There are other ways to the
Source, other symbolic chains involving the *blancheur* which I have
treated elsewhere,[8] those comments having been further commented on
by Derrida, in *La Dissémination*, Part II.

As we observed in *Modes of Art* (p. 39), Eden can also be here and
now, at the zero-infinite center of our polypolar crossroads—the point of
origin of the Cartesian grid—as it is in Kierkegaardian Instants and the
eternal present—out of time—of Proust's privileged moments at their
peak, when memory has been transcended. Mallarmé, far more than has

---

[8] In *L'Oeuvre de Mallarmé*, pp. 137–140; also in the present volume, Appendix A.

been realized, is a poet of *life*, in exactly this sense. A passage from the present study of the sonnet goes:

> And yet we, no more than the swan, would not really leave, not while we have our pride and strength. Like Wallace Stevens standing on the wind-swept hill, we, too, cry, even as the air pangs our lungs: "This health is holy," or Rimbaud's "que salubre est le vent!" The first line of Mallarmé's sonnet is a pure inhalation of this pathetic, tender, but also bracing, per-sistent (*vivace*) and heady challenge:
>
> [O] The virgin, hardy and beautiful today

It is limpidly evident from this one celebrated line that Mallarmé is a poet of reality in the sense that Wallace Stevens is said to be—phe-nomenological, immediately present, a poet of being—and that critics who try to shove him into a corner of idealism, and they are many, simply do not know what they are talking about. The poetic "music" with which the sonnet begins is in the key tone of *life*: the *vie* in *vierge* together with the direct meaning of *vivace* (and *vivre*, below), plus all the echoes of *vie* in *hiver*, *ivre*, *givre*, *souvient*, *délivre* which interlock, crystallize to-gether to form the solid ice-block (*glacier*), the "transparent" marvel of this art. The suggestion of past life—lost paradise—is also implied, in the "cygne d'autrefois se souvient," as in "ce vivant d'autrefois" (*Mal-larmé lycéen*[9]). But, as in the formula "ce civilisé édennique" of *La Musique et les Lettres*, there is a paradox, a vibrancy between past and present, transcended, as in Proust, in the artistic faith of an eternal pres-ent, out of time, of the poem, "simplement, la vie vierge, en sa synthèse et loin illuminant tout" (*Sur Poe*).

This is the moment of *Les Fenêtres*, when the dying old man looks backward in time to his youth and through and beyond it to "le ciel an-térieur où fleurit la Beauté." And yet, "ivre, il vit"—the nucleus of the swan sonnet ("le divin cygne," as Valéry called it) is already here. Even if that is only an instant of the poem, it is potentially the summing up of its total effect, its tone, its simultaneous, static and ecstatic, epiphanous being. Similarly, the peak and focus of Baudelaire's *Les Fenêtres* (writ-ten *after* Mallarmé's poem of that name) is "derrière une vitre . . . vit la vie, rêve la vie, souffre la vie." In both these poets, it is surely no acci-dent that a *vitre* is a place where one lives (*vit*), keenly feels the pres-ence of *vie*, with the added possibility of an erotic undertone in *vit*, plus the concentrated effect of the *i*.

The dialectic of life at its full, as in Camus' lyrical essays, quivering between presence and absence, love and death, runs throughout Mal-

[9] Gallimard, 1954, p. 190.

larmé's oeuvre. It is the vibrant presence, so fragile and beautiful—the supreme paradox—of his homage to the painting of Berthe Morisot:

> Féerie, oui, quotidienne—sans distance, par l'inspiration, plus que le plein air enflant un glissement, le matin ou après-midi, de cygnes à nous; ni au delà que ne s'acclimate, des ailes detournée et de tous paradis, l'enthousiaste innéité de la jeunesse dans une profondeur de journée.

This movement toward the immediacy of the present is not really a reflection of any shallowness on Berthe Morisot's part but rather an expression of sympathy and affinity: in many a poem, Mallarmé rejects the vainglory of traditional transcendence and, in a complex manoeuvre, having found no metaphysical resting place either on the axis of aspiration or that of normal bourgeois activity, turns to his simple core of everyday being and impulse, life. This is the meaning of *Les Fenêtres*, of the prose poem *La Gloire*—"l'intrus royal qui n'aura eu qu'à venir pour l'être"—or *Bucolique*—"se percevoir simple, infiniment, sur la terre"—of the healthy laughter in *Victorieusement fui* and so on; it is a theme—really more than a theme: that is too limited a formula for Mallarmé's universe, which is ubiquitous in our poet. Just because the *paradis* is explicitly ignored in the passage of Morisot or implicitly in the other works does not mean that it cannot return in a subtly transformed essence as that "profondeur de journée." "On ne peut se passer d'Eden," of that present sort, the living paradise of the poem: "Quel génie pour être un poète! . . . Simplement la vie, vierge . . ." (*Sur Poe*).

In *Les Fenêtres* the "Ivre, il vit" represents this poetic plenitude, if only potentially. Although it is an early poem, it is a major step toward his mature manner and contains an immense amount of richly suggestive imagery, words reaching out in so many directions toward other words, moving toward the crystallizations of the *Jeu suprême*, on its way to *Prose (pour des Esseintes)* and ultimately the *Coup de Dés*.

Because Mallarmé's universe is so freely open every part to every other, one hesitates to speak of a theme; indeed, Jean-Pierre Richard and others have been criticized by contemporary critics for treating him thematically. Still, in an epilogue, leading gradually into the fullness and complexity of the total work, we may be excused for seeking some main ways through it, some Ariadne threads to cling to. These "ways" or "threads" naturally pass through crossroads, those crucial points where so much of reality, of the universe, seem to converge—those *intersections* of his central *toile d'araignée* image summing up his vision. In *La Musique et les Lettres* where he projects his future Work he speaks of that cosmic network ("tout l'être pareil") and of the microcosmic poetic images to which we alluded earlier—the favorite symbols—in the following terms: "l'ambiguïté de quelques figures belles aux intersections."

The window is among the most privileged of such images, and if we are careful not to force things but, instead, to emulate him in "yielding the initiative to the words" (or images) we may quietly find ourselves, somewhere along the critical way leading from one such image to another, growing in awareness of his splendid totality.

The way begins with a near-nothingness, a memory of lost beauty, a mere tone. Certain childhood experiences hint at it. In the crisis of being —Hamlet's agonizing "to be or not to be"—when we, at a crossroads of growth, are not sure we will make it—can one go on?—which is the fountainhead of poetry like Mallarmé's, one is bereft, stripped naked back to the source of being (nonbeing). On the way down and back, one goes through childhood memories of awesome power: the luminous sucked-out grape-skins of the faun, the *matin oublié des prophètes* in *Hérodiade*, the lost-paradisial mother's milk of *Don du poème* . . . "L'Enfant déshérité s'enivre du soleil" (Baudelaire)—at such intimate moments the poet is born, or reborn. That is what Mallarmé's windows are originally about.

There are literary windows before Mallarmé, including some French ones,[10] but his have an unprecedented poetic intensity. They are precisely, this "cristal par le monstre insulté," a new yet old, light yet weighty crystallization of reality into art.

In *Les Fenêtres* of 1863 the complex structuring process, bringing further dimensions of art, is already well advanced. Primarily, the core of the poem, its central symbol, is an absolutely naive childish view of a window transfigured into a network of mature vision. What does the child see there? The pure source, limpid as air and light, from which it was born, but caught and frozen in a palpable concretion of earthly being, the pane of glass. This is the spiritual place of the poem and its very weighty, sensual, material place as well. Here, the ambiguity of *glace* as *verre* (*de fenêtre, de miroir*) and as *eau gelée* is operative and

---

[10] Examples: *The Song of Songs, Le lai du laustic* of Marie de France, Ronsard's sonnet to Hélène no. XXVIII, Julien Sorel's tower-window, Fabrice's prison-window. Baudelaire's prose poem *Les Fenêtres* was published shortly *after* Mallarmé's *Les Fenêtres*. It emphasizes the dialectical *Aufhebung* through constriction (frame) and partial barrier (pane) of what is glimpsed through it. This is implied in Mallarmé's elite little window-theaters as well: "La chambre singulière en un cadre" (*Ouverture ancienne*). Baudelaire and Mallarmé are both looking in at this point but at other times out; it comes to much the same thing. We have discussed some further valences of the image in *The Writer's Way in France*, pp. 370–372 (Proust's voyeur windows) and 374–375 (the stained glass of Combray etc.). And we have many pages on it in the present study.

relates, for example, the solid block of a poet's whole life-experience—
"le transparent glacier des vols qui n'ont pas fui" (*Le vierge, le vivace...*)
—to the deep mirror—"eau froide ... dans ton cadre gelée"—with its
shadowy memories suspended there like leaves in a frozen lake (*Hérodiade*).

That block, incidentally, prepares cubism (Picasso came to Paris
partly because of Mallarmé) and carries the angelic breath and reality
of Mallarméan space, the champagne of summer in ice.

I am reminded of those chips we used to split off the great blocks
of the old-fashioned ice chest and sucked like a wafer in an oral communion with the all. Or of those lollipops or popsicles we held up to
the sun between licks and from which one "suçait la clarté" exactly
as the Faun did with his bunch of grapes; that is to say we devoured them
with our eyes as much as our mouths. This was our true religion.

The old man of the poem reverts to this cult: [11]

> Et la bouche fiévreuse et d'azur bleu vorace,
> Telle jeune, elle alla respirer son trésor,
> Une peau virginale et de jadis! encrasse
> D'un long baiser amer les tièdes carreaux d'or.

Nothing is more obvious than the substitution of the lollipop for the
maternal breast. And the further displacement to the window-pane in an
impoverished, pathetic and frustrated attempt is a rather common phenomenon in my memory. Before developing this constellation of imagery
more broadly, I owe a word of tribute to Charles Mauron who was the
first to observe it critically, at least in faint outline.

The mother was the first of those intermediaries between ourselves
and the Origin toward which we must mount from time to time to be
born again spiritually. Not only does the infant consume (a part of)
her in sucking her breast to pass through her to that source, but he would
eat her entire, the little cannibal, if he could. "Mangez la dame": we
find this funny and elliptical formula amid the fragments of *Le Livre*,
with "dix francs pour elle." "Soif de tes yeux" is a closely corollary phrase
from the same text, which brings us back to the pane, rendezvous of this
whole network: air, light, water, milk, milky azure, *glace*, vitreous eyes,
pane. Hence, for example:

> Si tu me vois les yeux perdus au paradis,
> C'est quand je me souviens de ton lait bu jadis
> (*Hérodiade, Scène*)

---

[11] We note, in passing, the overtone of *jeûne* in *jeune*; this is one of Mallarmé's major
themes, for example in *Le Livre*.

Or:

> presseras-tu le sein
> Par qui coule en blancheur sibylline la femme
> Pour les lèvres que l'air du vierge azur affame?
> (*Don du poème*)

Here it is the maternal milk the baby-poem hungers for, but the underlying play between azure and milk becomes evident from the phrase
"d'azur bleu vorace." Later, Verlaine will sing of "le ciel comme du lait"
(*Sagesse*, XIII): Mallarmé himself had early spoken of the "ciel
lacté" (*Ce que disaient . . .*). The music of the intimately feminine voice
enters the network naturally—*la berceuse*—and recalls the association
of a "damsel with a dulcimer" and "the milk of paradise" in Coleridge's
Kubla Khan. There is a subtle association of *muse-musique-suce* which is
crystallized in the stained-glass of the maternal *Sainte*, "musicienne du
silence," where the whiteness of the pure page functions poetically.[12]
Then there is, in *Les Fenêtres*:

> leur verre, lavé d'éternelles rosées
> Que dore le matin chaste de l'Infini

which contrasts in a way with "la femme allaitant ses petits" of the preceding strophe. Dew could be a sublime milk, nectar, or soma (universal
sap or milk of the Vedas) or amniotic water drunk by the virtual infant.[13]

In this communion the child, or man, seeks, like the *Pitre châtié*, to
be reborn:

> Yeaux, lacs avec ma simple ivresse de renaître
> . . . .
> J'ai troué dans le mur de toile une fenêtre

This is a baptism, through the eyes, associated with water and then with
a pane, a sort of frigid water or "eau perfide des glaciers," whence he
would surge up renewed. The rhyme *fenêtre-naître* (Baudelaire had
used it in *Paysage*), with an element *être*, is very active here. Through
the window one would plunge again into that primordial water which
is represented by amniotic fluid (waters of birth) in woman. The sexual
act enters the game with the lower part of the abdomen, the place of

---

[12] The core of this is the remarkable French *u*, combining relaxed, pendulous receptacle shape and tense sound; see our discussion of it here, pp. 273–274. The *x* is
discussed on page 276.

[13] *La rosée* is one of the generative images of *Les Dieux antiques* (Pléiade ed., p.
1167, etc.).

birth, of the total emptiness of the Source, but localized in a womb-like hollow.[14] Thereupon arises a whole series of beautiful linked images: the window, being essentially the *trou* which the clown penetrates (the eye-vagina association is classic), becomes the entrance to the eternal womb. The fact that panes, because of an eidetic impression, may appear swollen as in the "slotted window-bellied like the fig's fruit" of T. S. Eliot (*Ash Wednesday*) or certain medieval paintings, for example those of the Van Eycks, may explain in part this expression in one of Mallarmé's letters: "les carreaux bombés par les Rêves."[15] Far more important here is the mandolin, instrument of ideal creativity:

> une mandore
> Au creux néant musicien
> Telle que vers quelque fenêtre
> Selon nul ventre que le sien,
> Filial on aurait pu naître
> (*Une dentelle s'abolit*)

Narcissistically, it is the self that concerns the child at first, but from this site could also return a lost loved-one, a mother who died young or that distant princess she became. Hence Hérodiade is doubly bound to her window. In *L'Ouverture ancienne* she is the virginal, pure place of possible birth, and she could appear there. Though she is absent, the *vitrail* which opens onto her room in the fateful tower is full of her presence. Thus this fragment of the *Noces*:

> Non, nul jour—de la belle fenêtre
> Elle n'as pas aimé, cette princesse, naître
> Et cette mandoline au ventre [space] dit
> Pourquoi que sur le drap maternel du vieux lit . . .

All these elements are grouped in the difficult and miraculous sonnet *Une dentelle s'abolit* where it is a question of a *Jeu suprême* at different levels: struggle, dilemma or "conflict" between life and death, light and shadow at the moment of the possible birth of a day, a renewed being, an authentic creation.

How did this happen to the Hamlet-child of *Les Fenêtres*, or the old man he contains and becomes, or their later avatar in the sonnet?

---

[14] The ambiguity of the locus of birth—belly (pinpointed by the maternal navel) or vagina—is undoubtedly a major structure of thought. It implies a same-different relation between the median and the extreme, which we discussed in *Modes of Art*, p. 62.

[15] In *Propos sur la Poésie*, ed. Mondor, Monaco, 1946, p. 74. Cf. "bay windows" as bellies.

Summarily one may say that the child seeks the impossible, something like that union of contraries sought by mystics of all ages, for example between the here-and-now that one is reluctant to leave and the alluring beyond. Or between the part, concrete, finite, and the whole, diffuse and infinite. Or between the static and kinetic aspects of total reality. To unite stasis and kinesis would be an ideal marriage such as between *en-soi* and *pour-soi* dreamed of by philosophers from Hegel to Sartre; "la mer mêlée au soleil" of Rimbaud. Thus the sun "veut hâler" the pane of *Les Fenêtres*; it warms the stones. Remember that glass jar submerged in Proust's Vivonne? It irritated him because of this conflict between water and glass which he dreamed of biting exactly as did the old man of *Les Fenêtres*. Proust's child was hypnotized by that "perpetual allitera-tion between the water without consistency which the hands couldn't grasp and the glass without fluidity which the palate wouldn't be able to enjoy." The agonizing adolescent drama of *Hérodiade*, life-death, to be or not to be, is summed up in this play of contraries in the mirror; between stasis (the cold, rigid aspect) and kinesis (the fountain, the *trou profond*).

The *Jeu* of *Une dentelle s'abolit* is precisely that vibrancy between window and source, then all the levels of reality which emanate from this primordial dilemma according to an evolution parallel to the cosmogonic Becoming of the *Coup de Dés*: play between light and dark, love and death in the sexual act, the analogous rhythm of artistic creation, and so forth. All this is a *flottement* representing the never-definitive aspect of experience, a sort of coquetry or *Fiançailles* (*Coup de Dés*, page 5) that man carries on with the All during his existence. When the child of *Le Livre* wants to eat the lady, a voice tells him "No."

The curtains of the sonnet are the duplicity (*conflit*) plus the sym-bol of the duality which is an essence of femininity for Mallarmé, for ex-ample those twin panels which oscillate, the entrance of the tomb-womb of *Igitur*.[16] The sonnet's poetry depends largely on this ecstatic invitation and promise between the two feminine fragments: "virginité [la page blanche]—elle-même s'est comme divisée en ses fragments de candeur, preuves nuptiales [veil] de l'idée."[17] Regardless of what Satre thinks, for those who know how to abandon themselves with the naiveté of the true artist, the marriage sometimes takes place.

In the curtains lifted and billowed by the morning breeze there is a light suggestion of belly. In her commentary on the sonnet, Emilie Nou-let refers to "la lumière laiteuse de l'aube," and the lace curtains are themselves milky-white.[18] There could be born not only the poet or the

---

[16] See pp. 217 and 264 in this volume.
[17] Pléiade ed., p. 387.
[18] *Vingt poèmes de Stéphane Mallarmé*, Paris, 1967, p. 158.

poem but, beyond the mother or the sister who represents her youth—both having died early in Mallarmé's instance—there are the other loved-ones, at times male, for example his son Anatole, who died tragically little, or his friend Villiers. A suspicion of all this is found in the phantom of St. John who haunts the curtains according to various fragments of the *Noces*. Léon Cellier has invoked Poe's *Ligeia* here together with the "uncertain rustling" of the curtains in *The Raven*, translated by Mallarmé.[19] We note in passing that the window is a small theater—the place of encounter of all outdoors and the most intimate interior life, of the high and the low, and so forth—and that the curtains are easily assimilated to this image. An actor, dramatically, emerges from between theater curtains as if born: he *appears*, a phenomenon.

In *Les Fenêtres* the window becomes, subtly, a mirror—"je me mire et me vois ange"—offering that familiar spectral reflection which is visible at certain angles. The angelic phantom is a purified vision of himself, either before life, such as those innocent and embryonic creatures who exist only virtually as in the poetry of Blake or Hölderlin, or else after life, which comes to much the same thing. Now, there is a clear progression in the series door-window-mirror, a growing arrestation. The window is midway between the door and the mirror. With the full mirror there is a blockage, a reflection, a return upon the self like an embryo's or that related image of the ouroboros (curved serpent) which is at times Hérodiade's, the narcissistic princess before her looking-glass. Thus the "croisée vacante" of *Ses purs ongles* gives way to an even more static and empty image, that of the mirror in the background. There alone, at that zero umbilical point, could occur the union of opposites symbolized by the stars and night, like that "diamant de minuit" of *Igitur*. This site of renascence is the nodal point of a cross, which explains in part all the x's, especially in the extraordinary rhymes, and the word *croisée* itself. In spite of the ambiguity of the word "nue," the "défunte nue en le miroir" (with the "nixe") creates an atmosphere related to that of the mirror in *Frisson d'hiver*: "Et ta glace de Venise, profonde comme une froide fontaine . . . plus d'une femme a baigné dans cette eau le péché de sa beauté; et peut-être verrais-je un fantôme nu si je regardais longtemps." The "nudité" Hérodiade sees in her mirror is equally promising of an uncommon fecundity.

This *x* of a point of origin, a crossing, a multiplication is found at the center of Leonardo's cartouche "Sainte Anne and the Virgin" between the laps of the maternal pair, conjoined site of a supreme birth. Likewise, upon the enigmatic mouth of the sphinx-like Mona Lisa. In Mallarmé,

[19] *Mallarmé et la Morte qui parle*, Paris, 1959, pp. 31–32 et seq.

the cross is the syntactical form par excellence, representing what we have named "tetrapolarity" and the revolution it brought to the ancient triadic perspective of thought. Blanchot saw in this new opening of dialectic an absolute pivot—comparable only to Hegel's—of the Western tradition.[20] Derrida and others, as we know, took an important cue here.

We may speak of "polypolarity" beyond "tetrapolarity" in Mallarmé, but the paradoxical play between four fully interchangeable poles represents an enormous leap of vision and, accordingly, occupies a privileged position in his work, for example the famous "symphonique équation propre aux saisons" which stands for the armature of the *Coup de Dés*.

The "croisée d'où l'on tourne l'épaule à la vie" (*Les Fenêtres*) sums up the play between the horizontal axis of banal existence "où seuls les appétits mangent" and the vertical axis of death and transfiguration of the angelic poet. For Mallarmé as much as for Pascal angelism is a heresy: "l'ange fait la bête" and risks falling throughout eternity; there is no repose on either of the two axes. This is a crucifying dilemma.[21] The poet, like the swan of his celebrated sonnet, is caught, bent back on his central being: nothing, "la pièce principale ou rien" as he says in *La Musique et les Lettres*. This nodal point is the zero umbilicus through which we came into the world, the point we seek asymptotically throughout our days: quintessence, center of the life-death, past-future cross, null as that "fausse apparence de présent" in *Mimique*, empty ego of which Sartre and Lacan speak.[22] It is not really a "*dead* point" but a nullity, the nothing which is worse than the psychic death which precedes transfiguration. It is the *Rien* of page 10 of the *Coup de Dés* which is also "la neutralité identique du gouffre." But, like Pascal's *gouffre*, or Baudelaire's, or Proust's *néant*, it is also the "creux néant musicien," the womb of a supreme creativity.[23]

[20] In *L'Etretien infini*, Paris, 1969.
[21] This is the location of the altar of a cathedral. At that point one is nothing and is magnified to all, for which the expanded cathedral stands.
[22] Sartre in *Le Transcendance de l'Ego*, Lacan in "Le Stade du miroir."
[23] The mandala is sometimes seen as a tetrapolarity with its poles blown up into circles or spheres, each being a microcosm, including one in the middle which is the quintessential cosmos. Thus the world of nature passes vertically through an intermediary world at the center of the cross—the womb of artistic birth—into the world of the fully fashioned, ripe artistic product: bloom, fruit, bubble of fantasy, balloon, etc., at the top, just as, horizontally, past moves through the zero-womb of the present to the future. This tetrapolar scheme can be expanded into a polypolar one, adding a male-female polarity. The common origin of male and female which is reflected in the primitive concept of the penis-womb leads to ambiguity in the image of the place of creative process. A mandolin is a womb (round, static) but it also kinetically *emits*: it is an *instrument*. The basic idea of original androgyny is always there, but, as in life-forms, the accent varies to give important differences in imagery, e.g. the Faun's flute which contains a hollow ("womb") but is more

From it, the luminous rhythms of a totalization under way—the "compte total en formation" which is the last image of the *Coup de Dés*—arise *coup sur coup* in Mallarmé's art.

---

evidently linear ("phallic"). The stasis-kinesis-stasis ("dumbbell") pattern which prevails in all these instances runs through the *Coup de Dés*, concretized as an ivory tower joining a circular base to a crown of the *folie* (etym. *follis*, balloon) which rises through the Hamlet-figure from the global sea-base, and so on. Cf. ground-trunk-foliage. Most of Rodin's sculptural *oeuvre* is in this shape. Valéry projected an essay on instruments. The mandolin, or lute, develops into a key image of visual art, particularly cubist: Braque, Picasso, Gris.

3. REVISIONS

◊⊱◊⊱◊⊱◊⊱◊

Note: the first number refers to the page; the second to the line.

4, 4:   (after "cold-hot") : past-future
4, 38:   (after "body") :—or, cognately, between past and future, along the time-dimension involving the haunting nostalgia of a lost paradise—
13, 27:   This is a pastoral poem in a long tradition, with a direct hint of Theocritus in the allusion to Etna and Sicily.
13, 30:   The immediate and sharp brightness of *midi* is luxuriously prolonged by the *après*, adding a classically sustained calm of perpetuated (cf. *perpétuer*, below) pleasure through a summer afternoon.
15, 4:   The correct quote is: "Votre illustration [est allée] plus loin, vraiment, dans la nostalgie et dans la lumière."
16, 12:   *bien seul* indicates, incidentally, his narcissistic solitude.
20, 25:   (after "flesh") : (the *la* subtly refers to the feminine).
22, 18:   *monotone*: art as a substitute for more basic satisfactions can pall eventually, can seem to babble on tiresomely. The *ligne* (and *maligne* below) echoes the "omniprésente Ligne" (see p. 25).
29, 8:   (after "spectacle"): All this is anticipated but provides a feeling of gradual curving away of the afternoon, even as earlier lines suggested the rise from morning cool.
33, 22:   There is a tiny hint of oceanic salt (Latin *sal*, French *sel*) in the title.
53, 41:   Equally important is the *o* as in *O miroir*: the mirror before which she stands is a reflection of her pure femininity (the circle, the white space within); the *r* brings a touch of liquid grace to it.
54, 3:   For *diadème*, see M. L. p. 353.
57, 38:   *fuie un bel oiseau*: in addition to Hérodiade as swan-princess, this is an image of the lost paradise of childhood—"sweet bird of youth"—and beyond that, the dangerously deep memory of an even earlier, pre-natal, original Beauty.
            The crisis is fundamentally the crucial one in late ado-

lescence of growth from childhood to maturity (the girl's; the poet's creative equivalent). It is Hamlet's agonizing moment: to be or not to be; can one go on? In such a crisis one is bereft, stripped naked back to the source of being (non-being). On the way down and back, one goes through childhood memories, the nurse's milk and the like. At this level, adult religious forms—Christianity for Mallarmé— are mainly shucked off and one reverts to childhood— poetic, pagan—cults of ecstatic light and air, for example, the *matin oublié des prophètes* in the *Scène*, cf. the faun's delight in the luminosity of sucked-out grapeskins or "L'Enfant désherité s'enivre de soleil" (Baudelaire, *Bénédiction*).

Thus, although we take account of some lingering aspects of Mallarmé's "struggle with God" in our commentary, we do not believe one should overload the poem with a clutter of Christian references as some recent critics have done.

In the *Scène* the "pas un ange accompagnant ses pas" is one such mildly meaningful instance, and there are others. On the whole, Mallarmé's choice of an Oriental-Judaic heroine, named by himself, is part of a general Western turning to other—non-Christian—traditions (cf. Rimbaud's Orient; modern Zen, etc.). He wanted to be his own unmediated vision-recorder, a prophet in his own right. But Saint John, who is close to Mallarmé's final position in this regard (also in the *Coup de Dés*, as I study it) shows that the matter is complicated: he is not entirely devoid of Christian overtones.

60, 19:   Note the nuancé faded effect in the numerous diphthongs (*ei, ie, iei*).

62, 30:   (after "sachet"): Cf. the *os* and *froid* in *ostensoirs refroidis* a few lines below.

62, 34:   The following fragments from Baudelaire's *Voyage à Cythère* seem to be hovering in Mallarmé's memory: "Vénus . . . fantôme . . . planant comme un arôme."

64, 5:   The first two lines may be read as follows: "The old veiled dazzle of the strange gilt,/Languishing in voice," etc. Languishing would modify *éclat* in this reading.

66, 12:   The sickle shape of the *croissant*, echoing the *coupé* of the preceding line, may quietly allude to the weapon of execution in the *Cantique*.

69, 24:   *lions*: one approaches total crisis typically in this way, gingerly, by facing some specific danger, often in confrontation with an animal.

78, 19:   Flaubert's Salammbô, who is ritually involved with a snake, also deserves a mention here.

83, 42:   (after "Reaper") : Its shape may reflect the curving wing of a bird, hence *vols* (Mauron). Roger Fry traces it back to Kronos—Father Time—who used it to castrate Ouranos.

84, 8:   There is an overtone of *viol*; note cutting *v*'s.

85, 14:   (after Baudelaire): "quelque noir mélange" (*Tombeau d'Edgar Poe*);

85, 41:   We imagine a halo.

86, 40:   From *Salammbô*, Mallarmé could have retained the following: a virginal woman, reluctant to mature, who kills the man she loves; the snake; the dried up breasts of the nurse.

        Mallarmé's respect for Hugo is well established. He spoke admiringly of *Les Misérables*. In the Fifth Part, Book I, Chapter X, Hugo describes "une chambre virginale . . . C'est l'intérieur d'une fleur close, c'est une blancheur dans l'ombre, c'est la cellule intime d'un lys fermé qui ne doit pas être regardé par l'homme tant qu'il n'a pas été regardé par le soleil. La femme en bouton est sacrée. Ce lit innocent . . . cette gorge qui se voile devant un miroir . . . ces petits frissons de froid et de pudeur . . . L'oeil de l'homme doit être plus religieux encore devant le lever d'une jeune fille que devant le lever d'une étoile . . . Ici, contempler, c'est profaner.

        . . . la rose avait été faite par Dieu blanche, mais . . . Adam l'ayant regardée au moment ou elle s'entr'ouvrait, elle eut honte et devint rose."

        Every image here has its counterpart in *Les Noces d'Hérodiade*: the room, the closed flower, the lily, the rose, the bed, the sun before which the virgin opens first, the mirror and her nakedness, the shivering modesty, the sisterly star, the profaning male look; even the *entr' ouvrir* of virgin on her way to open maturity is in a fragment of the *Noces* . . .

        Of course, providing he was directly influenced, which is never sure—these images belong to the universe of poetic reality—Mallarmé, with assists from the memory of his virginal sister, made it all his own. Hugo's repetitive and rhapsodic manner is filtered into something subtler and finer. *N'empêche* and *quand même*; what a generous genius he was!

87, 47:   Keats, in a letter, says that the mind "sucks the teat" of the heart (see our "Keats and Mallarmé," *Comparative Literature Studies*, Vol. 7, no. 2).

95, 19:   *Postscript.* It appears, in retrospect, that Mauron and others (including myself) may have been unduly influenced by various stained-glass images in Mallarmé (plus the fact that the husband of Mme Brunet, to whom the poem was dedicated, was a stained-glass artisan; conceivably also a *sainte*-stain echo). Although the unity of effect is rather badly damaged thereby, it is possible that the saint is in an old *picture* ("image ancienne"), *by* a window ("A la fenêtre ... A ce vitrage"). The rest is basically unchanged.

    That Mallarmé thought the poem especially "mélodique" (and a "Chanson") is bothersome: the repetitions are indeed incantatory, and all good poems, including symbolist ones, have a linear melodic aspect (as well as a circular total-harmonious one), but the finest symbolist poems are primarily static, epiphanous, and that is the effect most of us particularly appreciate in this sonnet. Nor are we wrong to do so; Mallarmé's comment is off-the-cuff, not definitive, in a personal letter. His poem may well be more static than he thought at the time.

100, 5:   The descent echoes the mortality of the sun, the cosmic drama.

103, 7:   In *La Musique et les Lettres* Mallarmé spoke of the artist's task as being "nier l'indicible qui ment" (653).

104, 20: We further note the contrast between "*cet* homme" and "*Le* Maître"—the latter is more distinctive.

105, 4:   The mystery of naming, which implies the fundamental form-matter paradox of humanity, as in "the Word was with God and the Word was God," refers to Adam's original naming of God's creatures, in Eden.

108, 14: *séjour*: the abode of art as opposed to nature (*vrais bosquets*; cf. the *vrais bois* of the *Faune*).
    déjà: with the death of Gautier, the groves are already in their artistic abode.

111, 19: The *logis précieux* may also be the precious (in the sense of "preciosity") object, the fan, which liberates the verse written on it (in actual fact) when opened.

112, 14: Its position (*rejet*) *prolongs* the reassuring domestic mood of woman, wife, the on-going and stable though vibrant (*battement*) river of life (*toujours*, below). A reluctance to break this mood helps to account for the reservation being put in parenthesis.

112, 21:   *chagrin*: as in *Don du poème*, there is a veiled allusion to the guilt of the self-indulgent poet-husband, or of any careless man after whom a wife cleans up.

116, 7:   The poem ends with an appropriately static image, a crowning circle: a round bracelet.

118, 17:   The last few lines can also read: "if your naked jubilation plunges exultantly into the wave become you," i.e. the woman is now one with her sister-water (Richard).

121, 6:   The capital links it with *Terre* below: the sentimental early dream of an escape to an ideal realm has been dialectically modified to a dream within a humble earthly reality.

121, 18:   *plafonds*: the sterile limitations of mere space is implied in the physical "ceiling" like the "room" below (cf. the *froid plafond* of *Surgi de la croupe*).

122, 15:   The *S* of *Se* hints at the *torsion*, cf. the *torsion de sirène* of page 8 of the *Coup de Dés*.

122, 28:   It can also be the rare transitive usage of the verb "to lie," i.e. "a proud lie told by the shadows."

123, 39:   Antoine Fongaro has discovered another very likely source for some of the imagery in *Feuilles d'Automne*, no. 21:
   Le roi mystérieux de la pompe nocturne
   Que le ciel pour moi seul s'était illuminé!
Fongaro's fine article is in *Synthèses*, nos. 258–259.

125, 2:   (after "shiver"): in a moment of profound acceptance of life (the *vie* which is the key tone).

125, 9:   (after "*hiver*"):—containing anagrammatically and paradoxically the even more significant tone of *vie*—

125, 21:   The "fled swan" (or bird) of the *Ouverture* is very near to godhead, hence the singularly prestigious image of beauty-death and lost paradise of youth—the flown (ambiguously) "sweet bird of youth"—or of childhood or even further back, an exquisite life beyond, which we can only recall in Platonic "reminiscence" as we are born into this world "trailing clouds of glory." In Plato the aspiration to the divine source which is our profoundest fountainhead of inspiration, the nostalgia of the adult poet, was expressed archetypically through the image of the dying swan-song of Socrates (*Phaedo*); this is the rapturous theme of the wing-beat yearning to ideal eternal life in *Phaedrus*. The swan has accordingly haunted our whole tradition, coming down through memorable imagery in Dante, Leonardo, Ronsard, Shakespeare, and leaping to particular prominence with the Romantics (Lamartine, Hugo, Vigny) and the great Symbolists: Baudelaire (*Le Cygne*), Mallarmé (*Le vierge, le vivace*), and Valéry (the swan-god of *La Jeune Parque*).

Yeats, remembering no doubt his Mallarmé, has come very close to the main meaning of *Le vierge, le vivace* in the following lines from *Nineteen Hundred and Nineteen*:

The swan has leaped into the desolate heaven:
That image can bring wildness, bring a rage
To end all things, to end
What my laborious life imagined, even
The half-imagined, the half-written page;

That impossible beauty and past of wistful "failure" is what Mallarmé was singing his swan-sonnet about. And Yeats' magnificent *Leda and the Swan* portrays the godly power of the creature as Mallarmé's early *Léda* had tried to do and, before him, Ronsard's sonnets to Hélène.

Other birds share much of this prestige throughout our tradition, from the bestiaries through the Romantics again (Shelley, Keats) to Hopkins (*Windhover*) and, of course, Mallarmé (*Petit air II*, etc.). But the swan is pretty privileged. It is against this background that we can begin to understand the "fled bird," the "cygne inoubliable" of the *Ouverture ancienne d'Hérodiade* as well as the "divine swan" (Valéry) of the sonnet.

125, 32: The swan song is *not* sung, at the end; that would have created a linear movement, an asymmetric triumph, something too dramatic, too "kinetic" in the Joycean sense.

125, 42: The fuller resonance of this life-accepting tone in Mallarmé's *oeuvre* is explored in the Epilogue ("Mallarmé's Poetic Vision"), with specific reference to the swan-song.

127, 32: The vertical tension in *vierge* is complemented by an even deeper, more tantalizing dimension of tension in the element *vie*, which is the key tone of the whole poem, vibrating together with its anti-synthetical opposite, death (*hiver, agonie*). The *vie* is echoed by *vivace*, *vivre* (below) and all the other interlocking words mentioned above. The important intertextual network of this "theme" is explored in our Epilogue, e.g. "la vie, vierge" (872).

le bel aujourd'hui: to make a substantive of an adverb of time (or what we usually construe as such) is to arrest life-flow in an *ecstatic*, privileged moment, out of time.

129, 13:   *se délivre*: primarily, "frees himself"—meaning "tries to free himself"—and also, ambiguously, "surrenders himself." The latter meaning, rarer, harmonizes better with the negative context.

130, 9:   *chante*: the swan-song would have meant death as the price of paradise (as it did for Socrates in the *Phaedo*).

130, 26:   *vivre*: the ambiguity of directions is confirmed by a similar usage in *Les Fenêtres*: "ivre, il vit," combining both the ordinary life of an ailing man and the intense life of his vision.

131, 15:   *Mais non*: a mounting kinesis (*secouera*) has been abruptly cancelled.

131, 35:   As Camus says in *Le Mythe de Sisyphe*: "Il n'est pas de destin qui ne se surmonte par le mépris."

136, 17:   *Si* can also conceivably mean "so" ("so much yours").

139, 11:   (after "with"): *dé* ("thimble," from Latin *digitale*) and hence

140, 21:   Mallarmé had imitated the formula in "l'ennui pend ses drapeaux funèbres" (15).

141, 11:   (after "monument"): Cf: "le noble vol humain/Cendre ployée avec ces livres" (162).

141, 12:   The central image of the poem is a container (*amphore*, *ptyx*) which might be a holder of permanent life in art, a funereal womb of rebirth. This idea may owe something to a compelling echo of *urne* in *nocturne* (cf. the *fenêtre nocturne* of the letter to Cazalis), with a further association of *taciturne* (the silent room). Thus Verhaeren links a *calice* with *nocturne* and *taciturne* in *Pieusement* (*Les Débâcles*).

144, 29:   The word *oubli* is used referring to posthumous absence in *Igitur* (435) and the *Coup de Dés* (p. 11).

150, 11:   The *vive nue* is, in part, that natural or "live" nudity, or nude woman.

152, 12:   *écorche*: in the sense of "skins" this word may evoke an image of blood from the *rubis*.

Austin Gill has proposed a radically different interpretation, which runs as follows: the hair is a flame stolen (*vol*, in that sense) from the original Eros-flame—either by the poet who displays it in his sonnet (or before the crowd in the prose poem) or by the lady who wears it—that eternal *voleuse* as Mallarmé called her in the Huret interview, for wearing a beauty properly the poet's—and the rest of the poem says that it is a defamation of poetry—"Celle . . . qui accomplit par son chef"—to wish (*soupirer*) that antique amours (*nudité de héros tendre*) be continued (*continue*) in modern guise through a contemporary lady; no, that is over, poetry itself suffices. Thus the *front couronné* is the Banvillean idea of the poet crowned with laurel (Mallarmé did indeed celebrate this image in his "Symphonie littéraire"). The *occident* would be the modern decadence of the West when all this restitution is happening, as in *Le Phénomène futur*. Phew!

This interpretation makes for many difficulties when presented as *the* meaning: despite Gill, the hair is obviously still the core of the poem, persisting through the "la femme / Accomplit par son chef fulgurante l'exploit." The *se pose* refers easily to an idea of a flight alighting or going down, badly to Gill's notion that it means it "abdicates" in favor of a poet. The change from female hair to male brow is too abrupt and unpoetic, not at all typical of Mallarmé. It is far likelier that he had in mind here a subtle metamorphosis like the one from muse-hair to art in the *Tombeau de Charles Baudelaire*. Finally, the tone of the whole is violated by this exclusive slant: the celebration of woman (her hair) as a rival of art but also the unconscious source which it draws from is central to Mallarmé, as in *Victorieusement fui*, the early *Château de l'espérance*, *Quelle soie aux baumes de temps*, *De l'orient passé des Temps*, and the *Tombeau de Charles Baudelaire* as well as the prose poems *Le Phénomène futur* and *La Déclaration foraine*.

But if we accept Gill's version as a counterpointed theme, it does help explain some puzzling things: the *pour* in particular and the complex syntax in general. I must confess that I feel Mallarmé went too far in this poem.

154, 3: Compare "Tel, dans son intégrité restituée enfin, durable . . ." (507).

156, 17: *tombe*: clearly echoes *chu* and certainly helped give birth to that imagery of tombstone as meteorite.

157, 18: (after "version"): , and published it

171, 43: The core meaning here is: like all man's futile attempts to build something permanent on this earth, the external tombstone is as evanescent as the "roc évaporé en brumes" which is the final monument of mankind in the *Coup de Dés*. But the poetry of Verlaine, his spirit, is another affair . . . perhaps.

178, 40: (after "uses the"): image of cloth (not "word").

179, 35: *principal*: the *p*, here and in the next two words, emphasizes a (fallen) pride. See Appendix C.

193, 23: *poupe*: this supports the notion that the poem is primarily addressed to the young; Mallarmé, the aging poet, is left behind as in *Salut*: "Moi déjà sur la poupe."

203, 25: In *Igitur*, it is a question of poison, in connection with a Hamletic thought of suicide. Here too we have a phial-like vase in whose rounded base there is a deep dose of *Néant*. This shape of linear *col* and round base is comparably meaningful in both texts and generally in Mallarmé: the base is holistic (though circumscribed), deeply ambivalent, cyclical, "religious" in impact, "feminine" or redolent of (nothing) Being; the linear neck is more narrowly human, "male." The shape corresponds to the phallic erectness of the human—the spinal column, etc.—vs. the rounded emotional reservoir in belly or lower (e.g. in the male, the testes). Compare a mercury column in a thermometer with the total mercury source in the little round base: there, in the "rump," real zero could occur, or a hint of totality (as through the zero-*Néant*).

The *i* and *o* of *fiole* support the dialectic of line and circle, "male" and "female" in the *Igitur* text, so that the idea of fusion of opposites is embodied subtly in that word as in the anagram *folie* which clearly echoes it in *Igitur*: "La fiole vide, folie . . . ." But in this sonnet that union is far less sure.

208, 33: (after "stolen"): and awe-inspiring.

209, 27: Cf. the *Nul jour* of the fragment from *Hérodiade* we quote in relation to the mandolin below.

213, 6: Another possible sense is the "identité de deux fragments constitutifs" (333) referring to two rhyming lines.

213, 12: But cf. "le papier blême" (481).

213, 33: There is some hint too of the veil of the temple as in *Hommage* (*à Wagner*) and the passage on Hugo in "Crise de vers" (360).

214, 27: The lulling effect of *dore . . . ment dore . . . mandore* (and *telle que . . . quelque*) has to do with the nascent musicality.

215, 9:   The element *ment* here and in *mandore* helps to negate the promise; but the series of *m*'s is creative; see Appendix C.

243, 35:   *coeurs*: the proximity to *hymne* brings out an overtone of *choeurs*.

252, 29:   There is likely an overtone of *jeûne*, "fasting," as in the "dejeûnes ivre" of the *Cantique de Saint Jean* and the hungry artist of *L'Azur*, *Les Fenêtres*, and *Le Livre*.

264, 32:   The foregoing, of course, does not rule out other possible combinations of restless existence, "prevailing patterns," such as the important male-vertical-unity-circularity-metaphoric vs. female-horizontal-duality (multiplicity)-linearity-metonymic as concretized in the traditional single male versus two female pattern (e.g. in the *Faune*; cf. other polygamic structures).

BIBLIOGRAPHY

An extensive bibliography on Mallarmé is now easily available (for example, in J.-P. Richard's *L'Univers imaginaire de Mallarmé*); we are limiting, therefore, our list to those works bearing most directly on the *Poésies,* as we have studied them here.

I. *Mallarmé texts:*
(Note: there are a few references to unpublished letters, from various collections; these are gradually being published by Gallimard.)

Austin, Lloyd J. ed., *Les Gossips de Mallarmé.* Paris: Gallimard, 1963.

Davies, Gardner, ed., *Les Noces d'Hérodiade.* Paris: Gallimard, 1959.

Mallarmé, Stéphane. *Un Coup de Dés.* Paris: Gallimard, 1914.

Mallarmé, Stéphane. Original proofs of the projected Lahure edition (private collection).

Mallarmé, Stéphane. *Oeuvres complètes de Stéphane Mallarmé.* Editions de la Pléiade. Paris: Gallimard, 1945.

Mallarmé, Stéphane. *Igitur.* Paris: Gallimard, 1925.

Mallarmé, Stéphane. *Alternative.* NNRF (January 1, 1954), pp. 188-192.

Mondor, Henri. *Eugène Lefébure* (letters). Paris: Gallimard, 1951.

Mondor, Henri and Richard, Jean-Pierre, ed., *Correspondance 1862-1871.* Paris: Gallimard, 1959.

Mondor, Henri, ed., *Mallarmé lycéen.* Paris: Gallimard, 1954.

Mondor, Henri, ed., *Mallarmé, Documents iconographiques.* Geneva: Cailler, 1947.

Mondor, Henri, ed., *Mallarmé plus intime.* Paris: Gallimard, 1944.

Mondor, Henri, ed., *Propos sur la poésie.* Monaco: Editions du Rocher, 1946.

Richard, Jean-Pierre, ed., *Pour un tombeau d'Anatole.* Paris: Editions du seuil, 1961.

Ruchon, François, ed., *L'Amitié de Stéphane Mallarmé et de Georges Rodenbach* (letters). Geneva: Cailler, 1949.

Scherer, Jacques, ed., *Le "Livre" de Mallarmé*. Paris: Gallimard, 1957.

Vielé-Griffin, Francis. "Stéphane Mallarmé: Dialogue" *Mercure de France* (November 15, 1924), pp. 22-32.

II. *Books on Mallarmé:*

Ayda, Adile. *Le Drame Intérieur de Mallarmé*. Paris: Corti, 1955.

Beausire, Pierre. *Essai sur la poésie et la poétique de Mallarmé*. Lausanne: Roth, 1942.

————. *Mallarmé, Poésie et poétique*. Lausanne: Mermod, 1950.

Boulay, Daniel. *L'Obscurité esthétique de Mallarmé et Prose pour des Esseintes*. Paris: D. Boulay, 1960.

Cellier, Léon. *Mallarmé ou la Morte qui parle*. Paris: Presses Universitaires de France, 1959.

Chassé, Charles. *Lueurs sur Mallarmé*. Paris: Editions de la Nouvelle Revue Critique, 1940.

Chisholm, A. R. *Mallarmé's . . . Faune*. Melbourne: Melbourne University Press, 1958.

————. *Towards Hérodiade: A Literary Genealogy*. Melbourne: Melbourne University Press, 1934.

————. *Mallarmé's Grand Oeuvre*. Manchester: Manchester University Press, 1962.

Cohn, Robert G. *L'Oeuvre de Mallarmé: Un Coup de Dés*. Paris: Librairie Les Lettres, 1951.

Davies, Gardner. *Les Tombeaux de Mallarmé*. Paris: Corti, 1950.

Fowlie, Wallace. *Mallarmé*. Chicago: University of Chicago Press, 1953.

Gengoux, Jacques. *Le symbolisme de Mallarmé*. Paris: Nizet, 1950.

Goffin, Robert. *Mallarmé vivant*. Paris: Nizet, 1955.

Mauron, Charles. *Introduction à la psychanalyse de Mallarmé*. Neuchâtel: Baconnière, 1950.

————. *Mallarmé l'obscur*. Paris: Denoël, 1941.

Michaud, Guy. *Mallarmé: l'Homme et l'Oeuvre*. Paris: Hatier-Boivin, 1953.

Mondor, Henri. *Autres précisions sur Mallarmé*. Paris: Gallimard, 1961.

————. *Histoire d'un faune*. Paris: Gallimard, 1948.

————. *Vie de Mallarmé*. Paris: Gallimard, 1942.

Noulet, Emilie. *Mallarmé, Dix poèmes*. Geneva: Droz, 1948.

————. *L'Oeuvre poétique de Stéphane Mallarmé.* Geneva: Droz, 1940.

Soula, Camille. *Gloses sur Mallarmé.* Paris: Editions Diderot, 1947.

————. *La Poésie et la pensée de Stéphane Mallarmé.* Paris: Champion, 1929.

Thibaudet, Albert. *La Poésie de Stéphane Mallarmé.* Paris: Gallimard, 1930.

Wais, Kurt. *Mallarmé.* Munich: Beck'sche Verlag, 1952.

III. *Special Numbers of Reviews*
Empreintes (November-December, 1948), Brussels: L'Écran du Monde, 1948.

Empreintes. Numéro spécial, 10-11 (Brussels: L'Écran du Monde, 1952).

Les Lettres, nos. 9-11 (Paris, 1948).

Nouvelle revue française: "Hommage à Stéphane Mallarmé." (December 1, 1926).

Le Point: "Mallarmé." Lanzac. (February-April, 1944).

IV. *Books partly on Mallarmé*
Frétet, Jean. *L'Aliénation poetique.* Paris: J. B. Janin, 1946.

Ghil, René. *Les Dates et les Oeuvres.* Paris: Crès, 1923.

Gosse, Edmond. *French Profiles.* New York: Scribner's, 1914.

Montesquiou, Robert de. *Diptyque de Flandre, Triptyque de France,* Paris: Chilberre, 1923.

Moore, George. *Avowals.* London: Heinemann, 1924.

Renéville, Roland de. *L'Expérience poétique.* Paris: Gallimard, 1938.

Roujon, Henri. *La Galerie des bustes.* Paris: Rueff, 1908.

Weber, Jean-Paul. *Genèse de l'Oeuvre poétique.* Paris: Gallimard, 1960.

V. *Articles*
Adam, Antoine. "L'Après-midi d'un faune: Essai d'explication," *L'Information Littéraire* (July-October, 1940), pp. 137-140.

————. "Pour l'interprétation de Mallarmé" *Mélanges d'histoire littéraire offerts à Daniel Mornet.* Paris: Nizet, 1951, pp. 221-226.

Austin, Lloyd J. "Le principal pilier," *Revue d'Histoire littéraire* (April-June, 1951), pp. 154-180.

————. "Du nouveau sur la 'Prose pour des Esseintes.'"